CANADA'S
FIVE
CENTURIES

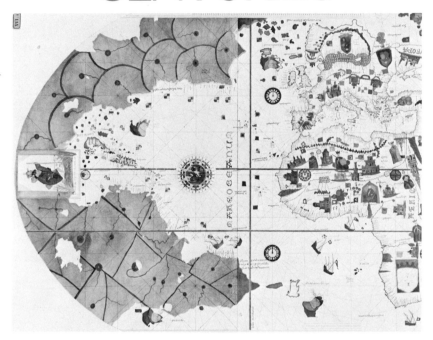

CANADA'S FIVE CENTURIES

From Discovery to Present Day

W. Kaye Lamb

S.M., Ph.D., LL.D., F.R.S.C.

McGraw-Hill
Company of Canada Limited

Toronto Montreal New York London Sydney
Mexico Johannesburg Panama Düsseldorf Singapore
Rio de Janeiro Kuala Lumpur New Delhi

ISBN 0-07-092907-6
123456789 AP 987654321

Printed and bound in Canada

PART I   10

Discovery and the First Century of Settlement
Canada to 1713

The Discovery   12
First Explorations   22
New France   32

PART II   48

The Struggle for Possession
1713 - 1783

New France After 1713   50
The British Rule and the American Threat   66
Canada to 1783   72

PART III   84

Expansion and Consolidation
1783 - 1867

Settlement   86
The Fur Trade   98
Threats Without and Within   108
The Maritimes to 1860   118
A Growing Canada   126

PART IV   150

The First Half Century of Confederation
1867 - 1919

Confederation   152
Settlement of the West   166
Urbanization and Industry   196
Internal Politics   218
The First World War and After   230

PART V   242

The Second Half Century of Confederation
1919 - 1970

Communications   244
Resources and Development   270
People and Politics   282
The Second World War and After   298

FORT WALSH. CYPRESS HILLS. 1878

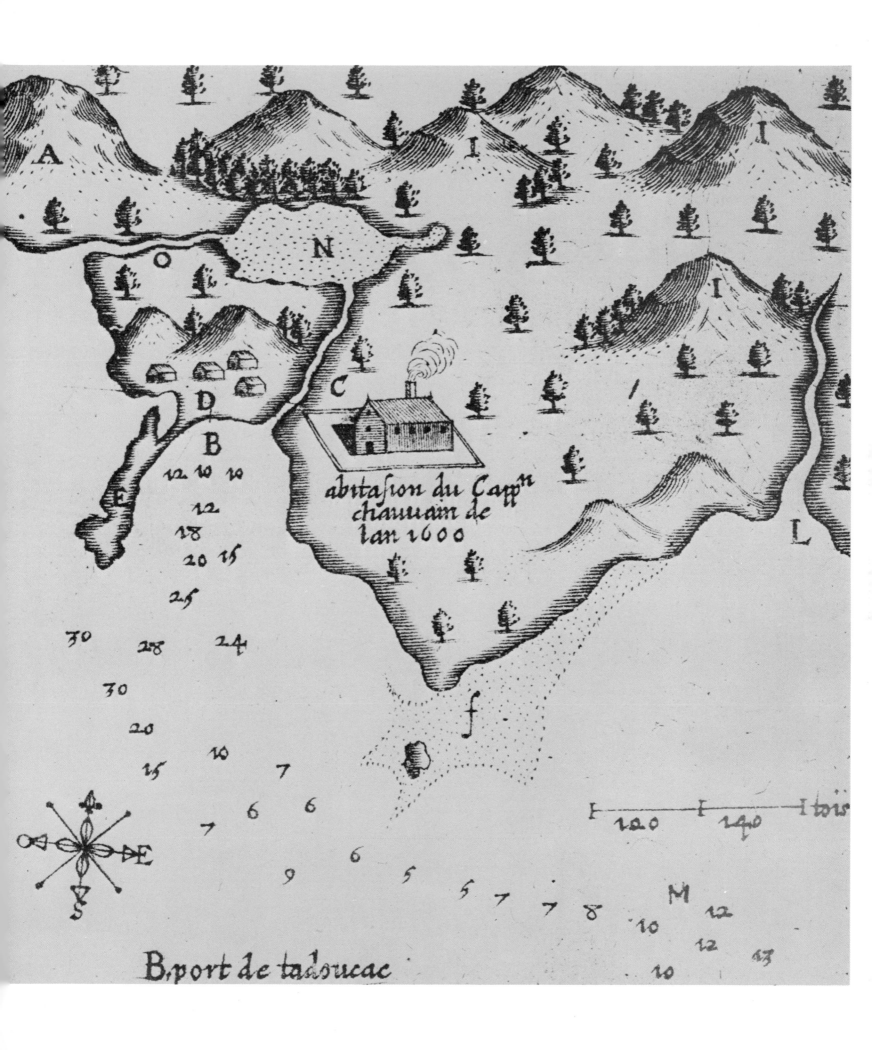

abitaſion du Capⁿ
chauuain de
lan 1600

B, port de tadoucac

Part I
DISCOVERY AND THE FIRST CENTURY OF SETTLEMENT CANADA TO 1713

Louis XIV

This striking likeness appeared on the medal struck to commemorate Frontenac's successful defence of Quebec against the attack by Phips in 1690, and it appeared again in 1713-14 on the medal that commemorated the Treaty of Utrecht.

CHAPTER 1

The Discovery

The Climate of Discovery

IT was doubtless inevitable that America should be discovered in the 15th century, and many circumstances can be cited to support this point of view.

In part they were political. For centuries after the decline of the Roman Empire western Europe was in a troubled and fragmented state and people were concerned primarily with things close to home. By the 15th century a great change had occurred. Spain, Portugal, France and England had all taken shape more or less as we know them today, and all were under the control of fairly stable ruling houses.

Roman map of the world, 77 B.C.

No original Roman maps of the world are known to have survived, but this reconstruction, the work of German scholars, is believed to reflect them accurately.

Public Archives of Canada

Something in the nature of a royal or national policy toward such matters as exploration had become possible.

The great outburst of learning and enlightenment known as the Renaissance was approaching its climax in Italy and was spreading rapidly to France and England. It engendered a new spirit of adventure and a lively curiosity about many things, including little known and unknown parts of the world. It was also—for the rich and powerful, at least—an age of prosperity in which spices and silks and other luxuries that came from the far east were in great demand. But a formidable wave of Turks and other Moslem invaders had swept westward into the middle east, North Africa and even Spain, and had disrupted the old-established trade routes to Asia. In Spain the tide of conquest was finally checked; a battle at Granada broke the power of the Moors and forced them to retreat to Africa. It is interesting to note that this battle was fought on January 2, 1492, just seven months before Columbus sailed on his first voyage of discovery.

If Asia could not be reached safely by land, the urge to explore and the demand for goods were sufficiently strong to encourage attempts to reach it by sea. The Portuguese took the lead in this endeavour, and during the last half of the 15th century they made a series of voyages down the west coast of Africa in the hope that they would be able to sail around the continent and then travel on to the Orient. This they were to succeed in doing in 1497-98, when Vasco da Gama made the first return voyage to India.

This around-Africa route was essentially a long and tedious coastal voyage; it involved serious dangers for cumbersome sailing ships, but those on board at least had the comfort of knowing that land was never very far away. Much more hazardous would be an attempt to reach Asia by sailing westward into the Atlantic, which was still an unknown ocean. But ships and methods of navigation had both improved in the course of the 15th century, and Columbus and others were prepared to attempt the voyage. "Within the period of a hundred years,"

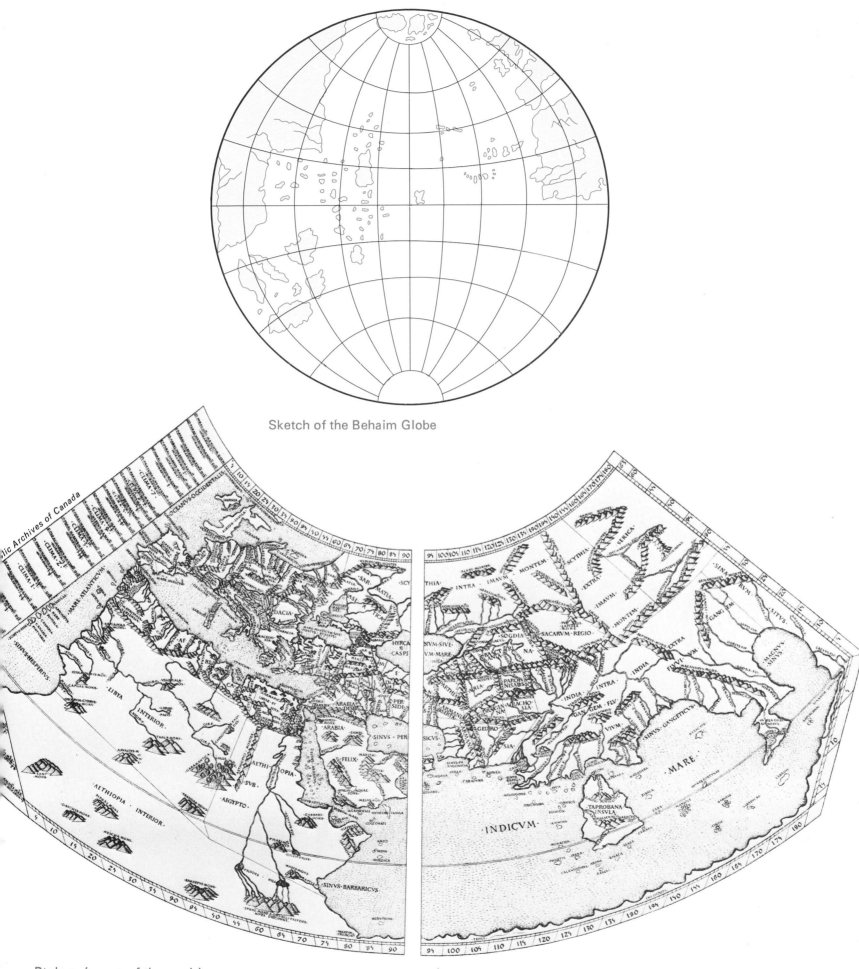

Sketch of the Behaim Globe

Ptolemy's map of the world

The advance in ship design

The earlier vessel is a "cog," a type of ship developed largely by the Hansa League ports in northern Germany. It was probably the most advanced design of the 14th century. The second model is the Golden Hind, *the ship in which Drake sailed around the world in 1577-80. Her design was far in advance of the "cog," and most of the improvements it represented had been made by the time Columbus sailed in 1492.*

Bjorn Landstrom tells us, "the sailing-ship had undergone more profound development than during the 5,500 years of its history that had passed and more than was to occur during 400 years to come."

Mariners were encouraged further by a stupendous but fortunate error in geographical knowledge. For fourteen centuries, geography had been almost completely dominated by the *Geographia* of Claudius Ptolemaeus (usually referred to as Ptolemy), compiled in Alexandria about A.D. 150. A most remarkable work for its time, it became virtually canonized through the centuries and was passed on from generation to generation as the unquestioned authority on the nature of the physical world.

Three aspects of Ptolemy's geography are important in the present connection. First, he believed that the habitable world consisted only of Europe, Asia and Africa—a single huge land mass surrounded by water. Secondly, he assumed that the world was round, and although this notion was long frowned upon by theologians, geographers had come to take it for granted. Finally, and most important, Ptolemy both overestimated the eastward extent of Asia and substantially underestimated the size of the globe. As a result, the early navigators who pored over his text could conclude that the distance from Spain to Japan, actually about 11,000 miles, was probably only about 3,000 miles. A voyage of that length, though hazardous, was practicable with the improved ships and navigation aids that were available; had Columbus and others had any inkling that Asia was in reality nearly four times as distant, their voyages would never have been

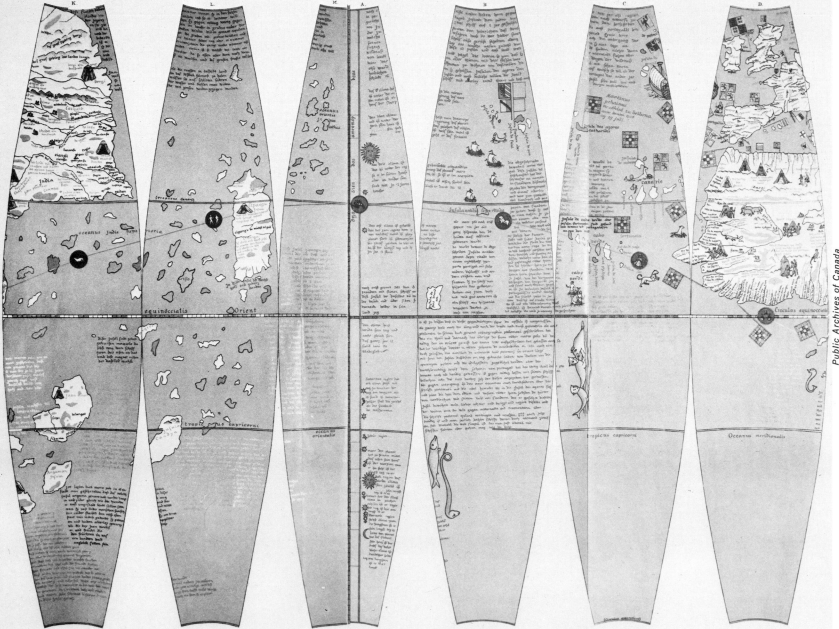

attempted. By coincidence, Columbus found outpost islands of North America about where he expected to sight land, and it was this circumstance that made him so confident that he had reached Asia when in fact he had travelled no farther than the Bahamas.

Printing was invented in the middle of the 15th century and Ptolemy's *Geographia* was printed only a few years after the appearance of Gutenberg's famous Bible. An edition published in Bologna, perhaps as early as 1462, was the first engraved atlas ever produced.

A globe made by Martin Behaim in Nürnberg in 1492—the oldest known to have survived—provides a convenient summary of geographical knowledge on the eve of the discovery of America. As in Ptolemy, the width of the ocean separating Europe from Asia is represented as being just over 3,000 miles.

The Many Discoveries of America

There are always people who are ready to disparage achievement, and the voyages of Christopher Columbus have not escaped their attention. He was not, they contend, the first person to cross the Atlantic and discover America; others—probably many others—had preceded him, notably the Vikings, who certainly reached the eastern coast of Canada nearly 500 years before Columbus sailed. But nothing can detract significantly from the drama and importance of the discovery made on October 12, 1492, when a

Western half of the Vinland map of 1440

sailor in the *Pinta,* the smallest but the fastest of Columbus's three little ships, sighted Watling Island, in the Bahamas, which Columbus called San Salvador. This voyage was not a sporadic or isolated effort; from it there followed the exploration, settlement and exploitation of North and South America that have continued ever since.

But the earlier voyages, real or apocryphal, are not without interest, and there is a surprising array of them. Egyptians reputedly sailed to Mexico 5,000 years ago, and may have been partly responsible for the remarkable civilizations that developed there. Some would have it that a party of Phoenicians, seeking religious freedom, crossed the Atlantic to New Hampshire as early as 480 B.C. Early Christians fleeing from Roman persecution allegedly sought refuge in Virginia in A.D. 64. St. Brendan, an Irish abbot and missionary, is said to have visited Iceland about A.D. 550, and some credit him with having ventured much farther afield, to Newfoundland and even to Bermuda and Florida. Be that as it may, the Irish definitely seem to have reached Iceland before A.D. 800, and a further story of Irish voyaging to America begins about that time. The Norsemen were invading Ireland, and a party that included a group of monks fled to the Shetland Islands. When the Norsemen later appeared there, they moved hastily to Iceland. The approach of the Vikings to Iceland caused the descendants of the Irish colonists to move on to Greenland about A.D. 870. A century later the sighting of a single Viking ship was sufficient to cause the colony to flee once again, this time to New England, where, the story goes, it survived for many years.

How much of this is fact and how much is fable we shall probably never know; each story has its ardent advocates. But there can be no question about the reality of the Viking voyages, although surviving details, based largely on two Icelandic sagas, are frequently vague and often confusing. As already noted, the Norsemen reached Iceland about 870 and founded a settlement there. In 982 Iceland-born Eirikr Thorvaldsson, better known as Eric the Red, was exiled for three years on a charge of homicide. Sailing westward in search of a refuge, he came to Greenland, where he was the first European to explore and settle. About the year 1000 Eric's son Leif Ericsson (Leifr Eiriksson) sailed still further westward on the famous voyage that was to bring him to the mainland of North America.

Leif received some guidance from one Bjarni Herjulfsson, who in 986 had been caught in a storm while sailing from Iceland to Greenland, and had been carried far to the south and west. He is thought to have sailed along the coasts of Newfoundland, Labrador, and Baffin Island before finally finding his way to Greenland. Leif followed much the same course, but in the reverse direction. He visited three regions, which in the sagas are called Helluland (Flagstoneland), Markland (Woodland) and Vinland. There has been endless discussion about the identity of these regions, but it seems fairly certain that Helluland was in Baffin Island and Markland

Viking ship

This Knarr-type seagoing cargo ship was the type in which the Vikings crossed the North Atlantic. Only one ship of this kind has yet been found; it was discovered as recently as 1962, and is now in the Viking Ship Museum at Roskilde, in Denmark. The missing parts of the wide, high-sided hull have been outlined in metal.

in Labrador. The name Vinland was long taken as meaning Wineland, and it was assumed that it must therefore refer to a country with a mild climate where grapes were found. The vicinity of Cape Cod seemed to be the most northerly part of the Atlantic coast to which this description could apply. This view has been challenged recently by Helge Ingstad, the Norwegian archaeologist, who has found and excavated the remains of buildings that are undoubtedly of Norse origin at L'Anse aux Meadows on the northern tip of Newfoundland. Ingstad points out that *vin* is the old Norse word for meadow, and that, in any event, wine can be made from berries as well as from grapes. In all probability L'Anse aux Meadows, where grasslands are extensive and wild berries abundant, was the Vinland of the sagas.

Leif spent the winter in Vinland and returned to Greenland in the spring. He made no further voyages, but two of his brothers—Thorvaldr and Thorsteinn—and his sister, Freydis, all visited Vinland or attempted to do so. Thorsteinn was killed by the Indians, and some years later Thorfinnr Thordarson, a well-to-do Icelandic merchant who had married Thornsteinn's widow, tried unsuccessfully to establish a settlement, first in Vinland and then at a bay called Straumfjord, which may have been the Baie des Sept-Iles in the Gulf of St. Lawrence.

After the Vikings the parade of alleged pre-Columbian discoverers of America continues, but they need not be detailed here. Much more interesting is a manuscript map dating from about 1440

Sectional drawing of Knarr ship
It was about 51 feet long and 14½ feet wide.

that was acquired by Yale University and published in 1965. This shows not only Iceland and Greenland, but to the west of Greenland, a substantial land mass with the inscription, in Latin: "Vinland Island, discovered by Bjarni and Leif in company." This is the earliest known map to show any part of Canada and of the North American mainland.

Belittlers of Columbus have contended that his first voyage was not the great leap in the dark that it professed to be; that he was aware of earlier voyages and knew that land lay at no vast distance to the west. Among other things they point to a voyage made about 1472 by one Joao Vaz Corte-Real, a Portuguese from the Azores. At the request of King Alfonso V of Portugal, the King of Denmark arranged to send Corte-Real to Iceland, Greenland and the lands beyond; but there is no proof that he made new discoveries of importance, news of which would have influenced Columbus's theories and plans.

Columbus sailed on a voyage that was a genuine venture into the unknown, and when he sighted the Bahamas he had no inkling that he had not reached Asia. The fact that he called the natives Indians and referred to the Islands as the Indies is surely proof enough of this.

There was an interesting sequel to Columbus's first voyage. The search for a sea route to Asia seemed to be so exclusively the concern of Spain and Portugal that Pope Alexander VI undertook to assign them areas of exploration and thereby avoid friction between them. The line of demarcation was first laid down on May 4, 1493, but was revised later under the terms of a convention signed by the two nations at Tordesillas on June 7, 1494. The amended line, which extended from pole to pole, was 370 leagues west of the Cape Verde Islands, very near to 50° west longitude. The only land on the mainland of the Americas east of this is the eastern part of Brazil, which was long a Portuguese possession. Everything west of it, including the whole of North America, was assigned to Spain. No provision was made for the interests and ambitions of other nations.

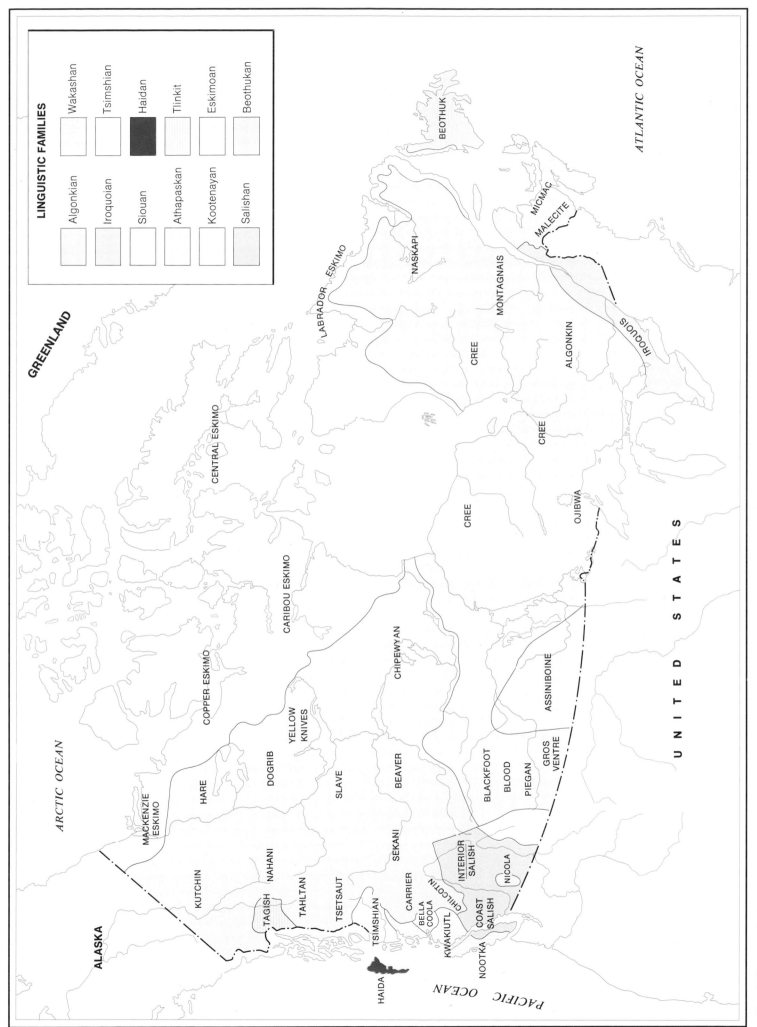

LINGUISTIC FAMILIES

Wakashan	Tsimshian	Haidan	Tlinkit	Eskimoan	Beothukan
Algonkian	Iroquoian	Siouan	Athapaskan	Kootenayan	Salishan

GREENLAND

ATLANTIC OCEAN

BEOTHUK

MICMAC

MALECITE

IROQUOIS

NASKAPI

LABRADOR ESKIMO

MONTAGNAIS

ALGONKIN

CREE

CENTRAL ESKIMO

CREE

CREE

OJIBWA

CARIBOU ESKIMO

COPPER ESKIMO

CHIPEWYAN

ASSINIBOINE

ARCTIC OCEAN

YELLOW KNIVES

DOGRIB

SLAVE

BEAVER

BLACKFOOT

GROS VENTRE

MACKENZIE ESKIMO

HARE

BLOOD

PIEGAN

KUTCHIN

NAHANI

SEKANI

INTERIOR SALISH

NICOLA

ALASKA

TAGISH

TAHLTAN

TSETSAUT

CARRIER

CHILCOTIN

TSIMSHIAN

BELLA COOLA

COAST SALISH

KWAKIUTL

NOOTKA

HAIDA

PACIFIC OCEAN

UNITED STATES

Indian Tribes at the Time of Discovery

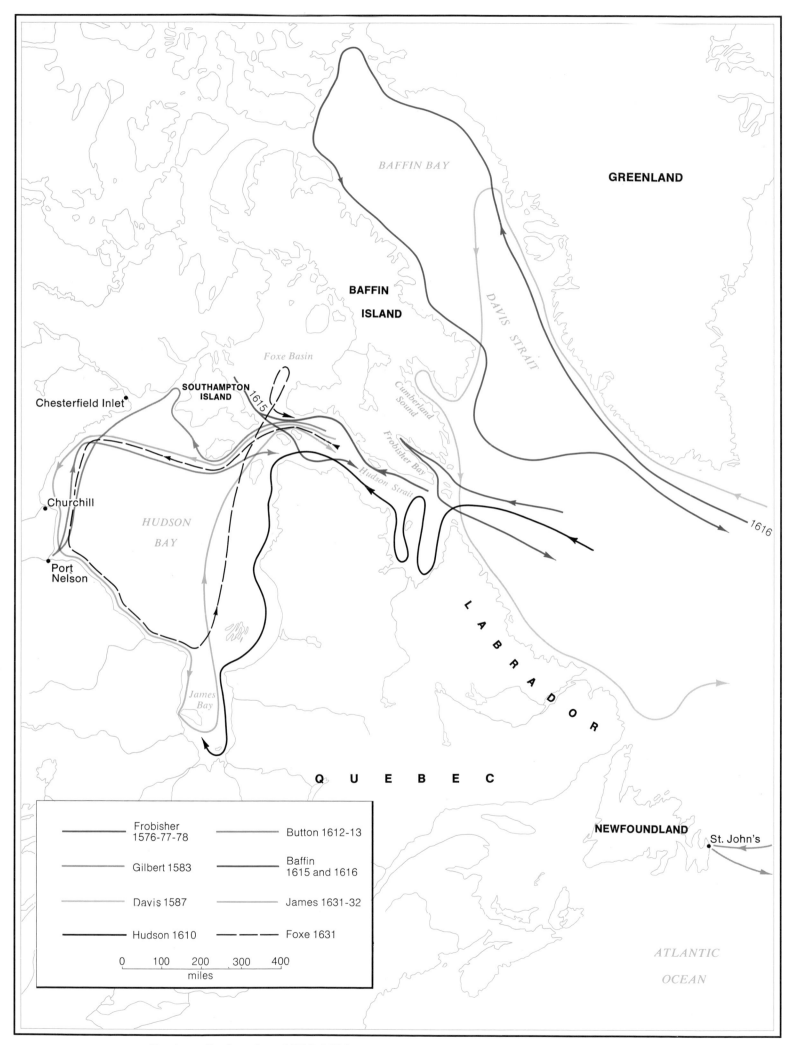

GREENLAND

BAFFIN BAY

BAFFIN

ISLAND

DAVIS STRAIT

Foxe Basin

Chesterfield Inlet

**SOUTHAMPTON
ISLAND**

1615

*Cumberland
Sound*

Frobisher Bay

Churchill

Hudson Strait

HUDSON

BAY

1616

Port
Nelson

L A B R A D O R

*James
Bay*

Q U E B E C

NEWFOUNDLAND

St. John's

Frobisher
1576-77-78

Gilbert 1583

Davis 1587

Hudson 1610

Button 1612-13

Baffin
1615 and 1616

James 1631-32

Foxe 1631

0   100   200   300   400
miles

ATLANTIC

OCEAN

Northern Exploration, 1576-1632

Canada As the White Man Found It

The early explorers found in North America a continent of contrasts. This was especially true of the climate, which varied from the near-tropical of Central America to the extreme Arctic climate in the far north, and was true also of the population. In Mexico the Spaniards discovered millions of people, including a highly developed Aztec empire with five or six million subjects. Farther north the continent was much more sparsely settled and cultures were much more primitive. At the time Columbus sailed, there were probably only about 900,000 Indians in the whole of what is now the United States, and no more than 220,000 Indians and Eskimo in the areas now comprising Canada.

The remote ancestors of Canada's Indians and Eskimo came to North America from Asia. In glacial times a land bridge existed between Siberia and Alaska. Later, when Bering Strait came into existence, its width was no more than 50 miles, and the Diomede Islands, in mid-channel, halved the distance that had to be traversed at one time. From Alaska the migrants worked their way eastward and southward by a variety of routes, including the Mackenzie River valley and the valleys of other rivers more to the west and south. As the figures given indicate, their descendants never became sufficiently numerous even to begin to populate the continent as a whole; patches of population grew up here and there where conditions seemed favourable, and for long periods there was little or no contact between many of them. This isolation explains the development of dozens of native languages that have virtually no kinship with one another, and many ways of life that often had surprisingly little in common.

The accompanying map of Canada shows the distribution of the major native tribes about the time they first came into contact with Europeans. As the white man arrived in eastern Canada long before

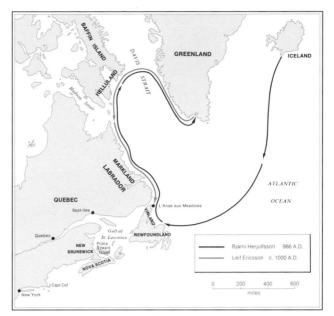

The Norse Voyages to Vinland

Excavations at L'Anse aux Meadows

Dr. Helge Ingstad

he reached the west, the map of the country east of Lake Superior shows the distribution of the tribes about 1525, or about the time of the voyages of Cabot and Cartier. The western part of the map shows the tribes as they are believed to have been distributed about 1725.

The physical nature of an area naturally went far to determine what a tribe ate, whether it lived in villages or led a nomadic life, and what kind of dwellings it built. Plains Indians based their life chiefly upon the buffalo, and as this made it necessary for them to be frequently on the move, they lived in teepees which were easy to carry from place to place. The Athapaskan tribes, living in a forest region farther north, depended chiefly on the caribou. The Pacific Coast Indians were primarily fish eaters, and although they were great travellers, they made their headquarters in permanent villages that included massive timber communal houses. Corn (maize), supplemented by beans and pumpkins, was the basic food of the Iroquoian Indians, including the Hurons. An agricultural society, they lived in villages, each surrounded by its cornfields. The village had to be moved from time to time when the fertility of the nearby land was exhausted. The Algonkian tribes, living in an enormous area, largely forested, stretching from the foothills of the Rocky Mountains to the Maritime Provinces, lived by both hunting and fishing, and were compelled in their search for food to move about, according to the season.

The Iroquoian group, which was to be so influential in the early history of Canada, included not only the Iroquois proper—the famous confederacy of five tribes, the Seneca, Cayuga, Onondaga, Oneida and Mohawk—who lived in the area south of Lake Ontario and the St. Lawrence River—but the Huron, Neutral and Tobacco Indians as well. In 1525 it seems that the Hurons occupied the whole north bank of the St. Lawrence to a point some distance east of Quebec, and on the south extended

19

Public Archives of Canada

Chart of the North Atlantic by Sigurdus Stephanius
The original of this interesting map showing Helluland, Markland and Vinland has been lost, but this copy, made in 1670, is preserved in the Royal Library in Copenhagen. The original was probably made in 1590, not 1570, the date given in the cartouche. The long peninsula marked "Promontorium Winlandiae" (Vinland) may well represent the northern part of Newfoundland. A similar map dated 1599 was discovered recently in Hungary by Helge Ingstad.

Geological Survey

Cree Indian camp on the prairie

The teepee was an ideal dwelling for the prairie Indian for their nomadic way of life. The framework consisted of saplings and some poles and the covering was made of buffalo and other hides. A typical teepee was about 15 feet in diameter.

into the Gaspé country. Certainly it seems probable that the Indians that Cartier met in the Gaspé and at the future sites of Quebec and Montreal were Huron-Iroquois. By the time Champlain arrived, three-quarters of a century later, they had withdrawn to Ontario, and their chief stronghold was in the area between Georgian Bay and Lake Simcoe that was later to be known as Huronia.

Thus tribal boundaries were not hard and fast but varied considerably from time to time. And the white man frequently contributed, at least indirectly, to these changes. The first tribe to obtain firearms possessed such an immense advantage over its neighbours that it could drive them out of long-held ancestral lands. In some cases the first tribe to secure horses enjoyed a kindred advantage. On the plains, horses and firearms in combination encouraged the growth of the belligerent bands of raiders who devoted much of their time to war and horse stealing.

For centuries after the white man came, the Indian and Eskimo populations of Canada steadily declined. In large part they were the victims of diseases brought from Europe against which they had had no chance to develop resistance. The Eskimo in particular fell victims to even the mildest of epidemics. In recent years, partly owing to greatly improved health services, both Indians and Eskimo have been multiplying rapidly. Indian population, which was only 136,00 in 1949, exceeded 225,000 in 1969, and the Eskimo have increased in number from 8,000 to over 15,000. Native population is back to the level at which it stood when Cabot and Cartier made their voyages.

Haida Indian village, Queen Charlotte Islands
This photograph of the village of Skidegate was taken in 1878. The West Coast Indian houses were the largest and most permanent dwellings built by Canadian Indians. Their economy was based chiefly on salmon and the cedar tree.

Geological Survey

CHAPTER 2

First Explorations

The Founding Voyages: Cabot and Cartier

JOHN CABOT, an Italian navigator and maker of maps and globes whose real name was Giovanni Caboto, arrived in England about 1495 and soon went to Bristol, which was then the centre of English interest in exploration westward. The names of several enterprising Bristol shipowners deserve to be better known than they are, notably Thomas Croft and John Jay, who in 1480—twelve years before Columbus sailed—sent a ship out into the Atlantic in search of land. She was driven back by storms, but a second attempt was made in 1481 and others followed. Details are vague, but it seems fairly certain that one of the expeditions, perhaps in 1494, did discover land, but what land it was we do not know.

Cabot, with Bristol backing, received letters patent from King Henry VII in 1496 authorizing him to make a voyage of discovery. He duly sailed but, like the ship that set out in 1480, was forced to return to port. The following spring he sailed on his second and world famous voyage. In the *Matthew* he left Bristol on May 20, 1497, and 35 days later, on June 24, sighted land. There, a contemporary source tells us, he "disembarked . . . with a crucifix and raised banners with the arms of the Holy Father and those of the King of England."

The location of this landfall has been the subject of endless controversy. Cape Breton in Nova Scotia and Cape Bonavista in Newfoundland both tenaciously claim the distinction, but it is unlikely that either claim is valid. New light was thrown on Cabot's voyage recently when a letter written in 1497 by one John Day came to light in the Spanish archives in Simancas. Day, who had been in England and had personal knowledge of the voyage, wrote to an unnamed correspondent in Spain who may have been Columbus himself. It had been assumed that Cabot, having sighted land, followed the coastline southward. The John Day letter and a harder look at other sources suggest that he sailed northward from his landfall and then sailed for home from the cape he believed to be nearest to Ireland. This means that he probably first sighted land in southern Nova Scotia, then sailed northward along the coast of Nova Scotia and Cape Breton, crossed over to Newfoundland, and took his departure from Cape Race. He was back in Bristol on August 6, and a few days later received a reward of £10 and a pension of £20 per annum from Henry VII for his discoveries. In 1498 Cabot made a further voyage, but few details are available and he himself apparently perished in the course of it.

Cabot was looking for a route to Asia, and if he did not find it he hoped at least to discover land that could be a staging-point on the way to the Far East. Of greater immediate interest in Bristol was his discovery of waters that teemed with fish—the famous fishing banks off Nova Scotia and Newfoundland. English fishermen were soon busily fishing there, and voyages from Bristol—for the most part unsung—continued. A "Company of Adventurers into the New Found Lands," with which John Jay was connected, sent out several ships between 1501 and 1505.

Trading ties between Bristol and Portugal were close, and King Manuel became interested in exploration, perhaps because he thought Cabot and others were invading areas that had been assigned to Portugal by the Treaty of Tordesillas in 1494. Portuguese fishermen had already begun to exploit the Newfoundland fishing banks, as they do to this day; Manuel was levying a tithe on them by 1501. The previous year Gaspar Corte-Real, son of Joao Vaz Corte-Real, who is said to have crossed the ocean in 1472, set out from Lisbon on a voyage of exploration. He got as far as Greenland, and some think that he continued on and sailed around Newfoundland, but there is no proof of this. In 1501 he made a second voyage and it seems clear that this time he did reach Labrador or Newfoundland. The ship in which he was travelling was lost, and in 1502

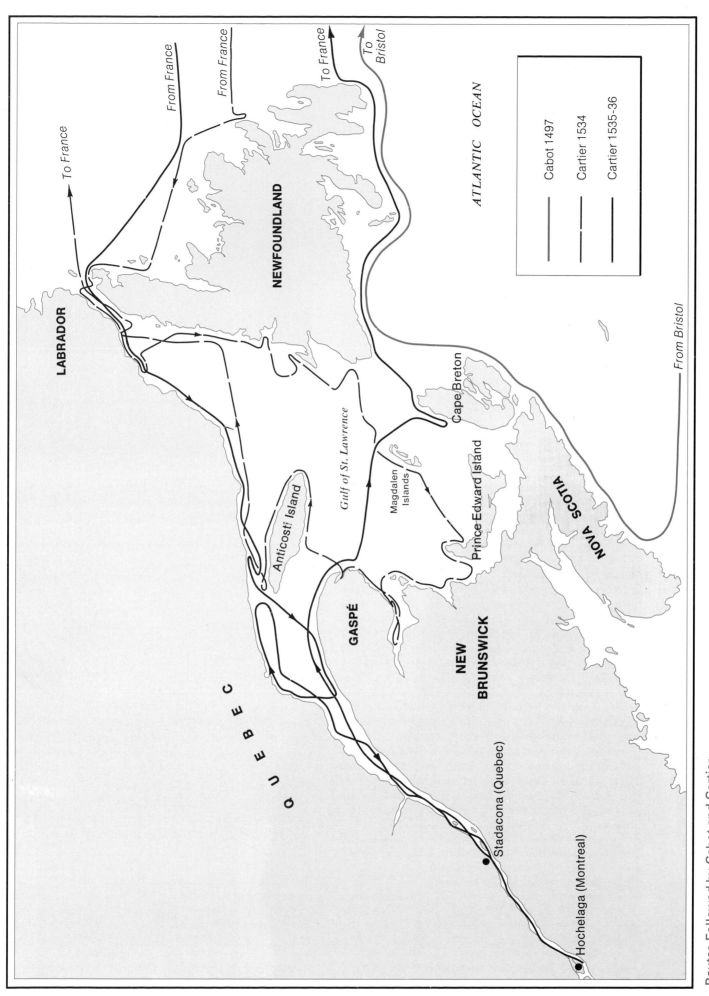

ATLANTIC OCEAN

LABRADOR

NEWFOUNDLAND

From France

From France

To France

To Bristol

From Bristol

Cabot 1497

Cartier 1534

Cartier 1535-36

Cape Breton

Gulf of St. Lawrence

Anticosti Island

Magdalen Islands

Prince Edward Island

NOVA SCOTIA

NEW BRUNSWICK

GASPÉ

QUEBEC

Stadacona (Quebec)

Hochelaga (Montreal)

Routes Followed by Cabot and Cartier

Portrait of Cartier in
Costumes français

Giovanni de Verrazzano
From an engraving by Guiseppe Zocchi (d. 1767), said to have been based on a painting in the Royal Gallery in Florence that has since disappeared.

his brother Miguel undertook a search for him. He may have visited St. John's harbour, but details are lacking as Miguel himself was lost on the return voyage. Twenty years later, in 1521, King Manuel gave a charter to Joao Alvares Fagundes, who sailed from Lisbon to discover new lands. He traced the southern coast of Newfoundland from Cape Race to Cape Ray, but whether he reached Cape Breton and entered the Gulf of St. Lawrence, as some have contended, is questionable.

Meanwhile the French had become interested in America. Breton fishermen were on the banks as early as 1504, and others from Normandy soon followed. In 1508 Thomas Aubert, a Dieppe sailor, crossed the Atlantic and brought back the first American Indians seen in France. King Francis I became anxious to have a share in the lands and treasures that Spain in particular was finding in the New World. The result was an official expedition under Giovanni da Verrazzano, a much-travelled Italian, who left Dieppe late in 1523, and sailed westward from Madeira early in 1524. A route to Asia was his prime objective, and he was hopeful that a passage would be found somewhere in the long and as yet unexplored stretch of coast between Florida and Nova Scotia. His landfall was probably in what is now North Carolina, and he worked his way northward to Newfoundland (making the first visit by a white man to the harbour of New York on the way) without finding any passage. Early in July he was back in Dieppe.

Jacques Cartier may have been with Verrazzano, but there is no proof of this. His own much more important and famous expeditions were made a decade later, in 1534 and 1535. He himself recorded them in considerable detail, and his journal is the earliest full-fledged travel narrative relating to Canada.

It is obvious that Cartier was following a well-beaten path when he sailed from his native town of St. Malo on April 20, 1534, and crossed the ocean to the Strait of Belle Isle. It was his purpose that set him apart from the many fishermen who had made the voyage, some of them doubtless several times. He came to go beyond the straits and to explore in the hope that he would find new lands for France, rich in gold and silver, and the long-sought route to Asia.

On this voyage Cartier spent two months feeling his way around the Gulf of St. Lawrence, which he was the first to describe and map in any detail. From Belle Isle he sailed down the west coast of Newfoundland, then crossed to the Magdalene Islands, travelled on to Prince Edward Island, and then went northward to the Bay of Chaleur and Gaspé. On July 24, on the shore of the Baie de Gaspé, he erected a large cross and took formal possession of the country in the name of the King of

Portrait of Cartier in Costumes français

This portrait of Cartier has appeared in countless textbooks, but the ancestory of the painting shows that there is only a remote possibility that it really resembles Cartier.

The portrait here reproduced, now in the Public Archives of Canada, was executed in 1860 by Theopile Hamel, a distinguished Canadian artist. It is a copy of a portrait in the Hôtel de Ville in St. Malo, Cartier's birthplace, painted by Francois Riss in 1839. Riss is said to have based his likeness on a pen-and-ink sketch in the Bibliotheque Nationale in Paris, but no such sketch can now be found. It is much more likely that his starting point was an illustration in Costumes français depuis Clovis jusqu'à nos jours, *published in Paris in 1836. Dr. Gustave Lanctôt, who has made a special study of Cartier portraits, thinks that the artist who executed this picture (probably Leopold Massard) based it in turn on a rough sketch that appears on the so-called Harleian map in the British Museum. This was certainly drawn very soon after Cartier's third voyage of 1541–42, and must have been based in part on data he supplied. It seems logical to assume that the central figure in the little group was intended to represent Cartier himself, and as he knew the French mapmakers of the day personally, it may well give an authentic impression of his general appearance. Unfortunately, it is too indistinct to give anything more.*

France. He then sailed on to Anticosti Island, and from there turned homeward and reached St. Malo on September 5.

On his second voyage, in 1535, Cartier became the discoverer of the St. Lawrence River, the great pathway to the interior of the continent that France was to control for two centuries and more. It was on August 13 that, guided by Indians, he started up the

Sir Martin Frobisher
Painted for the Cathay Company in 1577 by Cornelius Ketel, a Dutch painter working in England, this is the earliest authentic portrait of a British explorer of Canada. It was given to Oxford University in 1674, and is now in the Bodleian Library.

river, and on September 7 he reached the future site of Quebec, then occupied by an Indian village called Stadacona. On the 19th he began to push still further up the river, and on October 2 came to the village of Hochelaga, where Montreal now stands, and saw the Lachine Rapids, which barred the way to further easy travel.

Cartier had decided to spend the winter near Stadacona. He had no warning of the severity of the weather he and his men would have to endure, and they suffered intensely from the cold and from scurvy; 25 died before spring brought relief. He had to abandon one of his three ships, but finally sailed for home on May 6, 1536. It is noteworthy that on this return voyage he sailed south of Newfoundland, thus establishing the fact that it was a huge island.

Cartier planned a third voyage, but wars and other distractions in Europe led to long postponements. He sailed finally in May of 1541, this time under the orders of the Sieur de Roberval, who had been given the commission that Cartier himself had hoped to secure. He revisited Stadacona and Hochelaga and wintered again near Stadacona in a fledgling settlement christened Charlesbourg-Royal. But things seem not to have gone well and in June 1542 Cartier left for France. He took with him what he hoped were gold and diamonds, but which were in reality only iron pyrites and quartz. Roberval continued the colony briefly, but it was abandoned in 1543.

Cartier's career thus ended somewhat unhappily, but his fame rests securely upon his pioneering explorations of the Gulf of St. Lawrence, his discovery of the St. Lawrence River, and the fact that he and his men were the first exploring party since the Vikings to experience the rigours of an eastern Canadian winter.

The Explorers Turn Northward

By 1540 the immensity of the land barrier that lay to the west between Europe and Asia had become apparent. Explorers had ascertained that it consisted of two huge new continents, connected by an isthmus, which between them presented a continuous coastline from the far north to Cape Horn. Magellan, sailing across the Pacific in 1521, had found that in the south, at least, Asia was a much greater distance beyond the Americas than had been expected: the world was a substantially larger globe than it had been thought to be.

Except for the annual visits of her fishermen, France took no part in Canadian exploration for 60 years after Cartier's third voyage; she was preoccupied with affairs at home. In England, Queen Elizabeth came to the throne and by degrees a new spirit, adventurous and aggressive, spread among her merchants and seamen. Sir Francis Drake has become symbolic of the age, and on his famous buccaneering voyage around the world in 1577-79 it is probable that he sighted the west coast of British Columbia—the first white man to do so by a margin of almost two centuries.

Two other Elizabethans—Martin Frobisher and Sir Humphrey Gilbert—were the pioneers in a new era of British exploration. It was they who really began the long search for the North West Passage, which was in effect the search for a route to Asia around the northern end of the land barrier formed by the Americas. Cape Horn offered such a route at its southern end, but it was remote from England and using it would necessitate long voyages through waters that Spain regarded as her own. If a northern passage could be found, it would be both much shorter and in an area that the English could expect to control. Frobisher and his many successors started out with high hopes, but the hard facts of geography were to defeat them. North America extends much farther to the north than South

The earliest picture of Canadian Eskimo
Frobisher encountered Eskimo at Frobisher Inlet, on Baffin Island, and he brought a man and woman back to England. John White, the artist who made this water-colour drawing, seems to have sailed with Frobisher, and the drawings may have been made on the voyage or in England.

Sir Humphrey Gilbert
From an engraving by Willem and Magdalena van de Passe, one of a series published in 1620.

America does to the south, and this rendered hopeless the task of finding a northern passage that would be ice-free and navigable for more than a brief and uncertain period each year.

Frobisher set out with three small ships in June 1576. One was lost in a storm and a second turned back, but Frobisher struggled on alone in the *Gabriel*. From the coast of Greenland he sailed on to Baffin Island and entered Frobisher Bay, a great inlet that he hopefully took to be the strait separating America and Asia. Early in October he was back in London, where an assayer unfortunately professed to have found gold in some ore samples he had brought home. Frobisher's interest was thereby diverted from exploration to treasure hunting, and the voyages he made in 1577 and 1578 were devoted primarily to mining. In the end the hundreds of tons of ore carried to England from Frobisher Bay were found to be virtually valueless.

Gilbert—a half-brother of Sir Walter Raleigh —now took over the quest for a passage. In 1578 he was granted letters patent both for a voyage of discovery and the founding of a colony. After several

false starts and a preliminary voyage in 1580, Gilbert finally sailed with five ships in June 1583. One of them turned back, but the other four had assembled in St. John's harbour by August 3. Two days later Gilbert took formal possession for England of Newfoundland and all lands 200 leagues to the north and south of it. He had found 36 fishing vessels in the harbour—evidence of the extent of trans-atlantic traffic, even at this early date— and to emphasize his act of possession he issued fishing licences to them. At the end of August he left for home, full of plans to return the next year; but he and the little ship in which he embarked were lost at sea.

John Davis, a friend of Gilbert's, appears next on the scene. He was both an able commander and a highly qualified navigator, and his three voyages made an important contribution to knowledge of the northern coasts. After two more or less preliminary voyages in 1585 and 1586, Davis carried out his most notable explorations in 1587, when he traced the outline of the whole southern part of Davis Strait. Ice conditions were favourable, and he was able to sail up the west coast of Greenland as far as latitude 72°12'—much further north than anyone else had yet gone. He then crossed Davis Strait, followed the coast of Baffin Island southward, noted the entrances to Frobisher Bay and Hudson Strait, and continued on down the coast of Labrador.

After a pause of over twenty years, British exploration of Canada's northland was resumed in 1610 with one of the most famous of all Arctic voyages, that of Henry Hudson. Hudson had made a notable voyage the previous year for the Dutch East India Company, who had sent him to search for a northeast passage. Forced to turn back beyond the North Cape by ice, Hudson decided to cross the Atlantic and try to find a passage through North America. He rediscovered New York harbour, which Verrazzano had entered in 1524, and ascended the Hudson River as far as the site of Albany. In 1610 he followed in Davis's footsteps, sailed through Hudson Strait, and entered Hudson Bay, which he took to be the Pacific Ocean. Circumstances forced him to winter in James Bay, and difficulties that arose there revealed his weaknesses as a leader and disciplinarian. In June 1611, soon after the party left for home, the crew mutinied and put Hudson, his son, and the men who remained loyal to him adrift in a shallop. Though it ended in tragedy, Hudson's voyage was a notable and historic achievement and the great bay he discovered rightfully bears his name.

Other voyages followed. In 1612 Sir Thomas Button, looking for both Hudson and a northwest passage, crossed Hudson Bay, wintered at the mouth of the Nelson River, and then explored the bay's western shore in hopes of finding an opening. In 1615 William Baffin, a particularly able navigator, explored Hudson Bay as far as Southampton Island and became convinced—quite correctly—that there was no way out of it towards the west. The next year, 1616, he accomplished the remarkable feat of sailing around the entire shoreline of Baffin Bay; this took him to latitude 77°45', which remained the northern limit of exploration for well over two centuries.

Three other names deserve mention. Jens Munk, a Dane, led the only non-British expedition of the period into Hudson Bay in 1619. He spent a dreadful winter at the mouth of the Churchill River. Nevertheless he intended to return and found a colony, but the plan was never carried further. Some years later, in 1631, Thomas James, sailing from Bristol, and Luke Foxe, from London, both filled in blank spaces on the map of Hudson Bay and adjacent waters. James wintered in James Bay, and later wrote an account of his experiences that has become a classic; but it told so grim a tale that it discouraged others from undertaking further northern exploration for many years to come.

From many points of view this whole effort, from Frobisher's first voyage of 1576 to James's return to Bristol in 1632, was a failure. No passage was found and no treasure was unearthed. But these voyages had traced with fair accuracy the general outline of a vast portion of the Canadian northland, and the names of the navigators who accomplished this feat well deserve their prominence on the map of Canada.

Early Maps of Canada

The seven maps here reproduced in whole or in part show how Canada gradually emerged on the map of the world during the 16th century. At this time map-making was far from being an exact science; accurate surveys were virtually unknown. Adding to the confusion, cartographers were reluctant to leave blank spaces on their maps, and most of them filled in unexplored areas with features based on rumour, theory, or sheer imagination. As a result 16th century maps show Canada in an almost infinite variety of shapes and sizes. But Europe's conception of America did progress through definite stages, and the accompanying maps illustrate some of them.

The famous map of Juan de la Cosa, now preserved in the Museo Naval in Madrid, dates from about 1500. The portion showing the western parts of Europe and Africa, the Atlantic Ocean (which appears as a vast bay with the West Indies at its western end) and the New World is here reproduced. The enlarged inset shows part of the coast of North America. This runs in an east-west direction and is marked with five English flags. It seems certain that this is an attempt to record Cabot's discoveries of 1497. Some scholars think that it represents the area between Cape Canso, or Cape Breton Island, and Placentia Bay in Newfoundland. It seems more likely that it is intended to show the coastlines all the way from southern Nova Scotia to Cape Race.

In 1502 Amerigo Vespucci advanced the view that America was a new continent, distinct from Asia.

Public Archives of Canada

Thomas James
James Bay was named to commemorate his explorations. This engraving was based on an inset on the map included in his account of his travels, which is entitled The Strange and Dangerous Voyage of Captain Thomas James in his intended discovery of the North-West Passage into the South Seas *(London, 1633).*

He had his reward in 1507 when Martin Waldseemuller produced his famous map in which the New World was depicted as a separate entity and the name "America" was first placed upon it. North and South America, connected by an isthmus, were shown after a fashion, but it was Gerard Mercator, in a map printed in 1538, who first showed the two continents clearly and named them North and South America. The North American section of the remarkable world map published by Mercator in 1569 is shown in the accompanying illustration.

About the middle of the century, two Portuguese cartographers, Lopo and Diego Homen, pro-

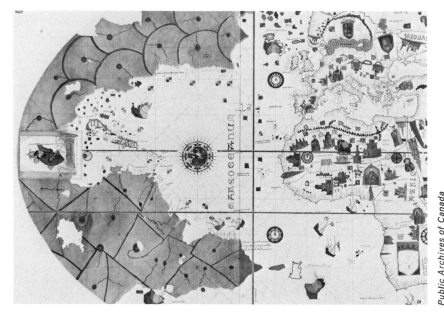

Public Archives of Canada

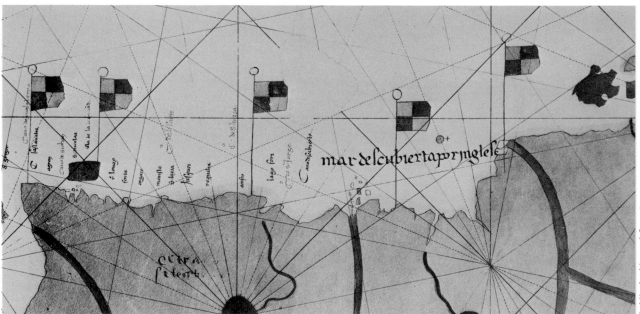

Public Archives of Canada

The La Cosa map, drawn about 1500. (See also frontispiece)

Cabot's discoveries on the La Cosa map

duced a series of notable maps. The section of one of them that depicts Nova Scotia and Cape Breton is here reproduced. Although drawn in 1558, this map undoubtedly records the discoveries made by Fagundes and probably other Portuguese explorers who visited the coast about 1520. It was upon this map that the Bay of Fundy (shown extending roughly to the north, instead of the east) first made its appearance.

Pierre Desceliers, one of a number of French cartographers who belonged to what is known as the Dieppe school of cartography, drew the picturesque map dated 1546. At first sight its details seem difficult to grasp because north is at the bottom instead of in its usual place at the top. Reversing the page will show that the map is an easily recognizable outline of northeastern North America in which Cartier's discoveries are recorded and such familiar

place names as Labrador, Terre Neuve (Newfoundland) and Canada appear.

The world map dated 1570 is from the first modern atlas, published that year in Antwerp by Abraham Ortelius. It is not difficult to distinguish fact from fiction in this map; stylized outlines and a scarcity of place names show the areas in which Ortelius had to use his imagination. The map is interesting because it shows the proper relationships between Europe, Africa and the Americas, and because it credits North America both with a vast expanse of territory and a strait separating it from Asia. The latter—the Strait of Anian—was purely imaginary, but its supposed existence had an important influence on exploration, and in the end Bering Strait, a real waterway, was found to exist roughly where Ortelius and others had placed the Strait of Anian.

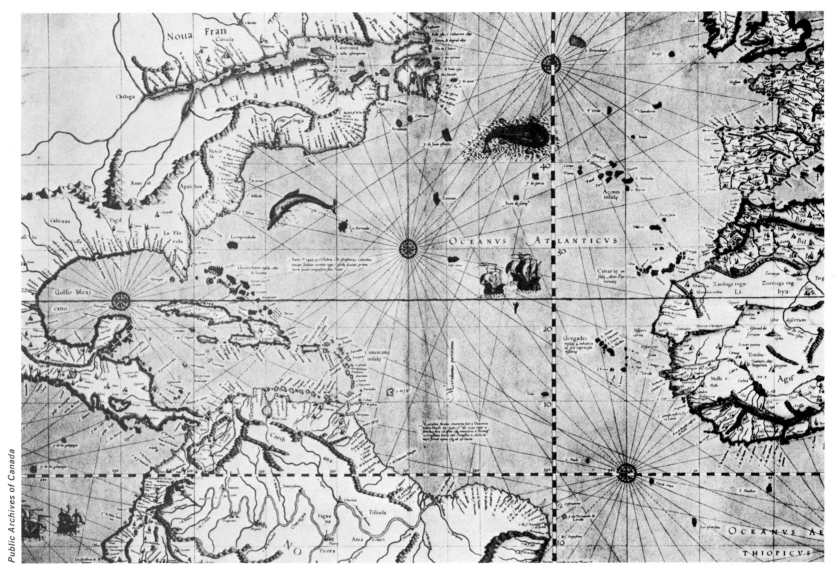

First appearance of the name ''America''
On Waldseemuller's world map of 1507 ''America'' appears on the southern part of South America.

Part of Mercator's world chart of 1569

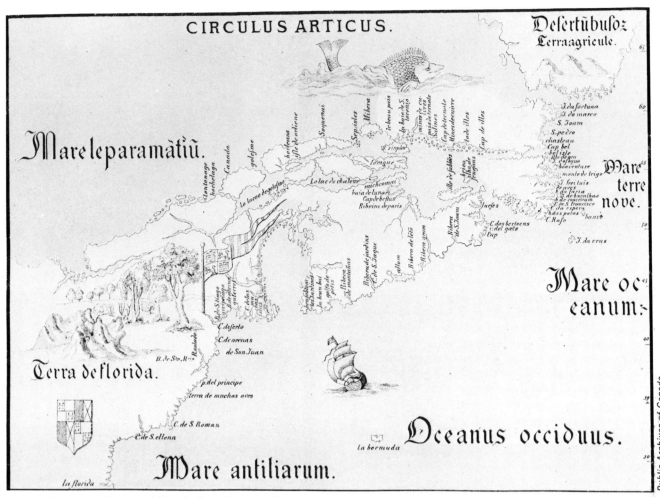

The Northeast Parts of North America by Homan

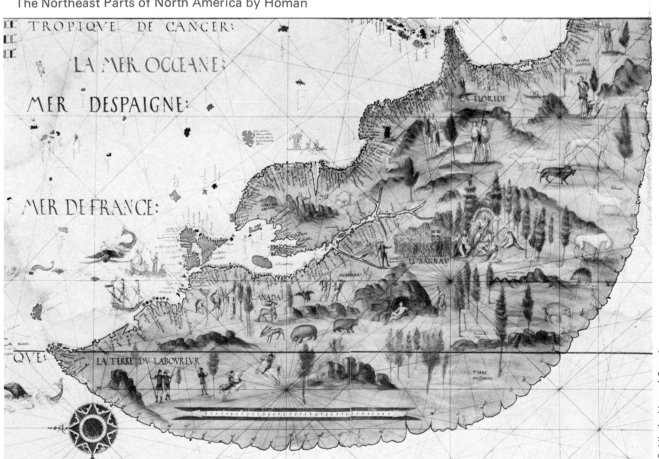

North America by Pierre Desceliers, 1546

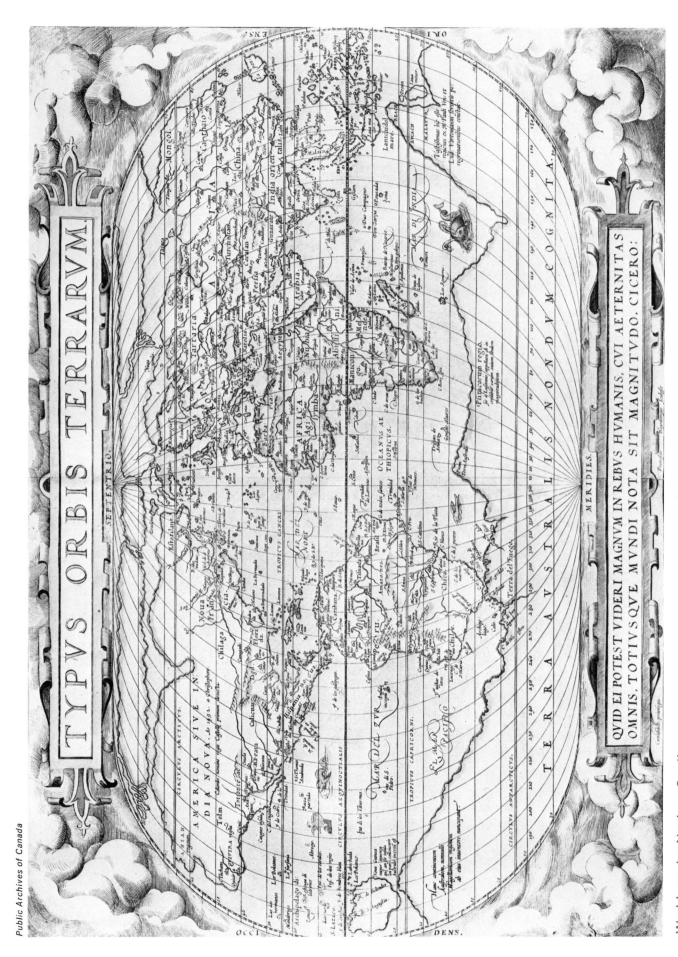

World map by Abraham Ortelius

CHAPTER 3

New France

Champlain: The Founding of New France

Told in brief, the story of Samuel de Champlain and the first French settlements in Canada may seem to be a simple, straightforward tale. In reality its background was complicated in the extreme. Voyages that are only vaguely known; monopolies that were plagued by rivals poaching on their privileges; trading companies that were much more imposing on paper than in reality, and whose nominal heads were constantly changing; fluctuating interest and support in France; war between France and England —these were among the things that made the lot of the colonizer anything but an easy one. Indeed, Champlain himself emerges as the only constant factor in the narrative; through good times and bad he retained his interest and faith in the future of Canada and held doggedly to his purposes. He richly deserves to be remembered and honoured as the founder of New France.

Little is known about Champlain's early career. He served for a time in the army, but geography and travel soon became his chief interests. Later he was to become a notable explorer and an accomplished mapmaker. His first important venture abroad was a two-year voyage to the West Indies, from which he returned in 1600 or 1601. In 1603 Aymar de Chaste held a trading monopoly, and Champlain joined an expedition he was sending to Canada. He went as an observer, not an employee, and in addition to visiting Tadoussac and the future sites of Quebec and Montreal, he was able to explore the lower reaches of both the Saguenay and Richelieu Rivers.

Champlain found the St. Lawrence attractive, but his interest shifted for some years to Acadia, where rich mines were believed to exist. By this time the trading monopoly was held by Pierre Du Gua de Monts, and Champlain may have persuaded him to try to found a settlement in Acadia instead of on the St. Lawrence. Once again Champlain had no official status in the expedition, but he sailed with it in 1604 and during the next three years shared in de Monts' efforts to establish a colony. A first miserable winter was spent on Ile Sainte-Croix (now Dochets Island) in the St. Croix River, an unfortunate site that had been chosen with ease of defence chiefly in mind. In 1605 the post was moved across the Bay of Fundy to Port Royal (now Annapolis Royal) in present-day Nova Scotia. Things went much better there, but owing to uncertainties about de Monts' trading privileges the colonists returned to France in 1607. While in Acadia Champlain had again devoted much time and attention to exploration, and he is believed to have examined virtually the whole of the coastline from Cape Breton to Cape Cod.

Champlain's interest now shifted back to the St. Lawrence and in 1608, this time serving officially as de Monts' lieutenant, he sailed up the river and founded Quebec. In retrospect this emerges as a momentous event, but at the time Quebec's very existence was precarious. For some years the colony had no more than a few dozen inhabitants; it was Champlain's activities as an explorer that made the period notable. In 1609 he agreed to accompany the local Indians on a foray against the Iroquois, which enabled him to explore the Richelieu River and Lake Champlain. In a brief battle fought near Lake George late in July his firearms, with which the Iroquois were unfamiliar, put the Iroquois to flight. Champlain is usually blamed for thus incurring the enmity of the powerful Iroquois confederacy, but a policy of neutrality was probably quite impracticable; the Indians in New France would not have remained friendly if he had refused to support them against their enemies.

In 1611 Champlain once again explored the St. Lawrence as far as the site of Montreal. He made some preparations to build a post there, but the plan was not carried out until 1642. In 1613 he ventured still farther afield and ascended the Ottawa River as far as Allumette Island, opposite the

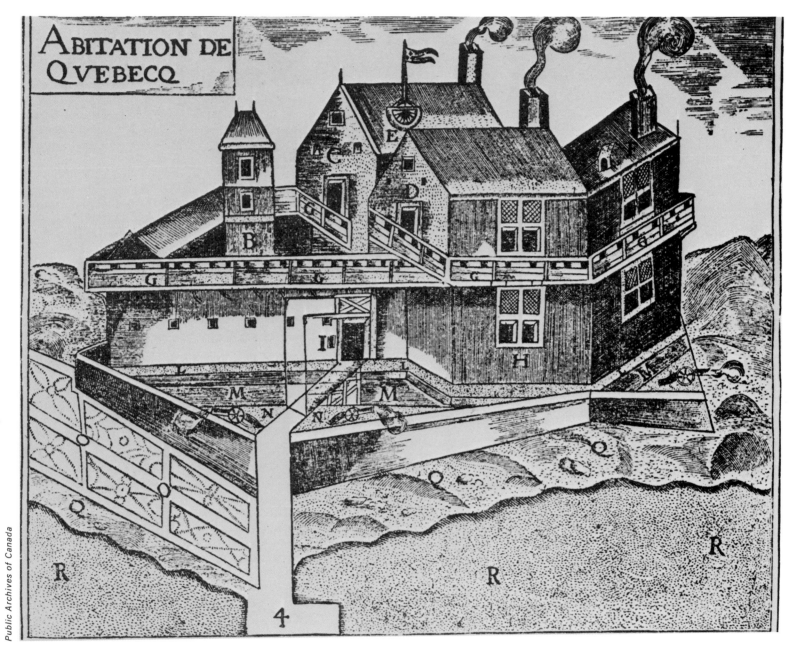

ABITATION DE QVEBECQ

The Habitation at Quebec

*This is Champlain's own drawing, first published
in the 1613 edition of his* Voyages.

Samuel de Champlain

Few imaginary portraits have become more familiar and few are more widely assumed to be genuine than this portrait of Champlain (upper left). But the original lithograph dates back no further than 1854, and was made from a painting by Louis César Joseph Ducornet, a French artist. There seems to be no doubt that when Ducornet looked about for a model he found and followed the portrait of Michel Porticelli, an Italian financier, engraved by Balthazar Moncornet in 1654. The picture of Champlain was the work of a man who was born deformed, without arms, but by using brushes with his mouth and toes Ducornet became an artist of some note.

Public Archives of Canada

Public Archives of Canada

present city of Pembroke. All this time he had been gathering information about the lakes and lands in the interior, and in 1615 he was able at last to put this knowledge to the test. Following what was later to become the main fur trade route to the west—the Ottawa River, the Mattawa, Lake Nipissing and French River—he reached Georgian Bay, the great eastern wing of Lake Huron. Following the coast southward he came to the central homeland of the Huron Indians, which lay between Georgian Bay and Lake Simcoe. Urged once more to join in an assault on the Iroquois, he descended the Trent River with a war party, crossed the eastern end of Lake Ontario, and travelled on into what is now New York State. Near the site of Syracuse the Hurons made a badly mismanaged attack on a fortified Iroquois village; the Hurons were repulsed and Champlain himself was wounded. He spent the winter with the Hurons and did not return to Quebec until the spring of 1616. In many ways this had been an unfortunate enterprise, but Champlain had gained a remarkable grasp of the geography of a vast region and soon incorporated it in his equally remarkable maps.

Champlain's great plans and ambitions for New France were perhaps best expressed in memoranda that he presented to the King and the Chambre de Commerce in Paris in 1618. But the companies that were assigned trading rights in the colony were unstable, and they were much more interested in profits than in settlement. In 1627 things seemed to take a turn for the better when the imposing Company of One Hundred Associates, headed by Cardinal Richelieu, came into existence; but war between France and England soon interfered with its activities. In 1628 an English expedition under the Kirke brothers pillaged the buildings at nearby Cap Tourmente and demanded the surrender of Quebec. Champlain resisted, but in 1629, when the Kirkes intercepted the French relief ships and made their demands a second time, he was forced to capitulate. Champlain was able to get to Paris, where he worked unceasingly to secure the return of Quebec to France. As the surrender to the Kirkes had actually taken place after peace had been concluded in Europe, his efforts were successful; New

France became French once again in 1632, under the terms of the Treaty of St. Germain-en-Laye.

When Champlain returned to Quebec in May of the following year, conditions there would have discouraged a lesser man; the town was virtually a ruin, and it is said that only 30 Frenchmen had remained during the English occupation. Champlain set about rebuilding the city and colony with his usual energy, and there was an optimistic ring to the reports he sent to France in 1634. But he was by this time at least 65 years of age and the effort and strains involved proved too great. In the fall of 1635 he was seized with paralysis; he died in Quebec on Christmas day.

The significance of Champlain's maps has been mentioned, but equally notable were the books in which he described his travels and sought to arouse interest in Acadia and New France. Most important are the three volumes of *Voyages* that he published in 1613, 1619 and 1632, all now prime items in any major collection of Canadiana.

Champlain was indefatigable in his efforts to promote the welfare and growth of New France. His voyagings are one example: he crossed the Atlantic at least 21 times in a period when the trip was most hazardous. Yet at the time of his death the population of Quebec was still less than one hundred. If it had not been for his determination it seems unlikely that the colony would have survived its first 27 troubled years.

New France Expands to the West and South

The exploration of the vast area now comprising Canada was a task that required three centuries to accomplish, even in a preliminary way. Columbus discovered America in 1492; Cabot touched Canada's eastern coast in 1497; but it was not until 1793 that Alexander Mackenzie completed the first journey across the full width of the continent, and, incidentally, across the Canada of today.

The French, having taken possession of the St. Lawrence River, one of the great waterways into the continent, soon ventured into the interior. Young Etienne Brulé, who seems to have come to Quebec with Champlain in 1608, ranks as the pioneer of French westward exploration. Indians who had come to trade at Quebec aroused his interest, and in 1610 Brulé asked Champlain for permission to return with them to their homeland and learn their language. Champlain agreed, and Brulé probably passed the winter with the Hurons. He thus became the first white man known to have seen Lake Huron, and, although details are vague, it seems certain that in the course of his many later journeys, he visited Lake Ontario, Lake Erie and Lake Superior as well.

Champlain's own travels westward have been noted. A few days before he arrived at the Huron villages in 1615, Father Joseph Le Caron, a Recollet

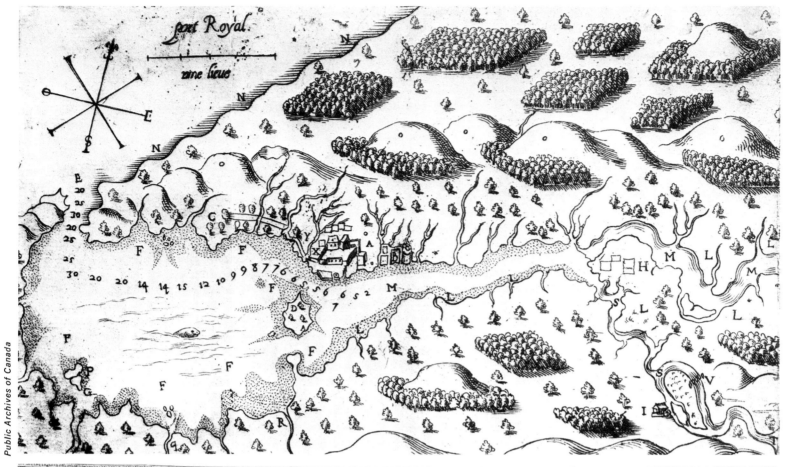

Champlain's map of the Annapolis Basin (above)
*The Habitation at Port Royal can be seen on the
north shore.*

Champlain's map of New France

priest, had reached them, and his appearance marked the beginning of a famous missionary effort that was to continue for a generation. At this time the Hurons lived in some eighteen villages scattered through the country between Georgian Bay and Lake Simcoe. Estimates of their numbers vary, but it was at least 20,000. The Recollets were joined by Jesuit missionaries, led by Father Jean de Brébeuf in 1626, and the famous Huronia mission is remembered chiefly as a Jesuit enterprise. The priests were compelled to abandon their work when the English captured Quebec in 1629, but it was resumed—this time by the Jesuits alone—in 1634. That year the first of the famous Jesuit *Relations* was printed in Paris—the beginning of the long series of descriptive reports on missionary activities that were published to arouse interest and attract financial support.

For years the Jesuits laboured steadily and with considerable success. Missions were established in a number of villages, and in 1639 Sainte-Marie, the famous headquarters mission, which has recently been excavated and restored, was built on the Wye River, near Midland. But the Iroquois, living to the south of Lake Ontario, were increasingly hostile, and became more and more determined to control or destroy the trade in furs carried on by the Hurons and the French. For a time they were content with raids on the Huron fur brigades that travelled to Montreal by way of the Ottawa or the St. Lawrence Rivers, but about 1647 the possession of firearms, which they secured from Dutch traders in the Hudson River valley, gave them a military superiority of which they quickly took advantage. In 1648 and 1649 they carried out a series of assaults on the Hurons that in effect destroyed the nation. Villages were burned, thousands of Hurons were massacred or captured, and five of the Jesuit missionaries, including Brébeuf, were tortured and killed. Some of the Hurons fled to Quebec; others found new homes as far afield as Oklahoma. Not content with these victories, the Iroquois next attacked the Tobacco and Neutral Indians, living in western Ontario, and destroyed or drove them out as well. Huronia and the regions south of it became virtually a waste land.

In spite of these disasters, French traders and missionaries worked their way farther and farther west. Most of them travelled by the Ottawa River—Lake Nipissing—Georgian Bay route that Champlain had followed and which was to be the classic route for centuries. In 1634 Jean Nicollet, a clerk and interpreter, had ventured into Lake Michigan and had explored Green Bay and some of the rivers of that region. More important were the travels of Médard Chouart des Groseilliers, an enterprising trader and explorer, who made a notable journey in 1654 that took him south from Georgian Bay to the future site of Detroit, across the Michigan peninsula to Lake Michigan, and up its western shore to Michilimackinac. Four years later, in 1659-60, in company with his brother-in-law, Pierre Radisson, Groseilliers followed the north shore of Georgian Bay to Sault Ste. Marie, and went on to explore the south shore of Lake Superior. He wintered with the Sioux Indians and then crossed the lake and followed its northern shore eastward to the Sault. Radisson afterwards claimed that he went north to Hudson Bay at this time, but it is extremely unlikely that he actually did so. It was by quite another route—the Saguenay River, Lake St. John and the Rupert River—that a French party that included Father Charles Albanel, a Jesuit missionary, finally reached Hudson Bay in 1672.

The following year important discoveries were made in the far west. In 1673 Louis Jolliet, a trader, accompanied again by the ubiquitous missionary, this time the Jesuit Jacques Marquette, travelled inland from Green Bay, discovered the Mississippi River, and descended it to within about 300 miles of its mouth. René-Robert Cavelier de la Salle completed its exploration when he travelled on to the mouth of the river in 1682 and there took possession of its whole enormous watershed in the name of King Louis XIV of France.

Seventy-five years after Champlain founded Quebec the French had thus gained a working knowledge of the geography of a large portion of what is now Eastern Canada, and their claims to the Mississippi valley made them hopeful that they could confine the English colonies on the Atlantic Coast, which were growing at an alarming rate, to the east side of the Appalachian Mountains.

Fur Trade in the 17th Century

Silks, spices, gold, silver and precious stones were the things the early explorers hoped to find in New France, but furs turned out to be the resource upon which the life of the colony depended. The fur trade was, indeed, vital because for many years New France produced little except furs for export. The quantity gathered was far greater than in the English colonies to the south. By the 1670s the annual fur harvest in New France in an average year included 60,000 to 80,000 beaver skins; the English harvest was only about one-tenth this number.

Of the various furs available, that of the beaver quickly became the most valuable and sought after. The demand for beaver skins was linked to the famous beaver hat, which grew steadily in popularity during the 17th century and had become a necessity in smart society by the end of it. The hats were fashioned from felt made from the soft, matted undercoat of the beaver's fur, and the best way of making felt was for long a trade secret jealously guarded by the Russians. As fur production grew, New France became indirectly dependent on Russia; the market in France could absorb only a fraction of the skins received, and fortunately most of the surplus could be disposed of profitably in Russia.

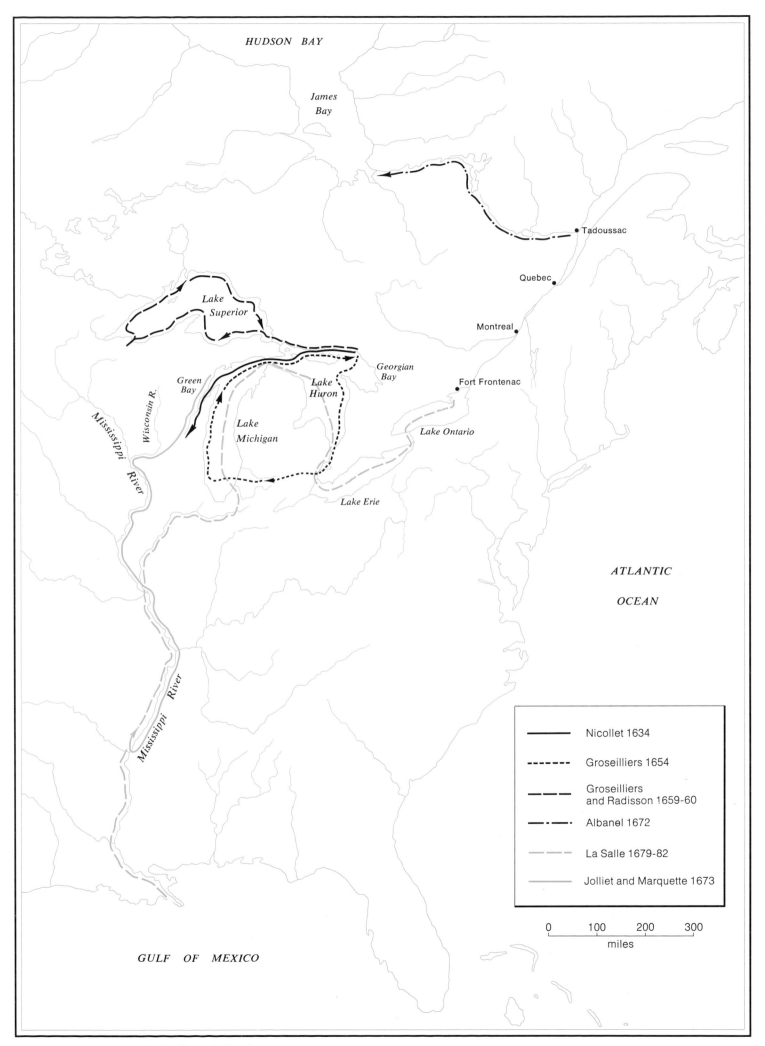

HUDSON BAY

James
Bay

Tadoussac

Quebec

Montreal

Lake
Superior

Georgian
Bay

Fort Frontenac

Green
Bay

Lake
Huron

Lake Ontario

Wisconsin R.

Lake
Michigan

Mississippi River

Lake Erie

ATLANTIC

OCEAN

Mississippi River

Mississippi River

——————	Nicollet 1634
- - - - - -	Groseilliers 1654
— — — —	Groseilliers and Radisson 1659-60
—·—·—·—	Albanel 1672
– – – –	La Salle 1679-82
——————	Jolliet and Marquette 1673

0   100   200   300

miles

GULF   OF   MEXICO

Approximate Routes of the French Explorers

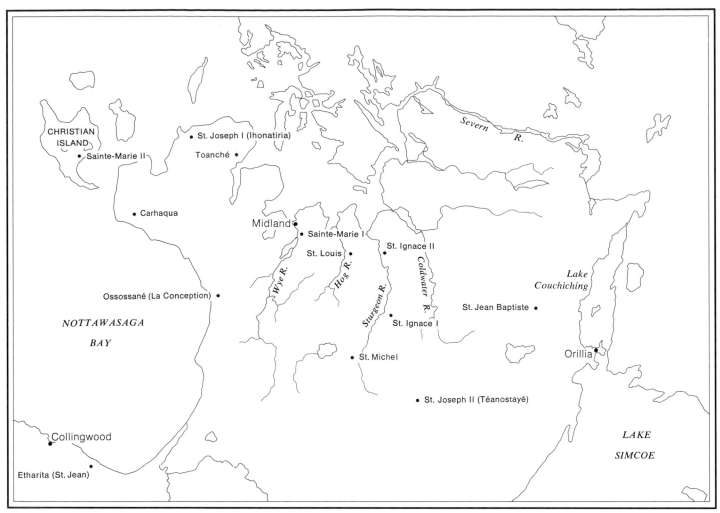

The Principal Missions and Villages in Huronia
(above)

Contemporary map of Huronia

This map was printed in 1660 as an inset on the map of New France in Du Creux's Historia Canadensis.

The trade began casually on ships along the coast; Tadoussac was the first important centre on land; Quebec quickly became another. One of the motives for the founding of Montreal in 1642 was the desirability of having a post farther west, and it soon became a key trading centre. At this time most of the furs were brought to market by the Indians themselves, but young Frenchmen—soon to be called *coureurs de bois*—were finding it profitable to go out into the western wilderness both to persuade the Indians to bring in their furs and to do some trading on their own. The freedom and other attractions of this life made serious drains on the very limited manpower available in New France and by hindering the development of agriculture and other resources increased the colony's dependence on furs.

The savage depredations of the Iroquois posed a very serious threat to the French fur trade. They began with attacks on parties of Indians bringing furs to Montreal or Quebec; the destruction of the Huron nation and its neighbours in 1648-50 was an attack on the source of these furs. The travels of French explorers in the succeeding decades, while partly an effort to find the still hoped-for route to a western sea and thence to Asia, were essentially a search for new sources of furs, and for the best locations for the inland trading posts and travel routes that would be needed to bring them to New France.

It is sometimes assumed that Champlain's efforts and the founding of Quebec had firmly established the St. Lawrence area as a French possession, and that the voyages of Hudson, Baffin, Davis and others had similarly established British sovereignty in Hudson Bay. In reality neither side was yet prepared to yield an inch to the other. About the time Richelieu was founding the Hundred Associates, the British Government gave a charter to a Canada Company whose purpose was to trade in the St. Lawrence and endeavour to dispossess the French. The Kirke brothers were associated with it, and their success in capturing Quebec in 1629 seemed to assure the Company's future. The restoration of Quebec to France in 1632 was a blow to its hopes, but the Kirkes received a renewal of their monopoly in 1633 and would have cheerfully assaulted Quebec again, had opportunity offered.

The French were equally stubborn in their efforts to keep the British out of Hudson Bay. Ironically, the chief reason the British were trading there was the treatment Groseilliers and Radisson had received from the French themselves. In an effort to conserve manpower, the authorities in New France were doing their best to check the exodus of young men to the Indian country. Groseilliers and Radisson had left without official permission when they began what proved to be their great voyage of discovery in 1659-60, and when they returned laden with furs, they were greeted with fines and taxes and perhaps even by confiscations and imprisonment. Groseilliers also came back convinced that Hudson Bay, which provided a sea route far into the heart of the continent, offered great trading advantages, and when he freed himself of entanglements he looked about for sponsors who would back a voyage to the Bay. New France, Gaspé, New England and France itself all failed to produce them, and he and Radisson went finally to London. There he awakened interest, but the Dutch War, the great fire of London in 1666 and the plague year all delayed the enterprise. At last, in June 1668, Groseilliers in the *Nonsuch* and Radisson in the *Eaglet* sailed from the Thames bound for Hudson Bay. Storms forced the *Eaglet* to turn back, but the little *Nonsuch*—a ketch only 36 feet in length—made the crossing successfully, wintered in Hudson Bay, and returned in October 1669 with a substantial cargo of furs. It is doubtful if she actually made a profit, but she had proven that the trade was practicable. On May 2, 1670, the Hudson's Bay Company—officially the "Governor and Company of Adventurers tradeing into Hudson's Bay"—received from King Charles II the historic charter that gave them a trade monopoly and virtual sovereignty over Rupert's Land, which embraced the whole of the immense watershed of Hudson Bay.

Within a dozen years four trading posts had been established—Rupert's House, Moose Factory and Albany Fort, all on James Bay, and Fort Nelson,

Sainte-Marie among the Hurons

This was the headquarters of the Jesuit missions in Huronia. Careful excavation revealed the ground plan of the original buildings and they have been reconstructed as they existed in 1649.

First page of the Hudson's Bay Company Charter,
of 1670

and ☙ **By the Grace**

and defender of the faith &c **To** to whome these present ...
...d Entirely Beloved Cousin Prince Rupert Count Palettyne of ...
...d & Christopher Duke of Albemarle William Earle of ...
... Ashley Sir John Robinson and Sir Robert Vyner Knight and ...
...ward Hungerford Knight of the Bath Sir Paule Neile Knight ...
...night James Hayes John Kirke ffrauncis Millington William ...
...itts Cittizen and Goldsmith of London have att theire owne greate ...
...Hudsons Bay in the Northwest part of America for the discovery ...
...the finding some Trade for ffurrs Mineralls and other ...
...undertaking have alreadie made such discoveries as doe ...
...esigne by meanes whereof there may probablely arise very ...
...he said Undertakers for theire further encouragement in the ...
...rant unto them and theire Successors the sole Trade and ...
...d Sound in whatsoever Latitude they shall bee that lye within ...
...ther with all the Land Countryes and Territoryes vpon the ...
...Creekes and Sound aforesaid which are not now actually possessed ...
...to or State **Now know wee** that wee being desirous to ...
...o and to encourage the said Undertaking have of our especiall ...
...d and confirmed And by these present for vs our heires and ...
...usin Prince Rupert Christopher Duke of Albemarle William ...
...hn Robinson Sir Robert Vyner Sir Peter Colleton Sir Edward ...
...rett James Hayes John Kirke ffrauncis Millington William ...
...tts shall bee admitted into the said Society as is hereafter ...
...u uttime by the name of the Governor and Company of ...
...he name of the Governor and Company of Adventurers of England ...
...and in nature reallie and fullie for ever for vs our heires and Successors ...
...these present and that by the name name of Governor & Company ...
...have perpetuall Succession And that they and theire Successors ...
...uglend Tradeing unto Hudsons Bay bee and att all tymes hereafter ...
...ue possesse enioy and retayne Land Rent priviledges liberties ...
...y and quality soever they bee to them and theire Successors ...
...enement and hereditament and to doe and execute all and ...
...nitty apperteyne to doe And that they and theire Successors ...
...f England Tradeing unto Hudsons Bay may pleade and bee ...
...ded in whatsoever Court and places before whatsoever ...
...singuler Actions Pletts Suites quarrells causes and demaund ...
...and former as any other our Liege people of this our Realme ...
...have purchase receive possesse enioy retayne give graunt ...
...e permitt and execute And that the said Governor and ...
...y and theire Successors unto have a Common Seale to serve ...
...hatt itt shall and may bee lawfull to the said Governor and ...
... tyme att theire will and pleasure to breake change and to ...

Further wee will and by these present for vs our heires ...
... henceforth one of the same Company to bee elected and ...
...sed which shall bee called the Governor of the said Company ...
...etten of theire number in such as hereafter in these present ...
...Company which Committee of seaven or any three of them ...
...ominated for the tyme being shall have the direction of the ...

Noble Death of Certain Fathers belonging to the
Society of Jesus in New France

*This famous engraving was published in 1660 in
the* Historia Canadensis, *by Father François Du*

*Creux, which is primarily a history of Jesuit
activities in New France. It is a composite picture,
showing incidents that took place in different*

places over the period 1646-50. The two figures in the right foreground are Father Jean de Brébeuf, founder of the Huron mission, and Father Gabriel Lalemant, who were captured by the Iroquois at St. Louis and tortured and put to death at St. Ignace II in March 1649.

Le Moyne d'Iberville (above left)

Member of a famous and numerous Canadian family, D'Iberville has been called the most renowned son of New France.

The "Nonsuch"

on the west shore of Hudson Bay. Each was at the mouth of a river down which Indians could travel easily with their furs. In 1684 Fort Nelson was replaced by York Factory, at the mouth of the neighbouring Hayes River, and in 1685 Severn Fort was built at the mouth of the Severn.

Meanwhile the French had begun what proved to be a long and determined effort to drive the British out of the Bay. Though England and France were at peace, hostilities broke out in Hudson Bay in 1682, and a series of clashes and seizures characterized the next 15 years. In 1686 Le Moyne d'Iberville, coming by land from New France, made the first of his celebrated attacks on the Hudson's Bay posts. By the end of it, all three posts on James Bay were in French hands. War was declared officially in 1689, and the following year D'Iberville returned by sea and captured Severn Fort; only York Factory remained in British possession. In 1693 British forces regained the James Bay posts, which was just as well, as D'Iberville, on a third foray, captured York Factory the next year. The British regained it briefly in 1696 but lost it again in 1697. From the latter year until 1714 Albany Fort was the sole post the Hudson's Bay Company held and occupied.

The Company was under a legal obligation to explore Rupert's Land, and in the midst of the French attacks Henry Kelsey, a remarkable young apprentice who took kindly to the wilderness and the Indian way of life, made two historic journeys. In 1689 he trudged north for 200 miles from the Churchill River in an unsuccessful attempt to make trading contacts with the Indians there. In 1690 he went up the Hayes River and began a pioneering journey westward that was to last for two years. Although his journal is available, the lack of place names makes it impossible to trace his route with much certainty. In all probability he saw Lake Winnipeg and Cedar Lake, and then travelled out on the plains for a distance he estimated to be about 600 miles. He thus became the first white man to see the Canadian prairies, and he was also the first to see the musk ox, the buffalo herds, and probably the grizzly bear.

In spite of its tribulations the Hudson's Bay Company managed to carry on a profitable trade and to pay dividends until 1690. But for the next 27 years—from 1691 to 1717—it paid none. Few corporations can have placed so prolonged a strain upon the loyalty of their shareholders and survived.

Tadoussac: the first trading post in New France

In 1600 Captain Pierre de Chauvin, a native of Dieppe, built a small trading post and tried unsuccessfully to found a colony at Tadoussac, at the mouth of the Saguenay River. Champlain drew this picture map.

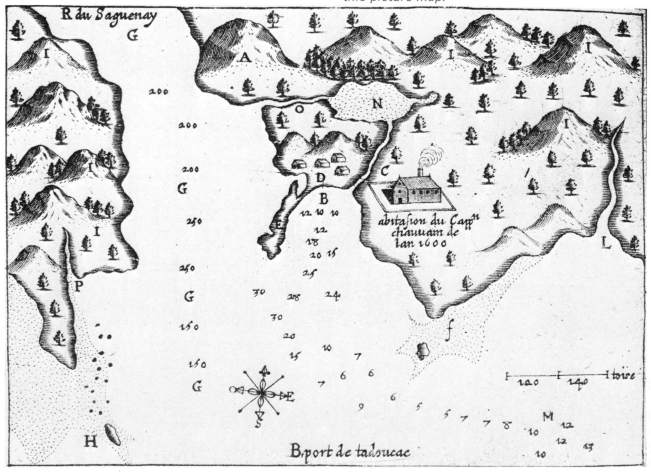

New France to the Treaty of Utrecht

During its first half century New France grew very slowly. In 1642 the population was still only about 200, and although it had increased to 2,500 by 1663, the colony was by then in a serious plight. The Iroquois, having destroyed or dispersed the Hurons, were harassing the French settlements, particularly Montreal, and paralyzing the fur trade, upon which the colony was almost entirely dependent.

Louis XIV and Colbert, his great minister, realized that something had to be done, and in 1663 New France became a royal province, with a governor and intendant. The famous Carignan-Salières regiment of veteran regular troops was sent to Canada to bolster its defences, and under the Sieur de Tracy, who arrived in 1665, and with the aid of local militia, it took such effective action that the Iroquois concluded a peace with the French in 1666 that was to endure for over 20 years. The King was generous with money and Colbert saw to it that New France had able administrators. Jean Talon, who has been dubbed "the great intendant," arrived in 1665 and made a determined effort to encourage the growth of agriculture, fishing and the timber trade. Although then, as now, the French were reluctant to leave France, some thousands of immigrants came to Canada, and by 1676 the population had grown to 8,500.

Colbert was anxious to see New France become a compact, well populated colony with a well diversified economy, but over the years this was found impossible to achieve. The country still had little in the way of marketable exports except furs, and the French did not abandon their hope of securing control of vast areas in the interior. These territorial ambitions, as well as the search for furs, lured young Canadians farther and farther to the west and south, as the travels and discoveries of Groseilliers, Radisson, La Salle and many others demonstrate.

Wars, both official and undeclared, erupted almost continually in the last fifteen years of the century. Hostilities between French and English, as already noted, had almost swept the British out of Hudson Bay. In 1689, the year war was declared in Europe, the Iroquois broke the peace with a murderous attack on the village of Lachine, above Montreal. It was not until 1696 that the Comte de Frontenac led an effective counterattack that destroyed the villages, cornfields and food reserves of the Onandagas and Oneidas and again removed the Iroquois menace. Meanwhile, in 1690, forces from New England had captured Port Royal, in Acadia, and had attempted to take Quebec. Fontenac was able to muster his troops and hold the city, and responded to Phips' demand that he should surrender with the famous answer that he had "no

reply to make . . . other than from the mouths of my cannon and muskets." A few days later the approach of winter forced Phips to withdraw. In 1696-97 D'Iberville, back from his victories in Hudson Bay, turned his attention to Newfoundland, where the French had established themselves at Placentia. He attacked and burned St. John's and smaller settlements along the coast, leaving the British with only a slender hold at Carbonear and Bonavista.

In many respects New France reached the peak of its fortunes about 1700. The Treaty of Ryswick of 1697 returned Acadia, the only loss of consequence that France had suffered in America, and did not disturb the commanding position she had achieved on Hudson Bay, in the west, and in the Mississippi Valley. The only serious problem was overproduction in the fur trade, and the great quantities of unsold skins that had accumulated as a result. This was a problem that was to persist for some years, as it took time for the markets to return to normal.

The last fifteen years of the 17th century saw French fortunes rise to promising heights; the first fifteen years of the new century were to see them begin to decline. The peace concluded between France and England in 1697 was broken in 1702 and the new war dragged on for eleven years. Hostilities were not continuous in America, but the years were punctuated by attacks and counterattacks, some of them ugly and few of them heroic. In 1704 the little town of Deerfield, in Massachusetts, was devastated in the best remembered of many raids by Indians and others on New England settlements. In 1710 Francis Nicholson made the most significant capture of the war when he took Port Royal, the key to Acadia. The following year Admiral Sir Hovenden Walker set out from Boston with a fleet of men-of-war and troop transports assembled for the purpose of taking Quebec. On this occasion the elements combined with errors in navigation to save New France; Walker lost eight of his ships on the Isle aux Oeufs in the Gulf of St. Lawrence and abandoned the attack.

Jean Baptiste Colbert

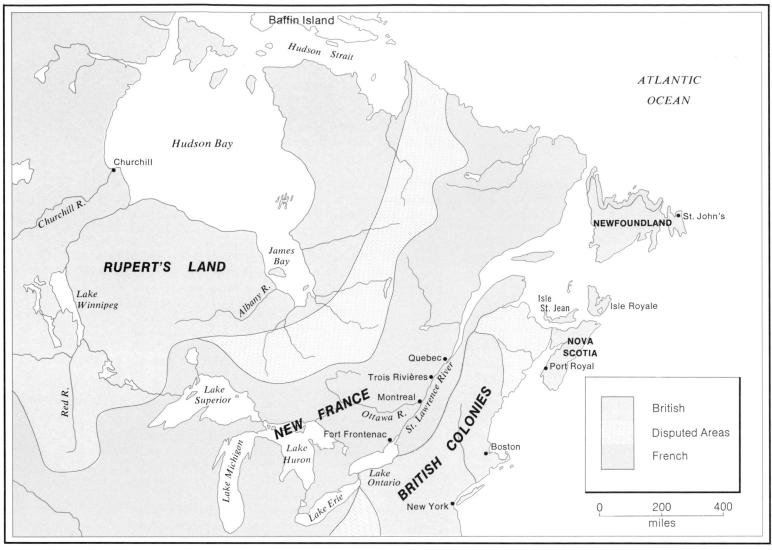

Canada after the Treaty of Utrecht, 1713

Jean Talon

As intendant, Talon virtually transformed the colony and its prospects, although his two terms of office totalled less than six years.

Alexandre de Prouville de Tracy

Quebec, about 1700

The Treaty of Utrecht, which ended the War of the Spanish Succession, and whose terms were governed primarily by European considerations, dealt several body blows to the French position in North America. It acknowledged British sovereignty in Hudson Bay; all the posts there were to be returned to the Hudson's Bay Company. Newfoundland was recognized as a British possession, but France retained, as she does to this day, the islands of St. Pierre and Miquelon, and she also kept the fishing rights along the north coast of Newfoundland that were to be a cause of friction for almost two centuries. Finally, Acadia, and its key settlement of Port Royal, were ceded to Britain, although Cape Breton Island, soon to be the site of the fortress of Louisbourg, was left in French hands. In sum, New France found herself for the first time confined within definite territorial limits, and the treaty enabled the British to establish themselves firmly to the north of her as well as to the south.

By 1719 the population of the colony had grown to 22,500. Relatively few immigrants had come to Canada since the time of Talon; the growth in population had been due to natural increase. By 1719 a high percentage of the people had thus been born in Canada; the first substantial generation of French-Canadians, rooted in this country, and in great part the generation from which the French-Canadians of today were to spring, had appeared on the Canadian scene.

Part II
THE STRUGGLE FOR
POSSESSION
1713-1783

The Royal Arms of France

This historic carving in wood, now in the Public Archives of Canada, was taken from the gates of Quebec on September 18, 1759, when the city surrendered to the British.

CHAPTER 4

New France After 1713

The French Fur Trade 1713–1760

THE commanding figure in the last three decades of the French fur trade was Pierre Gaultier de Varenne, Sieur de La Vérendrye, but there were important earlier developments in which he played no part.

It was certain that the Treaty of Utrecht would result in a sharp increase in competition from British traders, and the French acted quickly to anticipate it. Within five years of the signing of the treaty they had established or rebuilt strong posts at strategic points as far apart as Michilimackinac, Kaminisitiquia (the future site of Fort William), Fort Chartres (on the Mississippi River downstream from the mouth of the Missouri) and New Orleans. These and other posts strengthened their trading routes and defence lines to the west and to the south.

It soon became apparent that the British were no longer content to poach on the fur resources of New France through the intermediary of the Iroquois and freebooting white traders. In 1726 they built Fort Oswego, on the south shore of the eastern end of Lake Ontario, a move that the French looked upon as a clear invasion of their territory. Oswego offered severe competition not only because of its location, but because the trade goods it could offer the Indians were both better and cheaper than those available from the French traders. English-made kettles, knives, scissors, and needles were superior in quality, and this was important because these items were no longer novelties; they had been available so long that in many areas they had become part of the normal equipment of an Indian household, and quality counted. The attractions of Oswego and its wares became so great that the French were compelled to build a number of posts on the various travel routes that led to it in an effort to intercept the Indians and secure their furs. As late as 1749

Fort Rouillé was built on the site of Toronto with this purpose in mind, and in 1751 it was deemed wise to build a new post as far away as Sault Ste. Marie.

The French trade was better organized and more effectively controlled than it had been in earlier days. Adventurous young French-Canadians still took to the woods and the wilderness life, but recognized companies and licensed traders predominated. The volume of furs gathered after 1713 fluctuated somewhat but on the whole was relatively constant, and this helped solve marketing problems in France.

The old belief that a sea of some sort lay to the west that would provide a route to China was still very much alive, and the government of New France linked an obligation to explore with the granting of trading rights and monopolies. Thus when La Vérendrye was given command of the western posts in 1730, it was on the understanding that he would search for the western sea. No financial assistance was forthcoming; he was expected to meet the costs of exploration out of the profits of the fur trade. In the circumstances some conflict in priorities was inevitable; La Vérendrye was accused of placing much more emphasis on trade than on exploration. But he had to pay his way, and the Montreal merchants who provided his financial backing were naturally chiefly interested in profits. Nevertheless he and his associates made a major contribution to the exploration and development of the West.

La Vérendrye was assisted by his four sons and by a nephew, Christophe, Sieur de La Jemeraye. Their first objective was to extend the chain of French posts westward from Lake Superior, both in the interests of exploration and in an effort to intercept some of the furs that were finding their way to the Hudson's Bay Company, now firmly re-established on Hudson and James Bays. In 1731 La Jemeraye built Fort St. Pierre on Rainy Lake, and the following year Fort St. Charles was established

Page from La Vérendrye's journal

Journal en forme de Lettre, depuis le 20. de juillet 1738. de mon
Despard de michilimakina jusqu'en may 1739.

Envoyé a Monsieur le Marquis de Beauharnois, Commandeur des
ordres Militaire de St Louis, Gouverneur et Lieutenant General
de toute La Nouvelle france terres et pais de la Louisiane, par
son très humble serviteur Lauerendrye, Lieutenant d'une Compagnie
du Detachement de la marine En Canada, chargé de ses ordres pour
La Decouverte de la mer d'oüest.

J'eus l'honneur Monsieur L'année dernière de vous marquer mon
Despard de michilimakina, en six Canots, vingt deux hommes Esquipées
d'une maniere a pouvoir faire grande diligence, je me rendis au pais
plats le premier d'aoust le matin, le douziéme de mon Despard, j'y arreste
environ trois heures pour parler aux sauvages de votre part, je n'y trouvé
que le chef de gamanestigouya quelque vieillard, peu de jeunes gens,
j'auois deja Scû qu'il étoient tous partis pour aller chés les sioux, je fis
assembler ce qu'il y auoit d'hommes, Leurs fis un present de tabac et
blé, qu'il estime plus que les marchandises que L'on leurs donne a grand
marché, je Commancée mon discours par les blamer de ce qu'ils Estoient
allés En guerre, contre la parole qu'ils m'auoient Donnée L'année derniere
En passant chés eux, de n'erien Entreprendre que à mon retour que je
Leurs aporteis votre parole, que vous n'esties point dans le sentiment
pour le present qu'el on fit guerre, qu'un chaquein se teint tranquile
sur leurs terres, que vous auies vos raisons pour cela vous les feriés
auertir si vous auies besoin de leurs services, je leurs fis part
Ensuite des Nouvelles, dont ils sont fort curieux.

Le Chef me répondit sur l'heure, mon pere, ne sois pas fache Contre
Nous, le partis sont Loués Contre nostre volonté, C'est le Canard noir
sauuage de Mr de la Plante qui a voulu dire vraye, parlant auec de
beaux presents de la part de nôtre pere, ce que tu nous voye icy Nous
N'auons point voulu l'escouter, atendant ton retour, nous ne sommes
pas des enfans pour auoir deux paroles, tu a esté long temps auec nous
tu nous dois conoistre, nous auons toujours esté atachés a nostre pere, nous
le seront toujours, je les Encouragés dans ces bons sentiments, de n'escouter
par la suite que des chefs chargés de vos ordres, de bien chasser pour
fournir le besoin a leurs famille, que par votre bonté les françois leurs
venoit aporter sur leurs terres, je leurs dis a dieu voulant profiter d'un
bon tems le reste du jour, j'arrivée a gamanestigouya Le 5. je fis
publier vos ordres et Laissé Copie aux françois qui gardoit le fort,
Concernant ce poste, et de lekamamihouenne pour estre remis au sr de
marque qui y deuoit arriuer au premier jour, je partis le 6. au

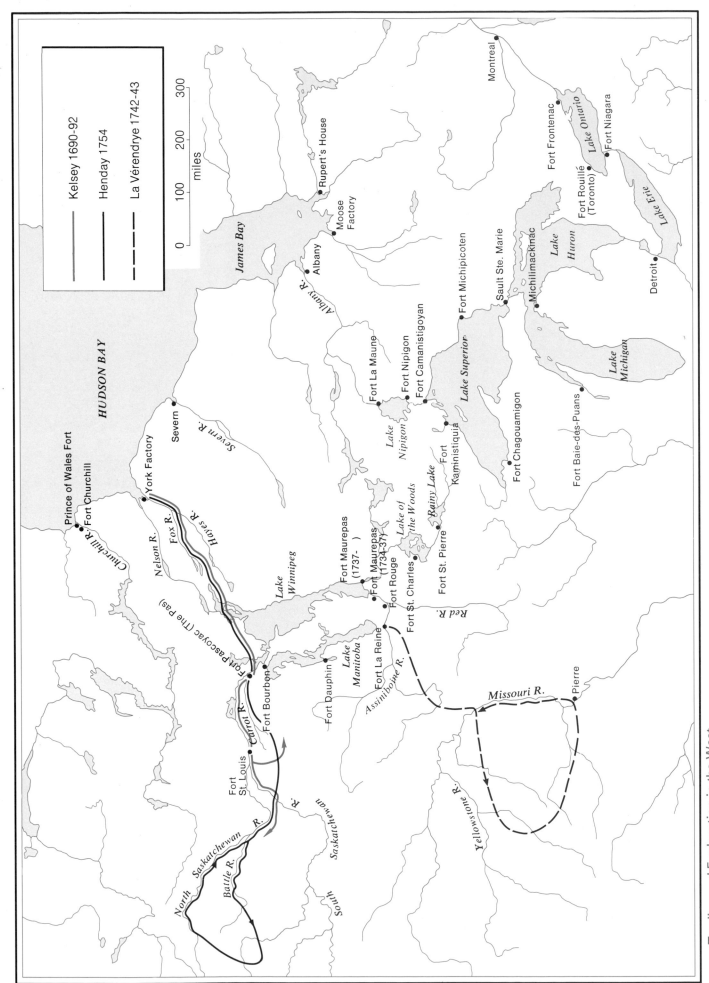

Legend:
- Kelsey 1690–92
- Henday 1754
- La Vérendrye 1742–43

miles
0   100   200   300

HUDSON BAY

James Bay

Prince of Wales Fort
Fort Churchill
Churchill R.

York Factory
Severn
Severn R.

Rupert's House
Moose Factory
Albany
Albany R.

Nelson R.
Fox R.
Hayes R.

Fort Pascoyac (The Pas)

Fort Bourbon

Lake Winnipeg

Fort Maurepas (1737–)
Fort Maurepas (1734–37)
Fort Rouge
Fort St. Charles

Fort La Maune
Fort Nipigon
Fort Camanistigoyan
Lake Nipigon
Fort Kaministiquia
Rainy Lake
Lake of the Woods
Fort St. Pierre

Fort Michipicoten
Sault Ste. Marie
Lake Superior
Fort Chagouamigon
Fort Baie-des-Puans

Michilimackinac
Lake Huron
Lake Michigan

Fort Frontenac
Fort Rouillé (Toronto)
Fort Niagara
Lake Ontario
Lake Erie
Detroit

Montreal

Fort St. Louis
North Saskatchewan R.
Battle R.
South Saskatchewan R.
Carrot R.

Fort Dauphin
Lake Manitoba
Fort La Reine
Assiniboine R.
Red R.

Missouri R.
Pierre
Yellowstone R.

Trading and Exploration in the West

The La Vérendrye Plaque   Statue of La Vérendrye at St. Boniface

on the Lake of the Woods. In 1734 a longer leap to the west was made and the first Fort Maurepas was built on the Red River, a few miles upstream from Lake Winnipeg. Later this post was moved to the mouth of the Winnipeg River. A setback came in 1736, when La Vérendrye lost his two most experienced lieutenants—his eldest son was murdered by Indians and La Jemeraye fell ill and died—but in 1738 he himself pushed on and built Fort La Reine on the Assiniboine River, near the site of Portage la Prairie. Later the same year, with both trade and exploration in mind, he struck off southward across the prairie and visited the Mandan Indians in North Dakota.

In 1739 the search shifted to the north. In the spring, La Vérendrye sent his son François, known as the Chevalier de La Vérendrye, to ascertain what rivers flowed into Lake Winnipeg, and the result was the discovery of the mouth of the Saskatchewan. The next step was the founding of two new posts in 1741—the first Fort Dauphin, near the mouth of the Mossy River, at the southern end of Lake Winnipegosis, and Fort Bourbon, on an island in Cedar Lake, near the mouth of the Saskatchewan.

It was in 1742 that the Chevalier, accompanied by his brother Louis Joseph, set out from Fort La Reine on the famous journey that is believed to have taken him within sight of the Rocky Mountains. The route followed cannot be traced in detail but it seems reasonably certain that he went first to the Mandan villages, next travelled southward at least as far as the Black Hills in South Dakota, and probably far enough west to see the Horn Mountains, an outlying range of the Rockies, in Wyoming. Returning eastward he came to the Missouri River, followed it north to the Mandan country, and from thence returned safely to Fort La Reine after an absence of two years and three months. Almost the whole of this great journey, which provided no clue to the whereabouts of a western sea, was made in the United States, and some confirmation of the route taken was secured in 1913 when a small lead plate, buried by the La Vérendryes, was discovered near the city of Pierre, the capital of South Dakota.

This journey proved to be the climax of the achievements of the La Vérendryes. Financial difficulties plagued them, and they withdrew from the West. Under later commanders of the western posts

Plan of the fortress of Louisbourg

two new forts were established on the Saskatchewan River—Fort Pasquia, near the mouth of the Pasquia River, in 1751, and Fort St. Louis, some distance below the junction of the north and south branches of the Saskatchewan. The latter was founded by St. Luc de la Corne, the last French commander of the *postes de l'ouest*. It has been said that a third post, Fort la Jonquière, was founded about 1751 far up the Saskatchewan; the Bow River and the site of Calgary have even been mentioned. But evidence is lacking, and it is very unlikely that any French post was built west of the forks of the river.

All this time the Hudson's Bay Company had continued to centre its activities on the posts around

Louisbourg under siege in 1758

From an engraving after the painting by Thomas Ince. The British fleet is in the background, standing offshore; the French fleet is in Louisbourg harbour, to the right.

the edge of the bays, but it was now feeling the effects of French competition. Furs that would normally have been brought to its posts were being intercepted, and the time had come when it had to consider moving inland. In 1754 Anthony Henday, famous as the discoverer of the Canadian Rockies, set out from York Factory on an expedition that was in many ways the counterpart of the 1742-43 journey of the La Vérendryes. Opinions differ as to his precise route, but he certainly ascended the Hayes River and its tributary the Fox, and reached the Saskatchewan near Fort Pasquia, which he visited. He seems then to have ascended the Carrot River, and after leaving it travelled westward in the company of Cree Indians until he sighted the Rockies, probably west of the site of Red Deer, in the Alberta of today. On his homeward journey he followed the North Saskatchewan most of the way. The round trip occupied a full year less three days, and Henday brought the Hudson's Bay Company invaluable information about the geography of the west, the Indians who inhabited it, its fur resources, and the activities of the Company's French competitors. Thereafter parties of Hudson's Bay traders travelled inland almost every year, and it would obviously be only a matter of time before they began to build trading posts inland as well.

The Military Defences of New France

Quebec was the centre of the military defences of New France. But although it was a fortress of formidable strength, neither Quebec nor the colony had the resources to support large-scale operations, or to withstand a prolonged assault, without receiv-

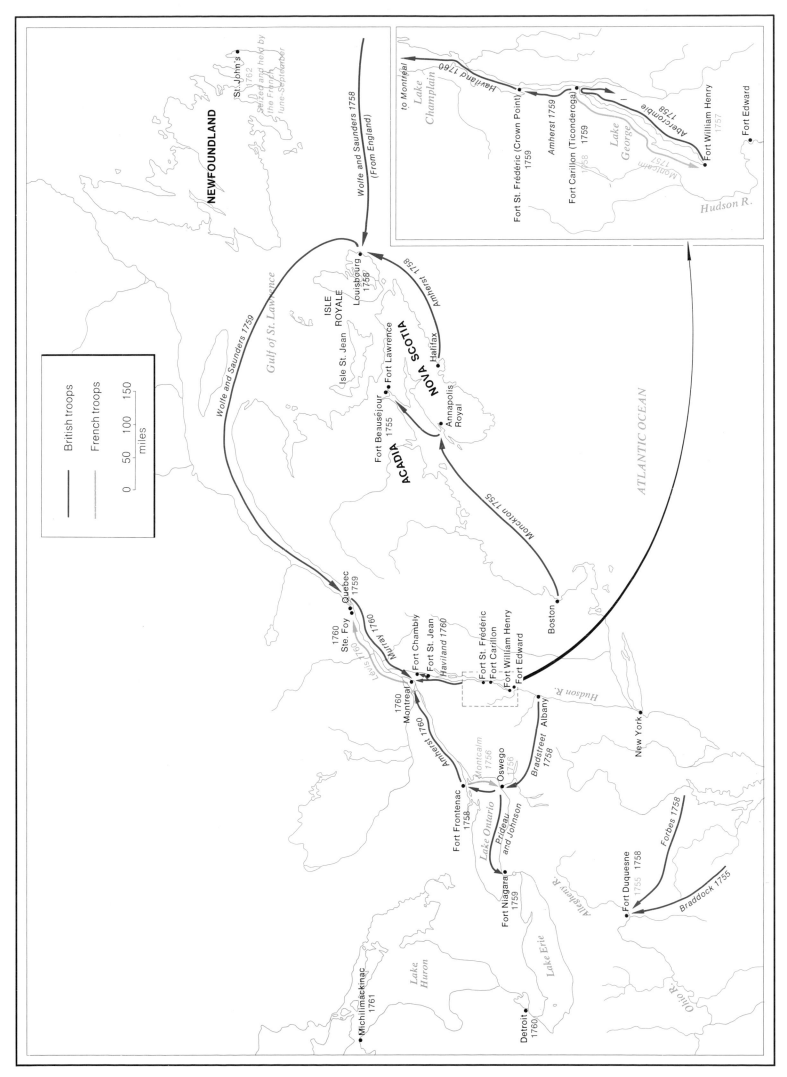

The Seven Years' War

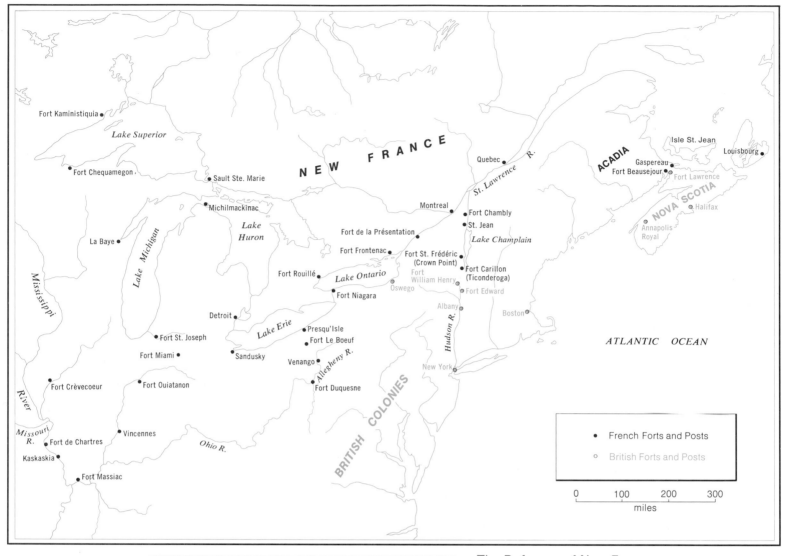

Fort Kaministiquia

Lake Superior

Fort Chequamegon

Sault Ste. Marie

Michilmackinac

Lake Huron

La Baye

Lake Michigan

Mississippi

River

Fort Crèvecoeur

Fort St. Joseph

Fort Miami

Sandusky

Detroit

Lake Erie

Presqu'Isle

Fort Le Boeuf

Venango

Allegheny R.

Fort Duquesne

Fort Ouiatanon

Vincennes

Missouri R.

Fort de Chartres

Kaskaskia

Fort Massiac

Ohio R.

BRITISH COLONIES

N E W   F R A N C E

Quebec

St. Lawrence R.

Montreal

Fort Chambly

St. Jean

Fort de la Présentation

Fort Frontenac

Fort St. Frédéric (Crown Point)

Lake Champlain

Fort Carillon (Ticonderoga)

Fort Rouillé

Lake Ontario

Fort William Henry

Fort Niagara

Oswego

Fort Edward

Albany

Hudson R.

Boston

New York

ACADIA

Isle St. Jean

Louisbourg

Gaspereau

Fort Beausejour

Fort Lawrence

NOVA SCOTIA

Halifax

Annapolis Royal

ATLANTIC   OCEAN

● French Forts and Posts

○ British Forts and Posts

0   100   200   300

miles

The Defences of New France

Louis XV

This official portrait of the last French King of Canada, painted by the famous Court painter Jean Baptiste Van Loo, is believed to have been sent by Louis XV himself to Quebec, where it hung in the Château St. Louis, the residence of the Governor of New France. After the fall of Quebec in 1759, it was apparently taken to England by an officer in Wolfe's army. In the present century it was acquired by Sir Leicester Harmsworth, who presented it to the Public Archives of Canada in 1923.

Public Archives of Canada

ing reinforcements and supplies from France. Control of the approaches to Quebec—the Gulf of St. Lawrence and the river itself—was therefore a vital consideration. It was for this reason that the French attached such importance to Cape Breton Island when the Treaty of Utrecht was negotiated. The treaty cost them Acadia and their hold on Newfoundland, but provided specifically that "the Island of Cape Breton shall hereafter belong of right to the King of France," and, quite as important, the King was to "have right to fortify any places there."

The French were soon busy building the great fortress and naval base of Louisbourg, designed to protect the gateway to Quebec. Oddly enough the site chosen was a small harbour known hitherto as Havre à l'Anglais (English Harbour) because it had been used extensively by English fishermen who crossed the Atlantic to fish for cod on the banks off Newfoundland and Nova Scotia. Construction of the fortress began in 1720 and continued for 20 years or more. The great walls enclosed an area of 57 acres, and the largest building, the handsome Château St. Louis, which contained the Governor's apartments, the officers' quarters and a chapel, was 360 feet long and surmounted by a graceful spire. The narrow harbour mouth was protected both by a fortified island and by an imposing Grand Battery on the shore opposite the entrance.

Louisbourg depended for most things directly on France. The Caen stone and much of the brick used in its construction came from France and most of its food and supplies were brought across the Atlantic. In peace time, it became of some importance as a trans-shipment point, with a trade in fish, furs, rum, molasses and other commodities. But its primary purpose was military, and from the first it was found that it suffered under one serious handicap: its location—isolated, and except in summer rather bleak and desolate—made it difficult to maintain the morale of the garrison.

In a report prepared in 1757, Louis Antoine de Bougainville, Montcalm's shrewd and observant *aide-de-camp*, listed 67 forts that were then garrisoned in New France. Most of these were primarily or exclusively trading posts, such as the forts the La Vérendryes had founded in the West. Those with a serious military purpose were placed strategically to block the rivers, lakes and valleys which were likely to be followed by invading forces from the British colonies to the south. Many were timber structures with wooden palisades, but a few, at points of key importance, were stone structures of quite elaborate design that resembled European fortresses of the day. Thus on the Richelieu River—Lake Champlain—Lake George route to the south the strongest defences were Fort Chambly, on the Richelieu, and Carillon (better known by its later name of Ticonderoga), at the northern end of Lake George. Both were of stone construction, as were Fort Frontenac and Fort Niagara which guarded the eastern end of Lake Ontario and the important Niagara portage. Further south the French had

Pierre de Riguad, Marquis de Vaudreuil
Appointed in 1755, Vaudreuil was the last Governor of New France, and the only native-born Canadian to hold the post.

Public Archives of Canada

tried for years to confine the British to the east of a line following the valleys of the Allegheny, Ohio and Mississippi rivers, and the forts there were located with this end in view.

In 1744, after 31 years of peace, war broke out once more between Britain and France. Canada itself was affected relatively little; the important event was a full-scale attack on Louisbourg in 1745, mounted from New England, where the existence of the French base had always been regarded as a dire menace. Led by William Pepperell, a merchant and politician turned general, the New Englanders succeeded in landing, to the surprise of the French, invested the fortress, battered it with their artillery and forced it to surrender after a siege lasting two months. Louisbourg had been found to be less formidable than expected; among other things the Grand Battery proved to be vulnerable from the rear, and after its capture its guns helped to breach the walls they were intended to defend. A large fleet sailed from Brest in 1746, in an effort to recoup French fortunes, but storms and shipwrecks so reduced its strength that it could take no effective action. Two years later, to the anger and disgust of New England, Louisbourg was returned to France by the Treaty of Aix-la-Chapelle.

In America both sides realized that only a brief breathing spell lay ahead, for the land-hungry British colonies were determined to expand westward into territory long claimed by the French. A clash became inevitable in 1749 when the Ohio Company of Virginia received a grant of some half million acres that extended to the Ohio River over a broad frontage of several hundred miles. On the Atlantic coast the fortress of Halifax was founded that same year to help counterbalance the strength of Louisbourg. New France for her part was busy strengthening her defence posts and adding to their number.

The lines were forming, and the battle would obviously soon be joined, whether or not a formal peace was maintained in Europe between France and Britain.

New France in 1760

A century and a half after Champlain founded Quebec, New France was still, except in physical extent, a pigmy colony. In 1754 the population was only about 55,000; it was no more than 65,000 in 1763. By contrast, the British colonies to the south, almost identical in age (Jamestown, Virginia, the first permanent English settlement, had been founded in 1607, just one year earlier than Quebec), had a population of a million and a half.

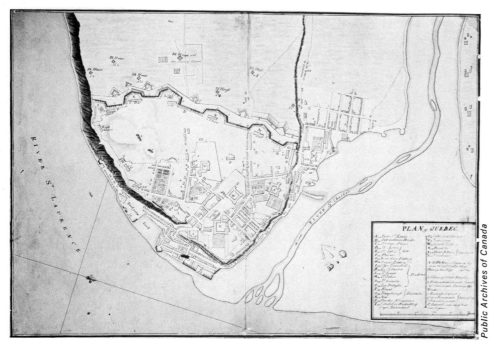

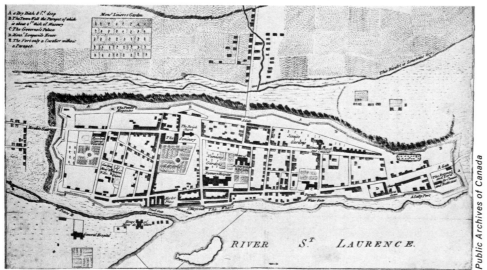

Plan of the city of Quebec, 1760 (above)

From a plan in the British military records of the time.

Plan of Montreal

Drawn by John Rocque in 1761.

Montreal was already the largest city in Canada; its population was about 8,500 in 1754, and that of Quebec, the only other large town, about 5,500. Most of the people of New France lived on farms, though many of the men supplemented farming by seasonal work of other kinds when it was available. Settlement was concentrated largely along both banks of the St. Lawrence River from above Montreal to below the Ile d'Orléans, and in a few subsidiary valleys, notably those of the Richelieu and the Ottawa. The land had been granted in large estates called seigneuries, and most of the farms were in the form of narrow strips running back from the rivers. Frontage on a river was important because it gave ready access to water transportation, and the back of a property was often occupied by a woodlot. Only here and there did settlement extend inland to a second row of holdings, behind those that bordered on the rivers.

The fur trade continued to be the most important industry. By degrees small supporting industries had developed, and more and more of the trade goods required by the fur traders were being made in New France instead of being imported. These gave employment to a wide variety of craftsmen, as diverse as dressmakers, silversmiths and blacksmiths. The canoe builders at Trois-Rivières should be included in the number, as fur traders purchased most of their wares.

Fishing was an important source of food and income, and during a hectic short season the seal fishery gave employment to hundreds of men. Seal oil was the chief product, with the seal skins being used to make moccasins. Shipbuilding was an industry of some moment, and produced both ocean-going ships and the small schooners that provided transportation and carried goods of all kinds on the St. Lawrence and other rivers and lakes. The famous Forges St-Maurice, near Trois-Rivières, made iron stoves, kettles, and other items for the local market.

In spite of these activities, New France could not pay her way. It is estimated that between 1749 and 1755 exports paid for only one-third of the goods imported. Military expenditures saved the day, for money was pouring into Canada from France to maintain the armed forces and to meet the cost of strengthening the colony's defences. If this had not been so, New France would have suffered from that very modern complaint, a balance of payments crisis.

It is important to note that very few immigrants came to New France from France after 1700; by 1750 the population was overwhelmingly Canadian-born. Their first and natural allegiance was thus to Canada; the attachment to France was secondary. By contrast, the social élite in the colony were largely French. Some of the seigneurs were Canadian-born, and so was the Marquis de Vaudreuil, the last Governor of New France; but as a group the more important officials, senior army officers, most of the seigneurs and many of the clergy had almost all come from France.

The system of government was scarcely more democratic than it was at the time in France. On the whole, however, it worked well, especially at the local parish level, where the two most influential persons were the captain of militia and the priest. In the last years of New France, government at the top levels was discredited by the wholesale corruption with which the name of François Bigot, the intendant, is associated. Bougainville dubbed Bigot and his associates "the Grand Society," and in view of their total disregard for the security of the colony and the welfare of its people considered them "an enemy a thousand times more dangerous than the English." Although this was an exaggeration, his journal records incidents that are shocking enough. The construction of vital defence works was fre-

Trois-Rivières in 1784

From an aquatint in King George III's Topographical Collection, now in the Map Room of the British Museum.

British Museum

quently delayed for long periods because officials and contractors were making huge profits from liquor sales and other sources that would cease when a job was completed. Most items and virtually all imports passed through the hands of some official, and advanced greatly in price before they were offered for sale. Thus at a time when the people of Quebec were facing starvation, food speculators went down the St. Lawrence to meet incoming ships and buy up all the supplies on board.

These conditions inevitably affected the morale of the people and the efficiency of the colony's defences, and as a result of them much of the money provided by the King was wasted. No wonder Bougainville wrote bitterly in August of 1758: "this land will perish after having ruined France through the monstrous abuses of these privileged select."

Laval University, in Quebec, traces its ancestry back to a college of arts and theology founded by Bishop Laval in 1663. In later years some schooling was available in the larger centres, mostly in seminaries and convents; but it is significant that there was still no printing press in New France when it surrendered to the British in 1760.

The Conquest of New France

The final contest for the possession of Canada may be said to have begun at Pickawillany, a remote little trading post built by New Englanders in western Ohio. Its existence was a cause of alarm and annoyance to the French, and in June 1752 Charles Langlade, leading 240 Indians and a few French,

"A General View of Quebec," by R. Short

This engraving shows Quebec as it was in 1761, just after the conquest.

Montreal

*The largest city in New France, from an engraving
by Thomas Patten, published in 1762.*

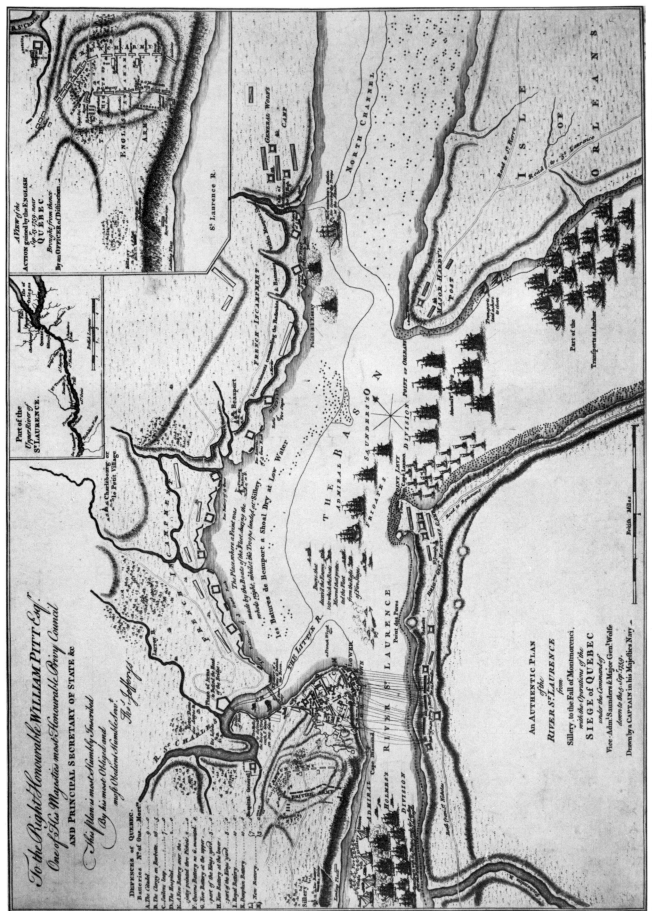

"An Authentic Plan" of the Siege of Quebec

Although the legend states that the plan illustrated operations only up to September 5, 1759, the French and British forces are shown facing one another on the Plains of Abraham, as they did on September 13, and a further view of the battle is given in the inset. It is interesting to compare this map with "A View of the Taking of Quebec," shown in colour on page ii. This engaging but highly imaginary engraving by an unknown artist was published in 1797.

surprised and captured the post and thereby temporarily checked the activities of the British in the Ohio valley. This pause enabled the French to build Fort Duquesne in 1754 at the junction of the Allegheny and Monongahela rivers—the future location of Pittsburgh. Later the same year young George Washington marched westward with a small force, expecting to find a British post on the site, and instead had to surrender to the French at nearby Fort Necessity.

There was still no war in Europe, but the tempo of operations in America increased in 1755. General Braddock took command of British forces and led an attack on Fort Duquesne. Braddock had great faith in the capabilities of his British regulars but no comprehension of wilderness fighting tactics, with the result that he himself died of wounds and two-thirds of his troops were killed or wounded when they were ambushed by the French and Indians.

The only British success of the year was in Acadia, where the French and British had built Fort Beauséjour and Fort Lawrence, facing one another near the present New Brunswick-Nova Scotia border. Brigadier General Robert Monckton took Fort Beauséjour and followed up his success by expelling the so-called neutral Acadians who had continued to live in Nova Scotia. Whether this step was either wise or a military necessity is still a matter of controversy, but the expulsion is one of several acts by the British that have left an indelible impression on the memory of French-Canadians.

War was declared between France and Britain in 1756, and the most important event of the year in America was the arrival of the Marquis de Montcalm, the brilliant new commander of the forces in New France. He made his presence felt in August, when he captured Fort Oswego, and with it gained control of shipping on Lake Ontario. Unfortunately friction soon developed between Montcalm and his nominal superior, the Canadian-born Marquis de Vaudreuil, Governor of the colony. The two were quite different in background and temperament, and lack of sympathy and cooperation between them became a serious military handicap for the French.

William Pitt's return to office and power in Britain in June 1757 had a decisive influence on the course of the war; it was he who inspired and directed its grand strategy. Pitt was interested in the extension and consolidation of Britain's colonial possessions, and he was prepared to give priority to the operations that would achieve these ends. During the next few years he kept military commitments in Europe to a minimum and assigned large military and naval forces and capable officers to the war in America. Hitherto warfare between New France and the British colonies had consisted essentially of raids and counter-raids. Pitt planned instead a series of coordinated attacks, all in substantial strength, that would force New France to divide its forces and fight on several fronts. He was well aware that the French could not hold out against a

Public Archives of Canada

Montcalm's last letter

Written on September 13, 1759, the day of the Battle of the Plains, presumably to General Townshend, this letter surrenders Quebec. Montcalm died early the following morning, and his mind was evidently somewhat confused, as Quebec in fact did not surrender until September 18. The original letter is in the Public Archives of Canada.

The Death of Wolfe, by Benjamin West

This highly effective picture, also shown in colour on the dust jacket, probably the most famous of all historical paintings, was first exhibited at the Royal Academy in 1771. It was purchased by Lord Grosvenor, whose descendant, the second Duke of Westminster, presented it to Canada in 1918, through Lord Beaverbrook, as a tribute to what Canada had done in the First World War. It now hangs in the National Gallery in Ottawa. In spite of this, the painting, in the words of Col. C. P.

Stacey, "is a remarkably untruthful production. Almost everything about it is historically wrong." The battle for Quebec was still in progress when Wolfe died, and "senior officers . . . had other things to do besides grouping themselves picturesquely about the dying general." At the most, five persons were in fact present. The wounded officer standing on the left is Brig. Monckton, who was shot before Wolfe, and was actually being conveyed to a ship when Wolfe died.

long campaign unless they received supplies and reinforcements from France, and naval squadrons were placed on the French coast and in North American waters to prevent transports from reaching Quebec.

It took some time for Pitt's plans to become effective and in the meantime Montcalm scored another striking success. In 1757 he besieged and took Fort William Henry, the fort built by the British at the south end of Lake George to counter-balance Fort Carillon, at its north end. To Montcalm's anger and distress the victory was marred by his Indian allies, who attacked British prisoners and massacred scores of them. Upon many occasions Indian allies were, indeed, nothing less than a necessary evil; on the whole it was better to have their support than to have them in the opposing forces, but to control them effectively was difficult and frequently impossible. At Fort William Henry they seized some 600 prisoners, and although Montcalm succeeded in ransoming 400 of them, the Indians took the rest to Montreal and held them there, in the heart of New France, until better terms could be wrung from the French.

In 1758 Montcalm won his last victory. General James Abercrombie made a massive but ill-managed assault on Fort Carillon (Ticonderoga) and withdrew when it was repulsed. But elsewhere the leaders and forces Pitt had provided gained the British important successes. Brig. Gen. John Forbes, after a long march westward through Pennsylvania, captured Fort Duquesne and so ended French hopes of retaining control of the Ohio valley. Lt. Col. John Bradstreet crossed Lake Ontario and took Fort Frontenac, thus severing French communications with other posts to the west. Most important of all, General Monckton and a naval force under Admiral Edward Boscawen invested Louisbourg and forced it to capitulate. Its reduction helped isolate New France, and so hastened its fall.

James Wolfe, a young brigadier only 31 years of age, had directed the siege of Louisbourg with notable resource and spirit, and in 1759 he was placed in command of the expedition assembled to attack Quebec. This was in effect a combined operation, as Wolfe received the closest support throughout from the fleet commanded by Admiral Sir Charles Saunders. Wolfe enjoyed the great advantage of mobility, and could move his ships about, thereby keeping the French in a state of wearisome uncertainty. A landing above Quebec was made finally on the night of September 12, and the famous Battle of the Plains of Abraham took place the next morning. The French were driven back into the city, both Wolfe and Montcalm were fatally wounded, and Quebec surrendered on September 18.

Strong French forces were still at large outside Quebec, and further fighting followed in 1760. In April the Chevalier de Lévis made an attempt to regain Quebec and came within an inch of succeeding. It became clear that the fate of the fortress would depend upon the nationality of the first

Lord Egremont

The death of Wolfe

This painting by Edward Penny comes much nearer to portraying reality than the great canvas by West. The original painting is at Petworth House, the seat of Lord Egremont.

Public Archives of Canada

Louis Joseph, Marquis de Montcalm

From the painting in the Public Archives, which is a copy of the portrait by an unknown artist in the possession of the family.

vessels to come up the St. Lawrence in the spring, and owing to the British naval blockade they were British.

A three-pronged approach to Montreal followed. Brig. Gen. James Murray advanced up the St. Lawrence from Quebec; Brig. Gen. William Haviland came down the Richelieu River from Lake Champlain; General Amherst, the commander-in-chief, marched eastward from Lake Ontario. Lévis and Vaudreuil were quite unable to meet such a massive assault and on September 8 they surrendered Montreal and all New France.

The war was over in Canada, but there was some activity elsewhere. In 1762 the French attacked and captured St. John's, Newfoundland, and held it briefly. The last French post to hold out was Fort de Chartres, far down the Mississippi River, about half way between Canada and New Orleans. Its flag did not come fluttering down until 1765, two years after the Treaty of Paris had ceded all French possessions in the northern part of North America, except the little islands of St. Pierre and Miquelon, to Britain.

While the terms of the treaty were under discussion there were those in both Britain and France who attached little value or importance to Canada. But William Pitt was not prepared to give up his colonial conquests, or to exchange Canada for a West Indies island that might produce immediate profits, and his influence made it certain that Britain would retain Canada.

British Rule and the American Threat

The First Years of British Rule

CIVIL government was not inaugurated in Canada until August 1764, nearly four years after the surrender at Montreal. The interval had been a period of military occupation. The French had been led to expect a reign of terror; instead, all three of the military district governors did their best to make life as nearly normal as circumstances permitted. General James Murray, at Quebec, was particularly well disposed toward the Canadians, and it was he who was appointed the first civil governor.

A proclamation dated October 7, 1763 had defined the new boundaries in the former French possessions. The colony of Quebec was relatively small, but it included the populated heart of New France. Its boundary ran from the Gulf of St. Lawrence up the St. John River to its headwaters, extended westward through Lake St. John to Lake Nipissing, ran thence to the St. Lawrence at the 45th parallel, and then followed that parallel to the height of land, which was the boundary eastward to the Bay of Chaleur and the Gulf. The Quebec-Labrador coast from the St. John River to Hudson Strait, Anticosti Island and the Magdalen Islands were added to Newfoundland, while what is now New Brunswick, the Island of St. John (Prince Edward Island) and Cape Breton all became part of an enlarged Nova Scotia. The rest of the former French areas, including the whole of the Great Lakes region, the Ohio valley and the lands east of the Mississippi, were thrown together in a vast Indian territory in which settlement was not to be permitted and in which trade could only be carried on by licence. The creation of this territory was regarded as an affront by the American colonies, as it implied that the British Government wished to confine them to the area east of the mountains, just as the French had tried to do.

This same proclamation, supplemented by instructions to Murray dated December 7, provided for the government of Quebec. Unfortunately the officials in London had assumed that New France could be fitted into the normal British colonial pattern. They took no account of the fact that the population was not only almost entirely French but also Roman Catholic which, under existing British laws, excluded them from many civil rights and all public offices. Murray quickly concluded that to hold an election for an assembly was therefore quite impracticable and he decided to institute rule by the governor and a council. Intended to be a tem-

General James Murray

''The Death of Montgomery before Quebec''
This painting is by the American artist John Trumbull, who studied under Benjamin West.

porary measure, this arrangement was destined to last nearly 30 years.

Though thoroughly well intentioned, Murray soon found himself in difficulties. The small but growing and aggressive British minority wanted power and preferential treatment; the French felt insecure with the future of their laws and institutions, and to some extent their religion still uncertain. Murray was recalled to London in 1766 to answer various charges, and although he emerged from the inquiries reasonably well he did not return to Canada.

Meanwhile a formidable Indian insurrection, led by Pontiac, an Ottawa chief, had erupted in the west. The causes were complex. Pontiac looked upon the British as invaders when they came to take possession of the western forts; the Indians were worried about their lands; the British had dropped the old French custom of offering gifts and hospitality at the trading posts; French officers and traders still active in the Mississippi valley encouraged opposition and revolt. Pontiac failed in an attempt to seize Detroit, but eight other posts, including Michilimackinac, were captured and most of the inhabitants killed in May and June of 1763. Pontiac tried to revive the war the next year but with little success. He learned that no more encouragement and assistance could be expected from the French, and he made peace at Detroit in August 1765. Fort de Chartres, on the Mississippi near the site of St. Louis, the last post to remain in French hands, was surrendered just two months later.

Murray's successor was Colonel Guy Carleton, who was appointed lieutenant-governor and commander-in-chief in 1766, and governor in 1768. His was a complex character—ambitious, competent, benevolent and authoritarian. He soon came to two conclusions. The first was that Quebec "must to the end of time be peopled by the Canadian (meaning the French-Canadian) race"; the second was that, if well treated, the Canadians would be ready to fight in defence of Quebec—a highly important consideration in Carleton's mind because of the rising spirit of discontent and rebellion in the American colonies. In other words, generous measures that met French grievances would not only be humanitarian but would be important as well from the military point of view.

Carleton went to England in 1770 to press these and other views and his efforts were chiefly responsible for the passing of the Quebec Act in 1774. This gave Roman Catholics in Canada complete civil equality, and legalized the levying of tithes by the Roman Catholic Church—remarkable provisions to be approved by a legislature in England where "Catholic emancipation" did not take place until 1829. French civil law again became the law of the land, although English criminal law was retained. Government was to continue to be by the governor and a council, as heretofore; there would still be no elected assembly. Boundary changes greatly enlarged the area included in Quebec. Labrador, Anticosti and the Magdalen Islands were added to it on the east; on the north it extended to the height of land that marked the limits of Rupert's Land, while it absorbed the former Indian reserve as far west as Lake Superior and southward to the Ohio River. These changes roused much resentment in the American colonies, which regarded them as a further attempt to restrict their expansion westward.

Carleton quickly discovered that although the Quebec Act had removed major grievances of the French, it did not have the expected result of making them more eager to defend their country. On the other hand, they showed little inclination to join the rebellion now obviously brewing in the Thirteen Colonies. Efforts to enlist their support were made by the Continental Congress in the fall of 1774, and in April 1775 a personal emissary came to Montreal to invite Quebec to send delegates to the May meeting of the Congress; but none attended. The truth appears to be that the French were not convinced that the severing of the connection with France was final. There had been many wars, and the next might well reverse international fortunes and place France in a position to demand the return of Canada. Neutrality under the generous terms of Carleton's Quebec Act seemed a prudent policy.

Actually, the intentions of the British Government were not as benevolent as the act made them appear; Carleton's instructions suggest that anglicization of the population was still the ultimate end in view. But Carleton, as was his way, acted only upon those instructions that he himself saw fit to implement, because of the military situation that soon faced him. On May 19, 1775, he heard that rebellion had broken out in Massachusetts. The next day he learned that the Americans were invading Canada by way of Lake Champlain.

Canada and the American Revolutionary War

At first sight the odds in favour of an American conquest of Canada seemed overwhelming. The population of the Thirteen Colonies had risen to about 2,500,000. That of Canada was scarcely 100,000, and it consisted in great part of French whose involuntary attachment to the British Crown dated back only a dozen years. And for the Americans the end in view was highly important. If they could seize Canada and assert their independence they would make themselves masters of most of North America, at least as far west as the Mississippi, and they would end forever the menace of raids and invasion from the north that had plagued New England for more than two centuries.

The invasion of Canada turned out to be a two-pronged attack. The first force approached by the familiar Lake Champlain route. In May 1775 Ethan Allen and Seth Warner, with a force of "Green Mountain Boys" (New Hampshire frontiersmen) surprised and captured Ticonderoga and Crown Point. (The garrisons numbered 30 and 12 respec-

Guy Carleton, 1st Lord Dorchester

tively.) Later the invasion began in earnest under Brig. Gen. Richard Montgomery. Fort Chambly surrendered on October 19; St. Johns was taken after a two-month siege on November 2. Carleton, who had counted too optimistically on French-Canadian support, evacuated Montreal and fell back on the time-tested strategy of holding Quebec and awaiting the arrival of reinforcements. Montgomery followed him and prepared to besiege the city. At Quebec he was joined by the second American invasion force, commanded by Benedict Arnold, which had arrived after a difficult march over a route that followed the Kennebec and Chaudière Rivers.

Time was of the essence; the Americans realized that Quebec must be taken before reinforcements could reach Carleton. Early on the morning of December 31, Montgomery led a gallant but unsuccessful assault on the Lower Town in which he himself was killed. At the same time Arnold attacked the city's approaches on the Charles River side, but he too was unsuccessful. These reverses did not end the siege, which continued until the spring of 1776, but relief of Quebec was certain, and the Americans began to retreat on May 5, the day the first British ships came up the St. Lawrence.

It seems clear that Carleton could have captured or annihilated the invading forces if he had pursued them, and his failure to do so was doubtless deliberate. The Declaration of Independence was not signed until July 4, and he appears to have been hopeful that some settlement could still be reached between Great Britain and the revolting colonies.

Sea power and the control of the river approach to Quebec had saved the city, and sea power, based on Halifax, played a major role in Nova Scotia as well. About 15,000 New Englanders had settled in Nova Scotia, and the Americans hoped that they would actively support the revolution. The naval and military forces based on Halifax prevented this from happening. In the fall of 1776 Jonathan Eddy raised a force in Massachusetts and attempted to capture Fort Cumberland (the former Fort Beauséjour) near the present Nova Scotia-New Brunswick border. His two assaults were repulsed in November, and the arrival of British reinforcements ended the siege.

At this time the fortunes of the Americans reached their lowest ebb. The Continental Congress was facing immense difficulties. It had no powers of taxation; most of its troops had joined up on short-term enlistments that were expiring; it was desperately short of arms and supplies. But the turn of the tide would soon be perceptible. In retrospect it is clear that the surprising defeat of the British force at Trenton, New Jersey, by Washington on December 26, 1776, marked the beginning of a new stage in the battle for independence.

Carleton had always felt that the most effective action that could be taken against the American colonies was a strong offensive down Lake Champlain, Lake George and the Hudson River to New York, which would in effect cut them in two. This was the plan finally adopted in 1777. If Carleton had been in command it might well have succeeded; unfortunately the leadership was entrusted to General "Gentleman Johnny" Burgoyne, who set out from Canada with a formidable force but was soon in difficulties. His advance was painfully slow; he was short of food and supplies; his army was reduced by losses in secondary actions. In addition the main British army in New York, under Sir William Howe, marched off toward Philadelphia instead of heading up the Hudson to help cut the Lake George–New York American lifeline. The result was that Burgoyne was defeated and compelled to surrender at Saratoga on October 17, 1777—a major British disaster that was infinitely encouraging to the Americans.

So far as Canada was concerned, most of the rest of the war was a matter of raids rather than battles. Troops and Indians united to harass American settlements and destroy food supplies. The damage done was sometimes substantial; on one occasion a thousand barns and 600,000 bushels of grain are said to have been destroyed. This was savage frontier warfare of the old kind, accompanied as usual by brutality, burnings and massacres. On the British side the best-known leaders were Sir John Johnson, Colonel John Butler, who raised a famous corps of Rangers, and Joseph Brant, a Mohawk chief. Four of the Iroquois tribes—the Mohawks, Cayugas, Senecas and Onondagas—had remained loyal to the British and contributed to the raiding forces. As their resources permitted, the Americans took countermeasures, and by 1779 they had gained effective control of the Ohio–Indiana–Illinois country that they had long coveted.

For the Americans the highlight of 1778 had been the official recognition of their independence by France in February. Later France was able to assist the colonies, and it was the support of a French fleet under De Grasse and French soldiers that forced the second major British surrender of the war, that of General Cornwallis at Yorktown in October 1781. Britain had many demands elsewhere, and the rebelling colonies were too populous and too large physically to be defeated by the armies that she was able and willing to devote to the task.

At the conference table the Americans tried to secure the cession of Canada, but Britain declined to agree. Canada, Nova Scotia, Newfoundland and Rupert's Land were all retained under the terms of the Treaty of Paris, signed on September 3, 1783.

Public Archives of Canada

Bourgoyne surrenders at Saratoga

Bourgoyne (left) is here shown surrendering his entire army of nearly 6,000 men to the American commander, Horatio Gates. This was one of the turning points in the American Revolutionary War.

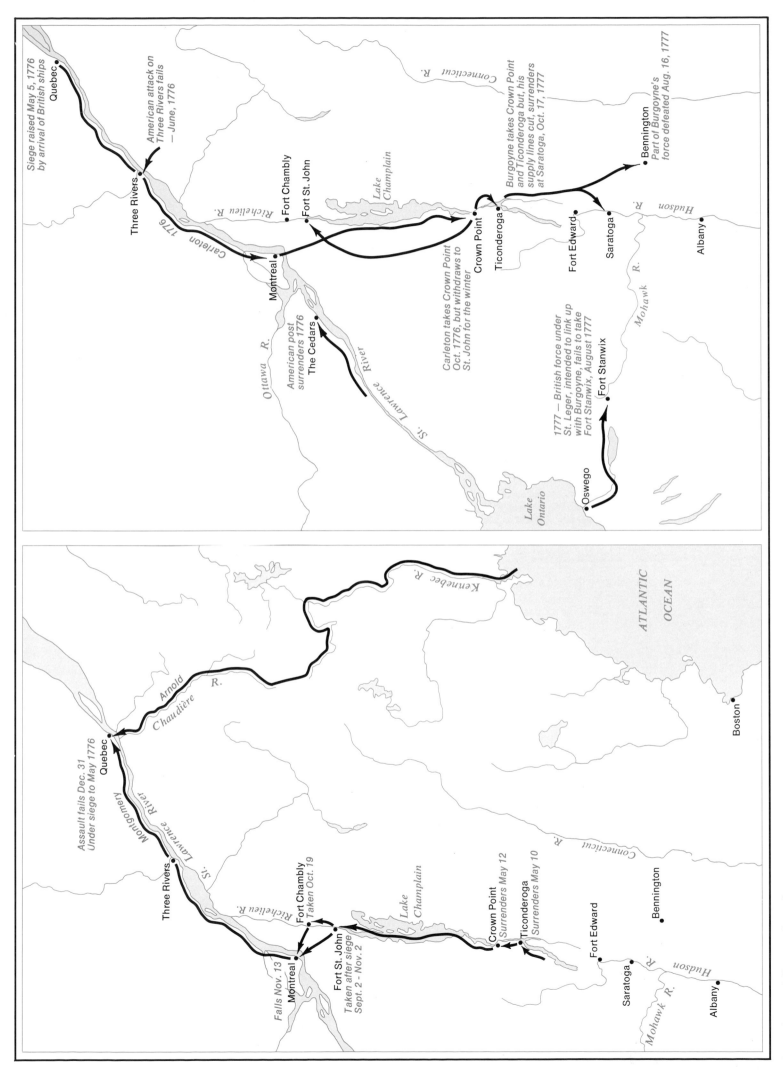

Invasion and Counterinvasion

Map labels (top panel):

Quebec

Siege raised May 5, 1776 by arrival of British ships

Three Rivers

American attack on Three Rivers fails — June, 1776

Fort Chambly

Fort St. John

Richelieu R.

Lake Champlain

Carleton 1776

Montreal

Connecticut R.

Crown Point

Ticonderoga

Carleton takes Crown Point Oct. 1776, but withdraws to St. John for the winter

Fort Edward

Saratoga

Hudson R.

Albany

Burgoyne takes Crown Point and Ticonderoga but, his supply lines cut, surrenders at Saratoga, Oct. 17, 1777

Bennington

Part of Burgoyne's force defeated Aug. 16, 1777

Mohawk R.

Ottawa R.

American post surrenders 1776

The Cedars

St. Lawrence River

Fort Stanwix

1777 — British force under St. Leger, intended to link up with Burgoyne, fails to take Fort Stanwix, August 1777

Oswego

Lake Ontario

Map labels (bottom panel):

ATLANTIC OCEAN

Kennebec R.

Arnold

Chaudière R.

Quebec

Assault fails Dec. 31 Under siege to May 1776

Montgomery

St. Lawrence River

Boston

Three Rivers

Falls Nov. 13

Montreal

Fort Chambly *Taken Oct. 19*

Fort St. John *Taken after siege Sept. 2 - Nov. 2*

Richelieu R.

Lake Champlain

Crown Point *Surrenders May 12*

Ticonderoga *Surrenders May 10*

Fort Edward

Connecticut R.

Bennington

Saratoga

Mohawk R.

Hudson R.

Albany

CHAPTER 6

Canada to 1783

Canada in 1783

THE Treaty of Paris gave Quebec (as Canada was still called officially) a new southern boundary. With minor adjustments, the major part of it—running from the Lake of the Woods to Lake Superior, and thence through the Great Lakes and the St. Lawrence River to the 45th parallel, which it followed eastward to the height of land—is still the boundary between Canada and the United States. The Canada of today was beginning to take shape.

The major point at issue had been the future of the rich lands east of the Mississippi and north of the Ohio River, which the American colonies had long wished to occupy. They had been the subject of much discussion, intrigue and even secret treaty-making. France and Spain were interested as well as Britain and the Americans. Spain would have liked to add them to Louisiana, which included the country west of the Mississippi River. France was ready to support Spain in the expectation that this would reduce Spanish pressure for concessions from France elsewhere. Britain, both for territorial reasons and because of the large French population in Canada, was anxious to check the growth of French influence in America. A concession to American ambitions and the loss of a huge and enormously valuable territory was the price she had to pay to attain this end.

An inaccurate map played an important part in the boundary negotiations. Little was known about many of the areas under discussion; surveys with any pretence to accuracy were few and far between. The British depended chiefly on "A Map of the British and French Dominions in North America" published in London in 1755 by John Mitchell. Thanks to its inaccuracies the extreme eastern and western ends of the new boundary gave rise to dis-

putes that were not settled for many years. In the east, the treaty stated that the boundary was to follow the St. Croix River to its source and then run north to the height of land between the Atlantic and the St. Lawrence River. The difficulty was that it was not certain which river was meant by the St Croix. In the west, the boundary was to run westward from the northwest angle of Lake of the Woods to the sources of the Mississippi—an impossible line, as the Mississippi did not extend that far north. An inset on the Mitchell map that covered the area in question was the cause of this latter mistake.

In 1783 the fur trade and British military expenditures were still the mainstays of the Canadian economy. British merchants and traders, among them a formidable group of Scots, had taken over the fur trade when the French withdrew, including its two most important assets—the birch bark canoe, which made travel and transport up rapid-infested waterways possible, and the French-Canadian voyageurs, who provided an incomparable labour force. Pontiac's insurrection had disrupted the trade in 1763 and 1764, and it was hampered for a time by unrealistic regulations requiring all trade to be conducted at trading posts. By 1767 rules were less stringent, peace had returned, and the British traders were ready to resume the push westward where the French had left off. In 1767 or 1768 James Finlay was in the Saskatchewan valley, where he had a trading post near the Nipawin Rapids, not far from the site of Fort St. Louis, the westernmost French fort. By 1773 traders were entering the West in numbers. Many of the furs they collected would otherwise have found their way to Hudson Bay, and the Hudson's Bay Company realized that the parties it had been sending inland were no longer adequate to cope with this competition.

Meanwhile the Company had been doing some exploring on its own account. Some of it was in search of the still elusive Northwest Passage. In 1762 it had explored Chesterfield Inlet, which it was hoped might be the entrance of a strait leading to

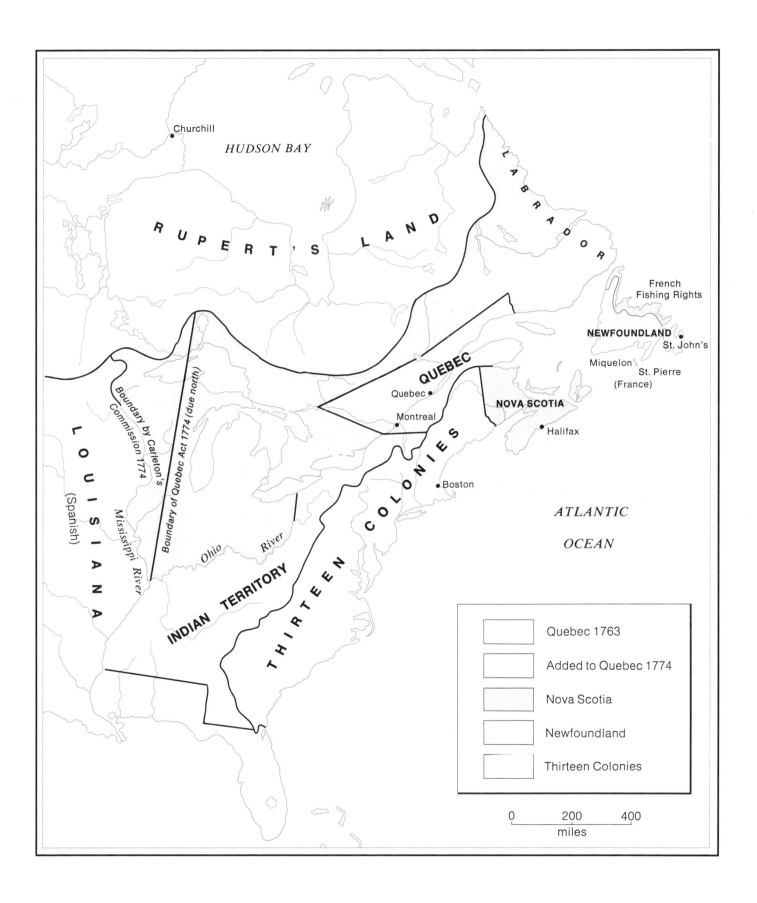

Churchill

HUDSON BAY

R U P E R T ' S   L A N D

LABRADOR

French Fishing Rights

NEWFOUNDLAND
St. John's

Miquelon
St. Pierre
(France)

QUEBEC

Quebec

NOVA SCOTIA

Montreal

Halifax

Boundary by Carleton's Commission 1774

Boundary of Quebec Act 1774 (due north)

LOUISIANA
(Spanish)

Mississippi River

Ohio   River

INDIAN   TERRITORY

T H I R T E E N   C O L O N I E S

Boston

ATLANTIC

OCEAN

	Quebec 1763
	Added to Quebec 1774
	Nova Scotia
	Newfoundland
	Thirteen Colonies

0   200   400
miles

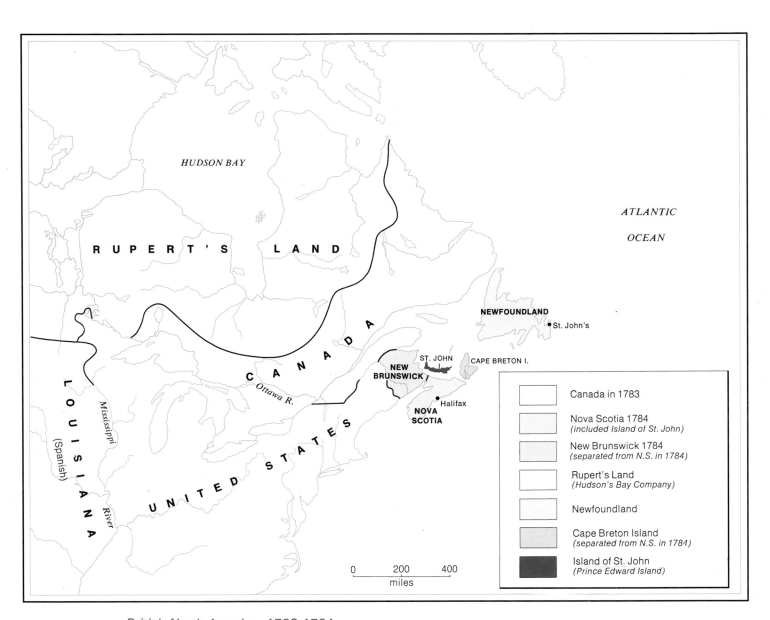

HUDSON BAY

ATLANTIC

OCEAN

R U P E R T ' S   L A N D

NEWFOUNDLAND
• St. John's

C A N A D A

ST. JOHN
CAPE BRETON I.

NEW
BRUNSWICK

Ottawa R.

NOVA
SCOTIA
• Halifax

L
O
U
I
S
I
A
N
A

Mississippi

(Spanish)

River

U N I T E D   S T A T E S

0   200   400
miles

	Canada in 1783
	Nova Scotia 1784 *(included Island of St. John)*
	New Brunswick 1784 *(separated from N.S. in 1784)*
	Rupert's Land *(Hudson's Bay Company)*
	Newfoundland
	Cape Breton Island *(separated from N.S. in 1784)*
	Island of St. John *(Prince Edward Island)*

British North America, 1783-1784

Public Archives of Canada

Public Archives of Canada

Joseph Frobisher (seen at left)

Samuel Hearne

This portrait is the frontispiece in the account of Hearne's travels that was published in London in 1795.

the Pacific. Later it took up the search for a northern river that Indian report credited with being rich in both furs and copper deposits. After two false starts Samuel Hearne set out from Churchill in December 1770 on the great journey that was to take him to the mouth of the Coppermine River in July 1771—the first trip made by a white man from Hudson Bay to the Arctic Ocean.

In 1774 Hearne undertook another important assignment—the building of Cumberland House, the Hudson's Bay Company's first permanent inland post. The site, on Cumberland Lake, just off the Saskatchewan River, was shrewdly chosen, and soon became a major crossroads of fur trade traffic from both Hudson Bay and Montreal.

The push westward continued and extended to the Churchill River (usually called the English River at this time). In 1776 Joseph and Thomas Frobisher were trading at Frog Portage, and later in the year Thomas built a post on Lac Ile-à-la-Crosse. Finally, in 1778, Peter Pond crossed the Methy Portage, entered the watershed of the Mackenzie River, and built a post on the Athabasca River, about 30 miles from Lake Athabasca. The scene for the long battle between the Hudson's Bay Company and the "pedlars" from Montreal, as the company had dubbed them, was thus set by 1780.

Neither the pedlars nor the other British

traders in Montreal were happy about conditions there. When the Quebec Act had established French civil law, Carleton had been instructed to take steps to see that some accommodation was made to meet the special needs of the merchants who were accustomed to British commercial law; but these instructions Carleton had chosen to ignore. His successor in 1778, General Sir Frederick Haldimand, was honest and kindly, but not one to welcome differences of opinion. Nor had he any great sympathy with the problems of the merchants, especially in time of war. If, for example, goods being imported were held up because of the leisurely habits of naval convoys, he could see no great excuse for grievance. These tensions were matched by others of quite a different sort in the French community. When France declared war on Britain in 1778, hopes ran high that Canada might again become a French possession. Rumours flew that the Americans were planning another invasion and that a French fleet would soon come up the St. Lawrence. Neither move was attempted, because a captured Canada would have to go either to the French or the Americans, and neither wished to see it in the possession of the other. This was not evident at the time, and New France continued to hope that it might be returned to France at the conference table if not by combat; but it was not to be.

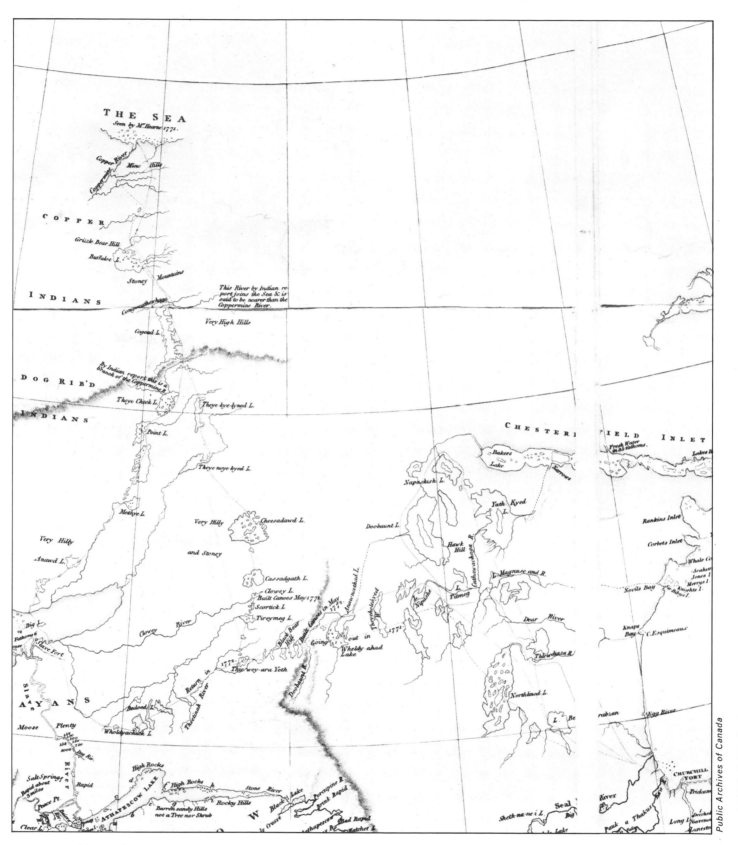

Hearne's track to the Arctic

Part of "A Map exhibiting all the New Discoveries in the Interior Part of North America," issued in 1795 by the famous cartographer Aaron Arrowsmith, showing Hearne's route from Churchill to the Arctic.

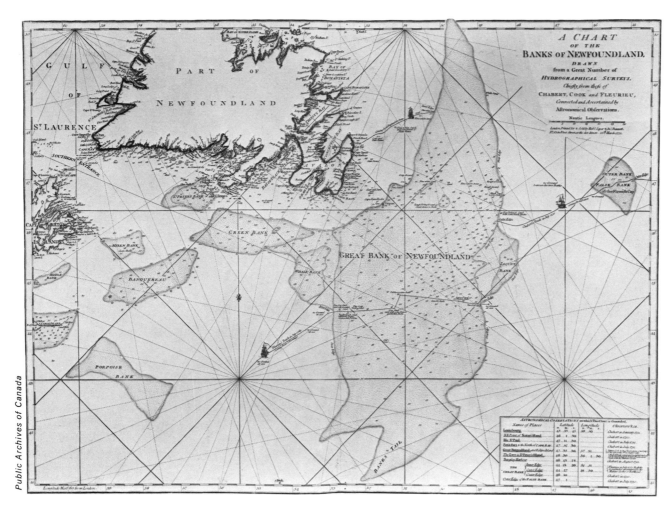

Cook's map of the Newfoundland fishing banks
It is frequently forgotten that Captain James Cook played a part in the history of eastern as well as western Canada. He took part in the naval operations against Quebec in 1759, and after the conquest carried out surveys on the St. Lawrence River, Halifax harbour and the coasts of Newfoundland and Labrador.

The Atlantic Provinces: 1775-1783

For two centuries and more the great attraction of the areas now comprising the Atlantic provinces lay in their fisheries. English, French, Portuguese, and for a time Spanish fishermen frequented the bays and banks of Newfoundland and Nova Scotia in great numbers, and to these were later added fishermen from New England. In addition to their economic importance the naval powers regarded the fisheries as an invaluable "nursery of seamen" that created a manpower reserve upon which they could draw in time of war. This explains the tenacity with which France fought to retain fishing rights in Canadian waters in spite of the loss of New France and Acadia.

In England activity in the Newfoundland fisheries centred in the West Country, in such ports as Poole, Topsham and Dartmouth. Both the merchants there and the authorities in London were convinced that shore settlements would harm the trade, and colonization on the island was forbidden or officially frowned upon for many years. But villages of sorts sprang up here and there in spite of

this, partly because the merchants themselves would recruit low-grade labourers in England and Ireland and abandon them in Newfoundland at the end of the season. In 1713 the resident population seems to have been about 3,000; by 1750 it had risen to about 7,000, and St. John's had grown into a trading post of some importance. For many years the Royal Navy had sent an annual convoy to protect the fisheries, and the officer commanding took some interest in maintaining law and order during the fishing season. In 1729 this officer was at last given more formal responsibility and the title of Governor, but there was still no provision for any control during the winter months.

The capture of St. John's by the French in 1762 has been noted; it was there that the French flag came down for the last time in what is now Canada. Newfoundland's population grew more rapidly in war time; it was about 16,000 in 1764, but increased very little in the following decade.

The peace treaty of 1763 gave France the islands of St. Pierre and Miquelon as shore bases for her fishermen, and fishing rights on the northern coast. The treaties of 1783 made further concessions to the French and also to the Americans that were to cause discontent for many years. The "French shore" on the northern coast was to end at Cape St. John, but it was extended to include the whole of the western coast, down to Cape Ray. The Ameri-

Public Archives of Canada

"Ye manner of Fishing for, Curing & Drying Cod at Newfoundland"

This famous engraving is an inset on a map by Herman Moll published in 1719.

cans were to be free to fish on the bays and banks of Newfoundland and Nova Scotia as usual, and could land in uninhabited bays in Nova Scotia, the Magdalen Islands and Labrador for the purpose of curing or drying their catch.

For a few years after 1763 Nova Scotia included both New Brunswick and the Island of St. John—the future Prince Edward Island. When the French were expelled in 1758 the Island had been left virtually without a population; only 30 families

"Charlotte-Town on the Island of St. John's 1778"

This water colour by C. Randle is one of the earliest views of the city.

were living there in 1764. In 1767 the British Government decided to divided it into large lots that would be granted to persons who had some claim on the patronage of the Crown, and the whole Island was duly granted to 67 proprietors. Absentee landlords were no more popular or successful there than elsewhere, but it was only a century later, after Confederation, that the Island got rid of the last of them. Equally extraordinary were provisions made for the civil government of the Island. In 1769, when the population was still only 250, it became a separate colony, with full-fledged provision for a governor, lieutenant-governor, executive council, legislative council, supreme court and elected assembly. Never was more government provided for fewer people.

In Nova Scotia itself, efforts were made after the expulsion of the Acadians to persuade New Englanders to take up their vacated lands. This the New Englanders were reluctant to do at first, because they feared French attacks and because there was no provision for representative government—a matter upon which they felt very strongly. The French threat was removed in 1758 when Louisbourg fell, and the same year the House of Assembly of Nova Scotia—the first elected legislature in Canada—met in Halifax on October 2. Thus reassured, about 15,000 New Englanders had moved to the colony before the outbreak of the American Revolution, where they founded Yarmouth, Barrington, Liverpool and other villages, and also settled in Chignecto. Meanwhile German immigrants had founded Lunenburg and Scottish highlanders had settled in the Pictou area. In what was soon to become New Brunswick, settlement began in the valley of the St. John River, but on a very modest scale; the population there was still less than 3,000 in 1775. Since 1764 Acadians had been allowed to return, and a considerable number did so and settled chiefly on the Bay of Chaleur.

When the American colonies revolted, the attitude of the New Englanders caused some anxiety, but it soon became evident that they preferred neutrality. They had a stake in the country, and the presence of strong British forces, and later the depredations of American privateers along the coast,

Public Archives of Canada

made them more and more sympathetic to the British cause. Fort Howe was built in 1777 at the mouth of the St. John River to increase the security of the settlements in the river valley. Their refusal to take the oath of allegiance had been the final straw that had led to the expulsion of the Acadians; the New Englanders seem to have taken the oath without hesitation when it was required of them. In Liverpool, for example, only one person refused when the people were asked to take the oath in the first days of 1776.

The Far West Coast

In early days the sea voyage from Europe to the Northwest Coast of North America was one of the longest and most hazardous that a sailing ship could undertake. This explains in part why several million people of European extraction were living on the eastern side of the continent before a white man first set foot in what is now British Columbia. The discovery of the west coast had to wait until explorers could set out from harbours relatively near at hand, which in practice meant from Russian ports in Kamchatka or Spanish bases in Mexico and California.

Meanwhile imaginative mapmakers hazarded guesses as to the shape and features of this part of America. About 1560 maps began to feature a Strait of Anian that separated Asia and North America and was supposed to be the beginning of a passage to the Atlantic. A Portuguese mariner, Lorenzo Maldonado, claimed to have sailed through it in 1588. Some years later Juan de Fuca, a Greek in the Spanish service, contended that he had sailed for twenty days in a strait he found at about latitude 48°. Early in the 18th century cartographers placed a huge Sea of the West on the map of Western Canada, with channels connecting it with the Pacific and eastern Arctic or Hudson Bay. As if to confirm this, a narrative by one Bartholomew de Fonte, published in 1708, described how he had sailed from the Pacific to the Atlantic through a series of rivers and lakes in 1640. As late as 1726 Swift could publish a map in *Gulliver's Travels* placing the land of Brobdingnag in Alaska, and no one could say him nay.

There was one genuine voyage in this era of romances. In 1579 Francis Drake, having harried the Spanish settlements on the coast of Central and South America, decided to return to England by way of the fabled Strait of Anian. In the North Pacific he changed his mind, and the winds and currents of the Pacific being what they are, it is reasonably certain that he sighted the mountains on Vancouver Island as he sailed southward—the first European to do so.

The Russians were the first to begin serious exploration. In 1728 Vitus Bering, a Dane in their service, sailed from Kamchatka through the strait that bears his name, but did not identify the coast of America. His second voyage was delayed for various reasons until 1741. This time he had two ships, the second commanded by Peter Chirikof, but storms soon separated them. Both ships sighted Mount St. Elias and followed parts of the coast of Alaska, and both parties met with misfortune. On the return voyage Bering's own ship was wrecked on Bering Island, and he and many of the crew died there. Chirikof sailed down the coast and sent two parties ashore south of the future sight of Sitka; both failed to return and presumably were massacred by the natives.

Despite his misfortunes, Chirikof was able to bring home furs. In the following years Russian traders appeared on many of the Aleutian Islands, and in 1768-69 they were visited by an official expedition under Captain Krenitzin.

Word of these Russian activities filtered through to Spain, and fears arose that they would soon be extended southward into areas that Spain regarded as her preserve. In April 1773 the Viceroy of New Spain was ordered to explore the Northwest Coast, to safeguard Spanish interests there, and he was told that officers were being sent out to take charge of the expeditions. Early in the following year, without waiting for the officers to arrive, the Viceroy sent Juan Perez north in the *Santiago*. Perez

Public Archives of Canada

Captain James Cook
From an engraving of the portrait by Nathanial Dance.

Town and Harbour of Halifax
From the engraving by R. Short, made about 1761.

Public Archives of Canada

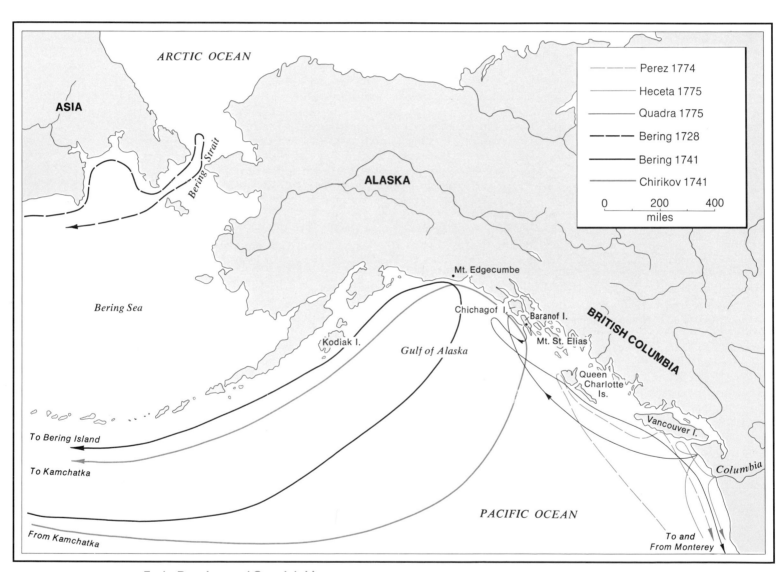

ARCTIC OCEAN

ASIA

Bering Strait

ALASKA

Bering Sea

Mt. Edgecumbe

Chichagof I.

Baranof I.

Mt. St. Elias

BRITISH COLUMBIA

Kodiak I.

Gulf of Alaska

Queen Charlotte Is.

Vancouver I.

To Bering Island

Columbia

To Kamchatka

PACIFIC OCEAN

From Kamchatka

To and From Monterey

Perez 1774
Heceta 1775
Quadra 1775
Bering 1728
Bering 1741
Chirikov 1741

0   200   400
miles

Early Russian and Spanish Voyages

"The Inside of a House in Nootka Sound"

From an engraving of a drawing by John Webber, who was with Cook in 1778.

had been a pilot on the Manila–Acapulco route, and he was instructed to try to reach latitude 60°, which would have brought him to Mount St. Elias. The *Santiago* got away from Monterey on June 11, and Perez first sighted land—the Queen Charlotte Islands—on July 14. He spent four days off Dixon Entrance, north of the islands, then headed for home. He thought he had reached 55° north, but he actually fell somewhat short of this. On the way south he paused off a roadstead that may have been Nootka Sound. Some trading was done with the Indians there, and also in Alaska, but Perez made no landing.

By the following year the officers from Spain had arrived, and Bruno de Hezeta was captain of the *Santiago*, with Perez his second-in-command, when she again sailed northward from Monterey in May 1775. She was accompanied by the little schooner *Sonora*, commanded by Juan Francisco de la Bodega y Quadra (usually referred to as Quadra). Landings were made in Trinidad Bay in northern California, and near Point Grenville in northern Washington, but storms separated the ships when they put back to sea. Hezeta ventured only far enough north to see some of the mountains on Vancouver Island and then sailed for Monterey. Quadra, on the other hand, headed north, but did not sight land until the middle of August, when he reached Sitka Sound and saw nearby Mount Edgecumbe. His farthest point north seems to have been 58°, near Cross Sound. Here sickness amongst the crew and bad weather compelled him to turn homeward. He

saw the coast at several points, but once again no landing was made on the west coast of Canada.

The next visitor to arrive was Britain's most famous navigator, Captain James Cook. The British were still vitally interested in a passage from the Atlantic to the Pacific and Cook was instructed to search for it from the Pacific side of the continent. He left Plymouth with two ships, the *Discovery* and *Resolution*, on July 12, 1776. This was his third great voyage of discovery, and it is interesting to note that he had heard about the explorations of Perez and Quadra before he sailed. He was also aware of Hearne's visit to the Arctic—a point of major importance, since it showed that any passage through the Arctic must be north of the latitude of the mouth of the Coppermine River. Actually Hearne had made an error in his observations (a surprising mistake for a former naval officer) and had located the river-mouth nearly 200 miles further north than its true position but, as it happened, this did not affect Cook's movements.

Cook's survey of the coast has been criticized as cursory, but it was strictly in accordance with his secret instructions, which directed him to proceed as quickly as possible to latitude 65° and search for the passage beyond it; he was "not to lose any time in exploring rivers or inlets, or upon any other account" until he reached that point. There was added reason for haste because Cook had been delayed on the long voyage via the Cape of Good Hope and Australia, and he did not sight the Oregon coast until March 7, 1778. Bad weather obliged him to keep out to sea, but on March 22 he sighted and named Cape Flattery, and a week later he found in Nootka Sound a secure and well-

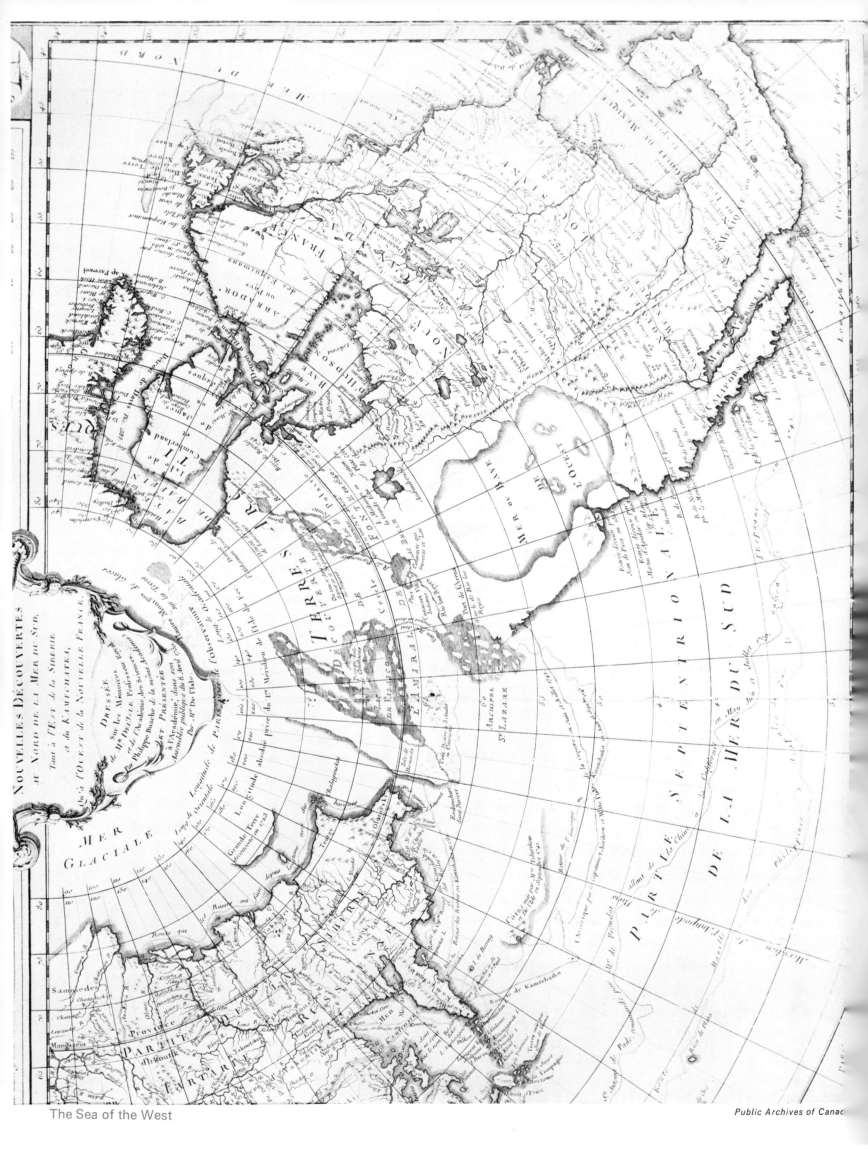

The Sea of the West

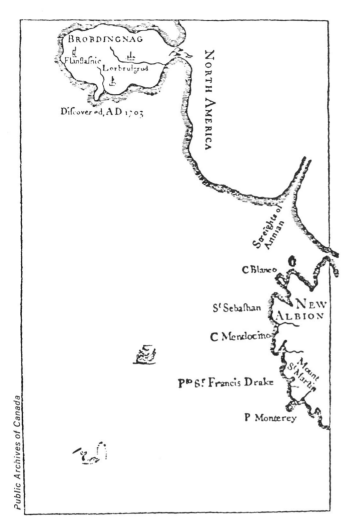

timbered anchorage, where the rotten masts and spars of his ship could be replaced. This was the first recorded landing of Europeans on Canada's west coast.

Four weeks later Cook sailed northward to carry out his survey, in the course of which he traced the coast of Alaska from Sitka to Bering Strait. When he sailed on past the straits, a solid barrier of ice blocked his progress at latitude 70°45' and he was compelled to turn about. Later he went south to winter in the Sandwich (Hawaiian) Islands, which he had discovered in January; and there he was murdered by natives in February 1779.

It has been said that Cook saw less of the coast of British Columbia than the Spaniards, but his account of the natives at Nootka Sound is incomparably the best and most complete description made by any expedition at this time. And Cook's voyage was to have momentous consequences, for his crews discovered, when they later reached China, that the furs they had traded somewhat casually at Nootka had an amazingly high market value, news of which led quickly to a period of great activity in trading and exploration all along the coast.

The land of Brobdingnag, as shown in the first edition of Gulliver's Travels, 1726.

Part III
EXPANSION AND CONSOLIDATION 1783-1867

The Great Seal of Canada, Queen Victoria

CHAPTER 7

Settlement

The Loyalist Migration to Canada

N 1782, as on many other occasions, the approach of peace produced problems, one of them being the future of the thousands of Loyalists who had taken refuge in British-held New York. Many of these people were as firm believers in complete self-government for the colonies as were the revolutionaries; they were merely reluctant to see the link with Britain broken and believed the goal could be achieved without formal independence. But the revolutionaries were singleminded and intolerant; one had to agree with them completely or take the consequences, and for many Loyalists (Tories, as the Americans called them) this had meant persecution, physical abuse, confiscation and in effect deportation. The British commissioners made every effort to gain concessions for them during the treaty negotiations, but the Congress had little or no control over the individual states with regard to such matters, and the promise to "earnestly recommend" fair treatment had little or no effect.

In 1782 the British Government sent Sir Guy Carleton to New York in the double capacity of military commander-in-chief and commissioner to liquidate the war. Looking about for a solution to the Loyalist problem, Carleton's attention soon centred on Nova Scotia—a British colony relatively near at hand, with vacant lands in which a new population could be settled. Even before the treaty of peace was signed, the first shiploads of Loyalists had sailed, and by the end of 1782 about 35,000 had landed in Nova Scotia. Inevitably difficulties arose, in part because many arrived before any official provision had been made for their care.

About 20,000 of these Loyalists came to Nova Scotia proper, where they were to be a major influence in life and politics for many years to come. The other 15,000 went to what was to become New Brunswick, many of them to the St. John River valley. Loyalist military units were an important element in this migration; soldiers and their dependants to the number of about 3,000 settled between Fredericton and Woodstock.

Most of these people had come from New York and New Jersey. Many of them had been town-dwellers, and not a few had been well-to-do. For them the transition to pioneering and frontier life was not easy. The picture was somewhat different in Canada. A trickle of Loyalist refugees had been arriving while the Revolutionary War was in progress; a small Loyalist settlement had grown up at Niagara by 1781. In all, about 7,000 Loyalists came to the St. Lawrence and Great Lakes valley, of whom 6,000 settled west of Montreal. The largest settlement on the lower river was in the vicinity of Sorel. Officially the Eastern Townships were closed to Loyalist settlers, but some acquired land there in spite of this. Once again the military units were an important element. The King's Royal Regiment of New York settled along the St. Lawrence between Lake St. Francis and Kingston; Butler's Rangers received lands in the Niagara region. At this same time provision also had to be made for the Mohawk Indians and the other Iroquois tribes who had been loyal to the British Crown; their old tribal lands in the United States had been confiscated, and they found a new home in the Grand River Valley. It has been said that "with rare exceptions, only Loyalists of humble origin" came to Ontario. Many of them were from upper New York State; most of them were farmers, well equipped to settle in a new land. In theory all Loyalists were to receive tools, implements, seeds and provisions to help them through the first difficult year or so; but in many instances these essentials were in short supply. In spite of this, most of the Loyalists in Canada succeeded in establishing themselves relatively quickly, although poor harvests in 1788 made 1789 a long-remembered "hungry year" for many.

It could hardly be expected that this population movement would be without political conse-

Cataraqui (Kingston) in August 1783

The Kingston area was largely deserted after the capture and destruction of Fort Frontenac in 1758, but was resettled by the Loyalists and later became the British naval base on Lake Ontario. The painting is by James Peachey.

Sir Frederick
Haldimand
*From the portrait by Sir
Joshua Reynolds.*

quences. In Nova Scotia, the officials in Halifax seemed remote and indifferent to the Loyalists in the St. John River valley and an agitation for a local government soon arose. This was granted in 1784 when the separate province of New Brunswick came into existence. The same year Cape Breton Island also became a separate colony, although no more than 400 Loyalists had settled there.

The Loyalists who came to the province of Quebec soon made it clear that they wanted three things—freehold land tenure (instead of the seigneurial tenures still prevalent in French Canada), English civil law and representative institutions. As most of them had settled west of Montreal, in four new districts, the idea of dividing the colony soon arose; since this would make it possible to grant these demands without disturbing the French population.

In 1786 Sir Guy Carleton, now Baron Dorchester, returned to Quebec as Governor. With him came his close associate, the new Chief Justice, William Smith. Smith was an ardent advocate of a federation of all the surviving British colonies, and he envisioned a new central authority with Dorchester as its head. But these views were not presented effectively in London, where the Constitutional Act was passed in June 1791. This divided Quebec into two provinces, each with an elected assembly, an appointed legislative council and an executive council. Dorchester, who had hoped to become Governor-General of British North America, found the office reduced to that of Governor-in-Chief. True, the heads of individual colonies became Lieutenant-Governors, but Dorchester was Chief only in the colony in which he was actually present —which in effect meant Lower Canada.

William Grenville, the Secretary of State responsible for the new Act, hoped that it would in great measure satisfy both the English and the French. What he overlooked was the fact that although only about 7,000 of the 145,000 people in Lower Canada were English, this minority included many of the most important and influential figures in the official, commercial and social life of Montreal and Quebec. They would not welcome an assembly in which the French had a large majority, and they were unhappy because, once again, no concessions had been made to their preferences in commercial law.

Surveys and Settlement

The sudden influx of Loyalists and disbanded troops posed many unprecedented problems for the colonial governments, especially in Nova Scotia and the old Province of Quebec. General Haldimand was Governor of Quebec when the first waves of settlers began to move into Ontario, and he struggled manfully to meet their needs, which were pressing and immediate.

Haldimand sent a Deputy Surveyor into each area where settlement was intended, whose duty it was to survey properties and then distribute them by lot to the persons who were to receive them. The acreage to which military claimants were entitled varied with their rank: a "common soldier" received 200 acres, a corporal 400, a captain 3,000, and field officers 5,000 acres. Loyalists received 200 acres, with supplementary grants for sons and daughters. As would be expected, the military claimants tended to settle in groups, so that certain regiments are closely associated with the early history of specific localities.

It was Haldimand who decided that the basis of land surveys in what became Upper Canada should be the township. Theoretically a township was supposed to be 10 miles square, but there were many exceptions. In some areas—along the Detroit River, for example, where settlements had grown up in the French period—existing properties had to be taken into account. Lots had to front on a river or lake in a sensible way, and the same was true of important roads, some of which had been built in advance of land surveys. After Upper Canada came into existence in 1791, Crown Reserves and Clergy Reserves were set aside in every township. As each was to total one-seventh of the land, this meant that over a quarter of the whole area was withheld from settlement. The properties making up the reserves were scattered throughout the township, and these vacant lands made such cooperative projects as road building very difficult. From the first the reserves were a source of constant annoyance, but many years passed before they disappeared entirely. The bulk of the Upper Canada Crown Reserves, totalling over 1,384,000 acres, were finally sold to the Canada Company in 1825. The much smaller reserves in Lower Canada—just over 250,000 acres—were acquired by the British American Land Company and sold off for settlement. Sale of the Upper Canada Clergy Reserves began in 1827, and by 1854 they had all been secularized. The same year the old system of seigneurial tenure, dating far back into the early days of New France, was abolished in Lower Canada.

Colonel Simcoe, the first Lieutenant-Governor of Upper Canada, took a keen interest in settlement and in particular realized the vital importance of roads. It was he who had Dundas Street (as the highway was called) surveyed from Burlington Bay to the Thames River, and who began to build Yonge Street north from Lake Ontario to Holland Landing.

Perhaps the most extraordinary story of Loyalist settlement relates to Shelburne, Nova Scotia. Many of the people who arrived there from New York were city folk, and somehow the hope and conviction grew up that Shelburne could be a new metropolis. The first town lots were located in May of 1783; by February 1784 no fewer than 1,130 houses and stores had been built, and by the autumn over 3,000 were completed. Population soared to about 12,000, and there was even talk of moving the capital from Halifax. But neither the town itself nor the surrounding country had the resources needed to support a community of this size, and as soon as the aid given to Loyalists by the government ran out, Shelburne began to decline rapidly. By 1818 there were only 300 people left in the town.

The story of pioneer settlement was much the same everywhere. A crude shanty provided a first shelter; as clearings and cropped areas increased in size, it would be succeeded by a log cabin and barns of logs; later still these would give way to frame buildings. Two of the most sought after amenities were a grist-mill and a saw-mill; a river or stream usually provided the power for these and they were frequently built together. Churches, schools and small towns would follow in due course. Roads were always a vital thing, especially for farms some distance from large rivers or lakes: they provided the transportation that took crops to market, brought back supplies, and broke the isolation of the backwoods sufficiently to make life there bearable.

By 1855, or thereabouts, although it was not realized at the time, most of the prime farmlands in Upper Canada had been taken up. Settlement was pressing on the southern edge of the Laurentian Shield all the way from the Ottawa River to Lake Huron. Those in authority thought that all they had to do was to extend colonization northward, and with this in view a number of roads were hopefully thrust up into the Shield country. But no large extension of agricultural settlement followed, because the area was not capable of supporting it. This explains why so many immigrants from Europe stayed only briefly in Upper Canada, and then travelled on to the great open expanses of the American prairies. And it explains, too, why Upper Canada, realizing that it was becoming desperately in need of a hinterland, began to take a greater interest in what was to become Western Canada.

John Graves Simcoe

First Lieutenant-Governor of Upper Canada — the Ontario of today. Simcoe established the capital at Newark (Niagara), later he intended to move it to London, but it went to York (Toronto) instead in 1796-98.

Immigration Before Confederation

By 1806 the population of Lower Canada was about 250,000 and that of Upper Canada about 71,000. As the latter figure suggests, the few thousand Loyalists who had come to Upper Canada after the American Revolution were quickly outnumbered by other immigrants. Many of these came from the United States, and it was their attitude that had worried Brock when war broke out in 1812.

After the war it was only natural that for a time the authorities would not welcome American immigrants. By the time this attitude had changed, the Trans-Mississippi West was offering greater attractions to Americans than Canada could provide.

For half a century immigrants came almost entirely from Europe, where the hard times and distress that followed the Napoleonic Wars set in motion the great mass exodus to the New World that was to continue on a mounting scale until 1914. The great majority of the people went to the United States, and Canada discovered very early that many of those who did come to her shores were birds of

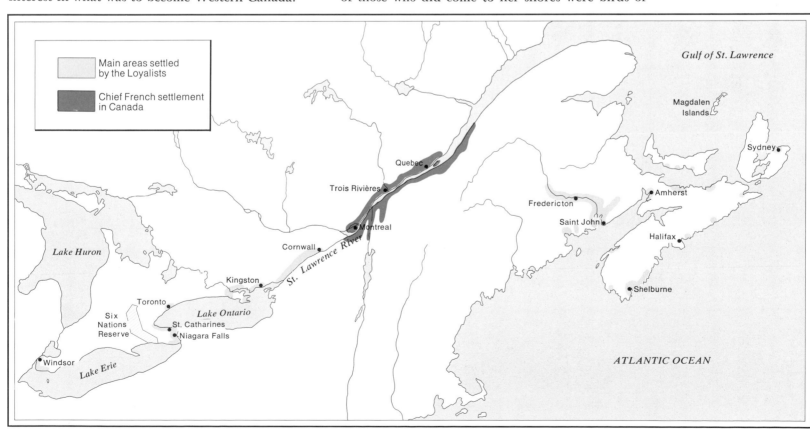

Main areas settled by the Loyalists

Chief French settlement in Canada

Gulf of St. Lawrence

Magdalen Islands

Sydney

Quebec

Trois Rivières

Fredericton

Amherst

Saint John

Montreal

Cornwall

Halifax

Lake Huron

St. Lawrence River

Kingston

Toronto

Lake Ontario

Six Nations Reserve

St. Catharines

Niagara Falls

Shelburne

Windsor

Lake Erie

ATLANTIC OCEAN

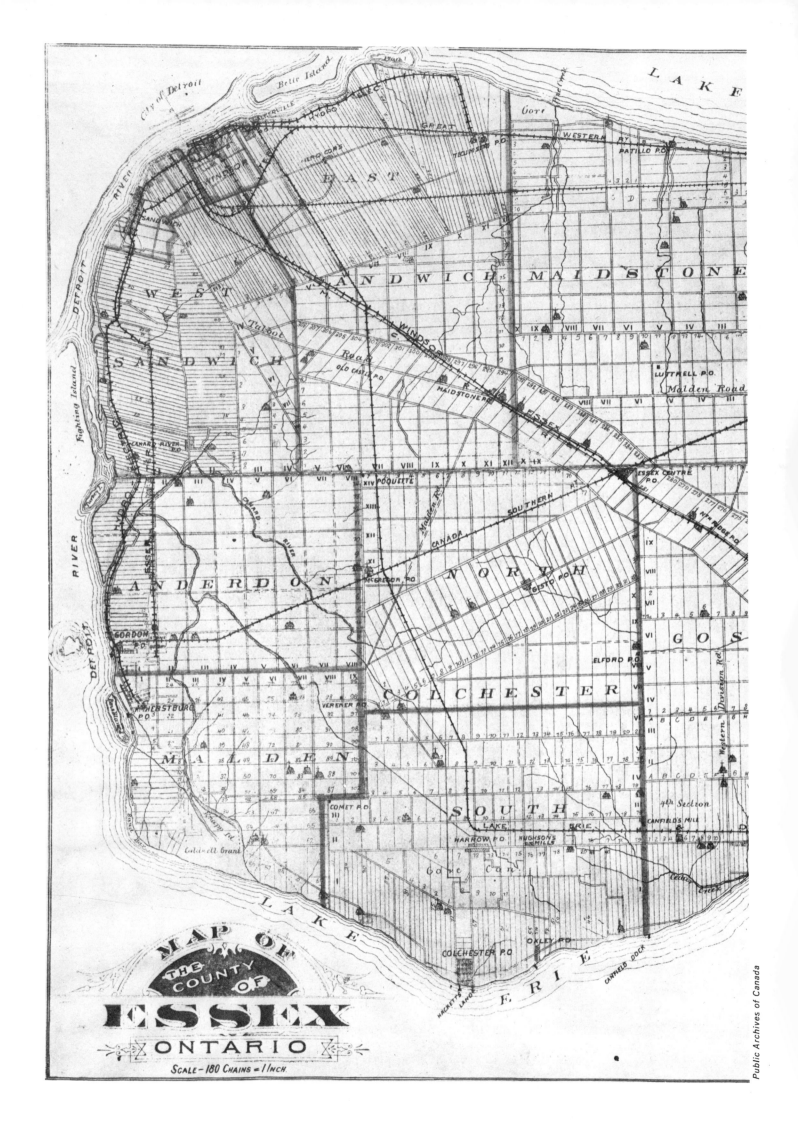

MAP OF
THE COUNTY OF
ESSEX
ONTARIO
SCALE—180 CHAINS = 1 INCH.

Western Half of Essex County

This map (at left) shows how the surveyors did their best to establish a regular pattern of properties, but had to vary it to take into account such things as earlier strip holdings dating back to the French period (in the northwest corner of the county), established roads, and sometimes rivers. The railways came later and simply cut across the plan in arbitrary fashion.

Loyalist encampment at Cornwall

Painted by James Peachey in June 1784. Cornwall was originally called New Johnstown, in honour of Sir John Johnson, but was renamed Cornwall in 1797.

Immigrants at Montreal, 1866

From the painting by William Raphael in the National Gallery of Canada. The scene is behind the Bonsecours Market.

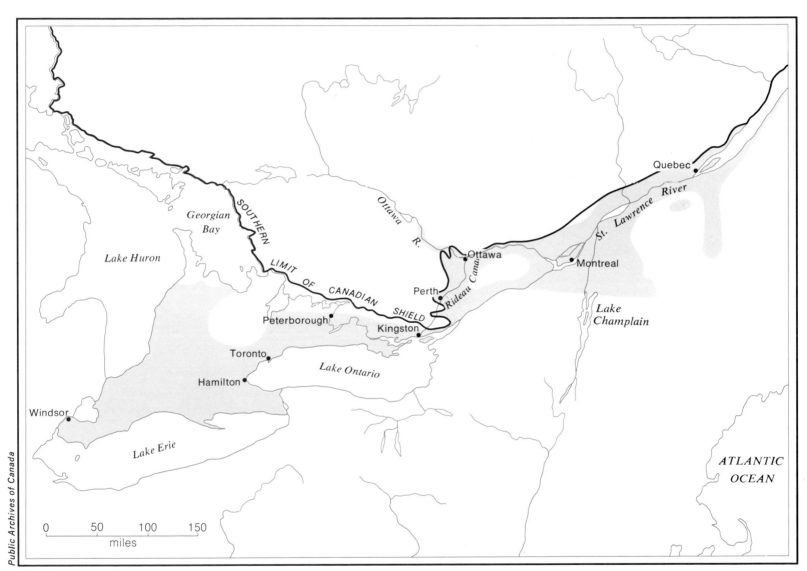

Georgian
Bay

Lake Huron

Ottawa R.

SOUTHERN

LIMIT OF CANADIAN SHIELD

Ottawa

Perth

Rideau Canal

St. Lawrence River

Quebec

Montreal

Lake
Champlain

Peterborough

Kingston

Toronto

Lake Ontario

Hamilton

Windsor

Lake Erie

ATLANTIC
OCEAN

0   50   100   150
miles

Pre-confederation Settlement Areas

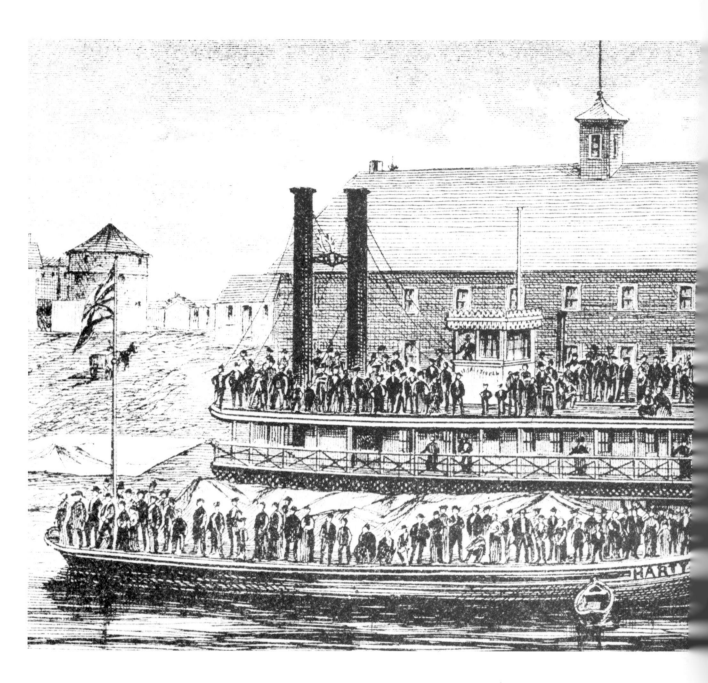

The arrival of the first Mennonites
The arrival at Fort Garry in 1874 of the first party of Mennonite settlers to reach the Canadian West. They had come down the Red River on the steamer International.

Public Archives of Canada

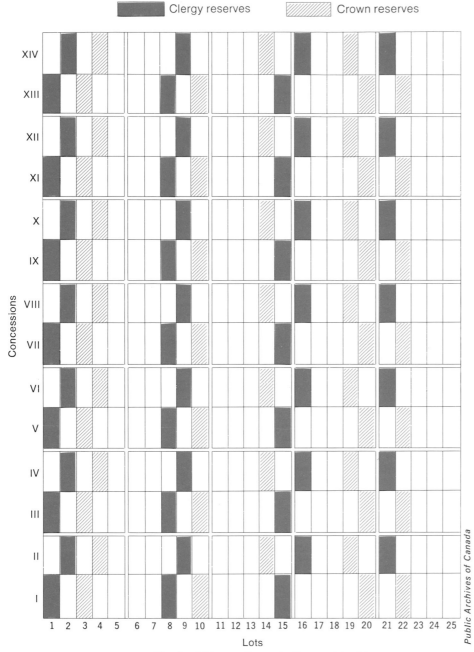

Clergy reserves   Crown reserves

Concessions: XIV, XIII, XII, XI, X, IX, VIII, VII, VI, V, IV, III, II, I

Lots: 1 2 3 4 5 6 7 8 9 10 11 12 13 14 15 16 17 18 19 20 21 22 23 24 25

Public Archives of Canada

Typical Upper Canada Township Plan

passage. Of the 120,000 immigrants who landed at Quebec in the years 1816-1828 no less than three-quarters are said to have moved on to the United States. This was probably the intended destination of most of them; ocean fares to Canada were very low, and they simply wished to take advantage of them.

Assisted immigration schemes supported by the British Government brought a number of groups to Upper Canada. In 1815 a party of 700 Scots founded Perth and settled in the country round about, where they were joined by 2,000 others in 1820. A few years later Peter Robinson headed a project that brought 2,000 Irish to the Peterborough area. Both settlements were successful, but the cost of assisted immigration was considered too high, and the Government withdrew its support.

Most of the assisted immigrants had been in dire economic straits. Those who came voluntarily included many English with some means who feared that conditions in Europe would become still worse, and who felt that it was wise to sell out and establish themselves elsewhere while they still had a little capital.

Two large settlement schemes in southern Ontario were noteworthy. In 1803 Colonel Thomas Talbot, an autocratic, eccentric, but immensely energetic character, received the 5,000-acre military land grant that was his due as a field officer. From this beginning, through the next 35 years, he built up an immense holding on the north shore of Lake Erie that extended all the way from Windsor to some distance east of St. Thomas, which was its administrative centre. Known as the Talbot Settlement, it had by 1837 a population that had grown to 30,000. North of the Settlement the Canada Company, whose founding was due to John Galt, the Scottish novelist, purchased over a million acres of Crown Reserves and added to them the million-acre Huron Tract, fronting on Lake Huron. Here population grew more slowly, but the cities of Goderich, Guelph and Stratford owe their origins to the Company. By 1834 it had sold 450,000 acres of its holdings. In 1833 a similar scheme was launched in Lower Canada, where the British American Land Company took up 800,000 acres in the Eastern Townships.

Upper Canada received many more immigrants than Lower Canada, partly because the old seigneurial tenures in the latter were not abolished until 1854. But there were problems in Upper Canada as well. The Government had tied up large areas in Crown and Clergy Reserves, and speculators had acquired huge tracts. When only 500,000 acres were actually under cultivation in the whole province, the reserves totalled 3,000,000 acres and speculators controlled some 5,000,000 acres. It took time to correct this state of affairs, but things had improved greatly before Confederation.

Only 12,000 immigrants came to Canada in 1828, but the flow increased sharply in the next few years. The total rose to 30,000 in 1830, and to 66,000 in 1832. The latter year saw the outbreak of a cholera epidemic that should have warned the authorities that much more would have to be done about sanitation, quarantine, hospitals and health generally. Conditions on board the immigrant ships were known to be very bad; most of them carried timber cargoes to Britain and on the return trip filled their holds with passengers accommodated in makeshift quarters of the most primitive and insanitary description.

The next and most tragic peak in immigration reflected the famine in Ireland, which caused widespread starvation and destitution in 1846-47. In 1846 immigrants landed at Quebec numbered 32,753, and in 1847 the total jumped to 84,445. Of the latter it is estimated that 70,000 were Irish. "Ship fever" (typhus) was common enough on immigrant ships at all times, but amongst the unfortunate Irish it became a raging epidemic. The Canadian quarantine station on Grosse Isle, a pleasant little island in the St. Lawrence, was totally inadequate to deal with it. Thousands of the sick could not even be landed; quarantined immigration ships lay anchored in the river in a line several miles long. It has been estimated that 17,000 persons had died at sea and that another 20,000 died in the St. Lawrence. The epidemic spread ashore, and although Quebec escaped relatively lightly, there were many deaths in Montreal.

From 1851 on, figures are available that make it possible to estimate the ebb and flow of immigration and emigration with some accuracy. In the decade 1851-61, immigrants numbered 209,000, and about 85,000 people left the country; the net population increase due to immigration was thus 124,000. In the following decade, however, immigrants totalled only 187,000 and emigrants numbered no less than 379,000. There was thus a net population loss of 192,000—and losses were to continue, decade by decade, until 1901. Canada's population grew during these years by natural increase not by immigration.

Yet increase it did. In 1841, at the time when Lower Canada and Upper Canada were being thrown together in the new United Province of Canada, the population of Lower Canada was 697,000 and that of Upper Canada 455,000. By the time of the 1851 census, Canada West (as Upper Canada had become) had added almost half a million people to its population, which had surpassed that of Canada East (Lower Canada)—952,000, as compared with 890,000. A decade later both had passed the million mark. In 1861 the population of Canada West was 1,396,000 and that of Canada East 1,111,000.

A map of settlement in the Canadas provides a striking illustration of the basic relationship between geography and colonization. The Pre-Cambrian Shield extends far south in the Quebec and

Public Archives of Canada

Colonal Thomas Talbot

From a portrait in the Lawson Memorial Library at the University of Western Ontario.

Ontario of today, leaving only a relatively narrow strip of fertile lands along the St. Lawrence River, the northern shore of Lake Ontario and Lake Erie, and the western shore of Lake Huron. For practical purposes the entire population of Canada West, and almost all that of Canada East, had settled within this restricted area, which to this day continues to be much the most heavily populated part of Canada.

CHAPTER 8

The Fur Trade

The Pacific Coast: The Maritime Fur Trade 1785-1820

IN addition to drawing world attention to the sea otter, when the skins collected by his crews fetched high prices in China, Captain Cook made two discoveries that were to figure largely in the maritime fur trade that resulted—Nootka Sound, on the west coast of Vancouver Island, and the Sandwich (Hawaiian) Islands. Most of the vessels bound for the coast called at both of them and many wintered in Hawaii, as Cook's own ships had done.

James Hanna brought the first trading vessel, appropriately named the *Sea Otter,* from China to Nootka in 1785. The following year there were at least eight ships on the coast. Three of them returned in 1787, and were joined by three new arrivals. All these ships were British, but they were already encountering difficulties that were soon to make it almost impossible for British ships to compete with traders of other nationalities. The natural market for furs secured on the Northwest Coast was China, but the East India Company held a monopoly of British trading rights there, and was willing to give other British traders access to the markets only on prohibitive terms. Some ships sought to avoid the monopoly by masquerading under other flags, but in general British ships found it very difficult to trade profitably.

The first of many American traders arrived at Nootka in 1788. Unlike the British, who could neither sell nor buy in China without the permission of the East India Company, the American ships, which came mostly from New England, were able to develop a highly profitable triangle trade between Boston, the Northwest Coast and China. They arrived on the coast well laden with liquor, arms and trinkets to trade for furs, sailed on to China, where they exchanged their furs for tea, silks and other Oriental luxuries, and then sailed home and sold these goods at high prices on the American market.

Spain still held firmly to the view that the entire coast belonged to her, at least as far north as Prince William Sound; and her chief fear was still Russian encroachment. In 1788 Don Estéban Martinez sailed from California with instructions to go as far as latitude 61° and to learn all he could about Russian intentions. The most alarming report he brought back was a rumour that they intended to build a post at Nootka Sound, and the Spanish decided forthwith to forestall this move by occupying the Sound themselves. This Martinez did in 1789, and a small fort and settlement were built that were to survive until 1795.

Unfortunately for Spain, Martinez seized at Nootka three British ships belonging to Capt. John Meares and his associates on the grounds that they were trespassing and poaching in Spanish waters. Meares, somewhat of a rascal but an engaging character, succeeded in raising such a furor in official circles in England that Spain and Great Britain were on the brink of war within a year. In the end Spain gave way and agreed to restore Meares' confiscated property and compensate him for his losses. Much more important, she agreed to drop her claims to the Northwest Coast, and to accept the British view that sovereignty had to be based upon occupation and settlement, and not on mere acts of possession or discovery. Both powers were to abandon Nootka, and trade on the coast was to be open to all.

Following the settlement with Spain, Britain sent out the famous expedition under Captain George Vancouver to make a detailed survey of the coast. In three seasons of meticulous work in 1792, 1793 and 1794, Vancouver compiled detailed charts that were a landmark in hydrographic surveying. Incidentally, as there remained a slight possibility that Alaska was a vast island, and that a passage to the Arctic might exist south of it, Vancouver was specially charged with the mission of ascertaining once and for all whether any such opening existed.

The Spanish village at Nootka Sound
The first European settlement in British Columbia, it was founded by Martinez in 1789, and abandoned in 1795.

Public Archives of Canada

The chronometer used by Cook and Vancouver

National Portrait Gallery

Captain George Vancouver

From the portrait attributed to L. F. Abbott in the National Portrait Gallery, London.

In October 1794 he was able to report that he had "truly determined the nonexistence of any water communication between this and the opposite side of America within the limits of an investigation beyond all doubt or disputation . . . ."

Up to this time British trading vessels had managed to participate in the maritime fur trade, but the outbreak of war with France in 1793, which was to continue with little interruption until 1815, proved to be a crushing handicap when added to the East India Company's monopoly. Of the 59 vessels known to have been on the coast in the decade 1795-1804 only 9 were British, and of 43 that traded in the succeeding 10 years only 3 were British; all the others were American. This state of affairs was to continue until ruthless killing and trading had virtually exterminated the sea otter, a point reached about 1825.

The ambitious moves made by the Russians during these years are frequently overlooked. In 1791 the Russian American Company began to take shape as an effective trading concern, and the same year it acquired an able chief in Aleksandre Baranof. Pushing southward, the company founded Sitka in 1799, and although it was captured and destroyed by the natives in 1802 it was rebuilt in 1805. Food supplies were always a serious problem for the posts in Alaska, and the Russian moves southward were motivated by a need for sources of supplies as well as territorial ambitions. At one time posts at Nootka Sound, at the mouth of the Columbia River, in California and in Hawaii were all planned, and two of them actually came into existence. In 1812 the Russians built Fort Ross, on

Bodega Bay, only 60 miles north of San Francisco, and it remained in their possession until 1840. From this vantage point traders poached for sea otter in Spanish waters, including San Francisco Bay. In 1814 a Russian vessel was wrecked and looted on the island of Kauai, in Hawaii, and the Russians seized the opportunity to extract concessions on Oahu which enabled them to build a block house and raise the Russian flag in Honolulu in 1816; but this post was short lived.

John Jacob Astor's Pacific Fur Company founded Astoria, at the mouth of the Columbia River, in 1811, but the outbreak of war between Britain and the United States in 1812 resulted in its sale to the North West Company in 1813. As this indicates, advances overland were at last beginning to influence events on the coast, and it was these advances that ultimately determined the future of the Northwest Coast.

The question of ownership, shelved by the Nootka Convention of 1790, soon reappeared. At one time Russia thought of claiming the entire coast southward to California, but this was revised in 1821, to a more modest claim to the coast as far as latitude 51°, or roughly to the northern tip of Vancouver Island. After much negotiation between Russia, Britain and the United States, a measure of recognition was given to a southern limit at 54°40′, in Dixon Entrance, the present boundary between Alaska and British Columbia. The future of the coast south of this point, to the Spanish possessions in California, still remained to be settled.

The Overland FurTrade

The "pedlars" from Montreal who were fanning out into the Canadian West quickly discovered that rivalry was both costly, because it raised prices, and dangerous, because some traders would go to almost any lengths to secure furs. In 1779 nine partnerships agreed to pool their operations for one year; other agreements followed, and by the winter of 1783-84 the famous North West Company had come into existence.

Its structure was unique, for it was a combination of a group of "wintering partners," who had charge of trading posts and operations in the interior, and agents and merchants in Montreal who purchased supplies and marketed the furs. Simon McTavish was the most influential agent in the first decades, and after his death in 1804 his nephew, William McGillivray, was almost as commanding a figure.

Like McTavish, most of the partners and clerks were Scottish, but the *engagés*—the men who did the heavy physical work involved in the trade— were almost all French-Canadians. Their strength and endurance were phenomenal, but so were the demands made upon them. Men and goods had to be transported by canoe over an endless succession of rivers and lakes; both canoes and cargoes had to be carried around the numerous rapids on the rivers. With this in mind, trade goods, provisions and furs were all put up in 90-pound packs. Most of the French voyageurs would carry two packs at a time; some even carried three. When travelling, the fur brigades lived on game and fish when they could, but both on the move and at their posts the basic food and emergency ration of the traders was pemmican—a compact, highly nutritious mixture of pounded meat and fat that would keep indefinitely.

The Nor'Westers were aggressive and enterprising, and their search for new sources of furs, and better transportation routes, resulted in the exploration of huge areas in the Northwest. In 1789 Alexander Mackenzie descended the Mackenzie River to the Arctic; in 1793 he ascended the Peace River, went up the Parsnip, discovered the Fraser River, descended it as far as Alexandria, and then made his way overland to the Bella Coola River and an arm of the Pacific. In 1805 Simon Fraser founded the first post west of the Rocky Mountains, on McLeod Lake; three years later he followed the Fraser from Fort George to its mouth. Meanwhile David Thompson, who served the company chiefly as a geographer, had surveyed innumerable lakes and rivers on the prairies, and between 1807 and 1811 he traced the entire course of the Columbia River from its source to its mouth. Thompson's famous map of Western Canada, the first representation of this vast region that could make any pretense to accuracy, was completed in 1814 and hung in the great hall of the North West Company's inland depot at Fort William.

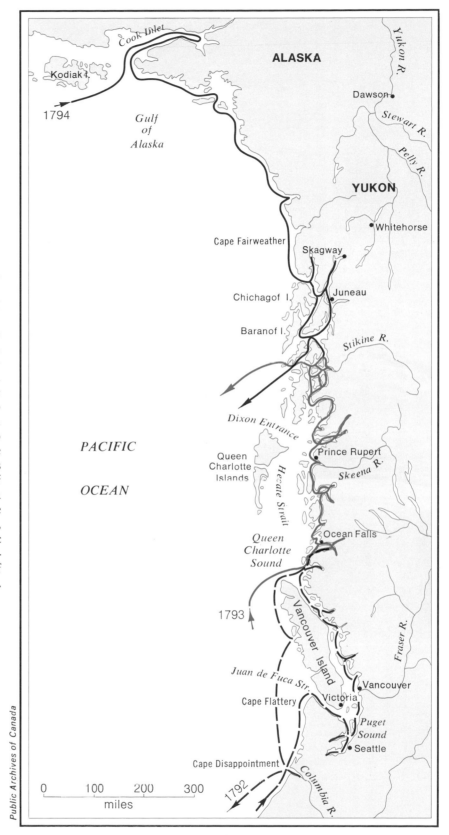

Public Archives of Canada

Vancouver's Survey of the West Coast

The Hudson's Bay Company, already over a century old, responded slowly but determinedly to the challenge of the pedlars. In the 25 years following the founding of Cumberland House in 1774 it built an extensive network of inland posts. It had

Public Archives of Canada

Public Archives of Canada

David Thompson (at left)

No authentic portrait of Thompson is known to exist, but his daughter stated that this picture of John Bunyan was so like her father that it could be accepted as a likeness of him.

Fort William in 1811 or 1812

This was the great inland depot of the North West Company.

certain advantages: it could bring goods cheaply by sea to Hudson Bay, in the heart of the continent; its lines of communication with its posts were shorter. But it was unable to establish itself in Athabasca, the richest fur country found by the Nor'Westers, and it did not cross the Rocky Mountains. The North West Company rapidly outstripped it in size; at one time the Nor'Westers gathered 11/13 of the total annual fur harvest, while Hudson's Bay Company's trade amounted to only 2/13 of the total. Nevertheless it had a corporate structure and financial reserves that made it a formidable opponent when competition and friction between the two companies became acute.

A clash became inevitable in 1811 when the Earl of Selkirk, who was interested in resettling Scottish Highlanders, secured sufficient control of the Hudson's Bay Company to cause it to make him an immense land grant in southern Manitoba and northern Minnesota. Admittedly, the area was within Rupert's Land, but the North West Company had never paid much practical attention to the famous charter of 1670, and Selkirk's grant not only lay right across the company's travel routes, but threatened one of the chief sources of its pemmican supplies as well. Violence resulted ultimately, notably in 1816, when the Governor of Selkirk's colony and a score of others lost their lives.

As in the beginning, competition again was proving to be both costly and dangerous. In its great days the North West Company had benefited greatly from the fact that its leading traders were not salaried employees; they were partners who shared in the burgeoning profits. But when the crisis came the fact became evident that those profits had all been distributed; there were no reserves to tide the company over. The Nor'Westers had to swallow their pride and negotiate with the Hudson's Bay

Company, and the so-called coalition that resulted in 1821 was in reality virtually a take-over by the older company.

The union would have pleased Sir Alexander Mackenzie, the first white man to cross the full width of North America. Ever since his journey to the Pacific in 1793, Mackenzie had contended that the fur trade should be in the hands of a single company that could receive supplies and ship its furs from either Hudson Bay or the mouth of the Columbia River, whichever happened to be more appropriate. He advocated, in fact, the coalition of the Hudson's Bay and North West companies that hard facts and violent competition finally brought about. Even the proposed Columbia River depot became a reality, for in 1813 the North West Company had purchased Astoria, at the mouth of the Columbia, from John Jacob Astor's Pacific Fur Company. Opposition to the scheme had come chiefly from those who had business interests in Montreal, as it was obvious that most of the commerce of a combined concern would be conducted through Hudson Bay. And so it proved in practice: the union of 1821 brought to a close the first great era of the fur trade, when it had been based in great measure on Montreal.

The Fur Trade 1821-1860

The union with the North West Company in 1821 created a greatly enlarged Hudson's Bay Company that enjoyed virtually complete command of the fur trade between Hudson Bay, the Great Lakes and the Rockies. To this was soon added a monopoly of British trading rights in the disputed territories west of the mountains, in New Caledonia (as the central interior of British Columbia was then called) and the Oregon Country.

Public Archives of Canada

Public Archives of Canada

National Gallery, Ottawa

The Red River Settlement

This sketch is believed to have been made by Lord Selkirk.

Simon McTavish (above right)

Sir Alexander Mackenzie (bottom right)

From the remarkable portrait by Sir Thomas Lawrence in the National Gallery of Canada.

The great figure of the period was George Simpson, who had been sent out from London by the Hudson's Bay Company as no more than a stop-gap appointee in 1820, but who demonstrated his unique fitness to direct the fur trade so quickly that he became Governor of the far-flung Northern Department, the Company's most important trading area, in 1821. Later he became Governor-in-Chief, responsible for all its operations in North America.

Simpson was energetic, tireless and a shrewd judge of men. He was dictatorial and a hard driver. Completely devoted to the cause of the Company's prosperity, he had a sharp eye for things that might increase or decrease profits. "It has been said," he wrote in a typical comment, "that Farming is no branch of the Fur Trade but I consider that every pursuit tending to leighten the Expence of the Trade is a branch thereof." The Governor and Committee in London at first supervised his activities fairly closely, but they ended by giving him virtually a free hand. It was in no small degree due to his efforts that for the last 35 years of his service the annual dividend of the company was never less than 10 percent and on some occasions was as high as 25 percent.

Simpson played a large part in the reorganization of the Company that followed the union of 1821. To a great extent Montreal's fears were fulfilled: supplies and furs were handled mostly through Hudson Bay or the depot on the Columbia River; but the Company had warehouses at Lachine and Simpson had an official residence there. Business meetings and council sessions were held at several of the Company's inland establishments, notably York Factory, Norway House and Fort Garry. All became imposing structures, resembling miniature palisaded or walled towns.

The new Hudson's Bay Company took over one important feature of the North West Company: its Chief Factors and Chief Traders, who corresponded to the Wintering Partners in the other concern, shared in the profits instead of receiving salaries. Simpson knew them all personally, for in a series of inspection trips he visited virtually every part of his vast trading territories and investigated problems and conditions on the spot. Duplicate and marginal posts were closed; new ones were built where trade promised to be profitable.

Simpson was a conservationist of sorts; reputedly he managed the country between the Great Lakes and the Rockies as if it were a vast fur farm, in which areas that were in danger of being trapped out were rested for a time, so that they could resume fur production later. But he could be ruthless when occasion offered. He shared British hopes that the Columbia River would become the international boundary in the Oregon Country, which meant that the area south of the river would become part of the United States. His first move there was to build a new district headquarters—Fort Vancouver—on the north bank of the Columbia; his second was to order intensive trapping in the lands to the south. He had two objects in view; to denude the area of furs while it was still open to the British, and to create a fur desert that would check the advance of rival American traders. Simpson also developed the trade along the Northwest Coast, and in 1839 entered into an agreement with the Russians that finally solved their supply problem. In return for a lease of trapping rights in what is now known as the Alaska Panhandle, the Hudson's Bay Company undertook to provide grain and other commodities that the Russians were most anxious to secure. This lease was renewed periodically and continued in force until the sale of Alaska to the United States in 1867.

The Hudson's Bay Company expanded in the east as well as the west. The King's Posts, a chain of trading posts on the lower St. Lawrence stretching

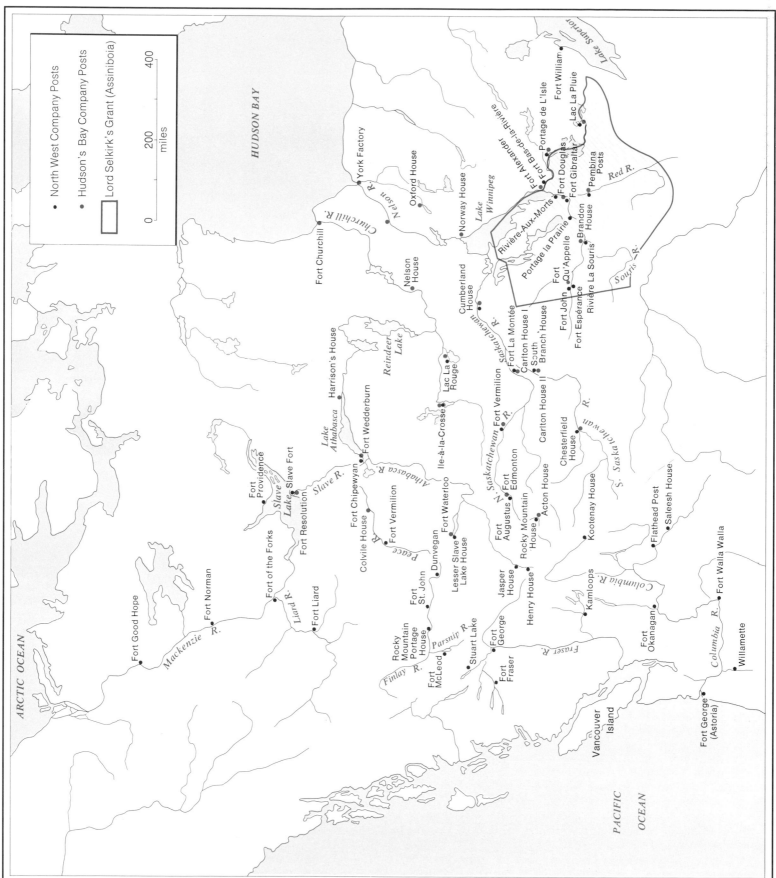

Fur Trade Rivalry in the West

Legend:
- North West Company Posts
- Hudson's Bay Company Posts
- Lord Selkirk's Grant (Assiniboia)

0 — 200 — 400 miles

ARCTIC OCEAN

HUDSON BAY

PACIFIC OCEAN

Lake Superior

Fort William
Portage de L'Isle
Lac La Pluie
Fort Bas-de-la-Rivière
Fort Alexander
Fort Douglas
Fort Gibraltar
Pembina Posts
Red R.
Lake Winnipeg
Rivière-Aux-Morts
Norway House
Portage la Prairie
Brandon House
Fort Qu'Appelle
Fort La Montée
Fort John
Fort Espérance
Rivière La Souris
Souris R.
Carlton House I
South Branch House
Carlton House II
Cumberland House
York Factory
Nelson R.
Oxford House
Churchill R.
Fort Churchill
Nelson House
Saskatchewan R.
Fort Vermilion
N. Saskatchewan R.
Fort Edmonton
Acton House
Chesterfield House
S. Saskatchewan R.
Kootenay House
Flathead Post
Saleesh House
Fort Walla Walla
Rocky Mountain House
Fort Augustus
Jasper House
Henry House
Kamloops
Columbia R.
Fort Okanagan
Willamette
Fort George (Astoria)
Fort George
Fort Fraser
Stuart Lake
Fort McLeod
Rocky Mountain Portage House
Finlay R.
Parsnip R.
Fraser R.
Vancouver Island
Reindeer Lake
Harrison's House
Lac La Rouge
Ile-à-la-Crosse
Lake Athabasca
Fort Wedderburn
Fort Chipewyan
Colvile House
Peace R.
Fort Vermilion
Fort Waterloo
Dunvegan
Fort St. John
Lesser Slave Lake House
Slave R.
Fort Resolution
Slave Lake
Slave Fort
Fort Providence
Fort of the Forks
Slave R.
Liard R.
Fort Liard
Fort Norman
Fort Good Hope
Mackenzie R.
Athabasca R.

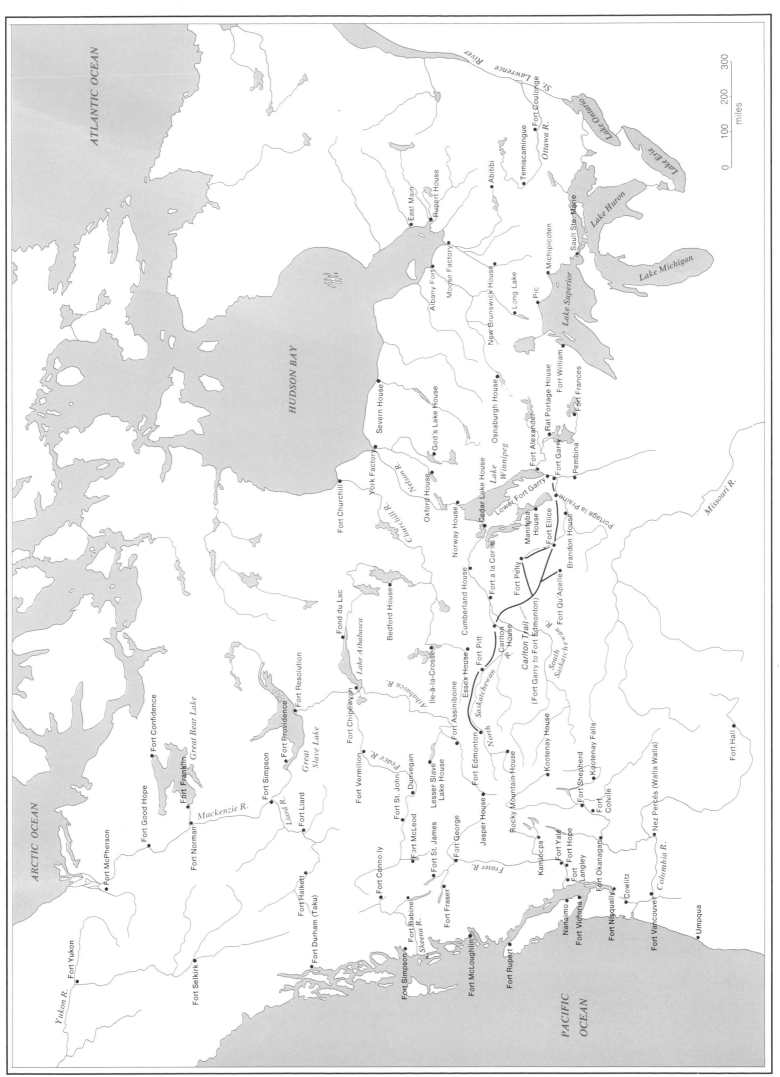

Trading Posts of the Hudson's Bay Company

Sir George Simpson

This mezzotint was made from the fine portrait by Stephen Pearce that hangs in the Company's London office.

from Tadoussac to Belle Isle, was leased by the Company in 1831, and in 1836 its own chain of forts was extended to Labrador. The operations of the Company had thus become truly continental in scope, extending to the Atlantic, the Arctic and the Pacific.

But there were signs of change in the air in Simpson's later years. The Red River Settlement, founded by Lord Selkirk, grew into a considerable colony—the first settlement of any size in the Canadian West. Fur traders were traditionally distrustful of settlers, and Red River was no exception. The Hudson's Bay Company bought Selkirk's proprietary rights from his heirs in 1834, but in spite of the authority this gave the Company, it was compelled to grant the settlers freedom to trade in furs in 1849. By that time trade and travel were developing between Red River and St. Paul, across the border to the south, and American interest in the vast stretches of unoccupied land in the Hudson's Bay territories was increasing. In the last years of Simpson's governorship the gold rush to the Fraser River, which began in 1858, completely transformed conditions west of the Rockies.

Clearly, the great era of the fur trade was ending. Simpson was too old to deal with drastic change, and his long career was drawing to a close. Because of his dictatorial ways and the style in which he travelled, especially after he was knighted in 1841, he had been dubbed the "Little Emperor." He died in 1860, aged 73, only a few days after he had entertained the Prince of Wales, the future Edward VII, at his summer home on Dorval Island.

Hudson's Bay Company

York Factory in 1853

Some of the establishments of the Hudson's Bay Company, such as this one, were extensive and imposing. They included the well-known stone fort at Lower Fort Garry, the Upper Fort on the site of Winnipeg, and Norway House.

CHAPTER 9

Threats Without and Within

The War of 1812

THE War of 1812 was a by-product of Britain's struggle with Napoleon; it broke out largely because the Americans resented the high-handed way in which the British searched neutral ships to make sure that they were not carrying supplies to the French. In addition, there was some feeling that the United States should seize the opportunity to take over Canada while Britain was heavily committed elsewhere.

On the face of it, this appeared easy to do. The population of the United States had risen to over 7,000,000; that of Canada was only a few hundred thousand. There were no more than 7,000 regular troops in Upper and Lower Canada, and the militia was for the most part virtually untrained. But there were some compensating factors. The United States did not go into the war a united nation; New England in particular was not enthusiastic and took little part in the hostilities. The American army was surprisingly small, with perhaps no more than 13,000 men in the regular forces. To begin with, the British had naval superiority on the Great Lakes —a matter of vital importance, since roads were so inadequate that soldiers and supplies had to be moved largely by water. Finally, in Upper Canada the forces were commanded by an officer of unusual courage and ability, Major-General Isaac Brock. He has been called the saviour of Canada and he well deserves the epithet.

Brock had been in Upper Canada since 1810. He felt sure that war would come, and set about bolstering defences as best he could. It was obvious that the commander-in-chief, General Sir George Prevost, would have to keep most of the regular troops in Lower Canada to defend Quebec, which was once again the vital stronghold through which

Canada could be reinforced. Nevertheless Brock felt that some effective action might be possible in Upper Canada. He felt, too, that it was highly important to gain the support of the Indians, and the best way of doing this would be to win a swift victory of some sort that would impress them. With this in mind, Brock's first action when war broke out in June 1812 was to inform Captain Charles Roberts, in command at St. Joseph Island, that he could attack Michilimackinac. Roberts set off promptly and the small American garrison, which had not heard of the war, surrendered on July 17. Though it was a victory over no more than 59 men, the fall of Michilimackinac impressed the Indians and attracted their support precisely as Brock hoped it would.

It had seemed almost certain that the first heavy American attack would come by way of Lake Champlain and the Richelieu River; its objective would be to capture Montreal, sever the St. Lawrence line of communications, and isolate Upper Canada. Instead, the Americans chose to attack in the Detroit and Niagara areas. As a first step, a force under Major-General William Hull had crossed the Detroit River on July 11 and settled down on Canadian soil. But Hull was old, inefficient and apprehensive; captured dispatches made Brock aware that the morale of the American troops and their commander was at a low ebb. Hull withdrew from Canada on August 11, and Brock boldly took the offensive. Five days later, when the British were about to attack Detroit, Hull surrendered.

Michilimackinac had won the support of the Indians; Detroit convinced the doubters in Upper Canada—and they were numerous—that effective defence was possible. That feeling was reinforced on October 13 at Queenston Heights, in the famous battle that cost Brock his life but turned back the American attempt at invasion at Niagara.

The fortunes of war were more varied in 1813. In April an American fleet carrying 1,700 men appeared off York (the future Toronto), the capital of Upper Canada, drove out the defenders and burned much of the town. Late in May an Ameri-

The Battle of Queenston Heights

From an interesting but highly inaccurate aquatint published in London and wrongly dated 1813, instead of 1812.

Prescott after the battle at the windmill

This sketch was made by Capt. H. F. Ainslie in 1839. The rebels crossed from Ogdensburg in November 1838, led by Nils Von Schoultz, a Pole. After they surrendered, Von Schoultz was tried at a court martial at Kingston and was sentenced to be hanged in spite of a valiant defence by his counsel, a young lawyer named John A. Macdonald.

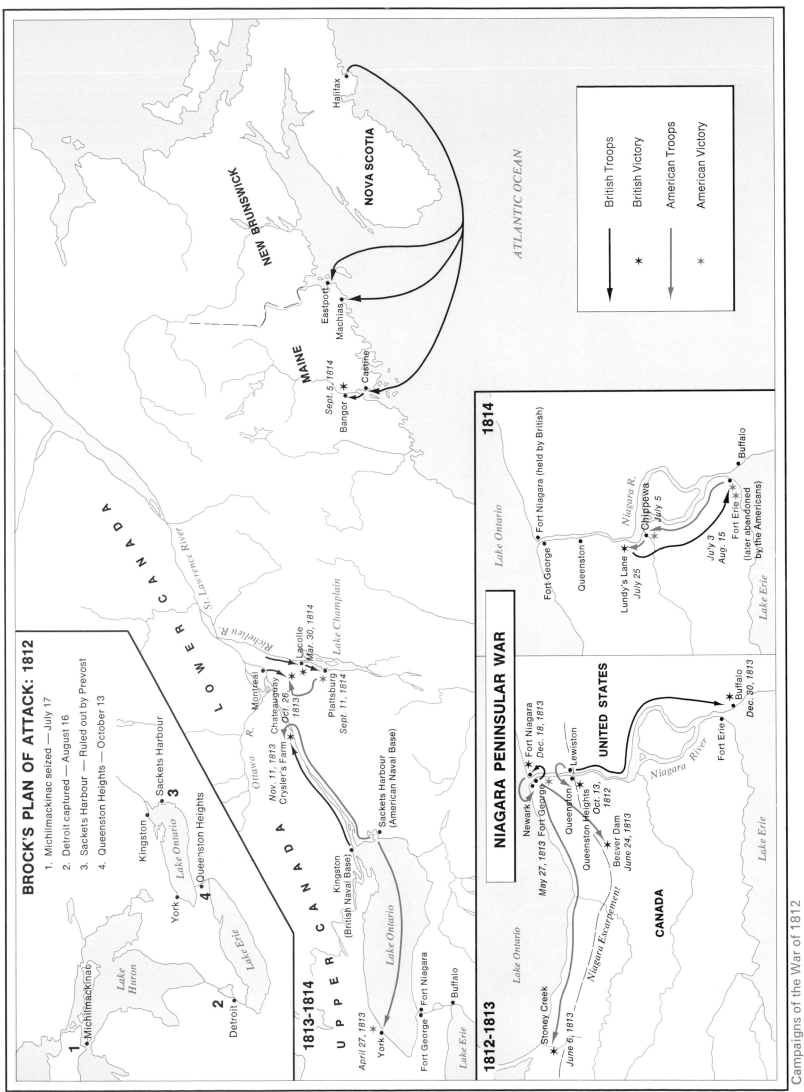

BROCK'S PLAN OF ATTACK: 1812

1. Michilimackinac seized — July 17
2. Detroit captured — August 16
3. Sackets Harbour — Ruled out by Prevost
4. Queenston Heights — October 13

1813-1814

UPPER CANADA

Michilimackinac

Lake Huron

Lake Erie

Detroit

York

April 27, 1813

Kingston

Sackets Harbour

4 Queenston Heights

Lake Ontario

Fort George

Fort Niagara

Buffalo

Lake Ontario

Sackets Harbour
(American Naval Base)

Kingston
(British Naval Base)

Ottawa R.

Montreal

St. Lawrence River

LOWER CANADA

Richelieu R.

Lacolle
Mar. 30, 1814

Crysler's Farm
Nov. 11, 1813

Chateauguay
Oct. 26, 1813

Plattsburg
Sept. 11, 1814

Lake Champlain

NEW BRUNSWICK

NOVA SCOTIA

Halifax

ATLANTIC OCEAN

Eastport

Machias

Castine

MAINE

Bangor

Sept. 5, 1814

Legend

→	British Troops
★	British Victory
→	American Troops
✦	American Victory

NIAGARA PENINSULAR WAR

1812-1813

Lake Ontario

CANADA

UNITED STATES

Stoney Creek
June 6, 1813

Niagara Escarpment

Newark
May 27, 1813

Fort Niagara
Dec. 18, 1813

Fort George

Lewiston

Queenston

Queenston Heights
Oct. 13, 1812

Beaver Dam
June 24, 1813

Niagara River

Fort Erie

Buffalo
Dec. 30, 1813

Lake Erie

1814

Lake Ontario

Fort Niagara (held by British)

Fort George

Queenston

Niagara R.

Lundy's Lane
July 25

Chippewa
July 5

Buffalo

Fort Erie
(later abandoned
by the Americans)

July 3
Aug. 15

Lake Erie

Campaigns of the War of 1812

Sir Isaac Brock

Brock was never aware that he had been knighted. The title was conferred upon him in London on October 10, 1812, just three days before his death at Queenston Heights.

can land force captured Fort George, at the mouth of the Niagara River, but in June, when it had advanced to the west it was halted in a night battle at Stoney Creek. In September the pendulum swung back when Commodore Perry won the famous naval engagement at Put-in-Bay that gave the Americans naval command of Lake Erie.

In the autumn the Americans launched the long-expected attack on Montreal. Two armies took part, one of which came down the St. Lawrence River from Lake Ontario while the other followed the familiar route down the Richelieu. Neither attained its objective. Late in October General Hampton, advancing from Lake Champlain, encountered a small defence force at Chateauguay, 15 miles from Montreal. It consisted mostly of French-Canadians and was commanded by Colonel Charles de Salaberry, who handled his troops skilfully and gave Hampton an exaggerated idea of their numbers. After a brief encounter, Hampton decided to withdraw. The St. Lawrence invasion army was turned back less than three weeks later, following a battle at Chrysler's Farm, near Cornwall.

A further British success came later in the year in the Niagara region. The Americans evacuated Fort George and on December 18 the British surprised and captured Fort Niagara, the American fort across the Niagara River. But in the summer of 1814 the Americans returned in force, determined to clear the British out of the peninsula and then advance eastward to York and Kingston. Their troops were now both better trained and better led, but the British had found in Lieut-Gen. Sir Gordon Drummond a commander who had many of the qualities of Brock. A hard-fought battle took place

Kingston naval dockyard in 1813

From a painting by F. Hall. The two large ships under construction were the Canada *and the* Wolfe, *which were never completed. They would have been larger than Nelson's* Victory.

at Lundy's Lane on July 28, and although neither side could claim a victory, the Americans retreated.

The security of Upper Canada was increased by the growth of British naval strength on Lake Ontario. A new flagship of surprising size was added to the British fleet—the three-decker *St. Lawrence*, which was larger and more heavily armed than Nelson's *Victory*. The Americans were soon building an even larger ship at Sackett's Harbour, but two sisters of the *St. Lawrence* under construction at Kingston would have more than redressed the balance.

A defeat at Plattsburg marred the year 1814 for the British. It should have been otherwise; 16,000 veterans of Wellington's peninsular war had arrived at Quebec in July and August and General Prevost had 11,000 of them with him when he set out to attack American posts and naval forces on Lake Champlain. But Prevost was neither an aggressive man nor an inspiring leader. When the British squadron on the lake was out-manoeuvred and defeated by the Americans, he abandoned the land operations as well and withdrew to Montreal.

Canadians tend to forget events of importance to them that took place outside the Montreal-Detroit area. On the Northwest Coast the war made it possible for the North West Company to acquire Astoria, and thereby extend its operations to the Pacific. The early capture of Michilimackinac was followed by the occupation of other posts over a large area to the south and west. An American force burned the warehouses of the North West Company at Sault Ste. Marie in July 1814, but its attempt to recapture Michilimackinac failed, and the same month the British captured the American fort at Prairie du Chien, on the Mississippi River. In August a British force landed in Maryland, advanced on Washington, and burned many buildings there, including the White House, in retaliation, it is said, for the burning of York. Finally, in Septem-

ber, Sir John Sherbrooke advanced across the disputed New Brunswick border and occupied much of Maine.

The Canadians might well feel that they were in a strong bargaining position when the commissioners met to negotiate peace terms, but the treaty between Britain and the United States signed at Ghent in December 1814 provided that all conquests by both sides were to be returned and the boundaries of 1812 restored.

The Rebellions of 1837

The plural form—Rebellions—is used deliberately, for although the uprisings in Upper and Lower Canada had features in common, in many respects they were quite different and distinct.

The causes of tension in Lower Canada were complex; they were economic, political, racial, and to some extent social. The French felt that the English dominated the province's economic life, and this was resented, especially at a time when the economy as a whole was not prosperous. The fur trade had declined sharply after the union of the Hudson's Bay and North West companies; the old pattern of agricultural production had been upset. The timber trade was flourishing, but it compensated only in part for declines in other activities.

The French had a large majority in the Assembly, but they felt that the Legislative and Executive Councils favoured the English and their commercial interests. The *habitants* were unhappy about the influx of English immigrants, fearing that the newcomers would take up lands they wanted for themselves. The Assembly included a large number of young professional men, especially lawyers, who had their way to make and were not averse to supporting a popular and radical cause. These factors together had given rise to strong French nationalist feelings that were represented by what became known as the Canadian Party—the *Patriotes*.

In 1815 Louis Joseph Papineau became its leader. Responsible government had been the party's chief aim, but through the years Papineau placed increasing emphasis on securing control of the government's funds, which he insisted must be voted by the Assembly. After 1830 he had also moved in the direction of republicanism on the American model, for he became convinced that the British Government was siding with the Councils in order to keep the French in a subordinate position.

The British Government had in fact been relatively neutral, but in spite of its own Reform Bill it still did not favour responsible government in the colonies. Resolutions introduced by Lord John Russell, the Colonial Secretary, in March 1837 made this clear, and they also empowered the Government of Lower Canada to make use of its funds, whether or not the Assembly approved.

Tempers rose, and they were not improved by severe repercussions in Canada from a financial crisis in the United States. Mass meetings were held in the autumn and one of them resulted in a clash between French and English groups. It seems certain that rebellion would soon have broken out in any event, but the first resort to arms took place almost by accident. Papineau was a remarkable orator and rabble rouser, but he was at heart a timid soul and dreaded the very violence he encouraged. In the hope that things would calm down, he left Montreal, taking other radical leaders with him. The authorities feared that they had gone to organize an insurrection and issued warrants for their arrest. On November 23 armed *Patriotes* repulsed the troops that had been sent to St. Denis to make the arrests.

This was to be the rebels' only military success, but this fact was hidden in the future, and it set the rebellion alight. Horrified, Papineau fled to the United States. Within a day or two a rebel gathering was defeated at St. Charles, and the *Patriotes* suffered their heaviest and bloodiest defeat at St. Eustache on December 14.

Meanwhile, partly as a result of the events in Lower Canada, violence had erupted in Toronto. In Upper Canada discontent had centred around the famous "Family Compact," the small, closely-knit group that controlled the Legislative and Executive Councils and the administration generally. Its two leading figures were the Rev. John Strachan, an Anglican cleric who wished to see his church become an established church in Canada, and John Beverley Robinson, who had been appointed Chief Justice in 1830. The Compact was opposed to popular government and favoured the existing system, in which they felt the two councils offered an appropriate counterbalance to the elected assembly.

There were many causes of friction, including land policy. Many felt that revenue from the Clergy Reserves should be used for educational purposes. Strachan wanted the whole of the reserves for the Anglican Church. This brought him into conflict with other denominations, notably the Methodists, who found a formidable champion in Egerton Ryerson. There were economic problems as well. The Erie Canal was draining off trade to the United States, and little was being done to enable the St. Lawrence route to compete with it. The virtual monopoly given to the Bank of Upper Canada aroused suspicion and resentment. Finally in 1837, Upper Canada, like Lower Canada, was caught in financial troubles caused by the crisis in the United States.

Politically, the opposition had come together in a group known as the Reformers. It included moderates, among them such men as William and Robert Baldwin, as well as a volatile firebrand and journalist, William Lyon Mackenzie. Their fortunes at the polls varied, and at every reverse Mackenzie became more and more extreme in his views. By 1835 the British Government felt that some concessions might be in order, and it sent out a new lieutenant-governor with this in mind. Unfortunately the person appointed was Sir Francis Bond Head, who was

A.D. 1837.

PROCLAMATION.

BY His Excellency SIR FRANCIS BOND HEAD,
Baronet, Lieutenant Governor of Upper Canada, &c. &c.

To the Queen's Faithful Subjects in Upper Canada.

In a time of profound peace, while every one was quietly following his occupations, feeling, secure under the protection of our Laws, a band of Rebels, instigated by a few malignant and disloyal men, has had the wickedness and audacity to assemble with Arms, and to attack and Murder the Queen's Subjects on the Highway—to Burn and Destroy their Property—to Rob the Public Mails—and to threaten to Plunder the Banks—and to Fire the City of Toronto.

Brave and Loyal People of Upper Canada. we have been long suffering from the acts and endeavours of concealed Traitors. but this is the first time that Rebellion has dared to shew itself openly in the land, in the absence of invasion by any Foreign Enemy.

Let every man do his duty now, and it will be the last time that we or our children shall see our lives or properties endangered, or the Authority of our Gracious Queen insulted by such treacherous and ungrateful men. MILITIA-MEN OF UPPER CANADA, no Country has ever shewn a finer example of Loyalty and Spirit than YOU have given upon this sudden call of Duty. Young and old of all ranks, are flocking to the Standard of their Country. What has taken place will enable our Queen to know Her Friends from Her Enemies—a public enemy is never so dangerous as a concealed Traitor—and now my friends let us complete well what is begun—let us not return to our rest till Treason and Traitors are revealed to the light of day, and rendered harmless throughout the land.

Be vigilant, patient and active—leave punishment to the Laws—our first object is, to arrest and secure all those who have been guilty of Rebellion. Murder and Robbery.—And to aid us in this, a Reward is hereby offered of

One Thousand Pounds,

to any one who will apprehend, and deliver up to Justice, WILLIAM LYON MACKENZE ; and FIVE HUNDRED POUNDS to any one who will apprehend, and deliver up to Justice, DAVID GIBSON—or SAMUEL LOUNT—or JESSE LLOYD—or SILAS FLETCHER—and the same reward and a free pardon will be given to any of their accomplices who will render this public service, except he or they shall have committed, in his own person, the crime of Murder or Arson.

And all, but the Leaders above-named, who have been seduced to join in this unnatural Rebellion, are hereby called to return to their duty to their Sovereign—to obey the Laws—and to live henceforward as good and faithful Subjects—and they will find the Government of their Queen as indulgent as it is jus

GOD SAVE THE QUEEN.

Thursday, 3 o'clock, P. M.
7th Dec. 1837

☞ The Party of Rebels, under their Chief Leaders, is wholly dispersed, and flying before the Loyal Militia. The only thing that remains to be done, is to find them, and arrest them.

R. STANTON, Printer to the QUEEN'S Most Excellent Majesty.

The price on Mackenzie's head

Poster offering a reward of a thousand pounds to anyone who would "apprehend and deliver up to Justice" William Lyon Mackenzie.

The battle at St. Eustache (top of page)

Here the rebels occupied the church, which is shown under attack in this lithograph published in 1840.

"The destruction of the 'Caroline'"

This picture by G. Tattersall was published in 1839. The Caroline did not go over Niagara Falls, as is frequently stated; she grounded and burned to the water's edge just above them, as here depicted.

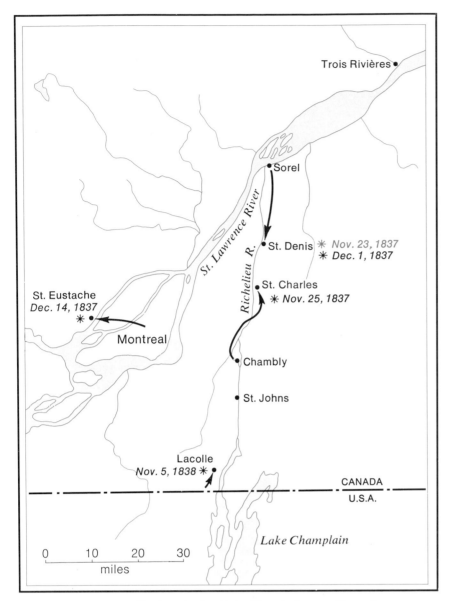

Trois Rivières •

• Sorel

St. Denis • ☀ *Nov. 23, 1837*
☀ *Dec. 1, 1837*

St. Charles •
☀ *Nov. 25, 1837*

St. Eustache
Dec. 14, 1837
☀ •

Montreal

• Chambly

• St. Johns

Lacolle
Nov. 5, 1838 ☀ •

CANADA
U.S.A.

Lake Champlain

0   10   20   30
miles

St. Lawrence River

Richelieu R.

Clashes in the Rebellion in Lower Canada

William Lyon Mackenzie

totally unsuited for the post. He first outraged the Reformers by appointing some of their number to the council but ignoring their views, then campaigned openly against them and helped defeat them in the election of 1836. Discouraged, the moderates held back, but Mackenzie, in a fury, began to think in terms of rebellion: by the autumn of 1837 he had men drilling with pikes and pitchforks. In October, Head, certain that all was well in Upper Canada, sent most of the troops available to Lower Canada, where trouble was obviously brewing. Mackenzie saw in their departure a golden opportunity to seize a defenceless government. Strongly republican by this time, he published a proposed constitution for a State of Upper Canada on November 15. News of the first clash in Lower Canada encouraged him to plan a march on Toronto, which took place on December 7. It was a total fiasco and Mackenzie fled to Buffalo. Later he and some followers established themselves on Navy Island, in the Niagara River.

Manifest Destiny—the theory that the United States was destined to rule all North America—was popular with Americans at this time, and the Canadian rebels were received sympathetically and given considerable encouragement and support. This increased sharply after Canadians seized the small American steamer *Caroline,* which had been carrying supplies to Navy Island, and set her afire. Various raids and small incursions occurred along the border, the two most serious being in November 1838. On November 4 a small force seeking to revive the rebellion in Lower Canada was turned back at Lacolle. Later in the month rebels landed at Prescott, in Upper Canada, and a spirited battle centred around a stone windmill in which they had taken refuge.

Lord Durham had been sent to Canada in 1838 as Governor-General and as a commissioner to inquire into Canadian problems and make recommendations. His classic *Report on the Affairs of British North America* was tabled in the spring of

1839. His chief proposals were two: that Upper and Lower Canada should be united to form a single province with one assembly, and that responsible government should be granted. The first of these the British Government accepted; the creation of the United Province of Canada was proclaimed in February 1841; but, to the dismay of the Reformers, responsible government was once again withheld.

Louis Joseph Papineau

This fine photograph of the leader of the Patriotes was taken late in life, when he was living in retirement on the seigneury at Montebello that is now the Seigneury Club.

Lord Durham (shown upper left)

From the portrait by Sir Thomas Lawrence in the Public Archives of Canada.

CHAPTER 10

The Maritimes

The Maritimes: 1812-1860

THESE years have been aptly termed an era of "wind, wood and water." The timber trade, shipbuilding, shipping and fishing combined to make the period one of almost continuous growth and prosperity in the maritimes, which many opponents of Confederation later looked back upon as a sort of golden age.

The War of 1812 occasioned the first prosperity. Trade flourished as never before. New England remained virtually neutral, and commercial contacts continued much as usual. Privateers and merchant ships furnished with letters of marque fared well; in all they are said to have made prizes of 207 American ships. Trade with the West Indies at one time doubled in only three years, with fish providing the chief item of trade in one direction and rum and molasses in the other.

These years saw the timber trade reach its peak in New Brunswick; shipbuilding flourished both there and in Nova Scotia, and in the latter shipowning increased rapidly. Over 1,300 vessels were owned in Nova Scotia by 1830 and by 1846 the total exceeded 2,800.

Prince Edward Island, formerly known as the Island of St. John (Ile St. Jean when it was a French possession), had received its present name in 1799. Cape Breton, which had become a separate colony in 1784, was reunited with Nova Scotia in 1820. Except for the disputed boundary between New Brunswick and Maine, the three provinces then existed as we know them today.

In all three there soon appeared the familiar demand for responsible government, and the usual struggle between an elected assembly on the one hand and the governor and an appointed council on the other. The clash was most acute and most interesting in Nova Scotia. There both the legislative and the executive power centred in the Council, which was soon dubbed the "Council of Twelve." To some degree it resembled the Family Compact in Upper Canada, inasmuch as it consisted of a closely knit group representing the interests of the bankers, the merchants and leading Anglicans. The opposition included farmers, small tradesmen, dissenters and Roman Catholics. In 1830 they found a leader in Joseph Howe, a young journalist and politician of great ability. A libel suit in 1836 made him widely known, and the same year he was elected to the Assembly. Some small concessions were made in 1839, and for a time Howe was a member of the Council; but the essential element of responsibility was not granted and in 1843 he resigned. Four years later the Reformers won the general election and it was realized that their demands must be met. In January 1848, when the Assembly passed a vote of no confidence, the Council resigned. The next month

Joseph Howe

He and Sir Charles Tupper are perhaps the best-known figures in the history of Nova Scotia.

Public Archives of Canada

Saint John in 1842

From an engraving based on a painting by William Henry Bartlett.

Public Archives of Canada

Colonial Building, Charlottetown

An example of the surprisingly imposing and attractive public buildings that had been erected in the Maritime Provinces prior to Confederation. This photograph was taken about the time of the Charlottetown Conference of 1864.

John B. Uniacke became premier and Howe became provincial secretary in the first responsible government in any overseas colony.

The struggle was less heated in New Brunswick than in Nova Scotia. Interest there was directed more to two matters of vital concern to the timber trade—land policy and the boundary with Maine. Control of public lands carried with it control of access to timber stands, and the point at issue became the terms upon which the governor and Council would surrender this control to the Assembly. The dispute with Maine suddenly took a serious turn in 1839, when some New Brunswick loggers began to fell trees on territory that Maine claimed. Troops were mustered by both sides, and although violence was avoided, the episode has been dignified with the title Aroostock War. The boundary was settled peaceably by Daniel Webster and Lord Ashburton in 1842.

By degrees a Reform Party and a strong demand for responsible government emerged, and the precedent set in Nova Scotia made ultimate success

certain. The concession was finally made in 1854, when Charles Fisher became premier of the first responsible administration. Prince Edward Island also gained responsible government the same year; George Coles, the Reform leader, was the Island's first premier. The battle had been won in Canada in 1849, and when Newfoundland was added to the list in 1855, all the colonies included in Eastern Canada had responsible governments—a matter that was to be of the greatest importance a few years later, when they began to consider some sort of federation.

Trade and railways were the chief preoccupations of Nova Scotia and New Brunswick in the later years. The Reciprocity Treaty of 1854 with the United States applied to the Maritimes as well as Canada, and had the effect of increasing substantially the flow of fish, timber, coal and agricultural products to American markets. There were high hopes that railways might soon link Halifax and Saint John with Quebec and Montreal, but for the moment the financial hurdles were found to be too high. Both provinces had to be content with local lines.

Exact figures are not available for the earlier years, but it is estimated that in 1806 the populations of Nova Scotia, New Brunswick and Prince Edward Island were respectively 65,000, 35,000 and 7,000, or a total of 107,000 in all. By 1825 the combined total had increased to about 205,000. At the

Charles Fisher

Leader of the first responsible ministry in New Brunswick, in 1854, and a decade later one of the Fathers of Confederation.

end of this prosperous period the census of 1861 showed that Nova Scotia had 330,000 people, New Brunswick 252,000 and Prince Edward Island 80,000, or a combined population of 662,000— almost half their population at the present time.

Newfoundland: 1783-1860

For many years Newfoundland was in the extraordinary position of being considered a British colony. The fisheries were long regarded as the only important consideration there, and settlement was frowned upon because it was thought to be detrimental to them. This view was held strongly by the West Country merchants who dominated the fisheries, and their powerful lobby in London saw to it that the official view coincided with theirs.

An anticolonization statute had been passed as early as 1698, and another was passed in 1789. Newfoundland had had Royal Governors since 1729, but officially the island was only a summer fishery, and the Governor sailed home when the season ended. As late as 1806 fishing "stages"—platforms used to dry fish—were "the only species of landed property recognized in law." The only title to land was the precarious one provided by occupancy.

But in spite of this a resident population grew up; by 1806 it numbered over 20,000. In 1812 the Governor, Sir John Duckworth, reported to London that the population "is now so great that any

George Coles

Coles formed the first responsible ministry in Prince Edward Island in 1851, and although the Island held aloof from Confederation in 1867, he is included in the "Fathers" as he attended the Charlottetown and Quebec conferences in 1864.

attempt to lessen it or even to check the rapidity of increase must be *completely vain*." For a few more years efforts were still made to discourage colonization; houses were torn down and their occupants shipped off to other colonies. But policy changes were in the offing. In 1817 the Governor became a year-round resident, and in 1819 Chief Justice Forbes made the all-important ruling that occupancy for purposes other than fishing was legal. In 1824 the British Parliament finally recognized Newfoundland as a British colony, and the following year a Council was appointed to advise the Governor. Growth in population had forced these issues: by 1830 there were 70,000 residents on the island.

It will be remembered that the French and Americans had attached much importance to the Newfoundland fisheries and had made successful efforts to have their fishing rights there recognized by treaty. The Treaty of Paris of 1783 not only confirmed the French title to the islands of St. Pierre and Miquelon, but gave them fishing rights along a "French Shore" that included part of the northern coast and the whole of the west coast. The west coast was also open to the Americans under the terms of an agreement made in 1818. In addition, the British had agreed not to permit settlement on that coast—a decision that had far-reaching results, as it was found later that about 80 percent of the potential farming land in Newfoundland was in the west. This made the island more than ever

St. John's in 1798

*From the drawing by H. P. Brenton in the Map
Room of the British Museum.*

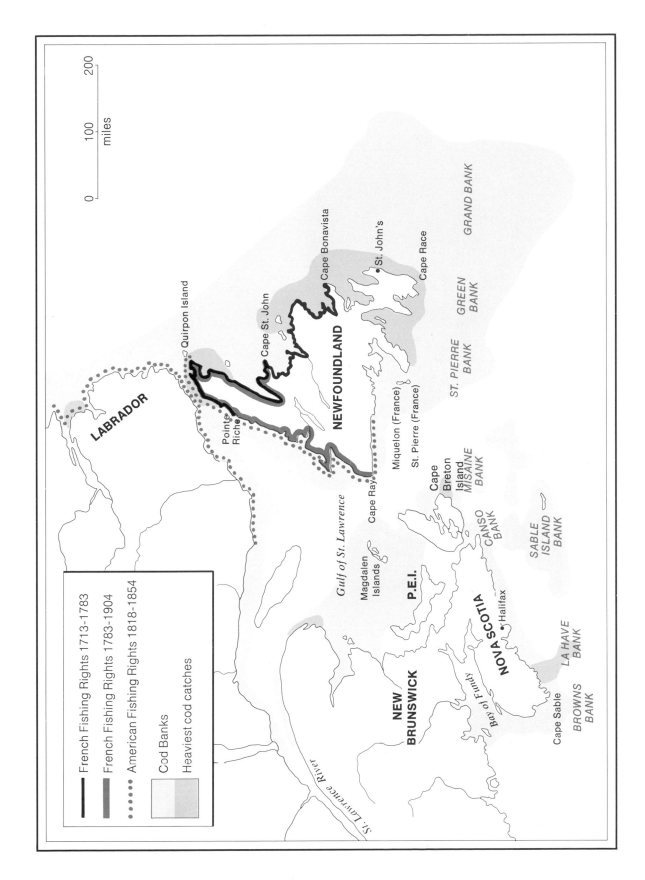

Legend:
- French Fishing Rights 1713–1783
- French Fishing Rights 1783–1904
- American Fishing Rights 1818–1854
- Cod Banks
- Heaviest cod catches

200

100

0

miles

LABRADOR

Quirpon Island

Pointe Riche

Cape St. John

NEWFOUNDLAND

Cape Bonavista

St. John's

Cape Race

GRAND BANK

GREEN BANK

ST. PIERRE BANK

Miquelon (France)

St. Pierre (France)

Gulf of St. Lawrence

Cape Ray

Cape Breton Island

MISAINE BANK

CANSO BANK

SABLE ISLAND BANK

Magdalen Islands

P.E.I.

NOVA SCOTIA

Halifax

LA HAVE BANK

BROWNS BANK

Cape Sable

Bay of Fundy

NEW BRUNSWICK

St. Lawrence River

Cormack's Route Across Newfoundland

Public Archives of Canada

Dr. William Carson

dependent on the fisheries, and probably also tended to discourage intercourse with Canada, since it kept the part of the country adjacent to Canada virtually vacant for many years.

Sealing was becoming an important supplement to fishing by 1800; in 1830 the annual harvest had grown to half a million pelts. Fishermen could share in this added source of income as the seals were taken before the fishing season began.

Sectarianism has played a major part in life in Newfoundland. This grew from a beginning in the 18th century when the churches recognized that in spite of official bans on colonization people were living on the island, many of them under most difficult conditions. The Anglican Society for the Propagation of the Gospel sent its first missionary as early as 1726, a Methodist arrived in 1765, and the Roman Catholics a few years later. As time passed and population grew, the various denominations became pre-eminent in different regions. The first schools

were provided by the churches and sectarian influence has been strong ever since. Inevitably, too, it was to become a force in politics.

Political development followed much the same basic pattern as elsewhere. Representative government was granted in 1832, largely through the efforts of Dr. William Carson, who had emerged as a strong Reform leader. Inevitably the elected assembly clashed with the appointed council, and a brief attempt to merge the two in a single-chamber legislature failed because the next logical demand of the reformers—responsible government—was denied.

When preparing his famous report on Canada, Lord Durham considered the state and future of Newfoundland. He found there "the ordinary colonial collision between the representative body on the one side, and the executive on the other." There as elsewhere the solution was responsible government, but because of Newfoundland's small size he felt that, like Prince Edward Island, it should become part of a federated British North America;

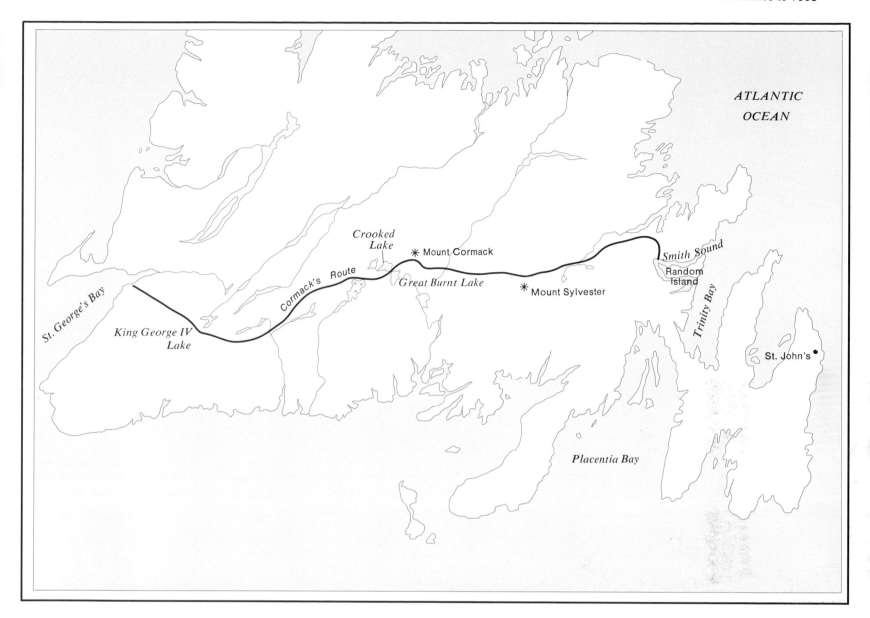

Fishing Rights in Newfoundland

this, he wrote, was "the only means of securing any proper attention to their interests." More than a century was to pass before this came about, but in 1855, after a troubled period marked by severe tensions and sectarian squabbling, Newfoundland did secure responsible government. The first premier under the new regime was Philip Francis Little, who had been born in Prince Edward Island.

Two years later a census showed that the population had grown to 124,000. In spite of setbacks that included a fire that almost completely destroyed the capital city of St. John's in 1846, Newfoundland was making progress.

An honoured name in Newfoundland history is that of William Epps Cormack. He is indeed Newfoundland's Alexander Mackenzie, for he made the first journey by a European across the island. In September and October of 1822 he travelled from Random Sound, in Trinity Bay, to St. George's Bay, on the west coast, and he later described the crossing

in a narrative first published in 1836. Cormack was only 26 at the time and had ahead of him a long career that would take him to Australia, New Zealand, California and finally British Columbia. There in 1860 he became a member of the first municipal council of New Westminster, the first city incorporated in B.C.

CHAPTER 11

A Growing Canada

Fur and Gold
West of the Rockies

THERE were nearly half a million people in the Canadas and the Atlantic Provinces before the first trading posts were built on what is now the mainland of British Columbia. Even on Vancouver Island the maritime fur traders rarely tarried long; they were essentially transients, interested in quick profits, who had hunted the sea otter to virtual extinction by 1825.

The explorers and traders of the North West Company went up the Peace, Athabasca and North Saskatchewan rivers, found routes and passes through the Rocky Mountains, and reached the upper waters of rivers flowing to the Pacific. It became apparent in time that the two important western streams were the Fraser and the Columbia, each draining a vast watershed, and each having a great array of tributary lakes and rivers. The remarkable journeys of Simon Fraser and David Thompson, in the course of which they descended these rivers to their mouths, have already been noted.

Forts were built at strategic points in the Fraser and Columbia watersheds, but the North West Company was not an aggressive trader in the area. There was little or no competition, and the battle with the Hudson's Bay Company east of the mountains was absorbing its energy and interest. For a time after the Hudson's Bay Company took over in 1821 there was little change, but George Simpson believed trade in the coastal region could be developed to advantage, and under his prodding it earned substantial profits.

Simpson hoped that the Columbia River would become the international boundary line, and to bolster British possession he had established a new headquarters depot, Fort Vancouver, on the north bank of the river near the mouth of the Willamette. But by 1843 it was evident that Oregon was a lost cause, and Fort Victoria was built on Vancouver Island as a contingency depot to which the district headquarters could be moved if need be. The transfer duly took place in 1849, three years after the 49th parallel had become the boundary.

The influx of American immigrants had been a major factor in the loss of Oregon, and in 1849 the British Government and the Hudson's Bay Company took the precaution of setting up a Crown Colony, under Company auspices, on Vancouver Island. Any chance that settlers might be attracted to the island was ruined by the gold rush in California, which completely absorbed attention for some years to come. A census taken in December 1854 records that the population of the colony was then no more than 774, of whom 232 were at Fort Victoria and 151 at Nanaimo, where extensive seams of coal had been discovered in 1850. Many of the rest lived on four large farms that helped to grow the agricultural products that the Hudson's Bay Company provided for the Russian American Company in Alaska. Incidentally, the close trading relations between the two made possible the negotiation of a neutrality pact covering the Pacific Coast when the Crimean War broke out in 1854.

The whole situation was changed dramatically by the discovery of gold in the Fraser River. In the spring and summer of 1858 between 20,000 and 30,000 miners and adventurers—almost all of them Americans—poured into Victoria and the valley of the Fraser; 4,700 are known to have landed in a single week in July. This posed a frightening problem for James Douglas, who was both Chief Factor of the Hudson's Bay Company and Governor of the Colony of Vancouver Island. He had seen Oregon lost, and he was determined that the experience should not be repeated on the island. A man of courage and resource, he did not hesitate to exercise authority on the mainland that he did not possess legally until a second Crown Colony was established there some months later. By a happy chance two ships of the Royal Navy were at hand, engaged in the boundary survey, and Douglas used them to keep firm control of the approaches to the Fraser

Trout Falls and portage on the Hayes River
From a water colour painted in 1819 by Robert Hood.

Hudson's Bay Company ships Prince of Wales *and* Eddystone *bartering furs with Eskimo in Hudson Bay. This water colour was painted in 1819 by Robert Hood, a member of Franklin's expedition of 1819-22. The party had travelled from England on the* Prince of Wales.

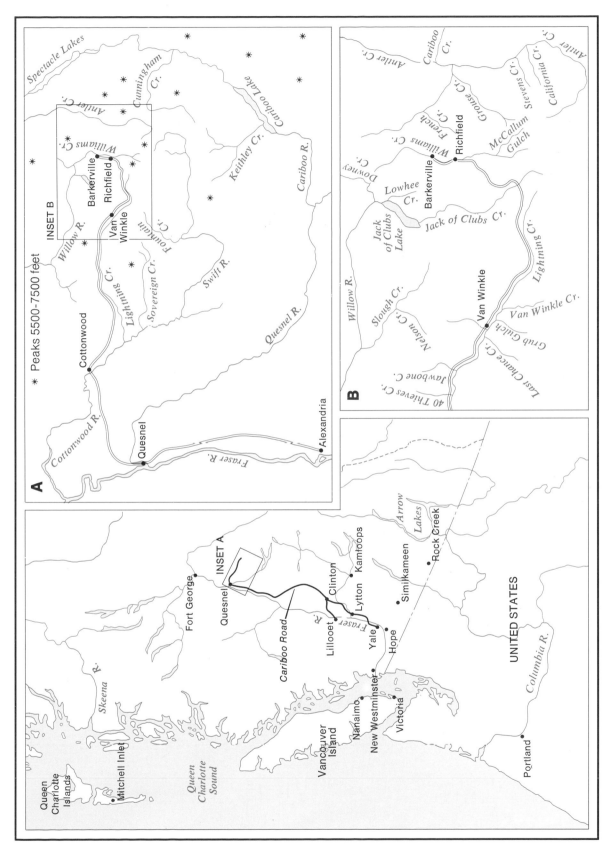

Gold Rush Days in British Columbia

Inset A

Spectacle Lakes
Cunningham Cr.
Cariboo Lake
Anter Cr.
Williams Cr.
INSET B
Barkerville
Richfield
Van Winkle
Willow R.
Keithley Cr.
Cariboo R.
Fountain
Lightning Cr.
Sovereign Cr.
Swift R.
Quesnel R.
Cottonwood
Cottonwood R.
Quesnel
Fraser R.
Alexandria

* Peaks 5500–7500 feet

A

Inset B

Anter Cr.
Cariboo Cr.
Grouse Cr.
Stevens Cr.
California Cr.
Antler Cr.
French Cr.
Williams Cr.
Richfield
McCallum Gulch
Downey Cr.
Barkerville
Lowhee Cr.
Jack of Clubs Lake
Jack of Clubs Cr.
Willow R.
Slough Cr.
Nelson Cr.
Van Winkle
Van Winkle Cr.
Grub Gulch
Last Chance Cr.
Jawbone C.
40 Thieves Cr.
Lightning Cr.

B

Main Map

Skeena R.
Queen Charlotte Islands
Mitchell Inlet
Queen Charlotte Sound
Fort George
INSET A
Quesnel
Cariboo Road
Lillooet
Fraser R.
Clinton
Kamloops
Lytton
Yale
Hope
Nanaimo
New Westminster
Victoria
Vancouver Island
Arrow Lakes
Similkameen
Rock Creek
UNITED STATES
Columbia R.
Portland

The Davis claim in Cariboo

The water wheel on the Davis claim on Williams Creek, in the Cariboo.

Sir James Douglas

River. As this was the only available supply route, it placed the miners at his mercy. As a result, the rush was remarkably orderly.

The first gold had been found in the lower canyon of the river, in the vicinity of Hope and Yale, but this was soon exhausted. Many miners left, but others moved upstream, seeking the legendary Mother Lode. The result was the discovery of the immensely rich deposits in the Cariboo, where the rush reached its height in 1862. To provide essential transportation Douglas arranged for the construction of the famous Cariboo Road, largely under the supervision of a small corps of Royal Engineers who had been sent from England to assist with law and order and public works.

Gold production continued at a high level for some years, but mining methods changed and employment fell off. A depression developed, and in 1866, for reasons of economy, Vancouver Island was annexed to the mainland colony of British Columbia. On the Island there had been a lively demand for responsible government, and as British Columbia had no assembly, the merger was a blow to the Reformers.

A few population figures are available for these early years. In 1861 Douglas reported that the population of Vancouver Island was 3,024; of these 2,350 lived in Victoria and the vicinity. In 1870 the total white population of the Island and mainland was estimated to be 10,586.

Early Canals in Canada

All canal building of importance in Canada has been on the St. Lawrence River and its tributaries, or on the Great Lakes. Between them, the river and the lakes provided a waterway reaching far into the continent; but navigation was broken by rapids, many of which could not be passed easily by anything except a canoe. As larger craft came into use, canals had to be built around the worst rapids before they could navigate freely.

A few canals were projected elsewhere, particularly in Nova Scotia. Before 1800 there was talk of a waterway across Nova Scotia that would link Halifax with Minas Basin and the Bay of Fundy. Much of it was actually built in the 1820s, but it was then abandoned and never completed. Another proposed canal would have connected the Bay of Fundy and the Gulf of St. Lawrence across the narrow Chignecto Peninsula, but this never progressed beyond the stage of preliminary surveys.

Canals to circumvent some of the rapids on the St. Lawrence were talked about during the French régime, but none was built. The first St. Lawrence waterways were four tiny canals built in the Soulanges area, upstream from Montreal, in 1779-1783. They had a depth of only 2½ feet and could accommodate nothing larger than a bateau. The only other canal completed in the 18th century was at Sault Ste. Marie, where in 1798 the North West Company opened a canal with a wooden lock 40 feet long that enabled loaded canoes to pass back and forth between Lake Huron and Lake Superior. In restored form, this little lock still exists.

The lock at the Sault is interesting because the fur traders really had no great need for canals; canoes, which could be carried around a rapid, met their transportation needs very well. Canals were expensive and, in theory, at least, some definite prospect of traffic and revenue was essential before they could be built. This meant that they would normally appear only after settlements had grown to some size, trade and commerce had developed, and there was need to move heavy or bulky products that could only be transported economically by water.

As it happened, much of the early canal building in Canada was due to two factors that had little to do with local traffic or circumstances. The first was military requirements. During the War of 1812 the moving of troops and supplies had been found to be a painfully slow and laborious business; the Army was anxious to have means of transportation that was both easier and, if possible, less exposed to American attack. The second factor was an ambition cherished for many years by the mercantile

Victoria in 1859 (top of page)

Barkerville in 1868

Barkerville, the most important of the towns that sprang into existence as a result of the Cariboo gold rush. Destroyed by fire in 1868, shortly after this photograph was taken, it was soon rebuilt.

The Cariboo Road in 1865 (shown at right)

The first canal at Sault Ste. Marie

Built by the North West Company in 1797-98, this little lock, which still exists in restored form, helped the canoes of the fur traders to bypass the rapids on the St. Marys River.

community in Montreal. The St. Lawrence–Great Lakes waterway seemed, on the map at least, to provide such a direct and obvious trade route to and from the interior that they hoped it would attract and funnel through Montreal not only the trade of Upper Canada and the Canadian West, but that of a large part of the American West as well. Until the War of 1812 Montreal traders had managed to maintain a substantial flow of furs to Montreal from the American territories south of the Great Lakes; the new commercial ambitions were thus simply a successor to the fur trade. The Americans, for their part, looked upon the Hudson River and its tributary the Mohawk as their natural route inland, and by 1800 plans were afoot for a canal that would connect the Mohawk River with Lake Erie and Lake Ontario. In 1801 Alexander Mackenzie, the explorer, submitted a memorandum to the British Government in which he pointed out that this project was intended "to make Albany what Montreal is intended by Nature to be, the Emporium of all the trade & commerce of . . . the Great Lakes . . . ." He urged that it be countered immediately by the construction of canals around the

rapids on the St. Lawrence between Montreal and Lake Ontario, but nothing was done. After many delays the Americans began to build the Erie Canal between Buffalo and Albany in 1817 and completed it in 1825. As Mackenzie feared, it did drain off much of the trade Montreal had hoped to secure, and Canadian canals came slowly into being in an effort to compete with it.

The first canal built was around the Lachine Rapids, the break in navigation nearest to Montreal. Completed in 1825, the first Lachine canal had 6 locks 100 feet in length. The next canal constructed enabled ships to bypass much the most formidable obstruction to navigation in the whole St. Lawrence–Great Lakes waterway—the Niagara escarpment and Niagara Falls, where the difference in water level between Lake Erie and Lake Ontario was no less than 330 feet. The original Welland Canal, which had 34 locks and extended from near Port Dalhousie, on Lake Ontario, to the Welland River, a tributary of the Niagara River, was opened in 1829. As navigation on the Niagara was found to be difficult, the canal was extended to Port Colborne, on Lake Erie, in 1833. It then had 40 locks, the smallest 110 feet in length.

The Rideau Canal was the next waterway completed. This was primarily a military undertaking and extended from Bytown (now Ottawa) on the Ottawa River to Kingston, on Lake Ontario, a

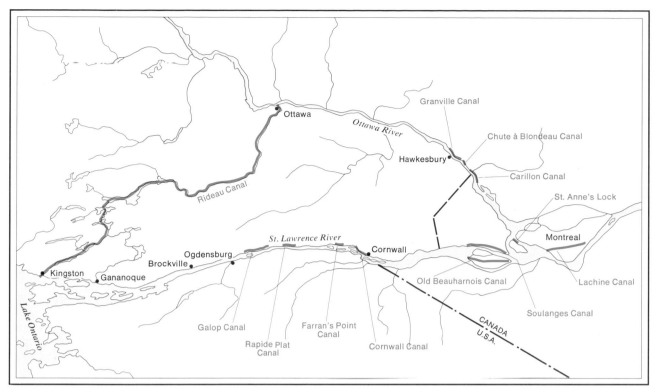

The Early St. Lawrence-Ottawa Canals

distance of 132 miles. Troops and supplies sent up the Ottawa River from Montreal and then taken down the canal would be much less vulnerable to American attack than on the direct route up the St. Lawrence. The canal made maximum use of the Rideau River and the Rideau Lakes, but nevertheless 33 locks were necessary, the standard length being 134 feet.

The pressing necessity was now for canals that would enable ships to pass the remaining rapids on the St. Lawrence between Lake Ontario and Lachine, and on the Ottawa River between Bytown and Montreal. These were not provided for a decade, but all came into being as a result of a burst of canal construction in the 1840s. On the Ottawa, canals around the rapids at St. Anne, Chute à Blondeau, Grenville and the Long Sault were all completed in 1843. The same year the Cornwall Canal, around the Long Sault on the St. Lawrence, was ready for service. The Beauharnois Canal, which superseded the four small pioneer canals at Soulanges, was completed in 1845 and in 1847-48 three canals upstream known collectively as the Williamsburg Canals were ready. These new St. Lawrence canals had locks 200 feet in length, with a water depth of 9 feet, and the Lachine Canal was enlarged in 1848 to correspond. The locks of the Welland Canal had already been enlarged in 1842-45 to a length of 150 feet and a water depth of 9 feet.

Two other canals deserve mention. The first was on the Richelieu River, around the rapids near Chambly. This caused the military authorities some worry because they felt it would facilitate the movements of American invaders as well as of Canadian trade. The second canal was an ambitious effort to link Lake Ontario with Georgian Bay by way of

the Trent River, the Kawartha Lakes and Lake Simcoe. The object was to avoid the long detour by way of Windsor. The first section was completed in 1833.

Viewed in relation to the actual traffic offering, almost all these canals were ahead of their time; they were quite unable to pay their way. But like many of the railways built in later days, they provided transportation facilities that were of immense value to the pioneers and in this way made an incalculable contribution to the development of Canada.

The Rideau Canal today

The only one of the early St. Lawrence-Ottawa canals that is still functioning, the Rideau Canal is now a popular waterway for pleasure craft. These are the well-known locks beside the Chateau Laurier in Ottawa. The large stone building almost hidden in the trees, now a museum, dates back to canal construction days.

135

Railway coach, early Grand Trunk style

This model was proudly exhibited by the Grand Trunk Railway at the Paris Exhibition of 1867.

Canada's First Railways

When railways were first being built, some doubts were expressed about their ability to operate in the severe Canadian winter. Experience showed that locomotives could keep steam up in subzero weather, and even before the days of snowplows, when drifts had to be dug out by hand, the trains managed to get through most of the time.

The advantages that the railways could bring were enormous. They offered all-weather travel, and provided a speed and ease of movement that no other means available could approach. They carried bulky products long distances to new markets, and in return brought back manufactured and imported goods. And they had a tremendous social impact as well, for they ended the relative isolation of countless communities on or near the railway lines. Not so long ago the arrival of the train was still the great event of the day in many small towns.

Canada's first railway was the Champlain & St. Lawrence, completed in 1836. Fourteen and a half miles in length, it ran from Laprairie, on the St. Lawrence above Montreal, to St. Johns, on the Richelieu River, and its primary purpose was to circumvent the Richelieu rapids. It was thus really a portage railway, and soon after it was built an attempt was made to build another portage railway that would provide transportation around Niagara Falls. Part of the line was opened in 1839, but the steep grades temporarily defeated the engineers. No line was completed at Niagara until 1854.

Many railway projects were talked about and a good many charters were secured, but little or no additional construction took place for a decade or more. Many of these projects were local or at most regional, but a few were more ambitious. The St. Andrews & Quebec Railway, chartered in 1836, was intended to connect New Brunswick with Canada, but it remained at the project stage for many years

and as late as 1868 the line had only struggled as far as Woodstock. In 1851 Joseph Howe and others thought they had secured backing and guarantees in Nova Scotia, Canada and Great Britain that would result in a railway from Halifax to Quebec, but the plan fell through. The first railway in the Atlantic Provinces was a six-mile company-owned line built by the General Mining Association to carry coal from its Albion Mine to the docks at Pictou. It was completed in 1838. The only public railways built in Nova Scotia before Confederation were between Halifax and Windsor, and Halifax and Truro. These were completed in 1858, and the latter was extended to Pictou in 1867.

The 1850s were the first great age of railway building in Canada. In part this was a reaction to what was happening in the United States, where railways were being built at a fantastic rate. Railway mileage there jumped from 9,000 miles in 1850 to 30,000 miles in 1860. This included a network that extended from New York to Buffalo, Detroit and Chicago, and to points as far west as the Kansas border. It was feared that these lines would drain off Canadian trade, just as the Erie Canal had done, and it was apparent that Canada must provide herself with through railways of her own as promptly as possible.

The first line built was from Montreal to the nearest ice-free port, which was Portland, Maine. The portion of the line in Canada was called the St. Lawrence & Atlantic Railway; the part in the United States was called the Atlantic & St. Lawrence. Through service began in 1853. The line ran through Sherbrooke and Richmond, and later a branch was added that ran from Richmond to Lévis, thus providing a link with Quebec City.

The next important construction was in western Ontario. The Great Western Railway completed a line from Niagara to Windsor, via Hamilton, and in 1855-56 it was linked with Toronto by the Hamilton & Toronto Railway. Meanwhile the Northern Railway had been built from Toronto to Collingwood, on Georgian Bay. In a sense the Northern was a portage railway, built in the hope that steamer services based on Collingwood would develop trade and traffic on the Great Lakes and in the West.

But the great event of the 1850s was the advent of the Grand Trunk Railway, which, as its name implied, aimed to provide the main through rail services in Canada. Chartered in 1852, it combined Canadian and British railway and financial interests and British contractors, notably Thomas Brassey and his associates. The Grand Trunk acquired a

The first locomotive in Nova Scotia (upper right)

The Samson, *which is still in existence, was acquired in 1838 to haul coal between the Albion Mine and the docks at Pictou, a distance of six miles.*

Hamilton's first railway station (bottom right)

This photograph of the depot of the Great Western Railway was taken in the 1850s.

number of lines, including the Montreal–Quebec–Portland lines of the St. Lawrence & Atlantic, and set about building a through railway from Montreal westward. The section from Montreal to Toronto was completed in 1856. It might have been expected that the Grand Trunk would have tried to acquire or cooperate with the Great Western, which already had a line from Toronto to Windsor, but it decided instead to go its own way, took over a partly built railway between Toronto and Guelph, and extended it to Stratford and Sarnia. This was completed in 1859. Later the Grand Trunk gained access to Detroit by building a branch line in the United States southward from Port Huron, which is across the St. Clair River from Sarnia.

The Grand Trunk also made additions to its eastern lines. The Richmond–Lévis line was extended along the south shore of the St. Lawrence as far as Rivière du Loup, while the famous Victoria Bridge, across the St. Lawrence at Montreal, was completed in 1860 and gave that city a much-needed convenient rail link with lines on the south shore.

Important local lines built in these same years included the Bytown & Prescott Railway, which in 1854 linked Bytown (Ottawa) with the main line of the Grand Trunk at Prescott, and the Brockville & Ottawa Railway, which ran from Brockville north to Almonte and Arnprior. In 1858 the Buffalo & Lake Huron Railway completed a line from Buffalo to Goderich, on the lake.

In 1866 there were still only 147 miles of railway in Nova Scotia, but there were 218 miles in New Brunswick, where the resoundingly named European & North American Railway had been completed from Saint John to Moncton and Shediac in 1860. By the same date there were nearly 2,200 miles in the United Province of Canada, and total expenditure on railway construction there had soared to no less than $146,000,000—a vast sum considering conditions and population at the time.

The beginnings of a railway system were thus in existence in 1867. True the Grand Trunk was already experiencing the first of the financial troubles that were to characterize its whole history, but lines had been built and trains were running. Like the canals, the railways may not have been financially profitable, but they were rendering an immense service; the country was receiving dividends of many sorts, even if the shareholders were not.

The Timber Trade and the Wooden Ship Era

Virtually every new settlement began with the felling of trees. Logs were needed to build a first shelter; fuel was essential for cooking and warmth. Most of the land suitable for agriculture was forested originally, and had to be cleared before crops could be planted. Along the St. Lawrence and the lower lakes in what is now Ontario there were magnificent stands of white pine that would have been worth a fortune in later years, but both markets and transportation were lacking in early days and most of the trees were burned to get rid of them. All the settler could hope for was a little revenue from the sale of ashes, if facilities were available to use them in making potash.

In the Maritime provinces spars were the first important export. Great quantities of masts and yards were required in Great Britain for the Royal Navy and also for merchant ships. Wars in Europe interfered with the flow of shipments from the Baltic and other usual sources, and as early as 1774 an official forest survey was carried out in Nova Scotia, including New Brunswick. Thereafter until about 1810 trees suitable for masts were reserved for naval purposes.

Next to develop was the trade in large squared timbers, which reached its height in the years between 1840 and 1860. Lumbering became an all-absorbing trade in the St. John River valley; the wages offered and its other attractions brought settlement and farming in many areas almost to a standstill. New Brunswick had to import most of its food, including even such items as wheat and potatoes. The other major source of squared timber was the valley of the Ottawa. Here farming and lumbering established a healthier relationship. The timbermen were in urgent need of farm products to feed their crews, and as they moved upriver, seeking new stands of timber, the farmers followed them, to mutual advantage. Prices were high enough to make farming attractive.

The squared timbers were lashed together to form cribs, and a number of cribs in turn formed the great timber rafts for which the Ottawa became famous. These floated down the Ottawa River and the St. Lawrence for hundreds of miles and most of them ended up at Wolfe's Cove, above Quebec, where the timbers were sold and loaded into the waiting timber ships. Other rafts came down the St. Lawrence from Lake Ontario, and these were frequently used as a means of carrying produce to the markets in Montreal and Quebec.

By degrees sawn lumber replaced squared timbers as the chief forest product. Some of it, notably heavy deals, was for export, but there was a rapidly growing home market as well. Settlers were anxious to replace their log houses and barns with frame buildings. There was the further point that squared timbers were very wasteful of wood and could be cut only from large trees; sawn lumber could come from a tree of almost any size, often including those a settler still had on his own property. A saw-mill soon came to be regarded as essential in a community; by 1854 there were 1,618 of them in Upper Canada alone.

In many places large trees grew near the water, and shipbuilding was a natural development. Pontgravé built two little ships at Port Royal in 1606, and many were built later in New France. A brig was built at Halifax in 1751 and a schooner was launched on the future site of Saint John in 1770.

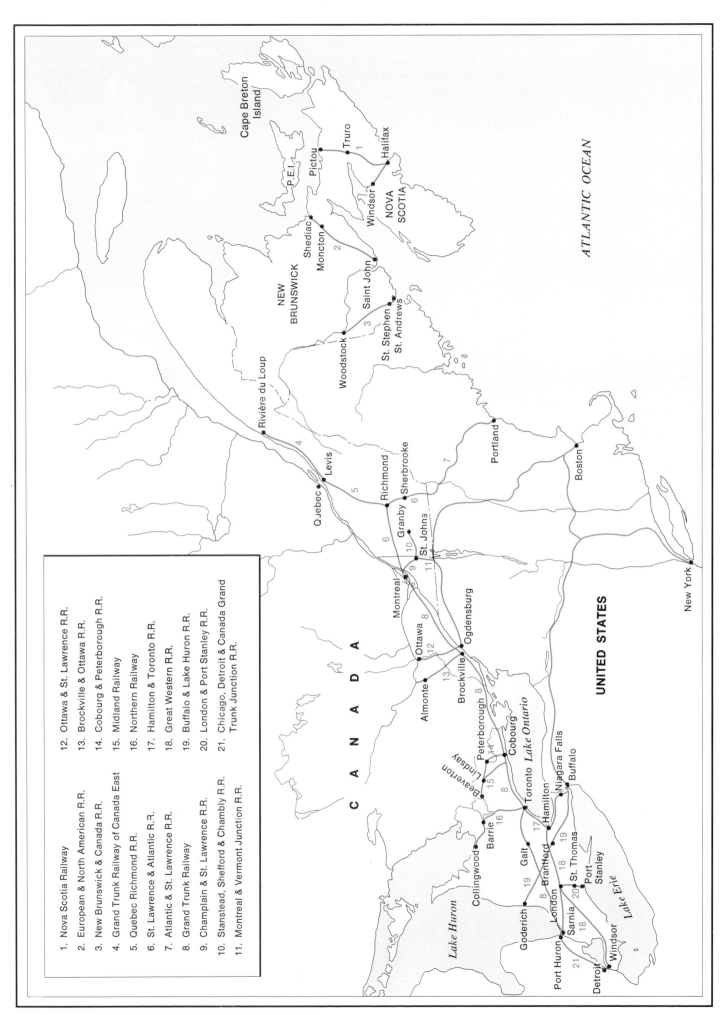

Early Canadian Railways, 1867

1. Nova Scotia Railway	12. Ottawa & St. Lawrence R.R.
2. European & North American R.R.	13. Brockville & Ottawa R.R.
3. New Brunswick & Canada R.R.	14. Cobourg & Peterborough R.R.
4. Grand Trunk Railway of Canada East	15. Midland Railway
5. Quebec Richmond R.R.	16. Northern Railway
6. St. Lawrence & Atlantic R.R.	17. Hamilton & Toronto R.R.
7. Atlantic & St. Lawrence R.R.	18. Great Western R.R.
8. Grand Trunk Railway	19. Buffalo & Lake Huron R.R.
9. Champlain & St. Lawrence R.R.	20. London & Port Stanley R.R.
10. Stanstead, Shefford & Chambly R.R.	21. Chicago, Detroit & Canada Grand
11. Montreal & Vermont Junction R.R.	Trunk Junction R.R.

Clipper ship "Marco Polo" (shown at top of page 140)
Built at St. John in 1851, many regarded her as the fastest sailing ship of her day.

Shipbuilding at Dorchester, N.B. (shown on page 140)
A typical scene with logs in the millpond, a saw-mill to cut them into timbers and planks, and a ship under construction on a slipway alongside.

The timber coves above Quebec (shown at top of page 141)
Squared timbers are being loaded through the special ports in the sailing ship's bow.

The last of the lumber rafts, Ottawa, 1908 (shown on page 141).

Referring to the Maritimes and Quebec in later years, F. W. Wallace wrote: "In the quiet coves and creeks of all four Provinces, vessels were being constructed almost in the forests. Little in the way of plant was required. A saw-mill, a good blacksmith outfit, and a gang of men handy with axe, adze, and auger, and a foreman shipwright formed the basis of a yard." In Europe ships were usually built of oak or teak, but Canadian oak was not durable. Tamarak was a favorite material, but pine and later spruce were also much used. Hulls of these woods were not supposed to last but many of them did, and a few sailed for half a century.

Many ships were built to carry timber and sometimes dried fish to market in England. Frequently they made only a single voyage and were sold at the end of it. At first many of them were crudely built, but later the best Canadian ships compared well with those from famous yards abroad. Shipbuilding suddenly became a booming industry in 1849, when the gold rush to California created an urgent demand for ships. The Australian gold rush in 1851 and the outbreak of the Crimean War increased it further. In 1853 some 80 ships of between 1,000 and 2,000 tons were launched in the four provinces, most of them for sale abroad.

A few of the ships built at this time have a place in maritime history. The *Marco Polo*, built at Saint John in 1851, was sold in Liverpool, refitted for the Australian emigrant trade, and in 1852 completed a round trip to Melbourne in the remarkable time of 5 months, 21 days. Some hailed her as the fastest ship afloat. The *White Star*, of 2,339 tons, the largest Canadian-built ship of the time, sailed in the Australian trade for the White Star Line.

Most of the ships built for sale came from yards in New Brunswick and Quebec. Nova Scotia, by contrast, built ships for local owners who operated them themselves. Thus it came about that although fewer ships were built in Nova Scotia, many more were owned there. Many of the smaller towns—Yarmouth, for example—became the home ports of substantial fleets. Figures are available for the year 1875 and these show that there were then 2,787 vessels on the Nova Scotia register totalling 480,000

tons, while 1,150 vessels of 295,000 tons were registered in New Brunswick, and 1,840 of 219,000 tons in Quebec. Canada was rapidly gaining stature as a mercantile power; by 1878, with 7,196 vessels of 1,333,015 tons on the register, she would rank fourth among the ship-owning nations of the world.

Arctic Exploration: 1818-1869

The half century before Confederation was a classic period in Arctic exploration. When it began, the mouth of the Coppermine River, discovered by Samuel Hearne in 1772, and the mouth of the Mackenzie, discovered by Alexander Mackenzie in 1789, were still the only known points on the northern coast of Canada west of Hudson Bay. By 1867 the whole of the coast and a good many of the Arctic islands had been added to the map of North America.

When the Napoleonic Wars ended, Britain found herself with a plethora of ships and men, and she was ready to devote a few of them to the age-long search for a Northwest Passage. In 1818 Captain John Ross was sent with two vessels to check the accuracy of Baffin's explorations of two centuries before. Ross vindicated Baffin and in the process explored the eastern coast of Baffin Island, and most of both shores of Baffin Bay, as far north as the narrows at Smith Sound.

The following summer Lieut. W. E. Parry, who had been second-in-command of the Ross expedition, left on a memorable two-year voyage in which he entered Lancaster Sound and explored much of what is now called Parry Channel, as far west as Melville Island. On a second expedition, in 1821-23, Parry traced most of the western coast of Foxe Basin, north of Hudson Bay. His discoveries on a third voyage, in 1824-25, were relatively minor, and added little to the map except part of the coast of Somerset Island.

Twenty years were to pass before the British Government sponsored another expedition by sea, but in 1829 Ross led a privately financed venture to the Arctic. Picking up more or less where Parry had stopped in 1825, he travelled south, down the east coast of the Boothia Peninsula. In the following years land parties explored part of the west coast and also crossed over to King William Island. Ross spent no less than four winters in the Arctic, and his expedition is notable on two other counts: he sailed in the first steam-driven vessel to visit the Arctic, the paddle steamer *Victoria*, which was a failure and was abandoned in 1832; and his nephew and second-in-command, James Clark Ross, discovered the magnetic pole, which in 1831 was located on the Boothia Peninsula.

Meanwhile expeditions that had approached the Arctic by land had added greatly to knowledge of the coastline. Lieut. John Franklin (later Sir John), having wintered on Great Bear Lake, reached the mouth of the Coppermine River in July 1821. From there he traced the coast eastward as far as

Turnagain Point, on the Kent Peninsula, and also explored Bathurst Inlet. It was Franklin who discovered that Hearne had made a mistake in his calculations in 1772, and had placed the mouth of the Coppermine much further north than it actually is.

In 1825-27 Franklin was back in the Arctic, this time following in the footsteps of Alexander Mackenzie. In the summer of 1826 he reached the mouth of the Mackenzie River, where his expedition divided to explore the coast to the east and the west. Dr. John Richardson led the eastbound party, which followed the Arctic shore from the Mackenzie to the Coppermine. Franklin travelled westward, where he hoped to meet a party from H.M.S. *Blossom*, which had entered the Arctic through Bering Strait. As it turned out, the two did not come within 160 miles of one another. Franklin had to turn back at Return Reef, within sight of Beechey Point, and the men from the *Blossom* went only as far as Point Barrow. But a vast stretch of the northern coast had been filled in, and the unknown sections were shrinking rapidly.

Anxiety about Ross, who had not been heard from in three years, resulted in another overland expedition in 1833-35 led by Lieut. George Back, who had accompanied Franklin to both the Coppermine and the Mackenzie. In 1834 he heard that Ross was safe, but he pressed on and explored the Great Fish River (the Back River of today) and the Chantrey Inlet, into which it empties.

The Hudson's Bay Company next enters the picture. In the years 1836-39 it sponsored two expeditions under Chief Factor Peter Warren Dease and Thomas Simpson, a cousin of Sir George Simpson. Dease was the senior of the two, but it was Simpson who did much of the actual exploring. In 1836 he travelled from Return Reef to Point Barrow, thus closing the 160-mile gap in the western Arctic coastline that Franklin had been compelled to leave unexplored. In 1838 Dease and Simpson were at the mouth of the Coppermine, bent on extending Franklin's survey eastward. This they did in the summers of 1838 and 1839, when they followed the coast to a point beyond Chantrey Inlet, and on the return journey explored parts of the south coasts of King William Island and Victoria Island.

In 1846-47 the Company sent a new and notable figure, Dr. John Rae, to the Arctic to resume the coastal survey. Rae's approach was from the east, through Repulse Bay, and then overland to Committee Bay and the Gulf of Boothia. He explored their western shores as far as Lord Mayor Bay, which linked up his survey with that made by Ross in 1829-33, and on the eastern coasts he went almost as far as Fury and Hecla Strait.

It is one of the ironies of Arctic history that, all unknown to Rae, the doomed ships of Sir John Franklin's celebrated expedition were lying icebound on one side of the Boothia Peninsula while he explored the other. When Rae was at Lord Mayor Bay in April 1847, the two were only about 150 miles apart.

Public Archives of Canada

The "Victoria" in the Arctic

In 1845 the British Government had decided once more to send an expedition by sea to search for the Northwest Passage. Franklin was placed in command, and his two ships, *Erebus* and *Terror,* were provisioned for a three-year voyage. They were last seen by a whaler on the coast of Greenland, but interviews with Eskimos and the discovery of relics, skeletons and one message gave a fairly clear outline of the expedition's misfortunes. The ships entered Lancaster Sound, and Franklin first sailed north into Wellington Channel. On the way back he circumnavigated Cornwallis Island and then wintered on Beechey Island. In 1846 he sailed westward through Barrow Strait and then turned south into Peel Sound. Franklin's hopes must have been high as he navigated the Sound and its continuation, Franklin Strait, because he was convinced that if he could reach the northern coastline, much of which he had himself explored, he would be able to sail westward to Bering Strait. But just north of King William Island, on what Franklin hoped would be the last lap of the voyage southward, his ships were caught in ice from which they were never extricated.

Tragedy struck in 1847: the ships remained immovable; disease seems to have broken out; Franklin himself died in June. Captain Francis Crozier succeeded to the command. As supplies dwindled, sickness increased and the ships remained fast. Crozier concluded that the only hope lay in abandoning them and trying to reach a Hudson's Bay post overland. It was a desperate venture, as the nearest post was 850 miles away, and all the 105 men who left the ships in April 1848 must have perished within a few months. Skeletons and relics have been found at various places along the west coast of King William Island, while others found at Starvation Cove, on the Adelaide Peninsula, show that some of the men reached the mainland. As for the ships, one seems to have sunk in Victoria Strait, and the other apparently was driven ashore, where it was picked to pieces by the Eskimos and demolished by ice.

Franklin's expedition is important chiefly because of the major discoveries made by the large number of rescue parties that were organized. Over a period of a dozen years sixteen expeditions under-

Public Archives of Canada

Hudson's Bay Company

explorers, and added new ones, notably Richardson, Rae, Ross, Austin, Kellett, M'Clure, Collinson and M'Clintock. The Admiralty's most imposing expedition was commanded by Captain Sir Edward Belcher, but his fame is somewhat marred by the premature abandonment of his four ships, in spite of the protests of his subordinates. One of them, the *Resolute*, later floated free of the ice, was reconditioned by the United States Navy, and courteously returned to Britain.

Canada's Five Capitals: 1841–1865

A curious feature of the United Province of Canada was the peregrinations of its capital. In 1841 Kingston was selected as the seat of government and a recently built hospital was hastily remodeled to accommodate parliament and departmental offices. However, in 1843 it was decided to move the capital to Montreal, where an old market building was refurbished to serve as a parliament house. This second home was burned in 1849 by a mob protesting the passing of the Rebellion Losses Bill, whereupon the capital moved to Toronto. There the government occupied the old parliament buildings of Upper Canada, which had been used in recent years as a lunatic asylum. But once again this was only a temporary measure, as it had been decided that when the life of the current parliament ended the government would migrate to Quebec. Thither it went in 1851. Even then no final decision had been taken regarding the location of the capital; until the matter was settled, the seat of government was to alternate between Quebec and Toronto. This it did for the next 15 years. In 1855 it returned to Toronto; in 1859 it moved back to Quebec.

By this time the absurdity of the situation was very apparent; the expense and dislocation caused by the transfer of the whole administration and civil service from one city to another every few years were too great to be tolerated much longer. As there seemed to be no hope of agreement on a site, the problem was referred to Queen Victoria, who, in 1857, decided in favour of Ottawa. The choice had some military merit; quite as important, it avoided pleasing one of the larger cities at the cost of mortally offending the others contending for the honour.

In Ottawa, therefore, the corner-stone of fine new parliament buildings was laid in 1860 by the Prince of Wales (later King Edward VII), and to them the government moved in the autumn of 1865.

Sad relics of the Franklin expedition

Chief Trader Paddy Gibson, of the Hudson's Bay Company, an authority on Franklin, found these skulls on King William Island as recently as 1931.

Sir John Franklin, R.N., the Arctic explorer (upper left)

took the search by sea and five by land. As the official view was that Franklin had most likely turned to the north rather than the south, long searches were carried out that added the coastlines of many of the larger islands to the map of the Arctic. But Lady Franklin held the view that Sir John had turned south, and it was the expeditions by land and those that she herself and her associates financed that finally ascertained Franklin's fate. In 1853 Dr. John Rae met Eskimos who gave him the first news of the disaster, and in 1855 the only surviving written record was found at Victory Point, on King William Island. Relics and skeletons have been found through the years, some as recently as the 1930s.

The accompanying map indicates in summary form the immense contribution made to knowledge of the Arctic by these expeditions. Among them was one conducted by the United States Navy in 1850-51 —the first American expedition to the Arctic. On the British side, the search had given increased lustre to many names already on the roster of Arctic

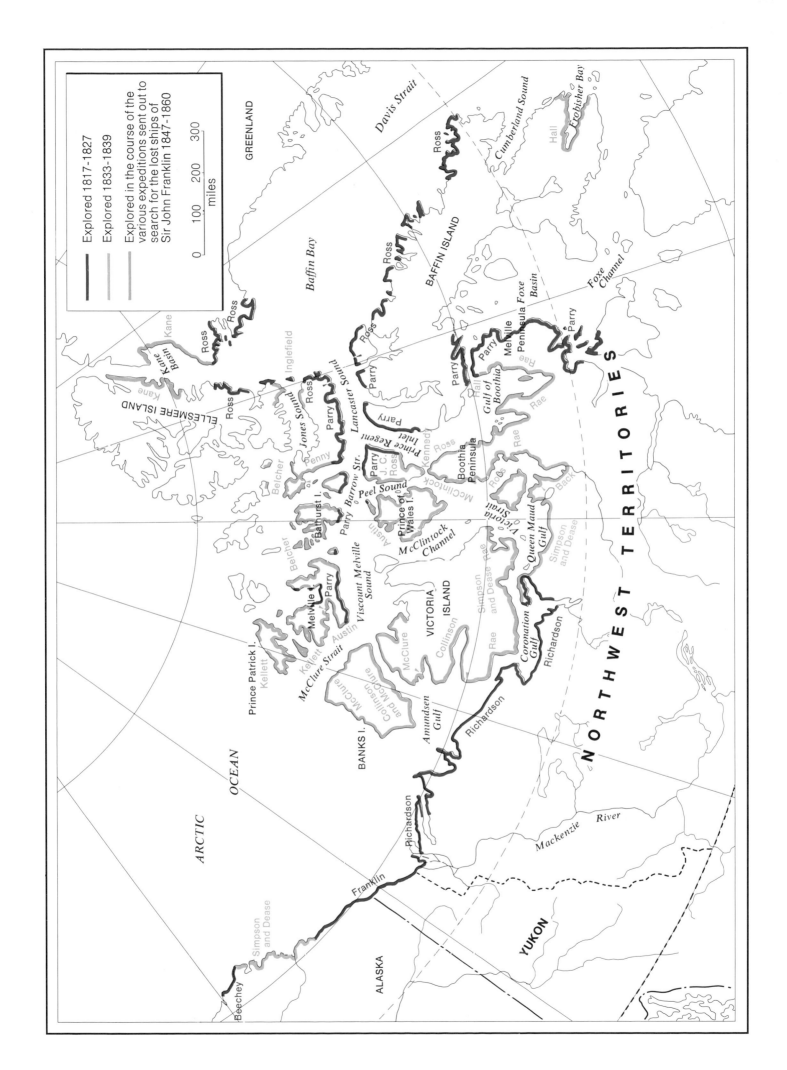

Arctic Exploration Before Confederation

Canada's Five Capitals   Quebec

These lithographs of Quebec, Montreal, Kingston, Toronto *and* Ottawa — *the five cities that were at one time or another the seat of government in Canada between 1841 and 1866 — were prepared about 1852 by Edwin Whitefield.*

Montreal

Kingston

Toronto

From a revised plate showing the first balloon   Ottawa
ascension over the capital, in 1858.

Part IV
THE FIRST HALF CENTURY OF CONFEDERATION 1867-1919

The Great Seals of Canada, Edward VII and George V

CHAPTER 12

Confederation

The Threat from the South

THE absorption of the North West Company by the Hudson's Bay Company in 1821 had the effect of isolating the West. The Company conducted its business through Hudson Bay, and the old links of the fur trade with Montreal were broken. The inhospitable wilderness north and west of Lake Superior formed a barrier that few ventured to cross.

Meanwhile settlers were pouring westward in the northern United States. Wisconsin was organized as a territory in 1836; by 1847 it contained 200,000 people, and in 1848 it became a full-fledged state. It was obvious that Minnesota would follow the same road: created a territory in 1849, it attained statehood in 1858. By that time St. Paul had become a considerable community with a population of nearly 10,000.

These were years in which a wave of expansionism swept the United States; "Manifest Destiny" (a phrase coined by a journalist in 1845) was in the air. Texas had been admitted to the union that year, the Oregon country was added in 1846; war with Mexico in 1846-48 added the whole area of the southwestern United States. It is not surprising that land-seeking Americans and immigrants began to cast their eyes to the north as well as to the west.

What they saw between Lake Superior and the Rockies was a vast open space, dotted with Hudson's Bay posts, but with only one settlement of any consequence—the Red River colony founded by Lord Selkirk. This had doubled in size after the 1821 union, as the merger had been followed by staff reductions, and many of the men preferred to remain in the West. By 1832 the population was 2,700; it had passed 5,000 by 1843 and was nearly 6,700 in 1855.

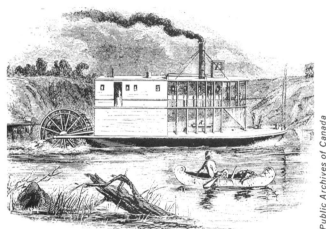

Public Archives of Canada

The pioneer steamer on the Red River

This was still not a large settlement, but it was larger than the Hudson's Bay Company could control effectively, especially when contacts began to build up with St. Paul and American markets to the south. In 1849 the Company was compelled to concede freedom of trade to the settlers, even in furs, in which it still held a legal monopoly. A well-travelled cart trail was soon established between Red River and St. Paul, and in 1859 St. Paul merchants financed the construction of the steamer *Anson Northrup* and placed her in service on the river to improve transportation to and from the settlement.

Concern about the future of the West had been growing in Canada, and in 1857 two official expeditions set out to explore it and judge its suitability for settlement. One of them was a Canadian party headed by Henry Youle Hind, of Toronto; the other was the better known Palliser expedition, sent out by the British Government with Captain John Palliser in command. In 1857-58 the parties crossed and recrossed the West. Their conclusion was that the valleys of the Red and Saskatchewan

Red River steamer ''Dakota''
Photographed at Dufferin, just north of the inter-national boundary. She and others like her pro-vided Red River's chief summertime link with the outside world until the coming of the railway.

Public Archives of Canada

The Red River cart

For many years these simple wooden carts, often drawn by oxen, were the principal means of moving freight both between Winnipeg and St. Paul and westward to Edmonton. By the time this photograph was taken in 1883 on Main Street, in Winnipeg, they were being superseded rapidly by river steamers and railways.

Rivers formed a vast fertile crescent that was well suited for agriculture. South of it lay what became known as "Palliser's Triangle"—today the southern part of Alberta and Saskatchewan—which Palliser felt was too dry and treeless for settlement. On the vital question of communications with Canada, Hind believed that travel routes between Lake Superior and Red River were feasible. Palliser, on the other hand, was convinced that the costs of construction would be prohibitive. Naturally the people in St. Paul welcomed the latter view and held to it tenaciously for many years. When the Canadian Pacific Railway was under construction, James J. Hill, Canadian-born but with railway interests centred in St. Paul, left the C.P.R. directorate because it insisted on building an all-Canadian line north of Lake Superior and thence westward to Red River. Hill wanted the line to cross into the United States at Sault Ste. Marie and be routed to the West

via St. Paul—a scheme that would have placed control of the line in American hands.

The outbreak of the Civil War in 1861 soon caused acute anxiety in British North America. The *Trent* incident in November brought Great Britain and the United States to the brink of hostilities. As the war progressed, the North built up the largest military forces that had ever been assembled, and when a Northern victory was clearly in prospect, Canadians began to wonder if that army, responding to the expansionist spirit, would turn presently and overwhelm them. The activities of Confederates in Canada, especially when they staged a border raid on St. Albans, Vermont, in October 1864, were rightly resented by the Americans. There was talk of cancelling the Reciprocity Treaty of 1854, and of ending the valuable privilege under which goods bound to or from Canada could cross the United States in bond.

Fortunately cool heads prevailed, and when the Civil War ended in 1865 the Northern troops were able to fulfil their greatest desire, which was to go home. But the United States took no special pains to curb the activities of the Fenian Brotherhood, a militant pro-Irish anti-British organization that had grown up in recent years. In 1866 and the following seven years threats and incidents and armed raids succeeded one another, and Canada had an unpleasant sense of insecurity. In the new capital city of

Ottawa, 500 British regular troops were housed in barracks not far from Parliament Hill from 1866 until 1870 to safeguard the government.

This combination of events exercised a profound influence on political developments in the 1860s. The individual colonies in British North America all at once felt their weakness and isolation. If they were to control their own future, and that of the great open spaces that lay to the west, it was clear that they must be able to speak with a stronger and more united voice. The military threat that was latent in the Civil War thus became a powerful force in support of the movement for Confederation.

Political Problems and Confederation

Confederation has been called the child of political deadlock, and to a considerable extent this was true. The system of government established in the United Province of Canada in 1841 got off to a reasonably good start, but in little more than a dozen years it was grinding to a halt.

The reluctance of the Colonial Office to grant responsible government made the inauguration of the new constitution difficult. Matters were complicated by the illness and death of three successive Governors-General. Lord Sydenham managed to form a ministry which though not responsible, was able to work with a majority in the Assembly, but he died within a few months. In 1842 Sir Charles Bagot offered places in the ministry to Louis Lafontaine and Robert Baldwin, the leading French and English Reformers, but they resigned late in 1843 owing to differences with Bagot's much more authoritarian successor, Sir Charles Metcalfe. It was the Earl of Elgin, able and liberal-minded, who became Governor-General in January 1847, who finally conceded responsible government. After an election at the end of the year the ministry was defeated in the Assembly, and in March 1848—six weeks after the first responsible ministry had taken office in Nova Scotia—Lord Elgin invited Baldwin and Lafontaine to form the new executive council. A year later he emphasized the concession by signing the Rebellion

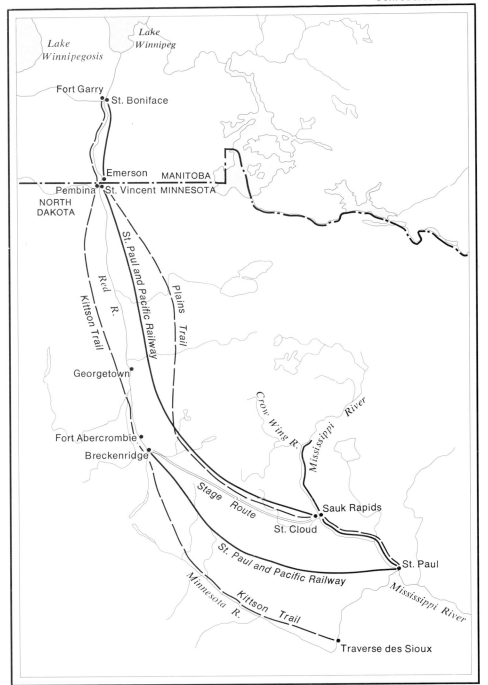

Travel Routes Between Fort Garry and St. Paul

Better transportation between Red River and St. Paul was a great convenience to the settler, but a major worry to Canadians. The expansionist spirit was strong in Minnesota, where many felt that the United States should push northward. In the 1840s the two chief routes from St. Paul to Fort Garry were the Kittson Trail (named after Norman Kittson, long a dominating figure in Red River transportation) and the Plains Trail. Travel over either was an ordeal, but the Plains Trail was the shorter and easier of the two.

The first steamer on the Red River sailed from Fort Abercrombie to Fort Garry and back in 1859.

Steamers also began to run on the Mississippi north of St. Paul, and presently a stage route followed a rough and ready road between the Mississippi and Red Rivers.

The St. Paul & Pacific Railway began building north and west from St. Paul in the 1860s, but its line to the Manitoba border was not completed until 1879. There it connected with the Pembina Branch Line of the future C.P.R., which ran from St. Boniface (across the Red River from Fort Garry and Winnipeg) to the border. These lines gave the Red River country rail communication with Eastern Canada, but only through the United States. An all-Canadian route to the East, which finally ended the annexationist threat, was not completed until 1885.

155

Public Archives of Canada

Sir Leonard Tilley (at left)
A Topley photograph taken in 1868.

Losses Bill, which had passed the House but had aroused such anger in some quarters that a mob burned the Parliament Buildings in Montreal and stoned Elgin in his carriage as he drove back to his residence.

Gradually the defects of the constitution became apparent. It provided for equal representation in the Assembly from Canada East and Canada West, a provision intended to keep the French-Canadians in a subordinate position and in time bring about their assimilation. It soon became clear that this expectation was illusory; the French and Roman Catholic majority in Canada East (Quebec) were as solidly entrenched as the English and Protestant majority in Canada West. This made it necessary for each ministry to have two co-equal heads, one representing each of the two sections of the United Province. Later, matters were complicated further by the doctrine of the "double majority"—the contention that no measure should be considered as having passed the House unless it had been approved by a majority of the members from each of the two parts of the Province.

Party lines were still loose, and for some years members may be said to have adhered to groups rather than to broadly based parties. Instability was the result; in the decade 1854-1864 there were ten administrations. In some instances the changes in personnel were relatively small, and one is reminded of the governments of the Third Republic in France.

By degrees a more substantial group or party began to take form, thanks in great part to John A.

Macdonald, a born politician who was first elected in 1844 and first served in a cabinet in 1847. The coalition he helped coax into existence became the nucleus of the Conservative Party, and it is significant that, with one brief interregnum, he served continuously in one ministry or another from 1854 to 1862. This was due in large part to an alliance he had formed with George Etienne Cartier, who had a substantial following in Canada East. The interregnum, which came in 1858, was occasioned by a crisis that had the important result of adding a third major figure to the succeeding Cartier-Macdonald ministry—Alexander Tilloch Galt. Galt was convinced that a union embracing all the British North American colonies had become essential, and with his adherence this became the policy of the government.

In the succeeding years George Brown, the formidable editor of the Toronto *Globe,* did much to increase the following of the Reformers, or Liberals, and he himself had been elected to the Assembly in 1851. Brown was restive under the existing constitution, which he felt carried the threat of French and Catholic domination and was unfair to Canada West, which had only the same number of members in the Assembly as Canada East, although its population had become substantially higher; he looked to a larger union as a solution to these problems.

Macdonald and Brown had long been bitter political opponents, but when a deadlock developed in the Assembly in 1864, they agreed to join forces in a new ministry—known to history as the "Great Coalition"—in which Cartier and Galt would be included, and whose purpose would be the achievement of Confederation.

Public Archives of Canada

Several forces were working towards this end. The American Civil War was posing a military threat; fear was growing that if Canada did not move quickly to secure the West, it would soon be absorbed into the United States. The British Government favoured the plan, but felt that the first step should be a union of the Maritime Provinces. With this in view, it had prompted the convening of a conference of the three provinces in Charlottetown in September 1864. Macdonald and his colleagues seized the occasion, invited themselves to the conference, and outlined their alternative proposal for a wider union to embrace all the colonies. The result was a second and larger conference at Quebec in October at which Canada, Nova Scotia, New Brunswick, Prince Edward Island and Newfoundland were all represented, and at which the essential features of the proposed federation were agreed upon in considerable detail.

There were still hurdles to surmount. Prince Edward Island and Newfoundland dropped out of the scheme. S. L. Tilley, the Premier of New Brunswick, was defeated in a general election by oppo-

nents who opposed Confederation, but this verdict was reversed before irreparable damage was done. Charles Tupper, Premier of Nova Scotia, was able to hold the line in a province that was proudly independent and not overly enthusiastic about sinking its identity in a larger entity. The four essential parts of the new federation—the two Canadas, Nova Scotia and New Brunswick—were thus all available when a delegation went to London late in 1866 to discuss the necessary legislation with the British Government. The British North America Act, introduced in the House of Lords in February 1867, received the Royal Assent on March 29, and came into effect by proclamation on July 1.

Canada in the modern sense had come into being.

Sir George Etienne Cartier (upper right)

The Charlottetown Conference (shown below)

The delegates gathered on the steps of Government House, in Charlottetown, in September 1864. Macdonald is in the middle, seated on the steps.

Sir John A. Macdonald
From a photograph taken in 1868.

First page of Macdonald's draft of the B.N.A. Act.

Be it therefore enacted &c

Union 1   It shall be lawful for Her Majesty with the advice of Her Privy Council to declare, (or to authorize the Governor General of British North America to declare) by Proclamation that the said Provinces of Canada, Nova Scotia and New Brunswick upon from and after a certain day in such Proclamation to be appointed, which day shall be within ____ Calendar months next after the passing of this Act. shall form and be one United ____ under the name of "The Kingdom of Canada" and henceforth the said Provinces shall constitute and be one Kingdom under the name aforesaid upon, from and after the day so appointed as aforesaid. —

2y Title — his Provisions should be omitted —

15 Months in Union act of 1840. — 2y.

Province Dependency Colony Dominion Vice Royalty Kingdom -

Executive 3
4 Resn

The Executive Government of the said Kingdom of Canada is and shall be Vested in Her Majesty the Queen her Heirs and successors. —

Command of Naval & Military Force

The Queen is and shall be Commander in Chief of the

Canada at Confederation

The Dominion that came into existence in 1867 consisted of four provinces—Ontario, Quebec, New Brunswick and Nova Scotia. The boundaries of the latter two were the same as they are now, but Ontario and Quebec extended northward only as far as the southern limit of Rupert's Land. The total area of the four was 350,188 square miles—less than a tenth of that of the Canada of today.

In Nova Scotia and New Brunswick provincial governments succeeded the old colonial regimes in Halifax and Fredericton. The Dominion Government took over the new Parliament Buildings in Ottawa; Toronto and Quebec became the capitals of Ontario and Quebec, which in terms of territory were slightly revised versions of Canada West (Upper Canada) and Canada East (Lower Canada).

There were still only a few railways in the Maritimes—indeed, one of the chief attractions of Confederation there had been the hope that the new federation would be able to arrange for the building of many more, including through lines to Quebec and Montreal. In Ontario and Quebec the rails extended from Rivière du Loup on the east to Windsor and Sarnia in the west, with branch lines running north to many points, including Ottawa, Peterborough, Collingwood and Goderich. Roads—at least of a sort—linked all the settlements of any size. The first complete series of St. Lawrence–Great Lakes canals was in operation, and vessels of modest size could travel from Lake Superior to the lower river. A network of telegraph lines provided quick communication, and after the first successful transatlantic cable was laid to Newfoundland in 1866, both Newfoundland itself and Europe were linked up with the lines in Canada. The new and enlarged Canada thus had the first beginnings of a modern system of transportation and communication.

It was essentially a rural country, in which farming and lumbering were the chief industries. Wheat and timber were much the most important exports. Both had suffered when Britain adopted a free trade policy and repealed the Corn Laws and ended the old system of preferences in 1846; but trade had revived when new markets were found in the United States. Shipping and shipbuilding were flourishing in Nova Scotia, but this prosperity was tied to wood and wind, and would soon begin to decline in the face of competition from larger and faster iron and steel vessels propelled by steam engines.

The total population in 1867 was about 3,500,000. By 1871, when the first census of the Dominion was taken, it had risen to 3,689,000. The racial background of the people is interesting. Those of French descent were the largest single group and numbered 1,083,000. The Irish ranked second, with a total of 846,000. There were 706,000 English and 550,000 Scots. (Irish, English and Scots between

them totalled 2,120,000.) Fifth place was held by those of German descent, 202,000 in number.

Communication would obviously be a pressing problem, as a railway between Quebec and the Maritimes was clearly a prime necessity. But the 1871 census had revealed a state of affairs that made it equally essential that Canada should look to the West. Population had increased by 33 percent in the decade 1851-61, but by only 14 percent between 1861 and 1871—this in spite of a sharp increase in immigration. It was evident that people were leaving Canada as well as entering it, and the emigrants included many native sons. The United States census of 1870 had shown that even at that early date the population there included nearly half a million native-born Canadians.

Climate may have accounted for some of this migration; the opportunities offered by a much bigger and more aggressive country doubtless attracted many then, as they do now. But the basic cause was a shortage of land. Almost everywhere in Ontario and Quebec settlement was pressing hard on the southern fringe of the Laurentian Shield, which in most instances marked the limit of good agricultural land. Immigrants and native sons alike could find none to settle upon and of necessity they looked elsewhere. Nor had Canada as yet any large-scale industrial centres where factories might offer alternative employment; in 1871 there were only 21 towns and cities in the whole country with a population of over 5,000. It was against this background that French-Canadians began to move in substantial numbers from Quebec to the factory towns in New England, and immigrants and native sons seeking land left Ontario by the thousands and moved on to the midwestern United States.

The answer to this problem would be for Canada to open up a hinterland of her own that could become a part of the Dominion and tributary to the original provinces that formed it. Rupert's Land would somehow have to be released from the clutches of the Hudson's Bay Company and then linked to Canada by a railway. The cost of such a railway would be enormous, especially as it was becoming certain that it would have to be extended right through to the Pacific Coast. British Columbia was in economic difficulties owing to the sharp decline in gold production; if she were not bolstered up reasonably promptly there was grave danger that she would gravitate to the United States. If Canada were ever to extend from ocean to ocean, as Sir John A. Macdonald and many others were anxious that she should, it was evident that there was no time to lose. The first priorities for the first years of Confederation were clear.

The Expansion of Confederation: 1867-1873

Little time was lost in opening negotiations for the acquisition of Rupert's Land. The chief terms of the

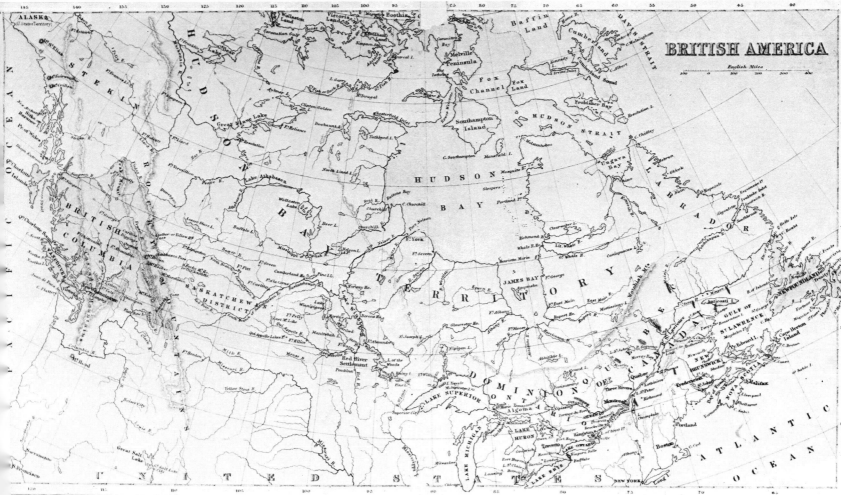

Canada in 1867

agreement concluded were: (1) that Canada would pay the Hudson's Bay Company the sum of £300,000; (2) that the Company would surrender its authority and proprietary rights to the British Government, which within a month would transfer Rupert's Land to Canada; and (3) that the Company would be entitled to a total of 50,000 acres contiguous to its trading posts, and to one-twentieth of the fertile lands in the area between Lake Winnipeg and the Rocky Mountains and south of the Saskatchewan River. Over the years this latter term gave the Company a little more than 6,600,000 acres of land.

The actual transfer was scheduled originally for December 1869, but by that date grave complications had arisen that necessitated postponement.

Neither Macdonald nor Cartier seems to have had any realization that Rupert's Land included not only vast wide-open spaces, but a long-settled community of substantial size. In 1835 the Red River settlement already had a population of 3,649; this had grown to 6,691 by 1855 and the first census of Manitoba, taken in 1870, would show a population of 11,903. Of this total nearly 10,000 were of mixed blood, more than half of them French-speaking Métis and most of them Roman Catholics.

The demand that Canada should take over the West centred in Ontario, and the people in Red River feared that they would be submerged in a sudden influx of English-speaking Protestants who would set up a new order on their own terms. These fears were fanned by a small but noisy and confident local "Canadian" party headed by Dr. J. C. Schultz. The Métis realized that their old semi-nomadic existence was doomed, but this made them all the more anxious to see that their lands, language and religion were safeguarded when Rupert's Land became part of Canada. They found a leader in Louis Riel, whose father had been a Métis leader before him, and who had recently returned to Red River after attending college in Montreal and spending some time in Minnesota.

Incredibly, neither the Hudson's Bay Company nor the British or Canadian governments took any steps to let the people in Red River know what was planned for them, and against this background of uncertainty—and before any formal transfer to Canada—two things happened that the Métis found profoundly disturbing. In August 1869 Col. J. S. Dennis arrived with a small staff to begin a land survey. He had no intention of disturbing any existing rights or properties, but unaware at first of local tensions, he had made the fatal mistake of associating with Schultz. Late in September the Hon. William McDougall—an ardent Ontario expansionist—was appointed Lieutenant-Governor, and was soon known to be on the way to Red River.

161

Public Archives of Canada

Riel decided that the time had come to act. The Métis were much concerned about their lands; Riel played upon this fear to rally them to his support. On October 11, one of his lieutenants forced one of the survey parties to suspend work; on the last day of the month McDougall, coming from Minnesota, was turned back at the border; on November 2, Riel seized Fort Garry, and in December a provisional government was set up, of which Riel became president. Later an elected convention came into being.

The whole complicated story cannot be told here; only the two chief points can be noted. The first was constructive. Riel and the convention drafted a bill of rights which, after a number of revisions, became in large part the basis of the Manitoba Act, passed in May 1870, which created the Province of Manitoba. The second was an act of violence—an appalling blunder that wrecked Riel's career and damned him forever in the eyes of English Canada. Métis forces had captured and confined various "Canadians" from time to time, including one Thomas Scott of Perth, Ontario. Scott proved to be a specially troublesome prisoner; it is probable that he enraged his captors by showing an open contempt for those of mixed blood. In any event, after the most summary of trials, he was executed on March 4, 1870.

Riel's purpose had been to resist, not to rebel; he simply opposed a transfer of Red River to Canada that took no account of the special interests of its inhabitants. The Manitoba Act gave him virtually everything he had wanted. But a military expedition to Red River had been in preparation since Riel had seized power; Scott's murder—as Ontario considered it to be—caused such indignation that it could not be cancelled. A force under Col. Garnet Wolseley, consisting of British Army regulars and two battalions of militia, one from Ontario and the other from Quebec, travelled laboriously westward over the old fur-trade canoe route and reached Fort Garry on August 24. Until it

The execution of Thomas Scott at Fort Garry
The Fathers of Confederation

The original of the familiar painting of the Fathers by Robert Harris was destroyed when the old centre block of the Parliament Buildings was burned in 1916. As its contribution to the celebration of the Centenary of Confederation, the Confederation Life Association commissioned this new version of the picture by Rex Woods and presented it to the Government of Canada.

The new painting varies considerably in detail from the old. Harris painted the original picture in 1883, and he tended to paint the surviving Fathers as he knew them at that time, rather than as they appeared in earlier days. Woods has sought to show the Fathers as nearly as possible as they were in 1867.

was close at hand, Riel seems not to have realized the position in which Scott's death had placed him; he fled to the United States only hours before Wolseley arrived.

In September a new Lieutenant-Governor, Adams G. Archibald, a quiet, capable Nova Scotian, set about organizing the government in the new Province of Manitoba—the famous "postage stamp," consisting of a modest little rectangle less than 13,000 square miles in extent. The rest of Rupert's Land formed a major part of the new Northwest Territories, under the direct control of the Government of Canada. They included the whole of the northern mainland to which Britain had title, and part of Baffin Island. To these the rest of the Arctic islands were added by a further transfer from Britain in 1880.

The acquisition of Rupert's Land extended Canada to the Rocky Mountains; beyond lay British Columbia, the last lap in the race to the Pacific. Anxiety about her future had been increased in the spring of 1867 when the United States purchased Alaska from Russia. An all-American Pacific Coast

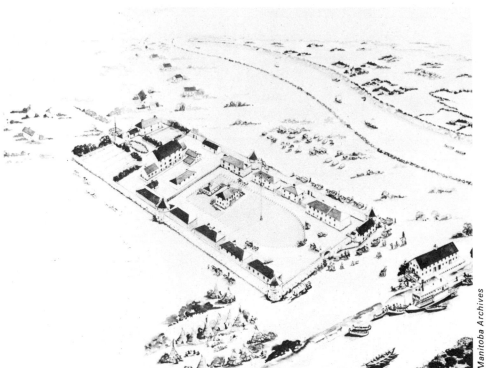

Fort Garry in 1867

A perspective drawing of the fort and its surroundings, showing the first beginnings of Winnipeg. The steamer Anson Northrup, *by this time renamed* Pioneer, *is shown at the wharf.*

Manitoba Archives

Canada in 1873

Louis Riel

From a photograph believed to have been taken a few years before the events of 1869-70 in Red River.

Joseph W. Trutch

From a Topley photograph taken in Ottawa in June of 1870, when Trutch and two other delegates from British Columbia were negotiating the terms of union between the colony and Canada. Trutch was the first Lieutenant-Governor of British Columbia, and inaugurated responsible government there, as this had not been granted previous to Confederation. He was knighted in 1889.

seemed a distinct possibility. The remoteness of Canada made many people wonder if this might not be a good thing. British Columbia was in dire straits economically because of the decline in gold production; she badly needed more population and new markets, and Canada seemed unable to provide either.

It is not surprising that an annexation movement sprang up; a petition was actually sent to the President of the United States late in 1869. But the agitation was supported mostly by foreigners, and it came too late to have much hope of success. By 1869 Canada was about to become the neighbour to the east, and the Colonial Office had stepped into the picture by appointing an able new governor, Anthony Musgrave, with instructions to bring British Columbia into Confederation. In May 1870 a delegation left Victoria for Ottawa to discuss terms. They had a wagon road in mind as one requirement; to their surprise they were offered a railroad. "They do not consider that they can hold the country without it," J. S. Helmcken, one of the delegates, wrote in his diary. "They agreed that a railway was necessary to Red River, ours . . . would only be an extension . . . " This provision disposed effectively of the bogey of remoteness, and the other terms were agreed upon without much difficulty. After the necessary ratifications had been secured in Ottawa and Victoria, British Columbia became the sixth province of the Dominion on July 20, 1871. With her adhesion, Macdonald's ambition was fulfilled; Canada extended from sea to sea.

In 1871 the white population of British Columbia was not much more than 10,000—a mere hand-

ful in a vast wilderness. Prince Edward Island by contrast, had 94,000 people, not far short of her present population. In 1867 the Islanders had preferred to keep their independence, but two matters finally moved them to seek outside help. The first was the age-old problem of absentee landlordism, dating back to the grants made in 1767. Many of the titles were still held abroad; they could be extinguished only by purchase, and the necessary funds were not available. The second problem was a railway, the contract for which had been awarded in a sudden burst of enthusiasm in 1870, but which threatened to become a heavy financial liability. Negotiations with Ottawa began in 1872 and were concluded the following spring, in time to permit Prince Edward Island to become the seventh province on July 1, 1873. The terms of entry were generous. Funds were provided to buy out the landlords; a debt allowance looked after the debts arising from the railway; Canada agreed to take over the railway itself, and in addition undertook to provide year-round service by steam vessels between the Island and the Mainland. Winter ice in Northumberland Strait was to make this last commitment difficult to fulfil; icebreakers capable of making the crossing in the worst conditions simply did not exist, and they were not to be available until 1913.

CHAPTER 13

Settlement of the West

Railways from Coast to Coast

CLAUSE 145 of the British North America Act declared with truth "that the Construction of the Intercolonial Railway" between Quebec and the Maritimes was "essential to the Consolidation of the Union"; without easy, rapid communication Confederation would not endure. The project had been discussed for a generation, but no way had been found to finance construction. The difficulty was that the line was unlikely to pay for a good many years to come. Canada and the Maritimes had few products to exchange, and Nova Scotia in particular was oriented towards the sea; the 1870s would be the golden age of her shipping and shipbuilding industries. The railroad was essential for political and military reasons, not for more immediate economic needs, and it was a loan from the British Government that made construction possible.

The only existing roads that would contribute to the Intercolonial were the Grand Trunk's line from Quebec to Rivière-du-Loup, the Nova Scotia Railway's line from Halifax to Truro and that of the European & North American Railway from Saint John to Moncton and Shediac. What was lacking was a through connecting line from Rivière-du-Loup to Moncton and Truro. By the route finally selected, the distance was almost exactly 500 miles.

That route was chosen in great part by the engineer-in-chief, Sandford Fleming, a Scot of outstanding ability who had been associated with railroading in Canada for over twenty years. The Intercolonial was government-owned, but politics interfered relatively little with the surveys for its route because much of the country it was to traverse was unoccupied; but it was otherwise when construction began. Fleming had to work under a Board of Railway Commissioners, and politics

William C. Van Horne

George Stephen took chief responsibility for the Canadian Pacific's political and financial problems; Van Horne was the driving personality behind actual management and construction. Stephen found the money and Van Horne built the railroad.

entered the picture at almost every turn. Fleming battled to defend his principles and standards with considerable success, and he was able to build a standard-gauge line with steel rails and many steel bridges instead of the broad-gauge line with iron rails and wooden bridges that was at one time in prospect. The whole line was ready for service in nine years and the first through train from Halifax arrived at Quebec on July 6, 1876.

By that time Fleming had been for five years the engineer in charge of surveys for the railway to the Pacific Coast that had been promised to British Columbia in the terms of union with Canada. Although this would be primarily a line to serve settlements in Red River and on the prairies, it had a political purpose of the highest importance as well. In 1864 the Northern Pacific Railway had been

Construction on the Intercolonial
This embankment, over 100 feet high, carried the railway over a deep ravine on the Nova Scotia section of the line.

Rock cut north of Lake Superior

It was conditions such as these that encouraged James J. Hill to think that the Canadian Government would have to abandon its all-Canadian route.

authorized by Congress and the Americans were confident that its construction would determine the fate of the Pacific Coast. "The opening by us first of a North Pacific Railroad," a Senate report declared in February 1869, "seals the destiny of British possessions west of the 91st meridian. Annexation will be but a question of time." Sir John Macdonald was well aware of this. "It is quite evident to me," he wrote in January 1870, " . . . that the United States

Government are resolved to do all they can short of war to get possession of the western territory, and we must take immediate and vigorous steps to counteract them. One of the first things to be done is to show unmistakably our resolve to build the Pacific Railway."

This was what lay back of the undertaking to build a railroad to British Columbia, and Sanford Fleming's survey crews began work the very day British Columbia became part of Canada. But actual construction was easier to plan than to carry out. The cost in relation to Canada's resources at the time would be enormous; the problem was how to carry out the project in a way the country could possibly afford. Undaunted, Macdonald negotiated

appalled by its cost, and he felt that construction should be postponed until the progress of settlement justified it; the country could make do with roads and rivers meanwhile. Fleming unconsciously aided this policy of delay by continuing a remarkable series of surveys over a huge area and through most of the passes in the Rocky Mountains; he seemed reluctant to call a halt and recommend a single route. The financial crash of 1873 and the depression that followed would have made it difficult for Mackenzie to do much, even if he had so wished. As a temporary expedient he resorted to construction under the direct supervision of his own Department of Public Works, and in August 1874 a first contract was let covering an 83-mile branch line in Manitoba from Selkirk to Pembina. The first locomotive for this branch, the famous *Countess of Dufferin,* was brought down the Red River to Winnipeg in October 1877.

A year later Macdonald was back in office and he at once tackled the railway problem, which had become a matter of great urgency. Owing to the long delays in construction British Columbia had been almost at the point of secession; quite as important, the Northern Pacific Railway, which had been halted by the depression, was about to resume construction and would certainly soon reach its Pacific terminus on Puget Sound.

In 1880 he at last found a syndicate that was willing to build the line. The leading members were George Stephen, President of the Bank of Montreal, R. B. Angus, and James J. Hill, of St. Paul. All three had already been active in the St. Paul & Pacific Railway, a highly profitable venture that linked St. Paul with Pembina and the branch C.P.R. line from Winnipeg. They soon recruited William Van Horne as general manager of the new Canadian Pacific Railway Company that was incorporated in February 1881. Hill, whose interests centred in St. Paul, dropped out when it became clear that Macdonald and Stephen were determined to build an all-Canadian line north of Lake Superior. Stephen, Angus and Van Horne became the triumvirate that pushed construction ahead, despite incredible physical and financial difficulties, and completed the line to Burrard Inlet in November 1885. Regular transcontinental train service began in 1886, and the Pacific terminus was established at the new city of Vancouver in 1887.

The terms of the contract provided for a cash subsidy of $25,000,000 and land grants totalling 25,000,000 acres. Far more money than the cash subsidy was required, and Macdonald and Stephen lived through many crises as Parliament became reluctant to provide further loans and guarantees, and the market became less interested in railway securities. Bankruptcy threatened for the last time only a matter of months before the completion of the line, but the immense undertaking was carried through successfully.

When the main line was opened in 1886 the capital and funded debt of the Canadian Pacific totalled over $96,000,000.

with a number of groups, notably a Canada Pacific Railway Company headed by Sir Hugh Allan, of Allan Line fame. But the same year it became known that Allan and associates had made very large contributions to Conservative campaign funds before the election of 1872, and the resulting "Pacific Scandal" caused the fall of the government. Macdonald's successor as Prime Minister was Alexander Mackenzie, who headed Canada's first Liberal ministry. There were those who said that Northern Pacific interests, anxious to block the construction of the Canadian Pacific had contributed substantially to Liberal campaign funds.

Certainly Mackenzie viewed the Pacific railway with little enthusiasm. A cautious Scot, he was

The first train in the Canadian West

Before the Canadian Pacific Railway Company was organized the Government of Canada built a "Pembina Branch" of the planned transcontinental, running from St. Boniface, south to the American border, where it connected to St. Paul. It was inaugurated in December 1878.

The first locomotive reaches Winnipeg
Loaded on a barge and pushed down the Red River by a sternwheeler, the historic Countess of Dufferin *arrived in Winnipeg in 1877. She now stands in a small park opposite the Canadian Pacific station in Winnipeg.*

Arrival of the first train in Vancouver

Hauled by lavishly decorated locomotive no. 374, this train arrived from Montreal on May 23, 1887, on the eve of Queen Victoria's birthday in her golden jubilee year. Trains had been running to Port Moody, further up Burrard Inlet, since the preceding July. Engine no. 374 is now preserved in Kitsilano Park, in Vancouver.

Law and Order in the West: The Mounted Police

There was little law and less law enforcement in the West in early days. In most places the fur traders would have been helpless in the face of a strong Indian attack, and there were enough instances in which a post was seized and its inhabitants were murdered to demonstrate the fact. But by degrees the traders established a tradition that usually protected them effectively. The Indians learned that even a lone white man represented something much stronger than himself—a power that would hunt them down and impose penalties for murder, thievery and destruction. And increasingly they were held in check by a further consideration—the traders were the only source of guns and goods that were soon virtually necessities of Indian life.

The need for law and order became much greater when intense rivalry developed between the Hudson's Bay Company and the North West Company. Clashes between competing traders led to violence and occasionally to murder. When a third contestant, the XY Company, appeared in 1799, some of the more conservative merchants concerned became seriously alarmed. John Richardson warned the government of Lower Canada in 1802 that he feared events "dreadful to contemplate" and pleaded for "a competent Jurisdiction . . . for the Investigation of Crimes and Criminal offences committed in the British part of the Indian Country."

This appeared to be provided by the Canada Jurisdiction Act, passed by the British Parliament in 1803. It empowered the Governor of Lower Canada to appoint "Justices of the Peace for the Indian Territories" who could make arrests and send suspects to Lower Canada for trial. In an effort to provide for unusual circumstances the Act went further and provided that *anyone* could make such arrests. But the only persons available to act as Justices were the fur traders themselves, and it was inevitable that some of them should use their legal authority to cripple their opponents. One famous instance occurred at Fort Chipewyan, where A. N. McLeod was in charge for the North West Company. In his capacity as a Justice of the Peace he arrested John Clarke, chief of the rival Hudson's Bay post, and for good measure contrived both to humiliate him before the Indians and arrest his staff, thus bringing all Hudson's Bay trading to a halt.

Arrests and counterarrests were frequent in the last stages of the struggle that ended with the coalition of 1821. Thereafter the Hudson's Bay Company became legally responsible for law and order, but little was done—indeed little was necessary—in a formal way except in Red River. When the Company assumed direct control of the settlement there in 1834, the number of Justices was increased, a

Horses stampeding in thunder storm

The journey of the Mounted Police across the southern prairies in 1874 was marked by many trials and tribulations. This wild stampede by their horses in a violent thunder and rain storm was one of them.

"On the Way to Manitoba" (top of page)

A sketch by Henri Julien, the noted cartoonist and caricaturist who accompanied some of the first recruits of the Mounted Police on their journey to the West.

General Court was set up in 1837, and Adam Thom, the first Recorder of Assiniboia, arrived in 1839. Elsewhere the establishment of a monopoly in the fur trade resulted in a large measure of peace and quiet.

Soon after Confederation it was evident that the West was entering an entirely new phase of development. The resistance in Red River led by Riel was only one of several indications that some effective means of law enforcement had become essential. Farther West, whisky traders from Montana were crossing the border and demoralizing the Indians. The Indians themselves were becoming restless, as many of them encountered changes that would alter their way of life. The fur trade was declining; the great herds of buffalo, upon which many of them had depended, would be virtually extinct by 1878; some of the treaties that would move them to reserves had already been signed. Finally, Canada had taken over the West with a view to settlement, and construction of a transcontinental railway would soon begin.

Public Archives of Canada

ORDER FOR
LAYING OUT KIT
For Inspection.
—DRESS.—

Summer :—*Serges, Breeches, Boots & Spurs, Side Arms, Carbines, Forage Caps.*

Winter: —*Serges, Breeches, Fur Caps, Moccasins & Stockings no spurs, Side Arms, Carbines.*

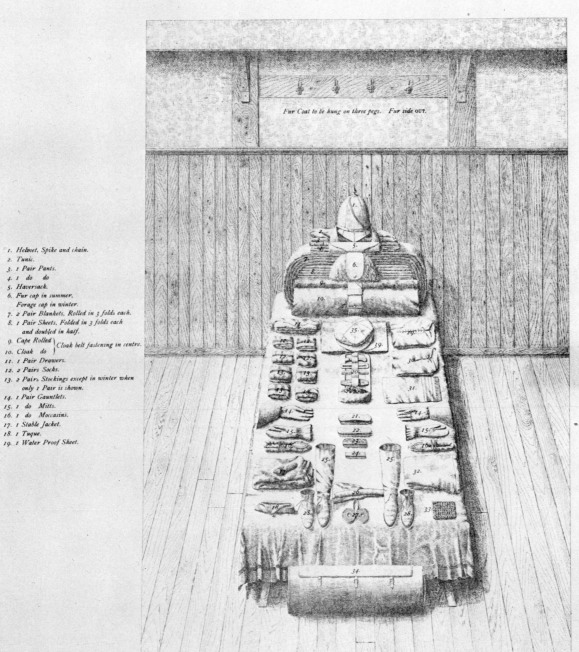

Fur Coat to be hung on three pegs.   Fur side OUT.

1. Helmet, Spike and chain.
2. Tunic.
3. 1 Pair Pants.
4. 1   do   do
5. Haversack.
6. Fur cap in summer,
   Forage cap in winter.
7. 2 Pair Blankets, Rolled in 3 folds each.
8. 1 Pair Sheets, Folded in 3 folds each
   and doubled in half.
9. Cape Rolled }
10. Cloak   do } Cloak belt fastening in centre.
11. 1 Pair Drawers.
12. 2 Pairs Socks.
13. 2 Pairs Stockings except in winter when
    only 1 Pair is shown.
14. 1 Pair Gauntlets.
15. 1 do   Mitts.
16. 1 do   Moccasins.
17. 1 Stable Jacket.
18. 1 Tuque.
19. 1 Water Proof Sheet.

20. 1 Holdall complete :—
    Shaving Brush.
    Button Brass.
    Comb.
    Razor and Case.
    Sponge.
21. 1 Clothes Brush.
22. 1 Polishing Brush.
23. 1 Blacking Brush.
24. 1 Brass Brush.
25. 1 Pair Boots (Long)
26. 1 Carbine Cover.
27. 1 Pair Blanket Straps.
28. 1 Pair Ankle Boots.
29. 1 Over Shirt.
30. 1 Under Shirt.
31. 1 Towel.
32. 1 Pair Stable Pants.
33. 1 Burnisher.
34. 1 Kit Bag.
35. 1 Stable Cap.

Note :—*Pillow, Palliasse, (filled with hay), 1 Blanket, 1 Rug, on the Bed according to diagram.*

When moccasins are worn, Spurs should be shewn on long Boots.

Knife, Fork, Spoon, Plate and Cup in mess.

1 Pair Sheets, 1 Towel, 1 Pair Socks at Wash.

All articles should be neatly folded with the numbers showing.

Original kit of the Mounted Police

This "Order" lists and pictures all the items in a constable's kit, and shows how each was to be arranged for inspection.

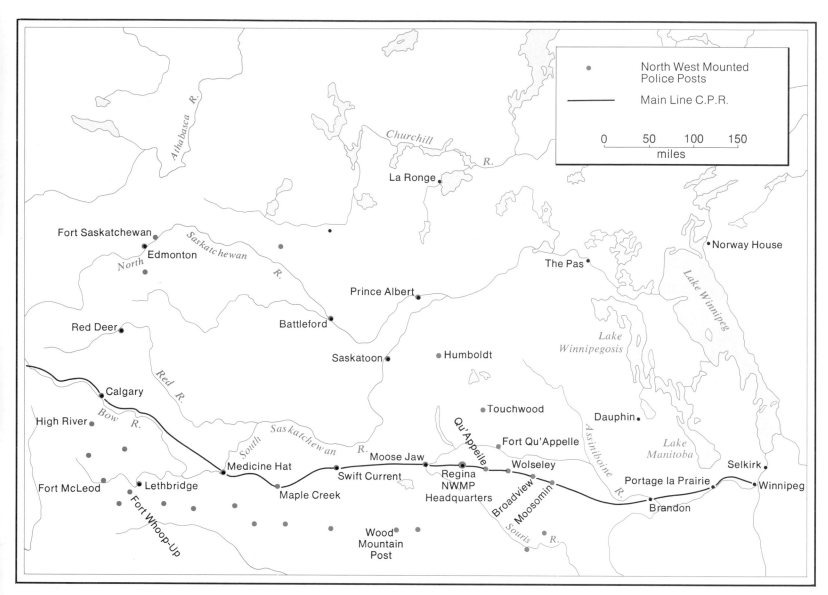

The North West
Mounted Police Posts,
1886

Regina in 1884 (right)
*The previous year the
little city had become
both the seat of the
Territorial Government
and the headquarters of
the North West Mount-
ed Police.*

Fort Whoop-up (left)
The notorious post built by American whisky pedlars south of Lethbridge. Here it is shown flying an American flag.

Fort Walsh
This important post was built in the Cypress Hills. It was abandoned in 1882 and replaced by a post at Maple Creek, on the railway.

FORT WALSH. CYPRESS HILLS 1878

In 1873 Sir John Macdonald introduced legislation that created the North West Mounted Police for the specific purpose of enforcing law and order in the Northwest Territories. It was a civilian force but was organized on a semimilitary basis. Recruiting began promptly and the pioneer contingents arrived in the West in 1874. The first of the famous "Mounties" travelled by train to Fargo, North Dakota, and then marched north to Dufferin, Manitoba, south of Winnipeg. Thence they proceeded west for 270 miles to Roche Percée, where they divided into two divisions. "A" Division went north to Fort Ellice and thence to Edmonton. "B" Division marched straight westward, and after a gruelling journey arrived in the area (in what is now southern Alberta) where the American whisky traders had been most active. There they built Fort McLeod, some 20 miles from the traders' notorious and aptly named Fort Whoop-up. The next year three other posts were established: Fort Walsh, in Saskatchewan's Cypress Hills, Fort Calgary, nucleus of the present city, and Fort Saskatchewan, on the North Saskatchewan River 20 miles downstream from Edmonton. From these beginnings grew a network of posts throughout the 800 miles of prairie land between Manitoba and the Rockies.

In time the Mounted Police became an almost legendary force, with a well-deserved reputation for bravery, fairness, persistence and success. For years they were not a large force (the strength originally authorized was only 300), and frequently they had to depend for their safety and effectiveness on personal courage and a tradition akin to that of the Hudson's Bay trader—the certainty that retribution would overtake anyone who molested them. Many of their responsibilities related to the North, the Indians, the Klondike gold rush, and other matters that had a romantic aura about them, and to this their horses and scarlet dress tunics (copied originally from the British Army) added attractive details, and helped to create the red-coated Mountie of fact and fiction.

The whisky traders were soon dealt with, and the Police settled down to the long task of watching over the transition of a huge area from a scantily peopled wilderness to a settled agricultural community. The thousands of workers employed in building the Canadian Pacific Railway inevitably included some rough characters, and the Police kept an eye on the construction camps—a responsibility that extended for a time into eastern British Columbia. Crises arose from time to time, notably the Northwest Rebellion of 1885, which they were unable to control unaided because of their small numbers, but in which they played an important part. Indian unrest in East Kootenay again brought the Mounted Police to British Columbia; a contingent spent a year there in 1887-88. The way in which a small force kept order in the Yukon during the Klondike gold rush that began in 1896 is well known. Incidentally, in the Rebellion, in Kootenay and in the Klondike the central figure in each case was Supt. Samuel B. Steele, later Major-General Sir

Samuel Steele. By 1904 the reputation of the force was such that King Edward VII conferred upon it the title of "Royal."

Both the Mounted Police and the infant Territorial Government had established their headquarters first at Livingstone, in the Swan River valley. In 1877 both moved to Battleford, and the further move to Regina came in 1883. Thirty-seven years later important changes were made. Conditions had altered greatly; the heavily settled areas of the old Northwest Territories had become the new provinces of Alberta, Saskatchewan and part of an enlarged Manitoba. In 1920 the Mounted Police and the Dominion Police, a protective and enforcement body, were united to form the Royal Canadian Mounted Police—the "R.C.M.P." of today—with headquarters in Ottawa. As the new title implied, the force would have responsibilities throughout Canada.

Through the years these have grown steadily. Quite apart from its work for the federal authorities, the R.C.M.P. has taken over police duties in all provinces except Ontario and Quebec, and has replaced local police in nearly 150 cities, towns and municipalities.

The Indians and Western Settlement

The buffalo on the coat of arms of the Province of Manitoba commemorates the vast herds of bison that once roamed the central plains of Canada. Their habits went far to determine the nomadic life of the Indians; the natives followed them, for they provided most of the essentials of existence. Clothing and leather could be made from their hides; their flesh was the Indians' staple food; even their dung was valuable, because it could be used as fuel.

Two changes threatened and eventually ended this way of life. The first was the destruction of the buffalo herds, which began in the United States as settlement spread westward. The Indians themselves contributed to it, for they delighted in prodigal buffalo hunts that slaughtered far more animals than could possibly be of any practical use to them. By the time of Confederation the numbers of buffalo were decreasing rapidly in Canada.

The second and even more important threat came from the spread of settlement. Canada had acquired Rupert's Land with settlement in view, and intended soon to build a railway through it. Something had to be done to come to terms with its Indian population.

The French had rarely recognized any Indian title to lands in Canada; they considered it was theirs by rights of exploration, occupation and conquest—a policy that probably was practicable only because the area occupied by French settlements was small.

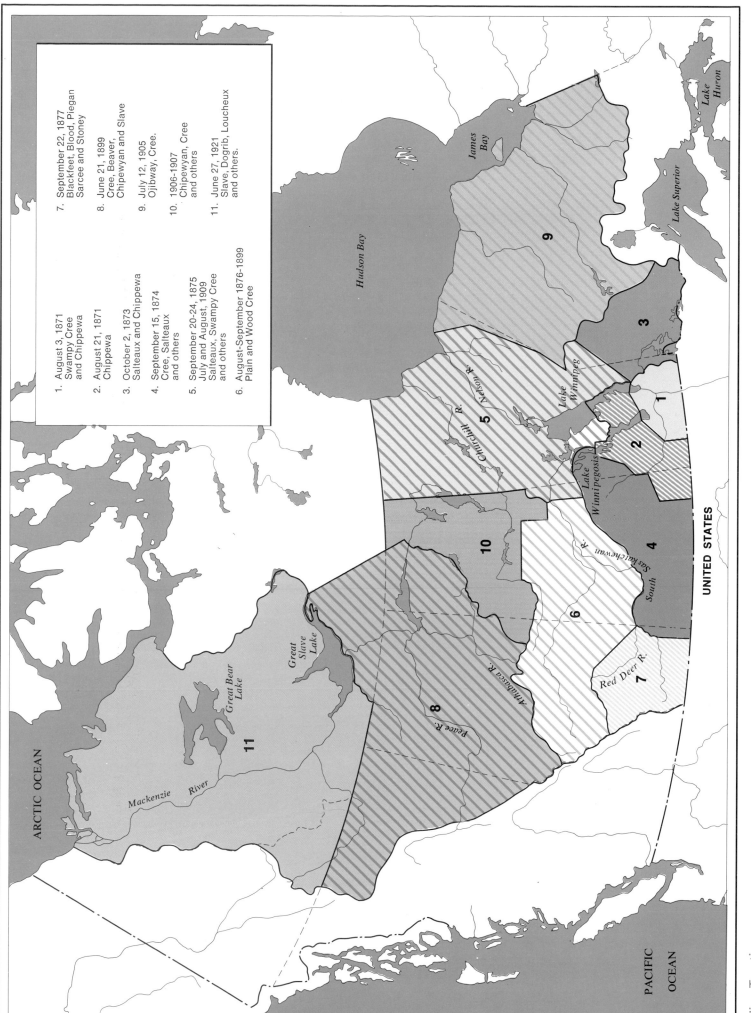

1. August 3, 1871
   Swampy Cree
   and Chippewa

2. August 21, 1871
   Chippewa

3. October 2, 1873
   Salteaux and Chippewa

4. September 15, 1874
   Cree, Salteaux
   and others

5. September 20-24, 1875
   July and August, 1909
   Salteaux, Swampy Cree
   and others

6. August-September 1876-1899
   Plain and Wood Cree

7. September 22, 1877
   Blackfeet, Blood, Piegan
   Sarcee and Stoney

8. June 21, 1899
   Cree, Beaver,
   Chipewyan and Slave

9. July 12, 1905
   Ojibway, Cree.

10. 1906-1907
    Chipewyan, Cree
    and others

11. June 27, 1921
    Slave, Dogrib, Loucheux
    and others.

ARCTIC OCEAN

Mackenzie River

Great Bear Lake

Great Slave Lake

11

Peace R.

8

Athabasca R.

Red Deer R.

7

6

Saskatchewan R.

South

4

10

Churchill R.

Nelson R.

5

Lake Winnipegosis

Lake Winnipeg

Hudson Bay

James Bay

9

3

1

2

UNITED STATES

PACIFIC OCEAN

Lake Superior

Lake Huron

Indian Treaties

The British, on the other hand, who were spreading in numbers over large areas, always tried to come to some agreement with the Indians, and to secure a formal transfer of titles to land—a policy that they felt was not only fairer to the natives, but of great importance in maintaining good relations with them. The Royal Proclamation issued in October 1763, after the signing of the treaty that ceded Canada to Britain, stated among other things that it was "just and reasonable and essential to our Interests, and the Security of our Colonies, that the several Nations or Tribes of Indians . . . should not be molested or disturbed in the Possession of such Parts of our dominions and territories, as not having been ceded to Us, are reserved to them as their Hunting Grounds . . . "

Only the Crown could expunge Indian land titles, and during the century that followed, as the spread of settlement made this necessary, it was accomplished by a long series of agreements and treaties. In time these covered the whole of Upper Canada.

It was this policy that was extended to Rupert's Land after 1870, and seven Indian treaties, identified by number, were concluded in the period 1871-77. The first two, signed in August 1871, covered the new and then very small province of Manitoba, and a larger range of territory west and north of it. In 1873 Treaty No. 3 dealt with Indian titles to most of the land between Manitoba and Lake Superior, and the following year No. 4 extended the treaty area westward to the Cypress Hills, near the present Saskatchewan—Alberta border. Almost all the lands so far covered had been south of 52° north latitude, or within about 215 miles of the American border. In 1875-76 treaties 5 and 6 extended the area further north, and in 1877 the last of the series carried it westward to the Rocky Mountains and the border of British Columbia.

The general pattern was everywhere the same. In return for ceding their lands to the Crown, the Indians were given reserves that would be theirs in perpetuity, unless the Government and the Indians agreed that it was to the Indians' advantage to lease or sell them. In addition, they received gifts, annuities, hunting privileges on Crown lands and other concessions.

Instituting the new regime was not easy. After long ages of untrammelled wandering, it was difficult for the Indians to adjust themselves to a relatively confined life, even though, as one official noted at the time, most of them realized that "the chase and the arrow no longer bring them the advantages of former times." Living in villages and engaging in agricultural pursuits were alike foreign to their nature and traditions.

Efforts were made to meet the wishes of the Indians regarding the location of reserves, and their size varied greatly according to the number of persons who were expected to live on them, the nature of the land, and so on. Special cases had to be met. The Indians near the Dawson route, the combination of roads, trails and waterways between Lake Superior and Lake Winnipeg, felt that its existence entitled them to special compensation. Vague promises that were alleged to have been made verbally at the time of treaty negotiations caused difficulties later. Special reserves had to be set aside for Sioux Indians who had taken refuge in British territory after a massacre in Minnesota in 1862. The surveyors sent to mark the limits of the new reserves did not find the task an easy one. One of the more picturesque problems encountered was the great desire of the Indians in the Cypress Hills to indulge in one last scalping and horse-stealing raid into the United States before they moved farther north to their new and permanent homes.

It is easy to criticize the reserve system, but it is difficult to suggest an alternative policy that could have been applied at the time. In 1875 there were only 10,305 Indians in the whole country between Lake Superior and the Cypress Hills. The Government was anxious to open the country for railroad construction and settlement, and to make it as certain as possible that neither would face native hostility. To establish Indians as wards of the Crown on lands, the possession of which was guaranteed to them, was an attractive solution.

Today there are about 2,200 Indian reserves of all shapes and sizes in Canada. They consist in all of about 6,000,000 acres, half of them in the three prairie provinces and most of the rest in Ontario and British Columbia. The system has had unfortunate results. It segregated and in many instances isolated the Indians and encouraged neither self-reliance nor initiative. But the balance sheet is by no means as negative as it has often been represented as being; complaints are apt to be loudest when conditions are improving because it has become apparent that improvement is possible. In 1900 the Indian population was only about 100,000. In recent decades, thanks to improved health services and better educational opportunities, it has increased rapidly. By 1954 the total had risen to over 151,000; it was over 204,000 by 1963, and is now about 250,000. It seems certain that the native population is now higher than it was when the first Europeans set foot in Canada.

The Northwest Rebellion of 1885

The Northwest Rebellion might well be renamed the unnecessary rebellion of 1885; it could easily have been avoided. Many warnings of possible trouble had been sent to Ottawa by the Mounted Police, Indian agents, the clergy and others. But Sir John Macdonald, the Prime Minister, placed his trust in advisers who did not appreciate the seriousness of the situation, and he had other things on his mind, including the final and most dangerous crisis in his long struggle to finance the building of the C.P.R.

As in Red River in 1869, the trouble centred around the Métis. In a measure history was about to repeat itself, for there were many from Manitoba in the new Métis settlements that had grown up along

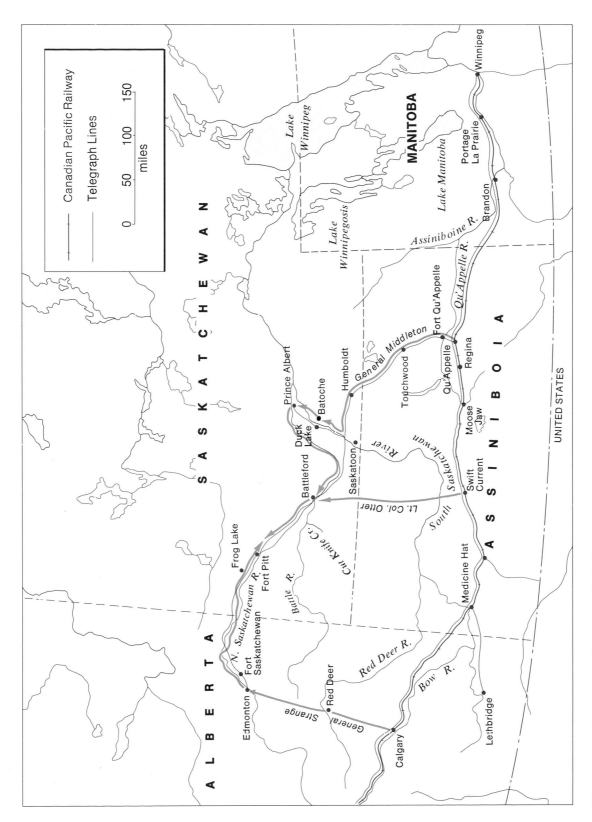

Legend:
- Canadian Pacific Railway
- Telegraph Lines

miles
0   50   100   150

ALBERTA

SASKATCHEWAN

MANITOBA

ASSINIBOIA

Edmonton

Fort Saskatchewan

Frog Lake

Fort Pitt

N. Saskatchewan R.

Battle R.

Cut Knife C. R.

Battleford

Duck Lake

Batoche

Prince Albert

Saskatoon

Humboldt

General Middleton

Fort Qu'Appelle

Saskatchewan River

South Saskatchewan

Touchwood

Qu'Appelle

Regina

Moose Jaw

Swift Current

Lt. Col. Otter

Medicine Hat

Bow R.

Red Deer R.

Red Deer

General Strange

Calgary

Lethbridge

Qu'Appelle R.

Assiniboine R.

Brandon

Portage La Prairie

Winnipeg

Lake Manitoba

Lake Winnipeg

Lake Winnipegosis

UNITED STATES

Military Operations in the Northwest Rebellion

Indian Treaty Conference in Manitoba

The terms of the treaties were worked out at discussions with Indian leaders that usually extended over several days. From the Canadian Illustrated News, *September 9, 1871.*

the South Saskatchewan River in the vicinity of Batoche. Economically their plight, like that of many of the Indians, was close to desperation. The buffalo, upon which they had depended in great part, had disappeared; crop failures had recently frustrated their attempts at farming. As in Red River, the advance of settlement and the arrival of land surveyors had made them fear both for their property rights, and for their freedom to roam about the prairies in their traditional nomadic way.

Their most prominent leader was Gabriel Dumont, in past days a great buffalo hunter. It was probably he who suggested that they should consult Louis Riel, who at the time was teaching in a Jesuit school in Montana. Riel came to Batoche in June 1884 and for a time urged that efforts be made to settle the grievances of the Métis by peaceful means.

Then by degrees a change occurred. In December he began to press what he regarded as his personal claims for compensation, and made it clear that he would disappear for a price. When this manoeuvre failed he became more and more belligerent in his views. Finally, in March 1885, he proclaimed a provisional government, with himself as its head and Dumont his adjutant general, and notified Superintendent Crozier of the Mounted Police that he would "commence without delay a war of extermination upon all those who have shown themselves hostile to our rights." At Duck Lake, on March 26, a Métis force under Dumont met and defeated police and volunteers under Crozier, who not only had to retreat but later found it necessary to evacuate Fort Carlton as well.

But Riel had reckoned without the telegraph and the railroad, both of which had penetrated the west since the Red River resistance of 1869-70. A fortnight before the armed clash occurred, Crozier had telegraphed his superiors, making the gravity of the position clear. At long last Ottawa became seriously alarmed, and General Middleton was on

Gabriel Dumont

Public Archives of Canada

Indian leaders in the Rebellion

Big Bear (front row, second from left) and Pound-maker, the two important Indian leaders, are here shown after their surrender. The group includes Capt. Deane (in white), a constable of the Mounted Police, and two Oblate missionaries.

his way west before the engagement at Duck Lake. There were still four gaps in the Canadian Pacific line north of Lake Superior, but when news of the Duck Lake reverse was received, William Van Horne, General Manager of the Canadian Pacific, not unmindful of the vital importance of financial aid from Parliament to complete the line, under-took to move troops from Ottawa to Fort Qu'Ap-pelle in eleven days. Actually, he bettered this schedule by a handsome margin. The first two bat-teries were in Winnipeg only four days after leaving Ottawa, in spite of deep snow and sub-zero weather that made crossing the gaps in the line a severe ordeal.

Perhaps the greatest uncertainty was the atti-tude of the Indians. Macdonald was fairly confident that there would be no general rising, and events proved that he was right; but Dumont's initial success had the effect of rallying some of the chiefs to his cause, notably two Cree leaders, Poundmaker and Big Bear. Poundmaker's followers overran and

pillaged the settlement at Battleford, but made no attempt to attack the Mounted Police compound in which the people had taken refuge. Big Bear seems to have taken up arms reluctantly, but a band of his warriors massacred nine persons at Frog Lake, including two priests.

Middleton's total force consisted of 363 regu-lars, 2,960 militia from the eastern provinces, 1,200 from Manitoba, and about 800 volunteers from the North West, a total of about 5,300 men in all. These he divided into three columns. He himself com-manded a force that marched north from Qu'Ap-pelle to Batoche and Prince Albert. A column under Colonel Otter proceeded north from Swift Current to relieve Battleford, while the third column, com-manded by General Strange, marched from Calgary to Edmonton. Middleton has been accused of being overly cautious, but most of his troops lacked train-ing and experience, and a number of small reverses and near reverses showed that he was right to take this into account. The decisive battle was a three-day engagement at Batoche. Here Middleton's caution finally exasperated the militia and they charged on their own initiative and swept the Métis out of their rifle pits. Three days later, on May 15, Riel surrendered and Poundmaker joined him on May 23. Farther west Big Bear succeeded in escap-ing, and Middleton made the mistake of sending militia on foot to pursue him instead of allowing

Encounter at Duck Lake

90th Rifles leaving Winnipeg for the front

The Battle of Batoche

the Mounted Police to do so. In the end Big Bear surrendered of his own accord on July 2.

What to do with Riel now became the burning issue. Unquestionably he had been guilty of treason and armed rebellion, and the trial at Regina could result only in a sentence of death. There were two possible grounds upon which a reprieve could be based. One was a plea of insanity; Riel's actions at times were clearly unbalanced, and he had spent the years 1876-78 in an asylum. The other was political expediency; his trial and conviction had aroused great concern in French Canada. Macdonald had three doctors visit Riel, and none gave any substantial support to the insanity plea. In one of the few major political miscalculations in his long career, Macdonald grossly underestimated the extent and the depth of the feeling among French-Canadians and let the death sentence stand. Most English-speaking Canadians agreed with him, but his decision destroyed the strength of the Conservative Party in Quebec.

Riel's rebellion and the completion of the Canadian Pacific Railway had repercussions, one on the other. There is no doubt that Van Horne's practical demonstration of the value of the railway in a time of emergency helped to persuade Parliament to make financial provision for its completion. Big Bear surrendered on July 2; the Canadian Pacific Bill passed on July 20. Ironically enough, the last spike was driven at Craigellachie on November 7, and Riel was hanged at Regina on the 16th.

Grain and the Golden West

There is an impression abroad that as soon as Canada acquired Rupert's Land settlers flocked in, and the Golden West, with its boundless wheat fields, came quickly into being. In truth, it was quite otherwise.

A Golden West required three things: wheat that would ripen in the normal frost-free season on the prairies, which in most areas meant only from 80 to 120 days; means of transport that could carry a crop to market, and farmers to raise it.

Seed grains were brought from abroad, including Russia, in an effort to solve the first problem, but it was a native variety, Red Fyfe, that gave prairie farmers a fairly reliable and satisfactory crop. Other varieties followed, the most famous being Marquis wheat, developed from a cross between Red Fyfe and a wheat from India by Dr. Charles Saunders, and first grown in quantity in 1909. It went a long way toward providing a variety that would mature early, yield well and produce grain of high quality. By 1920 nearly 90 percent of wheat acreage was growing Marquis, and it is still the standard variety by which others are judged. But the search for new and better wheats went on apace, for a variety that would ripen even

Red River cart train

Furs being portaged at Fort Smith in the Northwest Territories. The carts are a somewhat modernized version of the famous Red River carts.

a few days earlier would materially increase the area in which wheat could be grown. Moreover, wheat rust began to devastate crops, including Marquis, and rust-resistant varieties had to be found to combat it. New varieties to meet these needs included Garnet, Ruby, Rescue and Reward—names that suggest their value to the farmer.

Transportation was long a stumbling block. In 1870 some stretches of road and a trail—the Dawson route—led from Prince Arthur's Landing (later Port Arthur) to Winnipeg, and trails and steamers on the Red River, the latter operating only in summer time, connected Winnipeg with St. Paul, in Minnesota. The rail link between the two cities was not in operation until early in 1879. The basic

means of transport was still the Red River cart—a crude but easily made and serviceable two-wheeled cart, made entirely of wood, that was used even for treks as long as from Fort Garry to Edmonton. Versatile though it was, it was of little use in transporting grain in quantity, and it is scarcely surprising that no more than 15,000 acres were devoted to wheat growing in the West in 1875.

Farmers, the third essential, were also in short supply for a good many years, though the Government took steps to prepare for their arrival. In April 1871 an order-in-council outlined the land survey system that was to be used, with minor exceptions, throughout the West. A year later the first Dominion Land Act provided for free 160-acre homestead grants. Actually the freedom of choice available to a homesteader seeking free land was subject to some limitations. Each of the townships into which the public lands were surveyed was six miles square and consisted of 36 sections, each one mile square and

640 acres in area. Two of the 36 were reserved for educational purposes, and the Hudson's Bay Company, under the terms of the agreement whereby it relinquished its proprietary rights in Rupert's Land, was entitled to one-twentieth of the land in a large designated area, which meant that an average of not quite two sections in every township was assigned to the Company. Later, in 1880, the Canadian Pacific Railway received land grants that entitled it to every other section in certain areas.

But, at least to begin with, there was ample land available for homesteading. The disappointing thing was that few settlers applied for it. For this there were two chief reasons. The whole continent suffered from a depression in the years from 1873 to 1878, and this affected both migration and immigration. Equally serious, the easiest approach to the new Canadian West was through the United States, by way of St. Paul, and many a Manitoba-bound settler was lured away by the blandishments of

187

Public Archives of Canada

The first elevator at the Lakehead

Built by the Canadian Pacific at Port Arthur in 1883. The first Manitoba wheat was shipped that year. The steamer alongside is the Athabasca, which sailed the lakes for the railway for 63 years. Following a tax dispute with the city, the Canadian Pacific moved its operations to Fort William in 1889.

American land agents. As a result, the early homestead record was a dismal one. Up to October 31, 1874, only 1,376 applications were received, and only 499 were filed in 1875. It was inevitable that some homesteaders would later abandon their claims, but of the 1,875 applications received in 1874-75, no fewer than 1,043 were later cancelled. With the opening of the Winnipeg–St. Paul railway things improved considerably; 4,068 homestead applications were received in 1879.

Years passed before settlers began to arrive in the West in substantial numbers. In the years 1881-1886, Canada experienced a modest immigration boom. The peak year was 1884, when nearly 104,000 people came into the country, and in the six years 546,000 arrived. Yet it is estimated that in those same six years only 166,000 immigrants entered the North West, and the 1891 census would make it only too clear that people were still leaving Canada faster than new arrivals were being admitted. The net loss in the decade 1881-1891 was about 206,000, and the loss was to continue, although on a reduced scale, during the ensuing ten years. The modest rise in the population of Canada between 1871 and 1901 was due to natural increase, not to immigration.

Canadians as well as newcomers from Europe and the United States came to the West during this period. The figures are in part an estimate only, but the population of Manitoba and the Northwest Territories had risen to 118,706 in 1881 and more than doubled to 251,473 by 1891. More than 152,000 of the latter number were in Manitoba; people were still very thinly scattered further west. But circumstances both inside and outside Canada were changing, and, at long last, it would be a different story after 1900.

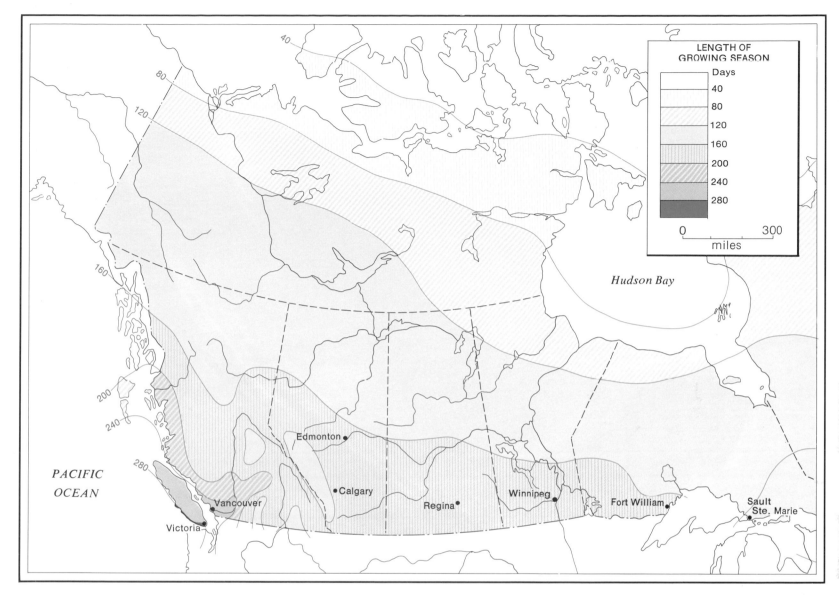

LENGTH OF
GROWING SEASON
Days
40
80
120
160
200
240
280

0   300
miles

Hudson Bay

*PACIFIC
OCEAN*

Edmonton •

• Calgary

Regina •

Winnipeg •

Fort William •

Sault
Ste. Marie

Vancouver

Victoria

The HighTide
of Immigration

The Growing Season in the West

The many thousands of immigrants who came to Canada in the years before the First World War were part of a much larger movement of population from most of the countries of Europe to the Americas. Immigration to the United States increased sharply after 1900, averaging over a million persons a year in the period 1905 to 1914, and in its peak years, 1907 and 1914, immigrants numbered over 1,200,000. Canada's problem was to secure a fair share of this mass immigration to the New World.

One great asset was an energetic minister, Clifford (later Sir Clifford) Sifton, in charge of the Department of the Interior. It was he who led the campaign to attract new settlers to Canada, and it was in full swing before he left the Cabinet in 1905. The Government, the Canadian Pacific Railway, the shipping companies and to some extent land

companies carried on a spirited and widespread propaganda campaign; in 1904, at the peak of the campaign, the Department of the Interior alone distributed 4,445,310 booklets, leaflets and maps in many countries and in many languages.

The prairies were made more attractive by the construction of branch railway lines, which pushed out in all directions, and by the coming of new railways, especially the Canadian Northern, which completed its main line from Winnipeg to Edmonton in 1905. Sifton was a Manitoban, and he was concerned about the millions of acres that were tied up by railway and other land grants, many of which had not yet been either chosen or surveyed. Partly for this reason the Laurier government abandoned the policy of assisting railways by grants of free land and substituted cash subsidies and bond guarantees—a policy that was to be expensive to the taxpayer in the long run, but kept lands free for settlement at a very critical time.

Bound for Canada (left)
Immigrants bound for Canada amuse themselves
on the foredeck of the first Empress of Britain.

The trek from the railway to the homestead

Waiting to go ashore

A sod house — first home in the West

In early days, bleached buffalo bones were plentiful. As they found a fairly ready sale, gathering them often provided a settler with his first cash crop.

The movement to Canada was helped by the growing scarcity of good unoccupied land in the United States. Indeed, a feature of the immigration boom was the number of people who moved from the United States to Canada. In 1901 they numbered only 5,197, but over 40,000 came in 1904 and over 107,000 in 1914. This was a particularly welcome influx, for many of those who came were experienced farmers who had some capital. Equally welcome was the return of many Canadians, which was another feature of the prewar years.

But the bulk of the newcomers were from Europe, and whereas most of those who had come previously had been from western and northern Europe, there now came a great influx of people from the south and east. It was at this time that ethnic pockets appeared in many localities on the prairies. Their variety appeared to be infinite. Group settlements made assimilation slower and more difficult, but it was only natural that people should tend to settle near others who spoke their language and had a similar background.

British Columbia shared in the population boom and soon had special assimilation problems of her own. Orientals had first come to Canada in significant numbers when railway contractors had brought in Chinese coolies to help build the Cana-

dian Pacific in British Columbia. Many of them had returned to China, but after 1880 there was always a substantial Chinese community in the province. After the turn of the century there was an influx of Japanese and later of East Indians. Presently it became apparent that some limitation of Oriental immigration was desirable, and by 1914 regulations and agreements had brought the influx under control.

A substantial movement to Canada from Great Britain took place at this time. Some were assisted immigrants, but many were young people with ambition who felt that the New World offered better opportunities than the old. As someone has expressed it, the mass migration of Europeans to America was a movement of hope, not one of despair, as it is sometimes represented as being. About 115,000 British immigrants arrived in Canada in 1910 and nearly 135,000 came in 1911.

In these same years a substantial population movement was also taking place within Canada itself. Finding in the West the hinterland they had long desired, thousands of easterners moved to the prairies.

The first fifteen years of the century saw an incredible transformation in western Canada. In 1901 the population of Manitoba, and the area that would soon become the provinces of Alberta and Saskatchewan, was only 419,512. A census taken in June 1906, ten months after the two new provinces had come into existence, showed that the total had more than doubled to 898,863 in only five years. By 1916 it had risen to 1,278,708, and in 1921 it was

Manitoba Archives

The old home and the new

The old house on the right, built of roughly squared timbers and with a roof of thatch, is replaced by the frame dwelling, with a shingle roof, on the left.

1,956,082. In the same twenty-year period the population of Canada's farthest west province—British Columbia—had grown from 178,657 in 1901 to 524,582 in 1921.

Of course east as well as west benefitted from the influx of immigrants. Each year from 1906 to 1914 more of the newcomers settled in Ontario than in any other province. But the settling of the west was of the first importance from the national point of view. André Siegfried once described Canada as being a strip of population glued to the American border. In 1901 that strip had been thin indeed for long distances; by 1911 it had widened and thickened sufficiently to bind the country together and make it an entity from sea to sea.

In these same decades, for the first time since Confederation, more people came to Canada than left it. The high tide of immigration began to rise in 1901; in the five years from 1904 to 1908 just over 900,000 immigrants arrived; in the ensuing five years (1909 to 1913) the total swelled to 1,568,-447. The peak year was 1913, when immigrants numbered 400,870. Not all the immigrants remained, and many Canadians continued to leave the country; but on balance there was a substantial gain. Over the twenty-year period from 1901 to 1921 a total of 3,371,000 people came to Canada and 2,424,000 emigrated, leaving a net contribution of 947,000 to the growth of the population.

Settlers arriving from the United States

This picturesque train of ox-drawn covered wagons brought settlers and their effects from the American West to Alberta. Migration took place by land as well as by sea.

CHAPTER 14

Urbanization and Industry

The Western Cities Emerge

O F Canada's seven largest western cities only two—Winnipeg and Victoria— existed even as small towns at the time of Confederation, and in 1891 three of them —Edmonton, Regina and Saskatoon—still had only a few hundred inhabitants. Yet by 1911 the seven already had a combined population of over 405,000, and by 1966 this had risen to over 1,629,000. There were 892,000 people in the Vancouver metropolitan area alone in 1966, and the next census will certainly show that the total has passed the million mark.

The origins of the seven were varied and interesting. Three of them—Winnipeg, Edmonton and Victoria—owe their beginnings to the fur trade. The site of Winnipeg, at the junction of the Red and Assiniboine rivers, was an obvious location for a trading post, and a succession of forts was built there. The French occupied the site for a time, but the first permanent post was Fort Gibraltar, founded in 1807 by the North West Company. Selkirk's Red River settlement scheme, which in effect was backed by the Hudson's Bay Company, led to bitterness and violence in the valley which did not end until the two companies joined forces in 1821. Later Fort Gibraltar was rebuilt and renamed Fort Garry, and it was around this new post that the little town of Winnipeg grew up.

By degrees Winnipeg became a trading and traffic centre for much more than the fur trade. First links were with St. Paul to the south, but the building of the Canadian Pacific Railway not only placed it on an east-west traffic route but made it the point of entry through which immigrants and supplies flowed to the prairies. In 1870 it had become the capital of the new province of Manitoba, and by 1901 its population was already over 42,000.

The rivalry between the Hudson's Bay and North West companies also figured in Edmonton's beginnings. As early as 1795 the two had built competing forts close together on the North Saskatchewan River 15 miles upstream from the site of the city, but in 1801 both were moved to the site itself. The Hudson's Bay post had been known as Fort Edmonton from the beginning, and the name was retained after the coalition in 1821. In time Fort Edmonton became the chief post in the region and was rebuilt on an imposing scale on a cliffside site about 200 feet above the river.

It was intended at first that the Canadian Pacific should follow a northern route from Winnipeg to the Yellowhead Pass, which would have taken it through Edmonton, but these hopes were disappointed when the line was relocated far to the south. Edmonton had to be content for the moment with a branch line from Calgary, completed in 1891, but the Canadian Northern linked it directly with Winnipeg in 1905. The same year its future was assured when it became the capital of the new province of Alberta.

Victoria was founded as Fort Victoria in 1843, when the Hudson's Bay Company decided that the days of British occupation of the Columbia River were probably numbered, and that it would be prudent to build an alternative Pacific Coast headquarters farther north. In 1849 it became the capital of the Crown Colony of Vancouver Island, and in 1858, when the Fraser River gold rush erupted suddenly on the adjacent mainland, its population jumped overnight from hundreds to thousands. After the excitement ebbed, island and mainland were united in British Columbia, and Victoria was its capital when British Columbia joined Canada in 1871. Its population was then 3,270.

If the change in route of the C.P.R. disappointed Edmonton, it led to the growth of new cities in the south. In 1878 the capital of the Northwest Territories and the headquarters of the North West Mounted Police had been fixed at Battleford, but it was obvious that settlement would centre for a time along the new railway, and the change in route

Calgary in 1881 (top of page)

Eighth Avenue, Calgary, in 1912

Fort Calgary was still just a stockaded police post in 1881; the main line of the Canadian Pacific was completed to Calgary only two years later and the town grew rapidly.

Vancouver in 1886 (top of page)

This photograph is said to have been taken only a month after the city had been swept by fire on June 13, and shows the remarkable speed with which it was rebuilt.

Vancouver in 1912

This is Granville Street, looking north, with the old Canadian Pacific station in the distance.

Winnipeg in 1914 (top of page)

Portage Avenue, showing the T. Eaton Company's new department store — one of the largest commercial structures in Canada at the time.

Regina in 1913

The view from the Parliament Buildings, with Wascana Lake in the foreground.

SASKATCHEWAN VALLEY ROUTE

CANADIAN NORTHERN

TIME TABLES

PORT ARTHUR
WINNIPEG
EMERSON
TO
MANITOBA

CARMAN	CARBERRY
BRANDON	NEEPAWA
HARTNEY	GLADSTONE
VIRDEN	DAUPHIN
PORTAGE LA PRAIRIE	SWAN RIVER

SASKATCHEWAN

MELFORT	HUMBOLT
PRINCE ALBERT	WARMAN
KAMSACK	N. BATTLEFORD

ALBERTA

LLOYDMINSTER	Fᵀ SASKATCHEWAN
VERMILION	EDMONTON

THROUGH FIRST CLASS SLEEPERS BETWEEN PORT ARTHUR & EDMONTON

DINING CAR SERVICE MEALS A LA CARTE

SASKATCHEWAN VALLEY ROUTE

CANADIAN NORTHERN

TIME TABLES

PORT ARTHUR
WINNIPEG
EMERSON
TO
MANITOBA

CARMAN	CARBERRY
BRANDON	NEEPAWA
HARTNEY	GLADSTONE
VIRDEN	DAUPHIN
PORTAGE LA PRAIRIE	SWAN RIVER

SASKATCHEWAN

MELFORT	HUMBOLT
PRINCE ALBERT	WARMAN
KAMSACK	N. BATTLEFORD

ALBERTA

LLOYDMINSTER	Fᵀ SASKATCHEWAN
VERMILION	EDMONTON

THROUGH FIRST CLASS SLEEPERS BETWEEN PORT ARTHUR & EDMONTON

DINING CAR SERVICE MEALS A LA CARTE

Railway Time-Table Cover

Canadian Pacific Express, 1926 (bottom left)

In the great days of steam: Canadian Pacific's Trans-Canada Limited, leaving Windsor Station, Montreal for Vancouver in 1926.

Saskatoon about 1910 (top of page)

The hotel, bank and business blocks shown here were all built between 1906 and 1909.

Edmonton, Jasper Avenue East, in 1914

Canadian Northern Express Co'y

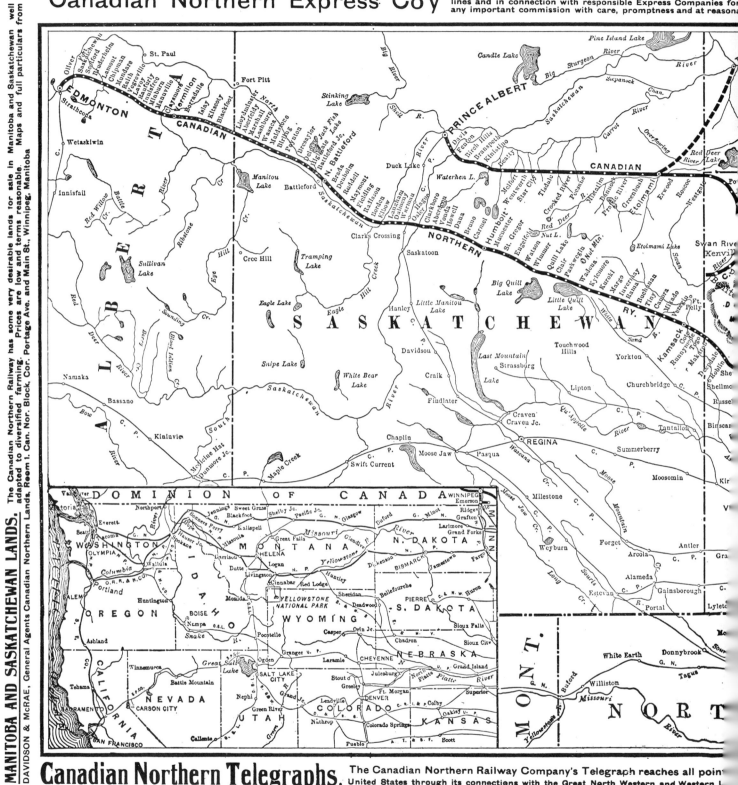

Canadian Northern Telegraphs.

The Canadian Northern in 1906

This system map was published in a timetable issued in July 1906. The main line then extended from Port Arthur through Winnipeg to Edmonton.

MAP OF THE

CANADIAN
NORTHERN
RAILWAY

AND CONNECTIONS

The Mackenzie and Mann partnership

placed Battleford inconveniently far to the north. No existing town was available to replace it, and the problem was solved by arbitrarily choosing a site that promised to be convenient. This happened to be where Wascana Creek crossed the railway, and there Regina came into being. Originally threatened with the name "Pile of Bones" because of the great number of bleached buffalo skeletons that dotted the surrounding prairie, it was rescued from this fate and named Regina by Princess Louise, daughter of Queen Victoria, in 1883.

Calgary had come into existence as Fort Calgary, a North West Mounted Police post, in September 1875. It had a strategic location at the junction of the Bow and Elbow rivers, but it was the railway, which reached it in 1883, that made its fortune. The same is true of Vancouver. Saw-mills had been in operation on Burrard Inlet since 1862, but there was little in the way of settlement until the completion of the Canadian Pacific in 1886. That year the little town was virtually wiped out by fire, but a period of frenzied building activity followed. By 1891 it already had a population of nearly 14,000, and Canadian Pacific *Empress* liners were sailing regularly to the Orient.

The seventh city—Saskatoon—originated in a quite different way. When immigration in the West began in earnest, various groups and companies acquired land and attempted to found settlements, with varied success. One of them was the Temperance Colonization Society of Ontario which acquired a land grant and planned to establish a temperance colony. The plan failed but its promoters had selected the site and name of Saskatoon, which began to develop slowly as a trading centre. A rail link with Regina was completed in 1890.

As mentioned elsewhere, the prairies developed less quickly than many suppose. Although Vancouver had 29,432 citizens in 1901, the other cities west of Winnipeg were still very small indeed. The population of the largest of them, Calgary, was 4,392, that of Edmonton was 4,176, and that of Regina only 2,249. It was only in the next dozen years that their real growth began, and it was after the Second World War that the four largest reached or far exceeded a quarter of a million people.

Shortly after Edmonton became the capital of Alberta, imposing Legislative Buildings for the new province arose just above and not far beyond Fort Edmonton. Although the palisades had been torn down, a group of the old fur trade buildings survived until 1915, offering a striking contrast between the old world of the West and the new. It is a thousand pities that no one thought of preserving the last of them as a period piece.

Railway Overexpansion

On the prairies the C.P.R. began life as a single line wending its lonely way through virtually unin-

habited country from Winnipeg to the Rockies. For a decade its development was slow, but thereafter the growth of the system was spectacular. The years from 1898 to the First World War have been called the golden age of the Canadian Pacific. Sir Thomas Shaughnessy—shrewd and able, filled with ambition but with his feet firmly on the ground—was its president, and his drive for expansion and improvement was reflected in many ways. Some of the most difficult stretches of line in the mountains were rebuilt or replaced by tunnels; locomotives and rolling stock increased rapidly in numbers and quality; the hotel chain was built or rebuilt; steamer services appeared on the Atlantic as well as the Pacific.

Shaughnessy's programme included a great number of branch lines on the prairies that both aided settlement and brought in revenue. But before long the C.P.R. discovered that two could play at the profitable branch-line game. Its chief rivals were William Mackenzie and Donald Mann who, as it happened, had first met as contractors in C.P.R. construction days. Mackenzie acquired control of a dormant local railway charter in Manitoba in 1895, and from this beginning a great railroad empire was to grow. In 1899 he and Mann consolidated their holding as the Canadian Northern Railway, and the little system soon began to expand in earnest. In 1901 it secured a long lease on the Manitoba government's line from Winnipeg to Emerson, which provided a link with American lines to the south. Late in 1902 the Canadian Pacific first felt its competition in a serious way when the C.N.R. completed a line from Winnipeg to Port Arthur, on Lake Superior. In the next few years it bought up various local lines in Ontario and Quebec and secured an entry into Ottawa, Montreal and Quebec City. Meanwhile it had been expanding westward as well, and by the end of 1905 Canadian Northern trains were running over a new main line to Edmonton.

By that time much more ambitious plans were in the air. Immigrants were pouring into Canada, the country was experiencing a great boom; grandiose railway projects were the order of the day. Sir John Macdonald and the Conservative Party had built the Canadian Pacific; Sir Wilfrid Laurier and the Liberals were attracted by the idea of sponsoring a second transcontinental railroad. The Canadian Northern was interested; so was Charles M. Hays, general manager of the Grand Trunk Railway, which had hitherto confined its activities to the eastern provinces. The logical course would seem to have been to make the new line a joint enterprise, but bad luck dogged the efforts of those who tried to bring this about. Perhaps, in any event, Mackenzie and Mann were too ambitious to be willing to share their enterprises with anyone else.

Out of these circumstances there grew two new transcontinental railway projects instead of just one. In 1903 the Government of Canada and the Grand Trunk signed agreements under which the Government would build a railway—the National

Transcontinental—from Winnipeg to Moncton, which would be leased by the Grand Trunk, while a subsidiary of the latter, the Grand Trunk Pacific, would build a line from Winnipeg to the Pacific Coast. The Yellowhead Pass was to be the route through the Rockies, and the Pacific terminus would be at Prince Rupert, near the mouth of the Skeena River. The total length of the line was about 3,550 miles.

Not to be outdone, the Canadian Northern pushed ahead with its own plans. These were less definite in detail than those of the Grand Trunk, yet slowly but surely its rails were extended, and gaps filled eastward and westward. Its plans embraced such imaginative projects as the Mount Royal tunnel in Montreal. In the west the line ran from Edmonton to the Yellowhead Pass (close to the Grand Trunk Pacific and frequently in sight of it) and, after some uncertainty as to route, it was decided that it should follow the Thompson and Fraser Rivers and end at Vancouver. The rival lines were opened within a few months of one another. The first Grand Trunk Pacific train arrived at Prince Rupert in April 1914; the last spike in the transcontinental line of the Canadian Northern was driven in January 1915, and the first passenger train travelled over the National Transcontinental from Quebec to Winnipeg in August 1915.

Both companies had made it clear that they hoped to compete with the Canadian Pacific on every front. On the Atlantic, the Canadian Northern placed the liners *Royal Edward* and *Royal George* in service to compete with the *Empresses;* the same year, on the Pacific Coast, the C.P.R. *Princesses* were faced with a fleet of Grand Trunk Pacific *Princes*. Adopting the château-style hotel, which the Canadian Pacific had originated, the Grand Trunk built the Château Laurier in Ottawa, and other hotels followed in Winnipeg and Edmonton.

Unfortunately both companies were in serious trouble by the time their lines were completed. The boom had collapsed, and had been followed by the outbreak of war. Money markets had tightened after 1911; traffic had failed to develop to the point at which it could pay interest charges, let alone return a profit. It was a bitter turn of events for Mackenzie and Mann, whose Canadian Northern had always been a sound business proposition before they developed delusions of transcontinental grandeur. The Grand Trunk was in an equally unhappy predicament. After an unprofitable half century it was at last enjoying prosperity when Hays manoeuvred it into the 1903 agreement with the Government. In the end the debts arising from their transcontinental ventures pulled down both corporations, and the Government, already deeply involved by bond guarantees and other liabilities, had no alternative but to take over the lines. First the Canadian Northern and then the Grand Trunk came under government control and in 1922 they were consolidated, along with the Intercolonial and other government-owned lines in the Canadian National Railways.

In the preceding decades railway builders had had a field day. In 1899, when Mackenzie and Mann formed their modest little Canadian Northern, there were 17,250 miles of railroad in Canada. When control passed to the Government in 1917, railway mileage had risen to 38,369—an increase of over 21,000 miles in only 18 years. It was far in excess of the real requirements of a nation with a population of only eight million, and was to give rise to the "railway problem" that bedevilled federal budgets for many years. But it opened up vast new areas of the country to settlement, and in a long-term view contributed substantially both to its growth and prosperity.

The Rival Transcontinentals in 1916

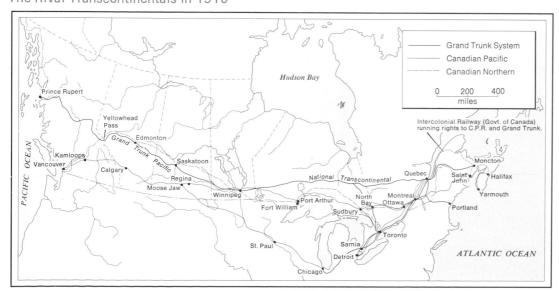

The Steamboat Era on Canada's Lakes and Rivers

Distributor III on the Mackenzie River (upper left)

Sternwheelers appeared on the Fraser River in 1858, on the Red in 1859, and on the Saskatchewan in the early 1870s. Thereafter for half a century they provided transportation over thousands of miles of western lakes and rivers. They survived longest in the North, on the Athabasca, Mackenzie, and Yukon rivers, and on Kootenay Lake, where service continued until as late as 1957.

The White Horse *(centre) steaming through the Five Finger Rapids on the Yukon River. Sternwheelers continued to run between Whitehorse and Dawson until 1954.*

Distributor III in winter quarters, hauled up on skids beyond the reach of ice (below)

A typical sternwheeler was 125 to 150 feet in length, could carry 150 to 200 tons of cargo, and was relatively cheap and easy to build. Her bottom was flat and her draft light — someone once remarked that a sternwheeler could navigate in a heavy dew! This was an important consideration on rivers where bars and channels were shifting constantly and seasonal change in water levels was often great. The position of the paddlewheel at the stern protected it from driftwood and made it possible for the steamer to poke her nose ashore where wharves did not exist but business offered, and then pull herself back into deep water. With the help of lines from shore she could battle her way upstream through rapids and canyons. Her life was short, as wooden hulls built of green timber deteriorated rapidly, but her engines usually went marching on. A classic example was the Distributor herself. In her first incarnation she was built in 1908 for service on the Skeena River. In 1913 her name and engines migrated to the North Thompson River, where a new Distributor took to the water. In 1920 they moved on to the Mackenzie River, where the Distributor III ran for 27 years.

Lumbering Over
Half a Century

A ten-horse team hauling logs on a skidroad. The skids were oiled or greased to make the logs slide along more easily. The picture was taken in Surrey, B.C. in 1885.

Techniques and equipment are all-important in industry. The first export sawmill in British Columbia, built in 1861 in a heavily timbered area on Vancouver Island, closed down only three years later because it was running out of logs. Trees there were in abundance, but most of them were so large that, with the primitive equipment available, the only way to bring them to the mill was to float them. This meant that only a narrow fringe of timber near the water could be logged. The skidroad, along which logs were dragged by oxen or horses, was the earliest solution to this problem.

Equipment soon became more elaborate and included private logging railways. The locomotive in this 1898 photograph is "Old Curly," brought to British Columbia in C.P.R. construction days and later employed in the woods for many years.

Vancouver City Archives and Surrey Museum

Vancouver City Archives and Surrey Museum

Power logging began after 1890, when the donkey engine came into use. This was a stationary steam engine, usually mounted on skids (as shown here) so that it could be moved readily from place to place. It hauled the logs out of the woods by means of a cable.

Interior of a shanty in the Ontario woods
A typical scene, pictured about 1890.

Fish:
Canada's Oldest Export

The fishing banks off Newfoundland and Nova Scotia attracted men across the Atlantic long before the trade in furs began. For a century or two furs were much more talked about, but fishing continued to be important, and is a major Canadian industry at the present day. In a recent year the landed value of fish was more than ten times the value of furs caught in the Canadian wilds, and even when the luxury furs produced on the fur farms were added, the value of fish was still nearly four times as great.

Cod was still king of the Atlantic fisheries at Confederation, and it was sufficiently important to cause lengthy disputes with both France and the United States, whose fishermen wanted free access to eastern Canadian waters and harbours. For some time after 1867 virtually the whole of Canada's deepsea fishing was carried on in the Atlantic. In 1876 the Atlantic fish catch was valued at $10,500,-000, while the catch on the Pacific Coast was worth no more than $123,000.

This state of affairs soon changed. Salmon was to become king of the Pacific fisheries, just as cod was on the Atlantic. The first salmon cannery on the Fraser River was established in 1869. In 1876 the season's pack was still only 9,847 cases, but it jumped to 113,600 cases in 1878. The salmon runs are subject to marked fluctuations from year to year, and the pack naturally reflected this. Peak years were 1882, when 225,000 cases were packed, 1889, when the total jumped to 414,000, and 1893, when production rose to 590,000 cases. An astonishing salmon run in 1897 pushed the total to just over a million cases; but this was exceptional, and although the total was twice surpassed, the average yield in the next decade was about 600,000 cases. By this time British Columbia was already contributing a quarter or more to the total value of the Canadian fish catch.

From the Fraser, fishermen and canneries had crept up the coast to many inlets and to the Skeena, Nass and other northern rivers. On that same northern coast, halibut (a near relative of the cod) was beginning to interest fishermen. Halibut was soon to rank second in importance to the salmon in the Pacific fisheries and its progress was helped greatly when the Grand Trunk Pacific Railway (now part of the Canadian National Railways) was completed to Prince Rupert in 1914 and a large cold storage plant was erected there.

Some thought was being given to the future; steps were being taken to restock the Fraser and other heavily fished rivers. Fish hatcheries were established, and by 1909 over 465,000,000 salmon fry had already been distributed. But time was to show that the conservation problem was really international in scope, and concerned the United States as much as it did Canada. What was the use of planting salmon fry by the million in the Fraser if the mature fish, seeking to return to the river some years later, were intercepted and fished to the point of depletion by American fishermen and fish traps? A kindred problem was arising with regard to the halibut, which was being over-fished by the fishermen of both countries. Eventually international agreements came to the rescue. A treaty signed in 1923 resulted in the establishment of the International Pacific Halibut Commission that regulated halibut fishing and quickly restored the prosperity of the industry. Similarly the International Pacific Salmon Commission watches over the salmon fishery based on the Fraser River, and conducts research relating to the industry in general.

Large-scale industrialization has developed in the fisheries as in so many other activities. Time was when a Fraser River fisherman needed little more than a rowboat and a fish net, but that day is long past. The gasoline engine aided the fishermen greatly, and led to the development of seiners and trollers that could work some distance offshore. But these new boats were much larger and much more expensive, and many were financed by companies rather than individuals. Similarly, in early days a cannery could be built and equipped for a few thousand dollars; but by degrees the small canneries that at one time dotted the rivers and inlets on the Pacific Coast disappeared and were replaced by a few elaborate, costly but efficient large-scale plants owned by large corporations. Mechanization has taken over at many points, and although production has increased greatly, total employment in the industry has dropped. In 1909 the total work force in the Pacific Coast fisheries was about 19,500. In 1967 there were 12,117 licenced fishermen in British Columbia.

On the Atlantic Coast the lordly cod found itself faced with both marketing problems and a rival for the leading place in the industry. Salted and dried fish had long been the basic product—lightly salted for the Mediterranean market, and more heavily salted for the trade in the Caribbean and elsewhere. Gradually the demand in the Mediterranean declined, and new products and new markets had to be developed. Refrigeration came to the rescue in part. It made it possible to send fish to new inland markets, and fresh-frozen fish and fish fillets were among the new items produced.

The rival to the cod was the lobster, which in some recent years has been the most valuable single item in the whole Canadian fish harvest. Cod, lobster and salmon have in fact been jockeying for first place, with halibut and the lowly scallop fourth and fifth on the list. The figures for the 1964 and 1965 seasons tell the tale. In 1964 the landed values of the catch of each was as follows: salmon, $30,244,-000; lobster, $24,244,000; cod, $22,055,000; halibut, $8,309,000; scallops, $7,278,000. In 1965 the order was: lobster, $26,632,000; salmon, $25,950,000; cod, $23,637,000; halibut, $11,112,000, and scallops, $10,-849,000. In each year herring was in sixth place with a catch valued at over $6,000,000.

Capt. Angus Walters

Public Archives of Canada

The schooner "Bluenose"

Long queen of the cod-fishing fleet, Lunenburg's beautiful Bluenose *won international races as well as plying her trade. Built in 1921, she was sold in 1942 and two years later was wrecked on a reef off Haiti. A replica was built in 1964.*

Nor must Canada's inland fisheries be forgotten. With a larger area of fresh water than any other country, the fisheries in lakes and rivers are important and will become increasingly so. In early days fish were the mainstay of many of the Indians, and at many posts the fur traders counted upon them heavily for subsistence; stories about fishing through the ice in winter are frequent in fur trade history. Then as now the whitefish was the most important catch, with pickerel and perch next in order. Total value of the inland commercial fish catch in 1965 was $14,589,000.

The annual harvest from ocean, lake and river is today truly a tremendous one. In 1966 it totalled no less than 1,300,000 tons of fish with a landed value of over $172,000,000.

211

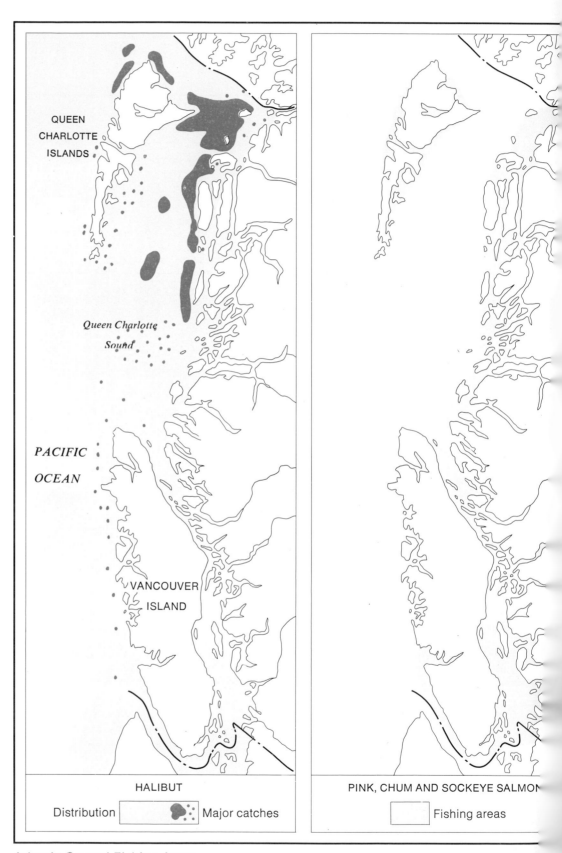

QUEEN
CHARLOTTE
ISLANDS

Queen Charlotte
Sound

PACIFIC

OCEAN

VANCOUVER

ISLAND

HALIBUT

Distribution ▢ 🔲 Major catches

PINK, CHUM AND SOCKEYE SALMON

▢ Fishing areas

Atlantic Coastal Fishing Areas

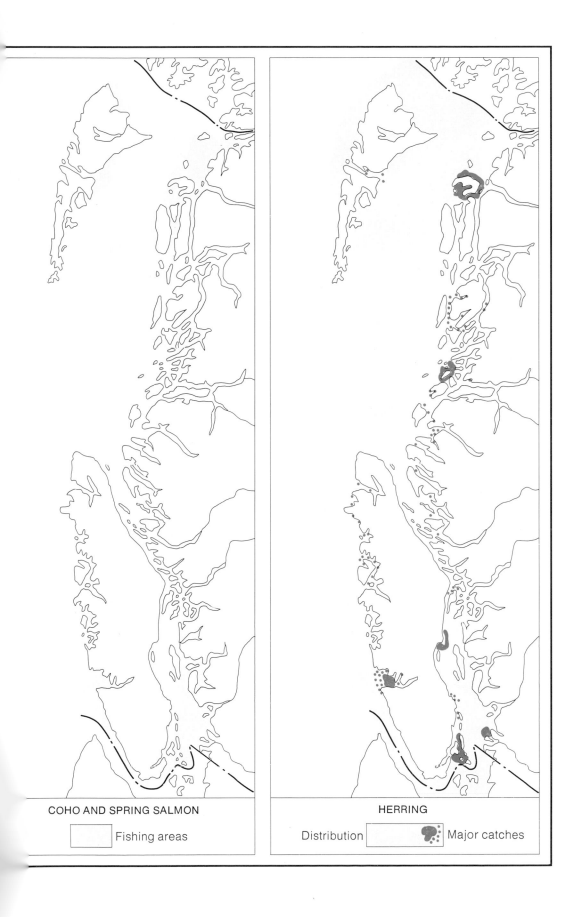

COHO AND SPRING SALMON

Fishing areas

HERRING

Distribution Major catches

Salmon fleet in the Fraser about 1905

Almost all fishing was then done by hand. The fishermen are waiting to hear the gun that signalled the moment when they could begin to throw out their nets. A scene of frenzied activity would follow.

Mails and Messages

Passengers, mail, and freight had to cross the ocean by ship until the coming of the aeroplane; but submarine cables and wireless telegraph (radio) made quick communication possible at a much earlier date. Here the famous steamer Great Eastern *is shown in 1866 at Heart's Content, Newfoundland, when she completed laying the first successful trans-Atlantic cable.*

Guglielmo Marconi, inventor of wireless, shown at upper right, in the Cabot Tower on Signal Hill, St. John's Newfoundland, where in December 1901 he received the first wireless signals transmitted across the Atlantic. Six years later the first commercial station capable of spanning the ocean was opened at Glace Bay, in Nova Scotia.

Surface travel between Canada and Europe reached its climax in 1931, when the 42,000-ton Canadian Pacific superliner Empress of Britain entered service. Her speed of over 24 knots enabled her to complete the voyage from Quebec to Southampton in less than five days. This great ship — much the largest ever built for service to Canada — was destroyed by bombs and torpedoes in 1940.

CHAPTER 15

Internal Politics

Defence: The Canadian Dilemma

I N 1867 national defence became a responsibility of the new Dominion government, and it soon became apparent that the responsibility would be a very real one. Early in 1870 Canada was notified that all British forces would soon be withdrawn, except the garrisons at the dockyards in Halifax and Esquimalt, which the Royal Navy would retain. Wolseley's Red River expedition in 1870 was the last military operation in Canada in which the British regulars took part, and all of them had sailed for home by the end of 1871.

Fortunately Great Britain and the United States had settled most of their differences the same year by concluding the Treaty of Washington, and Canada ceased to be apprehensive of an attack from the south. In spite of this, the passing of the first Militia Act in 1872 aroused some enthusiasm. An Active Militia with a maximum strength of 40,000 was authorized, to be recruited on a volunteer basis, and at one time over 37,000 men were actually enrolled. As most of them were mustered in training camps for only a few days each year, it became evident that a Permanent Force was also required. This had its first beginnings in 1871, but it was not authorized formally until 1883. Its original authorized strength was only 750, and although this was soon increased it was never more than 4,000 before the First World War.

The Militia was hard hit by the depression of the 1870s; appropriations were cut heavily and its strength declined steadily. It was faced, too, with a dilemma that was to become familiar—the unlikelihood of an attack on Canada, and, if one should come, the virtual impossibility of defending the country effectively with any forces that Canada was likely to have available. Nevertheless some useful

steps were taken. The proposal to set up a military college caught the personal interest of Alexander Mackenzie, when he was prime minister, and the Royal Military College at Kingston enrolled its first cadets and began its distinguished career in 1876. In 1882 an arsenal was established in Quebec, and within a few years Canada could provide herself with ammunition for small arms and with much of that required for artillery. But the Militia continued to decline, and by 1890 it had reached a very low ebb indeed.

External events gave it new life. Differences over Venezuela brought Britain and the United States within a measurable distance of war in 1895, and in the face of this threat the Militia secured a good deal of much needed new equipment. Four years later the South African War broke out, and Canada was invited to participate. Many English-Canadians strongly favoured sending Canadian troops; French-Canadian nationalists opposed the proposal with equal vigour. Laurier trod a middle path and announced that the Government would equip a volunteer force, not to exceed one thousand in number, and transport them to South Africa. Later other contingents followed and, at his own expense, Lord Strathcona raised and equipped the force of mounted rifles known as the Lord Strathcona Horse. In all a total of 7,368 men from Canada served in Africa, and another thousand relieved the Imperial troops on garrison duty at Halifax. They served with courage and distinction, and four of them were awarded the Victoria Cross. They served, moreover, as distinct and separate units throughout. The British had intended to use the Canadians as reinforcements for their own forces, but the proposal was not accepted.

Soon after the South African War ended it became clear that a crisis was on the horizon in Europe. The naval race between Britain and Germany had begun, and the tension was soon reflected in military circles even in Canada. A new and strengthened Militia Act was passed in 1904. In 1905 Brigadier P. H. N. (later Sir Percy) Lake was appointed to the new post of Chief of the General

Cavalry camp at Durban, South Africa
The Canadian Mounted Rifles appear in the left centre. The date was June 1902, just as the South African War was ending.

Staff, and in that position, and subsequently as Inspector-General, he did much to improve the quality and effectiveness of the Militia and Permanent Force, small in numbers though they were.

Britain was now concentrating her forces at home, and seeking to promote overall Imperial defence schemes that would include the forces of the self-governing Dominions. In 1906 the last of the Imperial garrison troops left Esquimalt and Halifax (where their departure severed a connection that had been unbroken since 1749), and in 1910 the dockyards themselves were turned over to Canada. Imperial Defence Conferences held in 1909 and 1911 resulted in important agreements on standardization of various sorts, but the Dominions held aloof from any unification of forces or command. A country with long coastlines and two dockyards obviously had to have ships, and in 1910 the Canadian Navy came into being. Two aging cruisers, the *Niobe* and the smaller *Rainbow,* were purchased that year from the Royal Navy. They have been much ridiculed, but they were well suited for training purposes and were intended for nothing more; a new naval force of five cruisers and six destroyers

Royal Navy squadron at Esquimalt, 1904

A typical scene in Esquimalt Harbour when it was still a Royal Navy base. Taken in 1904, this view shows the survey ship Egeria *(left), the cruisers* Bonaventure, Grafton *and* Flora, *and the sloop* Shearwater.

was supposed to be built forthwith. The new ships never materialized, and Borden's alternative proposal to assist Great Britain by contributing the cost of three battleships was defeated by the Liberal majority in the Senate.

Two small episodes deserve mention. In 1884 General Wolseley, who had led the expedition to Red River in 1870, was in command of a force in Egypt that was to go up the Nile and attempt to relieve General Gordon at Khartoum. Wolseley remembered the feats of the Canadian boatmen, and asked for their assistance in ascending the river. Some 400 men were recruited, for the most part lumbermen and Caughnawaga Indians. Strictly speaking they did not constitute a military unit, but it was the first occasion upon which a force from a self-governing colony served overseas.

Unlike the Nile campaign, the second expedition was very much Canada's own affair. There were a few Mounted Police in the Yukon area when the great gold rush to the Klondike began, but it was deemed wise to send a military force to ensure that law and sovereignty would be maintained. A Yukon Field Force, consisting of 203 volunteers from the Permanent Force, was recruited and dispatched in the summer of 1898. Unfortunately they had to travel by an all-Canadian route, and ships and trains could take them only as far as Glenora, on the Stikine River. From there they endured a dreadful overland march to Fort Selkirk and Dawson. Most of them were home again by 1900, but they had served a useful purpose at a critical time.

First Canadian Navy recruiting poster, 1911
(right)

The Yukon Field Force at Teslin Lake (shown
below)

*The gold discoveries in the Klondike region in
1897-98 attracted more than 40,000 people to the
Yukon, and a military force of 203 officers and
men were sent to help maintain law and order.*

Burning of the Parliament Buildings

On the evening of February 3, 1916, flames erupted suddenly in the reading room of the House of Commons, and fire swept through virtually the whole of the old centre block. This photograph was taken the next morning.

Political Leaders and Issues: 1867-1919

Three men dominated the Canadian political scene between Confederation and the treaty that ended the First World War—Sir John Macdonald, Sir Wilfrid Laurier and Sir Robert Borden. Between them they held the office of prime minister for no less than 42 of the 52 years.

Macdonald, having achieved Confederation, worked hard to complete it, and by 1873 Canada extended from Prince Edward Island to British Columbia. But that same year the "Pacific Scandal" —the disclosure that the first sydicate formed to build the Pacific Railway had contributed heavily to Conservative campaign funds in the election of 1872—forced him to resign. His Liberal successor, Alexander Mackenzie, held office for the next five years. The soul of integrity, Mackenzie was both cautious and lacking in imagination; a free trader, he believed that tariffs should be imposed only for revenue purposes, and was averse to any direct government aid to commerce and industry. His years in office happened to be a period of severe depression when many businesses were in difficulties. Macdonald, whom many had regarded as a spent force, shrewdly advocated tariff protection for Canadian industries (which he dubbed the "National Policy") and was returned to power in the fall of 1878.

The major achievement of his second and much longer term as prime minister, which was to last until his death in 1891, was the completion of the Canadian Pacific Railway. Mackenzie had regarded it as a project far in advance of its time; Macdonald felt that Confederation could not survive, let alone prosper, without it. By a supreme effort the line was built, but by the time regular train service had begun between Montreal and the Pacific Coast in 1886, troublesome issues were arising that began to undermine Macdonald's majority. A French-Canadian nationalist spirit had long been smouldering in Quebec, and the execution of Riel in 1885 fanned it into flames. Later the separate schools question in Manitoba aroused nationalist feeling still further. Macdonald won general elections in 1887 and again in 1891, just before his death, but the electorate was supporting a grand old political chieftain who had accomplished two miracles for Canada—Confederation and the C.P.R. —rather than his party, which was declining rapidly in popularity, especially in Quebec. Macdonald had no obvious successor, and his death was followed by a confused five-year period in which four Conservative prime ministers held office in uneasy succession.

Politics were led out of this wilderness by Wilfrid Laurier, an attractive and able French-Canadian who had become leader of the Liberal party in 1890. He won an easy victory in the election of 1896, and held office for fifteen years. For much of this time Canada enjoyed great prosperity, and it was the Laurier government that stimulated the great flow of population into the West, and subsidized the many railway projects that, whatever their merits, brought large amounts of capital into the country.

But, like Macdonald, Laurier had his problems as well as his great successes. Some of these stemmed from abroad. Participation in the South African War was one of them; Laurier tried to solve it and reduce French-Canadian nationalist opposition by agreeing to a Canadian volunteer force that would be paid for by Great Britain. Later the increasing tension between Britain and Germany led to efforts to persuade Canada to participate in Imperial defence. Laurier countered by the creation of a modest Canadian Navy.

Relations with both Britain and the United States were strained in 1903 by the award of the Alaska Boundary Commission, appointed to settle the dispute regarding the boundary between Alaska and British Columbia. The report, which accepted the American case, was supported by the three American members and the commissioner appointed by Great Britain; the two Canadian members declined to sign. Most Canadians felt that the American claims were unjustified and that the British commissioner had paid much more attention to Britain's wish to maintain good relations with the United States than to the strength of the Canadian counter case. This was one of the developments that led to the creation of a Department of External Affairs in Canada in 1909 and, to Laurier's cost, the anti-American feeling it engendered lingered on and played a part in the general election of 1911. The chief issue in the election was reciprocity in the trade with the United States, a proposal offered, somewhat surprisingly, by the Americans themselves. At first Laurier must have felt that victory was assured, but opposition mounted steadily. The prairie farmers, anxious to secure cheaper implements and machinery, strongly favoured reciprocity, but the railways and industry opposed it vehemently. These forces, plus anti-American sentiment, united to defeat Laurier and bring the Conservatives, under Robert Borden, into office.

Borden's term as prime minister, which lasted almost nine years, was dominated by the First World War. Politically, the crucial issue he faced was conscription—compulsory military service overseas. For several years it had appeared that sufficient volunteers would be forthcoming to maintain the Canadian divisions in France, but when Borden visited Europe in the spring of 1917 he became convinced that this was no longer true. In May he announced in the House of Commons that compulsory enlistment would be necessary, and the Military Service Act was passed in August. The political repercussions were enormous. French-Canadian nationalists were furious in their opposition, and riots later broke out in Quebec. Laurier had consistently supported the government's war effort,

Alexander Mackenzie (upper left)

The second Prime Minister of Canada, who held office from 1873 to 1878.

Sir Robert L. Borden (above)

Prime Minister of Canada from 1911 to 1919. This fine portrait by Sir William Orpen was painted in 1919, at the time of the Paris Peace Conference.

Anti-reciprocity cartoon, August 1911 (lower left)

HELPING SAM.

CANADIAN RESOURCES

Sir Wilfrid—"Whoa, now; Sam wants to milk you."

but he felt compelled to oppose conscription. The Liberals were badly divided on the issue, and a split in the party resulted. In October Borden reorganized his cabinet as a coalition in which Liberals were included, and his new administration, known as the Union Government, easily won the general election held in December, though Laurier won 62 of the 65 seats in Quebec.

The conscription crisis was of relatively short duration. The war ended sooner than many expected and fewer than 50,000 conscripts were actually sent overseas. The Union Government had been formed to meet a wartime emergency, and when that had been dealt with politicians began to move back to their former allegiances; the old familiar party lines soon reappeared. But the crisis had left scars, particularly in Quebec, that were destined to last for many years.

Sir John A. Macdonald in later years

Macdonald at Earnscliffe, his home in Ottawa, in 1888. He was then 73.

Public Archives of Canada

Newfoundland: 1867-1919

Officially the Fathers of Confederation included two Newfoundlanders—Frederick Bowker Carter and Ambrose Shca—but the advocates of union were defeated in the election of 1869, and Newfoundland was to continue its independent way for another eighty years.

It was a path beset with many thorns. The oldest of the island's problems—control of its fisheries—continued to be troublesome until the end of the century. The rights on the western "French shore" that Britain had granted to France in 1783 and to the United States in 1818 were constant subjects of friction and dispute. In 1881 Newfoundland was given full territorial jurisdiction over her western coast, but the fisheries continued to be the subject of agreements between Britain and France, and these Newfoundland declined to ratify. The issue was dealt with finally in 1904, when France relinquished her rights, which in effect had been purchased by Britain by the cession of territory in West Africa. The problem of the American rights under the convention of 1818 was referred in the end to The Hague Tribunal, which ruled in Newfoundand's favour in 1910.

For many years the interior of Newfoundland continued to be an unpeopled and inaccessible wilderness. A railway would obviously help greatly in opening up the country, but how to finance and build it was the problem. In 1881 work began on the first line on the island, which was to extend from St. John's westward and around Conception Bay to Harbour Grace. This was completed in 1884. During the next four years a second line was built across the Avalon Peninsula to Placentia. Work then began on the line that it was hoped would extend right across the island. An agreement concluded in 1890 brought into the picture Robert Reid, a railway and bridge builder of note, who among other things had built some of the difficult parts of the Canadian Pacific along the north shore of Lake Superior. In addition to building the railway, he undertook to operate both it and steamer services that provided essential communications for many settlements along the coasts. Although the depression and financial crises of the early 1890s brought work to a halt, it was later resumed and the line was completed in 1897. On June 29, 1898, the first through train steamed out of St. John's bound for Port aux Basques, well over 500 miles distant.

Fishing, with all its uncertainties, long continued to be the mainstay of the Newfoundland economy. To many its existence was vital, and a poor season could result in great hardship. Thanks in part to the railway, Newfoundland's forests began to offer a somewhat more certain source of employment and income. In 1897 a small pioneer pulp mill began operation at Black River, on Placentia Bay. It closed in a few years, but it had provided useful experience. In 1909 a newsprint plant was completed at Grand Falls by the Anglo-Newfoundland Development Company, a subsidiary of a group of British newspapers. This expanded into a major enterprise and took over a pulp mill that had been built at Bishop's Falls, eleven miles away. Paper from Grand Falls was shipped to England through Botwood, the port on Newfoundland's northern coast. In 1923 construction of a second major newsprint industry began at Corner Brook—then a small village, but destined to become Newfoundland's second largest city.

When Newfoundland rejected Confederation in 1869 its population was 146,500. By 1901 it had risen to nearly 221,000, and it increased slowly to 263,000 in 1921—about half the population of Toronto at that date. Life had been difficult at times, especially in the 1890s. On July 8, 1892, fire devastated more than two-thirds of St. John's, and it was estimated that not more than a quarter of the damage was covered by insurance. Most of the world suffered from hard times during the next few years, and Newfoundland endured more than most. Union with Canada was discussed again at this difficult time, but it met with no response from Mackenzie Bowell, the least imaginative and most ineffective of all Canadian prime ministers.

Newfoundland, like Canada, responded promptly when war broke out in 1914. Several thousand Newfoundlanders served in the naval forces. The first two infantry companies of a Newfoundland Contingent sailed in the same transports that carried the Canadian Expeditionary Force overseas in October. When the Contingent reached full battalion strength, it was sent to Gallipoli in the fall of 1915. Later it returned to France where it expanded into the Newfoundland (later the Royal Newfoundland) Regiment. In France the Regiment was to be involved in two tragic and bitterly fought actions in which it suffered heavily. The first was in the Battle of the Somme, near Beaumont Hamel, on July 1, 1916; the other was in the First Battle of Scarpe, fought at the time the Canadians were storming Vimy Ridge, in April 1917. Losses in the first engagement were so severe that July 1 has ever since been observed as Newfoundland's Memorial Day. In all more than 6,000 men served in the Regiment, and 3,720 of them were killed, wounded or taken prisoner.

Completion of the Newfoundland railway

This timetable was issued in December 1898, a few months after trains began running between St. John's and Port-aux-Basques, where the steamer Bruce *provided a connection with North Sydney. Passenger train service on this line ceased in 1969 and was replaced by a bus service on the Newfoundland section of the Trans-Canada Highway.*

NEWFOUNDLAND RAILWAY

SHORTEST SEA TRIP

SIX HOURS,

NEWFOUNDLAND TO CANADA.

S. S. Bruce.

R. G. REID, Proprietor, . . St. John's, Newfoundlan

OPERATING.

W. D. REID, General Manager. . St. John's, Newfoundlar

TRAFFIC.

H. D. REID, Assistant General Manager, St. John's, Newfoundla

TRANSPORTATION.

R. G. REID, JR., Superintendent, . St. John's, Newfoundla

G. H. MASSEY, Chief Engineer, . " "

H. A. MORINE, Freight and Pass. Agent, " "

H. McNEIL, Auditor, . . " "

H. S. CORMACK, Treasurer, . . " "

H. CRAWFORD, Purchasing Agent, " "

DECEMBER 1, 1898.

NEWFOUNDLAND
RAILWAY SYSTEM

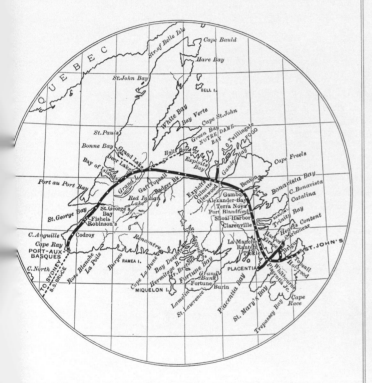

R.G. REID, Proprietor
❦ ST. JOHN'S ❦
NEWFOUNDLAND

THE SOUTH PUB. CO., ILLUSTRATORS AND PRINTERS, N. Y.

NEWFOUNDLAND RAILWAY
TIME TABLE.

MAIN LINE.

READ DOWN		MAIN LINE		READ UP	
No. 1. Express, Daily.	No. 7 Accom. Daily Except Sunday.	Stations.	Miles.	No. 8 Accom. Daily Except Sunday.	No. 2 Express, Daily Except Sunday.
lv **5.00** P.M.	**8.30** A.M.	......**St. John's**......	0	**9.30** P.M.	**11.00** A.M.
....	8.56	......* Dunnsmere	7	9.07	....
....	9.07	......* Irvine...........	10	8.55	....
5.43	9.27	......Topsail........	15	8.37	10.17
....	9.39	......* Manuels........	18	8.17	....
6.03	9.55	......Kelligrews........	22	8.03	9.55
....	10.14	......* Seal Cove	27	7.50	....
....	10.18	......* Duff's........	29	7.45	....
....	....	......*Brien's........		....	....
....	10.37	......Holyrood........	33	7.30	....
6.38	10.48	......* Woodford........	33	7.19	9.25
....	10.59	......Salmon Cove........	36	7.10	....
6.55	ar 11.20	......**Brigus Junction**......	39	lv 6.45	9 07
7.09	lv 11.30	......* Maher's........	44	ar 6.35	**8.48**
....	....	......*Hodge Water......	52	....	....
ar **7.50**	12.30 P.M.	......**Whitbourne**......	57	**5.45** P.M.	lv **8.10**
No. 1. Ex. Sun. Tues. Thur.	No. 5. Accom. Mon. Wed. Fri.			No. 6. Accom. Sun. Wed. Fri.	No. 2. Ex. Mon. Thur. Sat.
lv **8.00** P.M.	ar **7.50** A.M.	......**Whitbourne**......	57	ar **7.45** A.M. / lv **8.10**	**8.00** A.M.
	lv **8.15**				
8.25	8.42	......Placentia Junction......	64	6.22	7.30
8.49	9.10	......Long Harbor........	71	6.15	7.15
9.22	9.51	......Tickle Harbor......	82	6 15	6.55
9.46	10.15	......Rantem........	90	5.45	6.16
9.55	10.23	......La Manche........	92	5.35	6.10
10.21	10.53	......Arnold's Cove......	101	5.05	5.42
10.36	11.08	......Come-by-Chance......	105	4.50	5.30
11.17	11.55	......Northern Bight......	118	4 05	4.51
12.05 A.M.	**12.45** P.M.	......**Clarenville**......	132	**3.15**	**4.07**
12.15	12.53	......Shoal Harbor......	136	3.01	3.57
12.45	1.31	......Thorburn Lake......	145	2.27	3.27
ar **1.10**	2.00	......**Port Blandford**......	153	lv **2.00**	**3.05**
lv **1.20**	2.10			ar **1.50**	**2.55**
2.05	3.00	......Terra Nova........	167	1.00 A.M.	2.05
2.55	4.00	......Alexander Bay......	183	12.00	1.17
3.23	4 34	......Gambo........	192	11.28	12.53
4.05	5.25	......Benton........	206	10.35	12.13 A.M.
5.22	7.04	......Glenwood........	232	9.00	11 00
6.05	7.55	......Ouinette........	246	8.09	10.20
ar **6.30**	**8.30**	......**Exploits**......	256	lv **7.35**	**9.55**
lv **6.40**	**8.40**			ar **7.25**	**9.45**
7.15	9.21	......Bishop's Falls......	268	6.45	9.10
7.50	10.05	......Rushy Pond........	280	6.00	8.33
8.37	11.03	......Badger Brook......	296	5 00	7.45
9.30	12.03 A.M.	......Joe Gload Pond......	313	4.00	6.55
9.40	12.18	......St. Patrick's Brook......	317	3.45	6.40
10.00	12 42	......West Brook........	324	3.20	6.20
10.10	12.55	......Quarry........	327	3.07	6.10
10.35	1.24	......Gaff Topsail......	335	2.37	5.45
11.05	2.00	......Kitty's Brook......	345	2.00	5.15
11.44	2.45	......Howley........	359	1.15	4.33
12.01 P.M.	3.15	......Grand Lake........	365	12 46	4.15
12.34	3.55	......Deer Lake........	376	12.06 P.M.	3.42
1.09	4.37	......South Brook........	388	11.21	3.05
ar **2.05**	5.50	......**Bay of Islands**......	407	lv **10.10**	**2.05** P.M.
lv **2.15**	6.00			ar **10.00**	**1.55**
4.45	9.21	......St. George's Bay......	459	6.37	11.20
5.27	10.17	......Fischell's........	474	5.42	10.37
5 56	10.56	......Robinson's........	484	5.04	10.06
7.37	1.10 P.M.	......Codroy........	519	2.50	8 23
ar **9.00** P.M.	3.00	......**Port-aux-Basques**......	548	lv **1.00** A.M.	**7.00** A.M.
Mon. Wed. Fri.	Wed. Fri. Sun.	......**North Sydney**......	633	Tues. Thurs. Sat.	Wed. Fri. Sun.

* Flag stations.

S. S. Bruce leaves North Sydney after arrival I. C. R. Express, Tuesday, Thursday and Saturday evenings, and leaves Port Aux Basques after arrival of express from St. John's on Monday, Wednesday and Friday evenings.

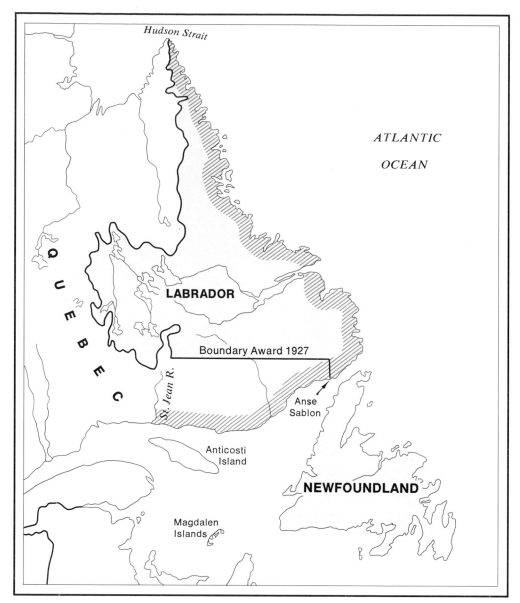

The Quebec-Labrador Boundary

This has a long and tangled history. In 1763 Anticosti Island, the Magdalen Islands and the coast of Labrador all the way from the St. Jean River to Hudson Strait were given to Newfoundland; but in 1774, at the time of the Quebec Act, all three were transferred to Quebec (as Canada was then called).

In 1809 the Labrador coast and Anticosti Island were given back to Newfoundland; but this decision was partially reversed in 1825, when Anticosti and the Labrador coast between the St. Jean River and Anse Sablon were again transferred to Quebec.

Controversy regarding the extent of Newfoundland's territorial rights in Labrador continued for a full century but was settled finally in 1927 by a decision of the Imperial Privy Council. This limited Newfoundland's coastal rights to the coast between Hudson Bay and Anse Sablon, but gave her title to a very large area inland.

St. John's after the great fire of 1892

Public Archives of Canada

This was the worst disaster in the history of Newfoundland. Over 2,000 houses and commercial buildings were destroyed and 11,000 persons were left homeless. The loss was estimated at $20,000,000, less than a quarter of which was insured.

CHAPTER 16

The First World War and After

Overseas
The First World War

WHEN, on August 2, 1914, Sir Robert Borden offered to send an expeditionary force overseas, and the British Government accepted the offer gratefully on August 6, neither can have had any inkling of the extent of the remarkable contribution that Canada was to make to the Allied cause in the First World War. From a population of only eight million, enlistments in the armed forces totalled 628,462, and of these 60,661 lost their lives.

All but a few thousand of the enlisted personnel were in the Army. The Canadian Navy had never been taken seriously, and its strength was only 330 when war broke out. Later this increased to over 9,000, and the Navy had 134 vessels in commission, mostly small craft engaged in antisubmarine patrols on the Atlantic Coast. More important was the Canadian contribution to the war in the air. There was no separate Canadian air force, but over 22,000 Canadians joined the Royal Flying Corps (later the Royal Air Force), and many of them served with great distinction. They included two of the most famous aces of the war—Major W. A. Bishop, who downed 72 enemy planes, and Major Raymond Collishaw, who shot down 60, totals not exceeded by any other Commonwealth airmen.

Army mobilization plans had been made before the war, but Colonel Sam Hughes, the energetic but unpredictable Minister of Militia, chose to improvise new ones. A training camp sprang into existence at Valcartier, near Quebec, and 35,000 volunteers, mostly from the militia, were soon assembled there. On October 3 the Canadian Expeditionary Force, 33,000 strong, sailed from Gaspé in 32 transports, bound for England, where they completed their training on Salisbury Plain. Early in January the first Canadian unit—the Princess Patricia's Light Infantry—arrived at the front, and by February the whole 1st Canadian Division was in France.

Of the many battles in which the Canadians fought in the next three years, four were outstanding—Ypres, the Somme, Vimy Ridge and Passchendaele. For the Canadians the battle at Ypres began on April 22, 1915, when the Germans launched their first attack using poison gas. French colonial troops on the Division's left flank fell back, creating a huge and dangerous salient, but the Canadians held firm under fearful conditions and both saved the day and established their reputation as a tough fighting force.

By the time the Canadians became involved in the long drawn out Battle of the Somme, the 2nd Division had arrived in France and had been united with the first to form the Canadian Corps. In May 1916 Lt.-Gen. Sir Julian Byng (later Viscount Byng of Vimy, and Governor-General of Canada) assumed command, and it was under him that the Corps fought on the Somme in September. Canadians there participated in the first attack in which tanks were used, but these were too few and inefficient to be effective. The Somme was one of the long, incredibly dreadful battles of attrition that characterized the western front in France for several years, and it seemed to produce nothing for either side but hundreds of thousands of casualties. It cost the Canadian Corps 24,029 men—killed, wounded, prisoners or missing.

The Battle of Vimy Ridge is regarded as a classic military operation. The Ridge itself is only about 350 feet high, but it dominates the Douai plain for miles around. The Germans had built strong defences and had defeated all attempts to capture it. By the time the Canadians were assigned to the task, the Canadian Corps had reached its full strength of four divisions, and constituted a formidable fighting force. The attack was prepared for with the utmost thoroughness; every man knew precisely what was expected of him. The main assault, preceded by a most effective artillery barrage, began early on the morning of April 9, 1917;

"Over the top"
One of the best-known photographs of the First World War, showing the fateful moment when Canadian troops went over the top to launch an attack during the Battle of the Somme, in 1916.

Sir Sam Hughes
Minister of Militia and Defence, 1911-16.

British and Canadian Commanders in France
Field Marshal Sir Douglas Haig (later Earl Haig), the British commander-in-chief, with Lieut.-Gen. Sir Arthur Currie, commander of the Canadian Corps.

virtually the whole of the famous Ridge had been captured by mid-day. The cost to the Corps was over 11,000 casualties, but it had taken more ground and more prisoners than any previous single British offensive.

In June the Corps received a Canadian commander—Lt.-Gen. Arthur (later Sir Arthur) Currie, an able officer whose abilities and accomplishments Canadians have been slow to appreciate. Perhaps this is partly because he was called upon late in October and early in November 1917 to lead the Canadian Corps in the attack on the ridge at Passchendaele. Physical conditions were indescribable and it was obvious from the first that nothing of consequence could be accomplished, but the French armies were faltering and diversionary action was essential. The Canadians displayed all the courage and stamina for which they had become noted, and they duly captured the Passchendaele ridge; but over 15,000 casualties were a heavy price to pay for an action that was basically a political move, and Passchendaele continues to be the most controversial episode in the career of the British commander-in-chief Earl Haig.

The Canadian Corps was not involved in the last great German offensive in the spring of 1918, but is was very active in the Allied counteroffensive that followed and ended the war. Amiens, Arras, the Canal du Nord and Cambrai were some of the points around which the Canadians fought battles and pushed forward. When the armistice came on November 11, they were on the outskirts of Mons, in Belgium, and in the course of the famous march into Germany a Canadian contingent crossed the Rhine at Bonn on December 13.

Once hostilities ended in France the great ambition of the Canadians was to get home as soon as possible. Most of them did so as soon as transportation could be arranged, but a few served for a time in distant and unexpected places. Some of the Allied politicians hoped for a time that intervention in Russia, where scattered elements were still opposing the Communists, might be effective, and small Canadian contingents were sent to Murmansk and Archangel, in northern Russia, and to Vladivostok, in Siberia. But these operations were short lived; all the troops had been evacuated by the summer and early autumn of 1919.

Canada's contribution to the First World War has been rightly termed "a staggering effort" for so small a country. The cost in lives had been high, but the rewards were great, for Canada emerged with her status as a distinct entity recognized not only within the Commonwealth but internationally as well.

The First World War and Canada

Canada was suffering from a depression in 1914; the period of great prosperity that had begun at the turn of the century had come to an end. At first the war promised to accentuate the slump, but by 1915 economic activity had begun to pick up, and a wartime boom soon developed.

Among other things, Europe needed food, for the war was upsetting home production and in some instances cutting off the normal sources of supply. Canadian wheat was in great demand, and the prairie farmers moved quickly to increase their crops. The acreage devoted to wheat growing was almost 80 percent higher in 1919 than it had been in 1913. Prices soared, and in 1917 the government intervened, assumed control of wheat stocks, and later established a Wheat Board to market the 1918 crop. Even so, the price of No. 1 Northern wheat, which had averaged $1.07 a bushel during the years 1910-16, rose to an average of $2.31 in 1917-20. Harvests were poor in the later war years, but at these prices the farmers still prospered.

Shells and ships were other vital wartime needs that Canada helped to supply. The prolonged battles on the western front required vast quantities of ammunition, and over 66,000,000 artillery shells were manufactured in Canadian factories. Ships were in great demand soon after the war began, and the shortage became more acute as the Germans developed their highly effective submarine campaign. By 1917 ships had become a matter of life or death for the Allied cause, and building yards began to mushroom not only on both coasts but on the Great Lakes as well. Many of the initial orders came from the Imperial Munitions Board, a purchasing agency of the British Government, but these were later followed by orders from the Governments of Canada and France and other sources.

This hastily improvised but highly successful shipbuilding effort lasted for five years, from 1917 to 1921. Standard type steel freighters with a carrying capacity of up to 8,800 tons were built by the deep-sea yards on both coasts, and on the Great Lakes a fleet of so-called "lakers" took to the water—steel ships built to the maximum dimensions that would enable them to squeeze through the canals between the lakes and the sea. One feature was a resurgence of wooden shipbuilding on the Pacific Coast. Steel was in short supply and ships of any sort were at such a premium that dozens of small wooden steamers, mostly ordered by the French Government, were included in the programme. More surprising still, sixteen wooden auxiliary schooners were built for private owners.

Public Archives of Canada

The mud of Passchendaele

Canadian gunners in the mud at Passchendaele.
From the painting by Alfred Bastien in the War
Collection of the National Gallery of Canada.

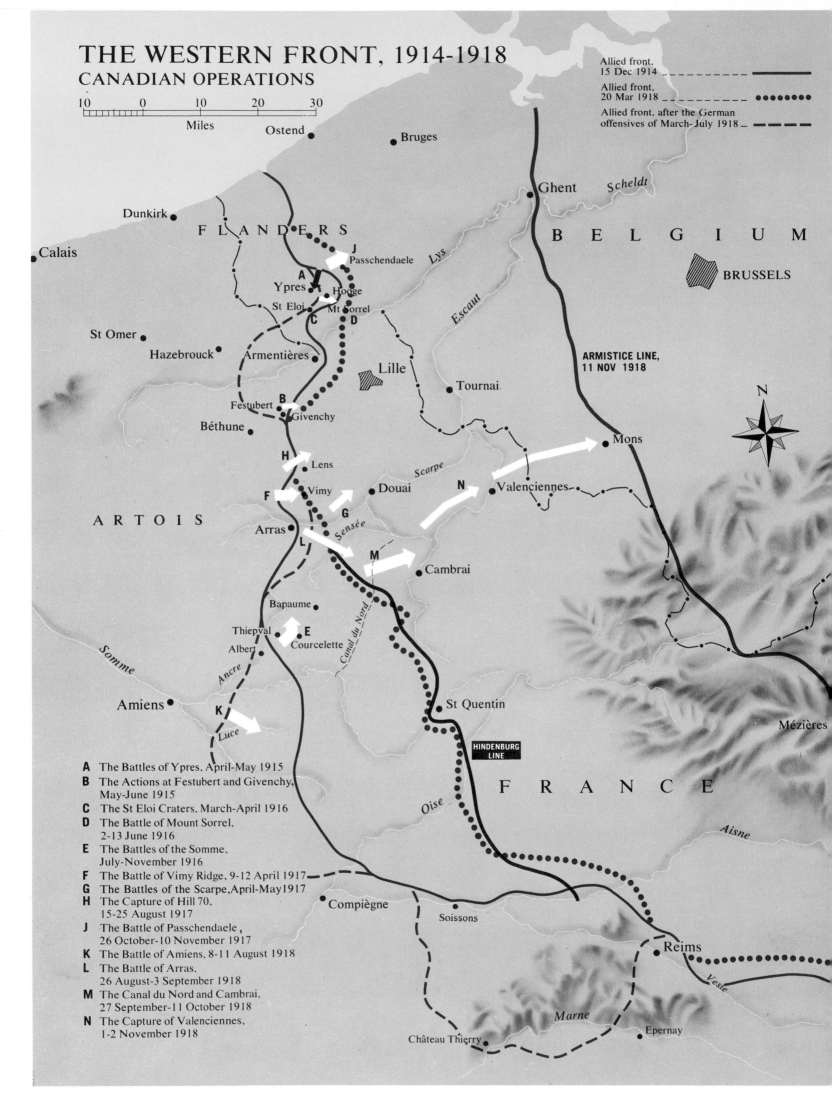

THE WESTERN FRONT, 1914-1918
CANADIAN OPERATIONS

10   0   10   20   30
Miles

Allied front,
15 Dec 1914 ——————

Allied front,
20 Mar 1918 ——————•••••••

Allied front, after the German
offensives of March-July 1918 ——————

ARMISTICE LINE,
11 NOV 1918

HINDENBURG
LINE

N

Countries / Regions: FLANDERS, BELGIUM, ARTOIS, FRANCE

Places: Ostend, Bruges, Ghent, Dunkirk, Calais, Passchendaele, Ypres, Hooge, St Eloi, Mt Sorrel, St Omer, Hazebrouck, Armentières, Lille, Tournai, BRUSSELS, Festubert, Givenchy, Béthune, Lens, Vimy, Douai, Valenciennes, Mons, Arras, Cambrai, Bapaume, Thiepval, Courcelette, Albert, St Quentin, Amiens, Compiègne, Soissons, Reims, Château Thierry, Epernay, Mézières

Rivers: Scheldt, Lys, Escaut, Scarpe, Sensée, Canal du Nord, Somme, Ancre, Luce, Oise, Aisne, Vesle, Marne

A The Battles of Ypres, April-May 1915
B The Actions at Festubert and Givenchy,
   May-June 1915
C The St Eloi Craters, March-April 1916
D The Battle of Mount Sorrel,
   2-13 June 1916
E The Battles of the Somme,
   July-November 1916
F The Battle of Vimy Ridge, 9-12 April 1917
G The Battles of the Scarpe, April-May 1917
H The Capture of Hill 70,
   15-25 August 1917
J The Battle of Passchendaele,
   26 October-10 November 1917
K The Battle of Amiens, 8-11 August 1918
L The Battle of Arras,
   26 August-3 September 1918
M The Canal du Nord and Cambrai,
   27 September-11 October 1918
N The Capture of Valenciennes,
   1-2 November 1918

The Western Front, 1914-1918

The ruins of Ypres

Lieutenant-Colonel "Billy" Bishop

-Col. W. A. Bishop, V.C., D.S.O. and Bar, M.C., F.C., of Owen Sound, Ontario, the highest scor- fighter pilot in the British Services in the First orld War. He was officially credited with having stroyed 72 enemy planes. In this censored otograph, taken in 1917, the identifying num- on his Nieuport 17 plane has been blacked out.

Air Training Plan — First War style (extreme left)
Student pilots grouped around a Curtiss JN-4 plane at a training centre in Canada.

JN-4 training planes at Leaside Airdrome (centre left)
These particular planes were the gifts of cities, etc., and are marked with the names of the donors.

Canadian troops entraining (left)
The 153rd Battalion leaving St. Thomas, Ontario. This became a familiar scene in all Canadian cities in which there were training camps.

The first Canadians arrive overseas, October 1914 (below)

Public Archives of Canada

Building submarines in Montreal

Twenty-four submarines — the only ones ever built in Canada — were constructed by Canadian Vickers for Britain, Russia and Spain. When the first of them were delivered, they became the first submarines ever to cross the Atlantic under their own power.

The orders from the Canadian Government came late in the day—deliberately so, as they were intended to provide a cushion of employment when the war ended. Some 62 ships were built in all, and most of them were operated by the Canadian Government Merchant Marine, which established services to many parts of the world. As long as ships were in short supply these services met with some success, but later they dwindled and finally disappeared in the face of normal peacetime competition.

The war contributed indirectly as well as directly to the growth and diversification of Canadian industry. Prosperity on the prairies and elsewhere resulted in a lively demand for many products. Many of the usual sources of imports were cut off, and Canadian factories began to make items that would normally have been secured from abroad. Both the home market and the capacity of domestic factories to supply it thus increased substantially during the war years.

Trade with the United States increased sharply at this time, partly because of greater production of such items as wood-pulp and newsprint, which were in demand there. During the prewar boom period most of the capital that poured into Canada for railway construction and other purposes had come from Great Britain. This source was now cut off, and American capital flowed in in its place. North-south economic and financial ties had become much closer by 1920 than they had been in 1910.

The Canadian war effort necessitated expenditures by the government on a scale far beyond anything experienced before 1914, but the country showed an astonishing ability to support this burden from its own resources. Between 1915 and 1919 a series of war loans was floated that yielded in sum the total—immense for that day—of $2,300,000,000. The national debt jumped correspondingly, but instead of being substantially a foreign debt as in prewar days, it became largely one owing to Canadians themselves.

Canada in 1919

Canada's substantial contribution to the Allied cause in the First World War gave her increased stature, both nationally and internationally. This quickly became evident during the diplomatic negotiations that followed the war in 1919. Canada was represented at the Paris Peace Conference by her own delegates, signed the Treaty of Versailles on her own behalf and, in January 1920, joined the League of Nations along with, but independently of, Great Britain.

The war had indeed swept her into the main stream of world events. Canadian troops had fought in South Africa 20 years before, but this had been an act of loyalty and patriotism; the war there had held no threat for Canada in any physical sense. As tension built up in Europe, Borden and others had been aware of its implications, but to the Canadian man in the street the issues and dangers involved still seemed remote. It was the war itself that made Canadians realize that their own future and independence were at stake.

"Standard" shipbuilding in Canada

These three ships were being fitted out at the Canadian Vickers yard, in Montreal.

In spite of this, neither the government nor the people showed much desire to retain more than the barest minimum of armed forces once the war was over. The comfortable and attractive theory that the war that would end war had just been fought and won held sway for the moment. The sole development of interest was the creation in 1920 of the Canadian Air Force, which would become the Royal Canadian Air Force in 1923. Having been brought into being, the R.C.A.F. cannot be said to have been pampered during its early years. In 1930 its enlisted strength was only 911. But it was not alone in receiving a minimum of financial support. That same year the enlisted strength of the permanent force of the Army, the Navy, and the Air Force combined was less than 6,000. In spite of an outstanding military record, Canada once again proved in the years between the wars that she was essentially an unmilitary nation.

In May 1919 Canadians were startled by the Winnipeg General Strike, the background of which was both interesting and complicated.

Industrially, Canada had developed greatly since 1914, but as the war ended production slumped. Contracts for war materials were completed or cancelled; foreign goods that had been kept out by the war began to flow in and compete with Canadian products that had had the market to themselves. Unemployment soared and labour unrest became serious and widespread. Many of the grievances were very real. Prices were high, hours long, and wages relatively low. Many employers were reluctant to accept the practice of collective bargaining. These were the matters in which the vast majority of the working men were interested, but there were those who wanted to interest them in political activities and, in some instances, revolutionary aims as well.

As industry expanded, labour unions had grown in number and strength, and the radicals saw in them a means of seizing power. Their weapon would be the sympathetic strike. If one or two unions went on strike, all other unions in the

The Peace Conference in session in Paris (above)

David Lloyd George, Aristide Briand, Charles Evans Hughes and Herbert Hoover are amongst those in attendance. Sir Robert Borden is second from the right at the table in the right foreground.

The Winnipeg strike of 1919 (below)

area would come out in sympathy. Ostensibly the aim would be to defeat the employers involved; actually, the intention was that the sympathetic strikes which would add up to a general strike, would paralyze the community and enable labour, in the persons of the radical leaders, to seize political power.

Over this whole prospect lay the shadow of the Russian Revolution. Many working men had welcomed it in all sincerity as a revolt against Czarist tyranny, and were much opposed to the anti-Soviet policy being followed by the Canadian Government. Naturally the Marxists among the radicals welcomed this attitude and tried to turn it to their advantage. Official circles, on the contrary, were highly suspicious of any sympathy with the Soviets, and regarded the aims and activities of the radicals as seditious conspiracy.

It was against this background that the One Big Union emerged in 1918-19. Clearly inspired by the radical International Workers of the World (the I.W.W.) in the United States, the O.B.U. aimed to organize all labour in one comprehensive union and, by use of the general strike, to make it the decisive weapon in a class war. Vancouver and Calgary were both scenes of O.B.U. activity, but it was in Winnipeg that its strategy was put to the test.

On May 1, 1919, metal workers and the building trades in the city went on strike; collective bargaining was the main issue. The Trades and Labour Council, having polled its member unions and found them sympathetic, called them all out in support on May 15. A virtually total general strike resulted. For a month Winnipeg struggled along as best it could and with surprisingly good temper. Negotiations were deadlocked because both the city

and the provincial government declined to negotiate unless the sympathetic strikes were called off. The federal government eventually became so concerned about the seditious aspect of the strike that on June 17 it ordered the arrest of eight of the strike leaders. The result was a mass demonstration on June 21, that developed into the Winnipeg Riot. The North West Mounted Police cleared the streets, but in the course of the disturbances one person was killed and a second fatally injured. Nevertheless the strike had been broken, and on the 25th it was called off.

The events in Winnipeg were the most notable manifestation of the unrest and uncertainty that were characteristic of 1919 and the years immediately following the First World War. It extended to the thousands of veterans who returned home to find that jobs were scarce and that careers interrupted by three or four years of war were difficult to resume. Canada and Canadians would require a few years to settle down and determine their course in the changed conditions that prevailed in the 1920s.

Like many other things, politics were to change. In February 1919 Sir Wilfrid Laurier died. He had been leader of the Liberal Party for no fewer than 32 years. It was known that Sir Robert Borden, wartime prime minister and leader of the Conservatives since 1901, was anxious to step down.

New leaders would appear, and they would play their parts on a new stage. The rebuilt Centre Block of the Parliament Buildings, though still lacking its great central tower, was otherwise complete. In February 1920, shortly before Borden retired, the Senate and House of Commons were able to leave the Victoria Museum, which had housed them since the fire in 1916, and move back to Parliament Hill.

Public Archives of Canada

The funeral of Sir Wilfrid Laurier (top of page)
The casket is being carried from the Basilica in Ottawa.

Rebuilding the Parliament Buildings
By 1919 the main structure of the new centre block was nearing completion. That year the Prince of Wales laid the cornerstone of the new central tower. The House of Commons was able to occupy its new chamber in February 1920, and the Peace Tower was completed in 1927 and dedicated on July 1, the 60th anniversary of Confederation.

Public Archives of Canada

Part V
THE SECOND HALF CENTURY OF CONFEDERATION 1919-1970

The Great Seals of Canada, George VI and Elizabeth II

CHAPTER 17

Communications

The Automobile Age Begins

For many years the railroads virtually ended long-distance travel by road. Good highways were rare, and no road vehicles were available that could compare remotely with railway trains in either speed or comfort. Locally, of course, roads continued to be as essential as ever. They were the means by which the farmer brought himself to town and his products to market. This was especially true on the prairies, where the roads that brought the grain wagons to the elevators were for all intents and purposes feeder lines for the railroads.

Then came the automobile. The first motor vehicle in Canada was an electric car built in Toronto in 1893. The first car propelled by a gasoline engine arrived in Hamilton in 1898. For a time purchasers had the choice of cars driven by steam, electricity or gasoline, but gasoline soon won out decisively.

The number of cars grew slowly at first. Registration of motor vehicles was introduced in Ontario in 1903; and at that time there were 220 cars in the province. As late as 1907 there were only 2,130 in all Canada. But changes were in the air. In 1904 the Ford Motor Company of Canada was formed to market and in some measure manufacture Ford cars in Canada, and in 1907 the McLaughlin Carriage Company in Oshawa, after building a car of its own, entered into a similar arrangement to assemble, build and market Buick cars. General Motors of Canada grew out of this latter agreement. But it was Henry Ford's Model T (the famous Tin Lizzie), introduced in 1908, and the mass production techniques that enabled him to produce 15,000,000 low-priced cars in 19 years, that marked the real beginning of the automobile age.

Automobiles were not welcomed everywhere. In Prince Edward Island they were banned entirely

Vancouver City Archives

The first service station in Canada

Built in Vancouver by the Imperial Oil Company in 1908. The gasoline reservoir was an ordinary 13-gallon kitchen hot-water tank, to which was attached 10 feet of garden hose.

for a time, and use was later restricted to certain roads three days a week. The last restrictions were not removed until 1919. But in Canada as a whole their numbers grew rapidly. There were 50,000 cars in the country in 1913, nearly 200,000 in 1917, and this total had more than doubled by 1920.

By that time some of the potentialities of the automobile were being realized. For the first time an individual was free to go where he pleased when he pleased. The isolation of life in the country began to disappear; neighbours could be reached much more easily, and towns were minutes instead of hours away. Social effects were becoming apparent. The automobile made it much easier for people to get together; they could pool their resources and facilities as never before. The little one-room schoolhouse, to cite one familiar example, began to give way to the better equipped consolidated school to which children were taken by bus. By degrees the automobile introduced a new kind of holiday travel, and developed a tourist trade that was to have a profound effect upon the Canadian economy.

Cars came to grief even in early days
This collision took place on South Granville Street in Vancouver, in 1914. Notice the broom used to sweep up small debris and broken glass.

The first horseless carriage in Vancouver

A foundry and machine shop equipped this imposing nine-passenger charabanc with a boiler and triple-expansion steam engine in 1899. It made only one trip, as this trial run showed that it was too heavy and clumsy to be practical.

Transcontinental touring in 1904

This English Napier car travelled by road from Boston to Minneapolis, where it was equipped with flanged wheels. It then took to the rails, and travelled to Moose Jaw over the tracks of the Soo Line, and thence to Vancouver over the main line of the Canadian Pacific. A total of 1,733 miles were travelled by road and 1,803 miles by rail, or 3,536 miles in all. On the railway the car was treated as a special train, and a conductor (here shown in the back seat) was always a passenger. This was the first car to cross the Canadian Rockies.

The first imported gasoline car in Canada (bottom right)

In 1898 John Moodie of Hamilton bought the second car turned out by the Winton factory and the first imported into Canada. His brother James, also a resident of Hamilton, bought a car of the same model. This photograph of Mr. and Mrs. James Moodie in their Winton was taken in 1899.

Vancouver City Archives

Hamilton Spectator

One of the great virtues of the Model T was its ability to negotiate bad roads. Surfaced highways were few and far between; most of the roads were earth or at best gravel; they were dusty in summer, and at some seasons incredibly muddy and virtually impassable. At one time all motor traffic was banned for a period of 40 days each spring in Nova Scotia when the frost was coming out of the ground. Such conditions were a constant annoyance to the motorist, who frequently found it difficult or even impossible to use his car for pleasure or his truck for business, and the demand for better roads became insistent. Roads had always been the responsibility of the provinces and municipalities, but Sir Robert Borden recognized that federal action was necessary as well. In 1919, while he was prime minister, Parliament passed the Canada Highways Act, which set aside $20,000,000 to assist in road improvement over a five-year period. Aid was to be given to the provinces on the shared-cost basis that was to become so familiar in later years.

A paved highway from Montreal 10 miles north-west to Ste. Rose, the first in Quebec, was completed in 1910; the 34-mile road south to Rouses Point, at the international boundary, was "macadamized" (a word of somewhat imprecise meaning) in 1912-13. Meanwhile Ontario had begun to build a paved highway between Toronto and Hamilton, a distance of 42 miles. When this was completed in 1915, it was one of the longest paved roads in the world.

Between 1920 and the outbreak of the Second World War in 1939, automobiles improved immensely in capability and reliability; the modern car may be said to have come into existence at that time. Quite as important, much safer and better-wearing tires became available. The high-speed truck and the long-distance passenger bus appeared.

Road transportation began to offer serious competition to the railways. The number of motor vehicles jumped spectacularly. From a total of 575,000 in 1923 the number rose to over a million in 1933, and in spite of the depression it reached 1,500,000 in 1940. All this traffic demanded more and better roads, and just before the war Ontario provided a portent for the future—a new Toronto–Hamilton highway, the Queen Elizabeth Way. Completed in 1939, this four-lane limited-access highway was the first freeway of the kind in North America.

The Queen Elizabeth Way was expensive, but there were compensations. The provinces had found in the automobile a new source of revenue. The first tax on gasoline was imposed in Alberta in 1922; by 1930 such taxes were bringing $23,000,000 to provincial treasuries. And much more was to come. By 1950 gasoline tax revenue exceeded $155,000,000 and licence fees brought in over $67,000,000 in addition.

Millions of Cars and Modern Highways

The number of motor vehicles registered in Canada first passed the million mark in 1928. In spite of depression and war there were over 2,000,000 registered in 1948. Thereafter the total jumped to over 5,000,000 in 1959, over 6,000,000 in 1963 and only three years later, to over 7,000,000 in 1966.

Cars have not only become much more numerous, but they have become larger and more powerful as well. The same is true of both buses and trucks. At one time capable of only short runs, they can now travel all over the continent, much of the time at the highest speed that the law allows. Cars, buses and trucks travel not only much faster but much farther than before. It is calculated that Canadians now drive their motor vehicles more than fifty billion miles each year. No wonder there is a constant demand for more and better roads!

When paved roads first appeared, most people thought that they were more or less permanent— that the job had been done once and for all. But more cars, faster cars, and above all heavier trucks will in time break up almost any surface. The Queen Elizabeth Way, Canada's first superhighway, was almost demolished by the wartime traffic to which it was subjected between 1939 and 1945. Most of the older main roads in Canada have already passed several times through a cycle that begins with a new surface, passes through a period of wear, tear and repair, and ends with another new surface.

As traffic builds up, routes as well as surfaces may need renewal. The chances are that when an old-established road was first paved its route was not disturbed—its sharp curves, steep hills and meanderings would all be retained. But presently it would become apparent that these were hazards that had to be eliminated, and the road would be re-routed at many points. Finally would come the realization that a completely new road would be much the best solution—one that would be straight and therefore as short as possible, and one on which curves and grades would conform to certain highway standards.

The attitude of towns and cities towards through highways is interesting. At one time they were most anxious to have trunk roads routed through their business districts, in the belief that this would bring them trade. (One is reminded of the scramble for railway stations in the 19th century.) But presently, as traffic increased, it was found that the highway caused more congestion than prosperity. The bypass road appeared; ready access to a highway was seen to be preferable to the highway itself.

Out of these circumstances grew, by degrees, modern highways. At first they seemed to be beyond Canada's means, except in a few heavily populated

Ontario Dept. of Highways

Ontario Dept. of Highways

Queen Elizabeth Way when completed in 1939 (top of page)

The Spadina interchange on Highway 401

areas. In the United States the Lincoln Highway Association began to plan a transcontinental paved road as early as 1913, but a comparable project was too costly for Canada to undertake for many years. By the end of World War II conditions had changed. Population had increased substantially; Canada's industrial capacity was far greater; road transportation had become highly important. Moreover, the war had shown that highways could be vital to national defence. This had been demonstrated dramatically when Alaska was threatened after the Japanese attack on Pearl Harbor. In the incredibly short period of eight months the United States pushed through a 1,500-mile road from Fort St. John, in northern British Columbia, to Fairbanks, Alaska. Improved and rebuilt after the war by Canadian Army engineers, this is now the famous Alaska Highway, 1,220 miles of which are in Canada.

In 1949 the Trans-Canada Highway Act was passed. Under its terms the Canadian Government undertook to pay half the cost of construction of a transcontinental road, providing its surface, width, bridges, gradients and curves met certain standards. The road builders found the greatest obstacles precisely where the railway builders had found them seventy years before—north of Lake Superior and in the Rocky Mountains and the other ranges of British Columbia. Costs here were so great that the subsidy was increased to 90 percent for some stretches of the road. In 1957 Saskatchewan, with 406 relatively easy miles to build, became the first province to complete its section of the highway. Although some work still remained to be done, the highway was officially opened on September 3, 1962. Its total length from Victoria, B.C. to St. John's Newfoundland is 4,860 miles—1,500 miles longer than the Lincoln Highway between New York and San Francisco.

The Trans-Canada Highway is in the South where population is concentrated. In the North the federal government has subsidized the building of the Mackenzie Highway, from Grimshaw, Alberta to Hay River, on Great Slave Lake. An extension runs on around the western end of the lake to Yellowknife on its north shore, and another extension will reach Fort Simpson on the Mackenzie River. Roads are vital for the development of the Canadian North, and in 1965 the Northern Road Network Program was launched to provide them— a scheme that calls for the expenditure of $10,000,000 a year for ten years. The North also benefitted from the preceding "Roads to Resources" program, which was announced in 1958, and resulted in the construction of nearly 5,000 miles of road in the ten provinces.

Canada's finest superhighway is Ontario's Macdonald-Cartier Freeway—highway 401—which extends from Windsor to the Quebec border, a distance of 510 miles. Connecting with it at Toronto, highway 400 runs north to Barrie, on Lake Simcoe. In places traffic has already caught up with the capacity of even such broad and unencumbered roads as these. For a 17-mile stretch through Toronto it has been necessary to expand highway 401 to no fewer than 12 lanes, and peak traffic on 400 is so dense that there is talk of making it a one-way road.

Each province has dealt with its road problems in its own way. The mountainous nature of the country makes road-building particularly difficult and costly in British Columbia, but old roads have been rebuilt to modern standards and many new ones—such as the highways west from Prince George to Prince Rupert and Kitimat, and north to Dawson Creek—have been added. For her superhighways Quebec has reverted to the old plan of toll roads, the prime examples being from Montreal north to Ste. Adèle, east to Berthierville and south through Sherbrooke to the international boundary. In the Maritimes an interesting development is the Canso Causeway, linking the Nova Scotia mainland and Cape Breton Island. In Newfoundland road-building has ended the isolation of many hundreds of communities, and the Newfoundland portion of the Trans-Canada Highway provides a paved road across the full width of the province.

Superhighways have invaded the cities themselves. Montreal's Metropolitan Boulevard, Ottawa's Queensway and Toronto's Gardiner Expressway are examples. But doubts are arising as to whether they really offer a solution for the gigantic problem of traffic congestion. They make it possible for cars to get out of the big cities much more easily, but they also encourage cars to come into the central congested areas. The private automobile, usually with only one or two passengers, takes far more room than seems reasonable, and instead of building more and more superstreets and multi-storied parking garages, it may be well to consider alternative means of transportation. Subways are helping in Toronto and Montreal; more and better commuter trains promise to help as well. We may yet see public transport take over completely in central areas, with a total ban on private vehicles.

The cost of all this road building has been prodigious, but so have been the results—occasionally bad, but on the whole very good. And if the automobile has not paid its way, it has at least made a substantial contribution to the cost of highways. In 1967 the various governments in Canada spent just under $1,400,000,000 on the construction and maintenance of roads, bridges and ferries. The same year provincial revenue from motor vehicles, including licence fees and gasoline taxes, amounted to the tidy sum of almost a billion dollars—$990,099,252, to be exact.

The First Twenty Years of Flying

Alexander Graham Bell, inventor of the telephone, was the father of aviation in Canada. Flying had long interested him and, like most of the pioneers in flight, he had made extensive experiments with kites. In 1907 he was joined at his summer home at Baddeck, on Bras d'Or Lake in Cape Breton Island, by two young engineering graduates of the University of Toronto, F. W. (Casey) Baldwin and John A. D. McCurdy; the latter's father had been Bell's secretary. Mrs. Bell suggested that they should form the Aerial Experiment Association to test the possibilities of flight, and, quite as important, she undertook to meet all the expenses involved.

Flying at this time was still very young indeed. The Wright brothers had made their first flight less than four years previously, in December 1903; Lincoln Beachey, who became a very well-known early American pilot, had made the first flight in Canada at Montreal on July 12, 1906. The Aerial

Experiment Association built four planes at Hammondsport, New York, and all of them were flown there successfully in 1908. Two have a special place in Canadian aviation history. The first of the four, the *Red Wing,* was flown by Casey Baldwin on May 12, when he became not only the first Canadian but the first British subject to fly a heavier-than-air craft. The last of the series, the famous *Silver Dart,* was flown by John McCurdy on December 8. In January the *Silver Dart* was shipped to Baddeck, and there on February 23, 1909, McCurdy made the historic flight that was both the first made in Canada by a Canadian and the first made by any British subject on British soil.

In August 1909 Baldwin and McCurdy took the *Silver Dart* and another machine, the *Baddeck I,* to Petawawa in an effort to interest the Canadian military authorities in aviation. Totally unsuitable flying fields and bad weather made the trials a failure and wrecked the *Silver Dart.* Even when war broke out in 1914 the military continued for a time to take scant interest in aviation. When Frank H. Ellis, one of the earliest Canadian flyers, offered his services he was told that "it was not anticipated" that there "would be any requirements for the service of aviators."

Frank Ellis has patiently pieced together the story of early flying in Canada, and the number of attempts that were made to build planes is remarkable. In those days the planes themselves could be built of wood, aluminum tubing, canvas, piano wire, bicycle wheels and other simple materials; the great difficulty was to secure an engine that would be sufficiently powerful, very light, and not prohibitively expensive. Pilots were not licensed and aircraft were not registered until 1920, and there was nothing to prevent anyone from having a try. Typical of many pioneers was W. W. Gibson, who built and flew what he called a twin-plane in Victoria in 1910, and followed it up with a multi-plane that made flights near Calgary in 1911. Gibson's unique achievement was the construction of the first successful aircraft engine produced in Canada—a six-cylinder motor that developed between 40 and 60 horsepower and weighed only 210 pounds. It was completed in Victoria and powered the twin-plane. Ellis himself was a notable pioneer on several counts and in July 1919 made the first parachute jump by a Canadian from an airplane flying in Canada.

Plane design had not progressed far before daring young pilots were trying to earn a living by exhibition flights, and by 1911 they had been seen in the sky over most of the larger Canadian cities. There were aviation meets in both Montreal and Toronto in 1910, and at Montreal the crowds were treated to the rare spectacle of three planes in the air at one time. They also witnessed a crash in which the airplane was demolished but the pilot walked away uninjured—a not unusual occurrence with the light, slow-speed planes of the time. But serious accidents did occur, and on August 6, 1913, Johnny Bryant, flying a Curtiss-type biplane, crashed to his death on the roof of a building in downtown Vic-

toria. This was Canada's first air fatality. The week before, at Minoru Park near Vancouver, his wife, Alys Bryant, had flown the same machine and had become the first woman to pilot a plane in Canada.

As the war progressed, and the potentialities of the aeroplane became better appreciated, planes and engines developed rapidly. As far as manufacturing was concerned, Canada's main achievement was to produce some 2,900 of the famous Curtiss JN4 biplanes, known as the Jenny. Today its wooden and wire fuselage looks very frail, but the Jenny was not only an excellent trainer but later was found to be a remarkably reliable and versatile aircraft. Thousands of Canadians served in the Royal Flying Corps (which became the Royal Air Force on April 1, 1918) and some of those who returned wondered about a civilian career in aviation. Jennys and some other aircraft were surplus and cheap, and all sorts of air ventures by veterans, varying all the way from stunt flying to attempts at commercial air services, were common in the years immediately after the First World War. There was even some sporadic carrying of air mail. Indeed, the first official air mail flight took place before the war ended, when Captain Brian Peck, an R.A.F. pilot, flew a Curtis JN4 with mail on board from Montreal to Toronto on June 24, 1918.

Several aspects of aviation at this time should be noted. First is the number of ambitious flights made or attempted soon after the war ended. The first trans-Atlantic flights are one example. An American NC4 seaplane, sole survivor of four planes that were intended to make the flight, landed at Plymouth on May 31, 1919, after an adventurous trip from Newfoundland by way of the Azores and Portugal. Alcock and Brown, in a converted Vickers Vimy bomber, made the first nonstop crossing from Newfoundland to Ireland just a fortnight later, on June 14-15. Between July 15 and October 20, four American planes made a round trip from New York to Nome, in Alaska, and flew through British Columbia and the Yukon in both directions. In August, Captain Ernest Hoy, a Vancouver airman, made the first flight over the Rocky Mountains. His plane was a war-surplus Jenny, and it took him 16 hours to fly from Vancouver to Calgary. The next year—1920—saw the first trans-Canada flight. The trip took only about 45 hours of flying time, but this was spread over 10 days, October 7 to 17. The pilot succeeded in travelling by air from Halifax to Vancouver, but his journey was characterized by delays, crackups, and several changes of plane.

This was the age of the bush pilots—of "Punch" Dickins and "Wop" May, and other venturesome pilots who began probing the wilds where there were no roads and no railroads. There were no landing fields either, and their planes were usually equipped with floats or skis, according to the season, so that the innumerable lakes of the North could be used as airfields. By degrees they and their successors were to usher in a new era, in which the isolation formerly inseparable from distant places vanished, and men, supplies, equipment

The first aircraft of Trans-Canada Airlines: one of the two Lockheed Electra 10As acquired when TCA took over Canadian Airways in 1937. One of these 10-passenger planes made TCA's first flight, Vancouver to Seattle.

After the Second World War, TCA acquired a fleet of Douglas DC-3 aircraft. The TCA version of this famous and versatile plane, over 10,000 of which served as military transports during the war, carried 21 passengers.

Luxury air travel in 1941: the interior of a Lockheed Lodestar. These 14-passenger planes were not pressurized, and when flying over the Rockies TCA passengers had to use oxygen masks.

In 1947 the entry into service of the four-engined North Star, a modified Canadian-built version of the Douglas DC-4, marked a great step forward in air travel in Canada. Fully pressurized and carrying 40 passengers, the North Star had a speed of 220 m.p.h. TCA used them on both domestic and overseas routes.

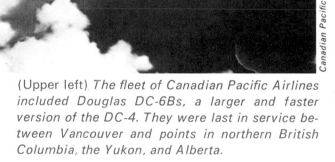

(Upper left) *The fleet of Canadian Pacific Airlines included Douglas DC-6Bs, a larger and faster version of the DC-4. They were last in service between Vancouver and points in northern British Columbia, the Yukon, and Alberta.*

The turboprop favoured by Canadian Pacific Airlines was the four-engined Bristol Britannia. Introduced in 1959, it flew on the company's far-flung international services from Vancouver to the Orient, Australia and South America.

(Upper right) *In 1955, TCA pioneered turbine air travel in North America when it introduced the Vickers Viscount turboprop aircraft. Comfortable and fast for its day, the Viscount could carry 40 passengers at 310 m.p.h. Five years later much larger turboprop Vickers Vanguards joined the fleet; they could carry 108 passengers at 425 m.p.h.*

(Right centre) *The name Air Canada replaced Trans-Canada Airlines in 1964, and Canadian Pacific Airlines became CP Air in 1969. In 1960 and succeeding years, both acquired Douglas DC-8 jetliners, capable of carrying 130 or more passengers at a speed of 550 to 600 m.p.h. Later both also added still larger "stretched" versions of the plane to their fleets. This view shows one of CP Air's "stretched" DC-8's in flight.*

(Right bottom) *For service on shorter routes, Air Canada is using the twin-jet DC-9, smaller than the DC-8 but almost as fast. CP Air has chosen two Boeing planes — the twin-jet 737, the first of which was delivered late in 1968, and the three-jet 727, which joined the fleet in 1970. A 727 is shown crossing the Rockies.*

and machinery could be flown to a new industry or community anywhere. In 1924 a regular air service, the first of its kind, began to carry mail, passengers and freight to the gold fields at Rouyn. In 1928 Dickins made the first flight over the Barren Lands, which took him as far north as Baker Lake, and then west to Fort Smith. The following year he flew all the way to Aklavik, on the fringe of the Arctic Ocean.

By this time aerial surveys were serving a wide variety of purposes. Forest fire patrols began at an early date, and development of cameras made it possible to survey forest resources by air. Planes were used to spot the seal herds off Newfoundland as early as 1924. In 1927-28 an aerial survey was made of Hudson Strait, and air photography has become a standard aid to the mapmaker, and has speeded up enormously the task of mapping Canada's vast area in detail.

A new generation of airplanes soon appeared in the North. Oddly enough, some of them were of German origin. Junkers all-metal mono-planes and Fokker Universals appeared, along with the Vickers Viking Mark IV (the first commercial amphibian in Canada), the Avro Avian and the Fairchild FC-2. A Curtiss subsidiary had built the Jenny in Canada during the war, and other factors followed in the peace. Canadian Vickers established an aircraft division in 1922 and began to produce the Viking; an Avro factory followed in 1927, a De Havilland plant that would soon produce Gypsy Moths opened in 1928, and Fairchild Aircraft Limited was established in 1929.

As already noted, pilots were first licensed and planes registered in 1920, when the Air Board was established and given regulatory powers. By the mid-twenties the day of the large-scale trancontinental airline was still a decade away, but commercial aviation, broken up into many small operations, was developing rapidly. In 1925 there were only 39 licensed civil aircraft in Canada; in 1929 there were 445. In 1925 civil aircraft carried 4,897 passengers, 1,080 pounds of mail, and 592-220 pounds of freight and express. In 1929 passengers numbered 124,875, the mail load had jumped to 474,199 pounds, while freight and express totalled 1,759,259 pounds.

Commercial aviation in Canada would soon be coming of age.

The Air Age Arrives

Flying progress was not just a matter of planes and pilots; many other factors were essential. Under the guidance of John A. Wilson, who had been secretary of the Air Board since 1920 and became Controller of Civil Aviation in 1927, many of them were provided in the two succeeding decades. The larger cities were encouraged to provide airports, and the Government itself set about the difficult and complicated task of providing a radio network, naviga-

tion aids, weather services and emergency landing fields—the latter not more than a hundred miles apart. The same physical obstructions that had proved formidable to the railways and road builders —the mountains in British Columbia and the rugged region north of Lake Superior—once again proved difficult and expensive to overcome.

By 1930 air services were becoming of consequence to the public. Nearly 500 tons of mail were carried by air that year, some to such places as the Magdalen Islands, on the Atlantic Coast, and Aklavik, in the Arctic, which were usually more or less isolated in winter. It was becoming clear that commercial aviation had a substantial future, and in 1933 the Canadian Pacific Railway, which as long before as 1919 had prudently secured a permit empowering it to own and operate aircraft, began to exercise these rights and to acquire a financial interest in various airlines that was to grow steadily during the next half dozen years.

National Museum of Science & Technology

Vickers Viking flying boat

The early days of aerial photography in Canada: this Vickers Viking flying boat helped to pioneer aerial surveying. The crew is shown with its primitive survival gear; note the emergency rations, the axe and the oil lantern. The camera is at the extreme left of the picture, which was taken at Victoria Beach, Manitoba, in 1924.

First flight in Canada of the "Silver Dart"
On February 23, 1909, piloted by J. A. D. McCurdy, the Silver Dart *rose into the air off the ice on the Bras d'Or Lakes in Cape Breton Island.*

A decisive step forward was taken in 1936 when the federal Department of Transport was created and the Hon. C. D. Howe became its first Minister. Howe was both interested in air transportation and ambitious for Canada, and under his guidance Trans-Canada Air Lines came into existence in 1937. On July 31 Howe himself was one of a party that made a twenty-hour all-day survey flight from Montreal to Vancouver. Its success showed that a transcontinental service was possible, but much equipment, staff and experience had to be acquired before it could be undertaken on a regular schedule. Meanwhile shorter distances could be covered, and on September 1, T.C.A. (as it soon became known) carried its first paying passengers from Vancouver to Seattle. The long-awaited passenger service between Montreal and Vancouver began on April 1, 1939, and was extended to Moncton in 1940 and to Halifax in 1941.

For a generation the fleet of Trans-Canada Air Lines (renamed Air Canada in 1964) has reflected the evolution of the modern air liner. Its first planes were Lockheed Electras, which inaugurated the trans-Canada flights. They carried 10 passengers, and took 17½ hours to make the trip from Montreal to Vancouver. As their cabins were not pressurized, passengers had to use oxygen masks when they crossed the Rockies. In 1941 the first Lockheed Lodestars were acquired; regarded as commodious in their day, they carried 14 passengers. After the war a whole fleet of Douglas DC-3's were purchased —the plane that had been such a wonderful workhorse in wartime, and which in its T.C.A. version carried 21 passengers in considerable comfort. The real breakthrough came in 1947, when T.C.A. secured its first large planes—the four-engined fully pressurized North Stars, which were a Canadian-built revised version of the Douglas DC-4. Lockheed Super Constellations were added to the fleet in 1954 —the last piston-driven planes the line acquired. Soon after came the Vickers "turbo-prop" Viscounts, the first turbine-driven air liners in North America. They were followed in 1960 by the larger Vickers Vanguards, but that same year ushered in the "pure jet" age, with the arrival of the Douglas DC-8 aircraft. Later came the smaller DC-9 for shorter routes, and "stretched" versions of both planes, the largest of which can carry 196 passengers and 25,000 pounds of cargo at nearly 600 miles per hour. Concordes are on order with which Air Canada expects to introduce supersonic flying in 1973.

Canadian Pacific Airlines (the "CP Air" of today) did not come formally into existence until 1942, but the Canadian Pacific had consolidated its air interests in 1939, when it assumed ownership of ten local and regional companies, mostly in the West and North. It was soon performing important war-

The Petawawa military trials

The Baddeck I at Petawawa in 1909, preparing for the trials that failed to impress or interest the Canadian military authorities.

time duties. These included flying schools under the British Commonwealth Air Training Plan, operation of overhaul and repair plants, and a large share in the ferrying of bombers across the Atlantic. Air Canada likewise became involved in trans-Atlantic flying in 1943, when it provided a wartime service with converted Lancaster bombers. Both companies emerged from the war with extensive experience of transoceanic flying and with ambitious plans to develop overseas services of their own. Air Canada was able to place North Stars in service between Montreal and the United Kingdom in 1947, and it has since extended its trans-Atlantic routes to Paris, Brussels, Copenhagen, Frankfurt, Zurich, Vienna and Moscow. In 1948 it turned southward, and now has services to Florida, Jamaica, Bermuda, Nassau and Trinidad. Canadian Pacific Airlines have a still more extended network that includes services from its operational centre in Vancouver to Tokyo and Hong Kong, to Hawaii, Fiji, New Zealand and Australia, to Mexico and South America, and by the polar route from Vancouver to Amsterdam. Other services to Europe extend from Montreal to Lisbon, Madrid, Rome and Athens. At home and abroad Air Canada planes operate over routes totalling 68,645 miles, while CP Air's routes total 57,346 miles; but Air Canada is proportionately much larger than these figures suggest. In 1968 it carried 6,393,124 passengers, whereas CP Air carried over 1,000,000—a total small only by comparison.

Not all Canada's flying is done by these two airlines. The high cost of modern aircraft has made it difficult for a small company to survive, but a number of regional airlines are flourishing. Largest of them is Pacific Western Airlines, which carried 401,955 passengers in 1967. Quebecair and its subsidiaries, which operate smaller aircraft, carried 223,697 passengers.

The first plane to cross the Canadian Rockies

This photograph was taken at Golden, B.C. The ceiling of the "Jenny" (JN-4) was so low that Captain Ernest Hoy sometimes had to fly around the mountains.

Faster and much larger planes, some of which will carry hundreds of passengers, are presenting serious problems on the ground. In the last decade the Department of Transport has built a whole series of magnificent new airports in Canada, but even the best of them are already proving to be too small. One of the newest, the International Airport at Toronto, is already handling over six million passengers a year, and in July 1969 Air Canada's traffic alone averaged 30,000 persons per day. A great new expansion programme is already under way which, among other things, will double the length of the main runways and provide an additional terminal building over half a mile long.

Like the automobile, the aeroplane has come of age, and congestion on the highways is quickly spreading to the airports and the airways.

By Land, Water and Air

Canada is in the midst of a revolution in transportation—an effort (in the words of the *Canada Year Book*) to achieve "an economic and efficient transportation system making the best use of all available modes of transportation at the lowest total cost." This is much easier said than done, for it involves decisions as to whether, in the national interest, a particular service can best be provided by rail, road, water, air or pipeline, all of which represent important vested interests.

For many years the railways were the only means of moving freight for any distance, except along the coasts, on the Great Lakes and on a few of the larger rivers, where ships were available. As late as 1945 they were still carrying about three-quarters of all intercity and long-distance freight. But in recent decades competition from other carriers has increased sharply, and although the tonnage of freight handled by the railways has risen

National Museum of Science & Technology

Some Aircraft Designed and Built in Canada

Shown above, the Vickers Vedette, a single-engined pusher biplane built by Canadian Vickers in Montreal. The first of the type was completed in 1925. Vedettes were used for many purposes, including forest protection services.

(Centre top) In the 1930s and 1940s Noorduyn Aircraft Limited, founded in Montreal by Bob Noorduyn, a Dutchman, built 1,500 Norseman

planes. A single-engined monoplane, it was specially designed for bush flying and proved highly successful in service. It could be equipped with floats (as here shown), wheels or skis, making operation possible on land or lakes in all seasons.

(Right top) In 1947 de Havilland Canada produced the first Beaver — a light all-purpose single-engined monoplane. Like the Norseman, it was designed with bush flying in mind, and many hundreds were built during the ensuing twenty years.

(Centre left) This remarkable but almost forgotten Canadian plane was the first jet transport to fly in North America. Built by A.V.Roe Canada

and known as the C-102, it took to the air for the first time on August 10, 1949. Unfortunately, although it aroused considerable interest and was much admired, it attracted no buyers and was never put in production.

(Centre right) *In 1951 de Havilland Canada introduced the Otter, a single-engined monoplane designed to carry heavier loads than the Beaver of 1947. In 1966 de Havilland produced the Twin Otter, a still larger all-purpose aircraft. Propelled by two turboprop engines, it can carry two tons of freight.*

(Bottom right) *Canadair CL-215 amphibian "water bomber," the only plane designed specifically to fight forest fires. It can drop six tons (1,200 gallons) of water and replenish its supply in only 16 seconds by scooping water from the surface of the ocean or a lake.*

somewhat, the proportion of the total traffic they carry has fallen. Less than half of it is now shipped by rail.

Competition from trucks has become severe. The railways have no rivals as carriers of heavy bulk freight (except oil) over long distances, but rates on these shipments are relatively low. Trucking services have skimmed off much of the more lucrative traffic in light and valuable shipments. In part this was because they could move goods directly from a warehouse in one city to a warehouse or customer in another city without intermediate handling; whereas the freight car, tied to its track, had to be loaded and unloaded in the railway yard at either end of the run. At one time the railways carried considerable quantities of oil, but long-distance pipelines, the first of which was built during the war, have

The engine roundhouse (shown above)

Once a familiar scene at railway divisional points in the days of steam: the "round house" in which locomotives were serviced and overhauled. This one could accommodate about 50 engines at a time.

The last days of steam on the C.P.R. (below left)

No. 3722, shown here on the trestle at Port McNicholl, made the last steam run in March 1960.

Canadian National turbotrain

The latest development in railway passenger service, this turbotrain was specially designed for the heavily travelled route between Montreal and Toronto.

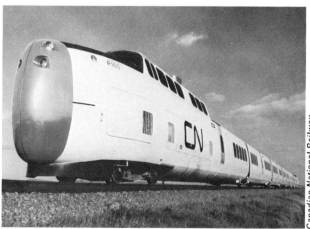

taken over most of this traffic and added to it on an immense scale.

There has been a sharp decline in railway passenger services. The peak year in passenger traffic was 1944, when the Canadian National and Canadian Pacific between them carried 54,389,000 revenue passengers; by 1967 the total had fallen to 24,488,000. Buses have taken away some passengers, but the major source of competition has been the private automobile. It is impossible to secure exact statistics, but it is estimated that in 1962 automobiles carried about 82 percent of the people who travelled from one city to another. The railways could have taken most of them more cheaply, but a car is preferred because of the freedom it affords to go when and where one pleases. Most of the people using cars, except motor tourists, travel a few hundred miles at the most; the railway's competition over longer distances is the aeroplane, which in 1962 carried about 8 percent of intercity travellers. Buses and trains thus carried only about 10 percent between them.

Most railroaders regard passenger traffic, except for commuter trains and a few heavily travelled runs between large cities, as a lost cause, but they have reacted with vigour and ingenuity to the challenge for freight. One major advance was the substitution of diesel-driven locomotives for the old steam engines. In 1946 only 29 diesels were in service and steam locomotives numbered 4,387, but diesels had displaced them completely by the early 1960s. Diesel engines required fewer stops and could haul heavier trains at higher speeds. In combination with electronically controlled yards, they have greatly speeded up service.

To counter competition from road transport, the railways have in some instances acquired truck and bus services of their own, and have developed the "piggyback" plan, using large trailers that can be loaded anywhere, like a truck, and can then be moved from city to city on a flat car. Large freight cars and cars designed to serve many special transport needs have helped to make shipment by rail more efficient and competitive. The growth of air travel and air freight had troubled the railways less because the two national airlines—Air Canada and Canadian Pacific Airlines—are their own subsidiaries.

In the days when they had a virtual monopoly, the railways had to be controlled in the public interest. Rates and almost every aspect of their operations became subject to elaborate regulations. To bring these controls into line with contemporary conditions has not been easy. Such a simple matter as closing an unprofitable branch line can be fraught with difficulties; isolated communities that have taken the permanent existence of the railway for granted may be left without alternative transportation. Even towns on a main line may suffer from such an improvement as the introduction of the diesel locomotive. In earlier days a main line was divided into divisions, with a divisional point at the end of each where the old steam engines could be changed or serviced. When the diesels appeared, capable of travelling much longer distances with a minimum of attention, many of the smaller divisional towns were hard hit.

The railroads have long contended that governments in effect subsidize their competitors. The Government of Canada built the St. Lawrence Seaway and the Trans-Canada Highway and founded Air Canada; governments at every level have built more and better roads. Part of their cost is recovered by tolls, licences and taxes, but only a part, and trucks, buses, airlines and pipelines are much less hampered by regulations than are the railroads.

The National Transportation Act, passed in 1967, endeavours to provide overall supervision for all forms of transportation. By degrees the railways will be freed of many restrictions and will be subsidized if uneconomic services must be maintained in the public interest. Control is vested in the Canadian Transport Commission, whose aim is to see that the various means of transport are used to the best advantage, and that the type available in a given area is the one best suited to meet its particular requirements.

Railway mileage in Canada was highest in 1959, when main and single lines totalled 44,209 miles and all lines 59,394 miles. The total has since declined, as many obsolete branch lines are being abandoned. But important new railways have been

Canadian Pacific

The "unit train"

Long "unit trains," consisting entirely of cars specially designed to carry a product in quantity, are becoming an important factor in railway operations. This 88-car Canadian Pacific train is carrying coal from East Kootenay to the docks at Roberts Bank, south of Vancouver.

Containers being unloaded at Montreal (above left)

Packaging freight in containers, usually 20 feet long and 8 feet wide and high, is revolutionizing cargo handling. The containers afford much better protection against damage and pilferage and can be loaded and unloaded so quickly that a ship's stay in port need be no longer than two days. More and more cargo is being carried in specially designed container ships, such as the Manchester Challenge, *here shown alongside the Montreal Container Terminal.*

built in recent years. The 360-mile Quebec, North Shore and Labrador Railway is a good example; it brings vast quantities of iron ore from the mines in the Knob Lake area to waiting bulk freighters at Sept-Iles. The Great Slave Railway has been built north to Hay River, on Great Slave Lake, and thence east to the mines at Pine Point. The Government of British Columbia found it profitable to extend its Pacific Great Eastern Railway first to Prince George and then to Dawson Creek and Fort St. John, in the Peace River country. Railroads continue to be essential to Canada, and for many purposes they are still the cheapest and most efficient form of transportation.

From the Great Lakes to the Sea

The spate of canal building that ended in 1848 gave Canada a seaway of sorts from Lake Huron to Montreal. It was superior to the Erie Canal, the rival it had been built to counter, but not much more could be said for it. Even at a time when ships were small, canals that could not accommodate vessels drawing more than nine feet of water were certain to prove inadequate before long.

(Upper right) *Unloading containers at Wolfe's Cove, Quebec. They are placed on trailer trucks for local and regional delivery and on railway flat cars for destinations at a distance.*

The Americans made an important contribution in 1855 when the state of Michigan completed the first canal around the rapids on the St. Marys River, at Sault Ste. Marie, between Lake Huron and Lake Superior. The water levels of lakes Erie, Huron and Michigan are so nearly the same that for navigation purposes they form one huge inland sea, and the new canal in effect added Lake Superior to them.

This became highly important towards the end of the century, when large quantities of iron ore and grain began to move from Lake Superior ports to the lower lakes. Big cargo ships can usually carry freight more cheaply than smaller ones, and the shipping companies were soon crying out for larger locks and deeper channels at the Sault. A new American lock with a water depth of 17 feet was opened in 1881, but the real breakthrough came in 1895-96, when Canada built a huge new lock 900 feet in length and 22 feet in depth, and the United States added one nearly as large. The result was a rapid increase in the size of ships and the development of the traditional type of Great Lakes freighter, with its engines right aft, a small deck house and bridge perched on its bow, and a long series of cargo holds in between. The 400-foot ship was built on the lakes in 1895; one over 500 feet in length was placed in service in 1904, and only two years later the first 600-foot vessel was completed. Thereafter for many years the typical large freighter was about 580 feet long and had a carrying capacity of about 12,000 tons.

Ships such as these could go no further east than Lake Erie; the Welland Canal and the canals on the St. Lawrence were much too small to enable them to reach Lake Ontario or Montreal. But some improvements had been made on these portions of the waterway. A twenty-year rebuilding programme completed in 1904 enlarged all locks to a length of

Public Archives of Canada

A typical "cannaller" the Kamloops

An Upper Lakes freighter, the Lemoyne

Engines and boilers were almost always in the stern of the Great Lakes freighters. This was long regarded as an oddity, but the plan has been adopted for many big deepsea freighters in recent years. The Lemoyne *was typical of the bulk carriers that were built in pre-Seaway days. She was 613 feet in length and for a time was the largest ship on the Great Lakes.*

Welland Canal locks

These three sets of twin locks on the Welland Canal, with a combined length of almost half a mile, raise or lower ships a total of 139.5 feet.

Seaway lock at Iroquois

The Iroquois Lock on the St. Lawrence Seaway. There are seven locks between Lake Ontario and Montreal (five in Canada and two in the United States); all are 766 feet long and can accommodate ships up to 730 feet in length.

at least 270 feet, with a minimum water depth of 14 feet. The immediate result was the appearance of fleets of little freighters about 250 feet long, which were as large as the new locks could accommodate. Known as "canallers" because they could move freely from the upper lakes through the canals to Toronto and Montreal, they were a familiar sight and an important part of Great Lakes shipping for half a century.

The 270-foot locks satisfied no one, but the cost of replacing them with larger ones would be prodigious. Two barriers stood between Lake Erie and the sea—the forbidding drop of 330 feet to Lake Ontario at Niagara, and the rapids on the St. Lawrence. In 1898 a private company proposed to by-pass both of them by building a completely new canal system that would follow the old historic route of the fur traders from Georgian Bay to Montreal, by way of the French and Ottawa rivers. Cost of construction was estimated at $100,000,000, and as the money could not be found the project never passed the planning stage.

Murray Bay in the Iroquois Lock
To take full advantage of the Seaway, shipowners have built ships as large as the locks can accommodate. Here the 730-foot Murray Bay *squeezes through the Iroquois Lock.*

In 1913 Canada was able at last to tackle the first of the two obstructions to navigation; work began on a new Welland Canal. Owing to the First World War and other difficulties, progress was delayed many times, but the rebuilding was completed finally in 1932. The old canal had no fewer than 26 locks; the new one had only 8, each 859 feet in length. With the completion of the new canal, Lake Ontario became part of the great inland sea through which the largest ships on the Great Lakes could now move at will.

Only one barrier now remained between the Lakes and the ocean, but in cost it would be the most formidable of all to overcome. As long ago as 1895 Canada and the United States had appointed a Deep Water Commission to study the possibility of building a full-fledged seaway. It reported favourably, but no practical steps were taken. In 1920 the International Joint Commission asked W. A. Bowden, who had designed the new Welland Canal, to make an engineering study of the seaway project, and his remarkable report was a landmark in the development of the scheme. But more than thirty years were to pass before actual construction began. The necessary treaty between Canada and the United States was signed in 1950, and the new St. Lawrence canals opened for traffic in April 1959. There are seven locks in all, five on the Canadian side of the river and two on the American. Techni-

Seaway Authority

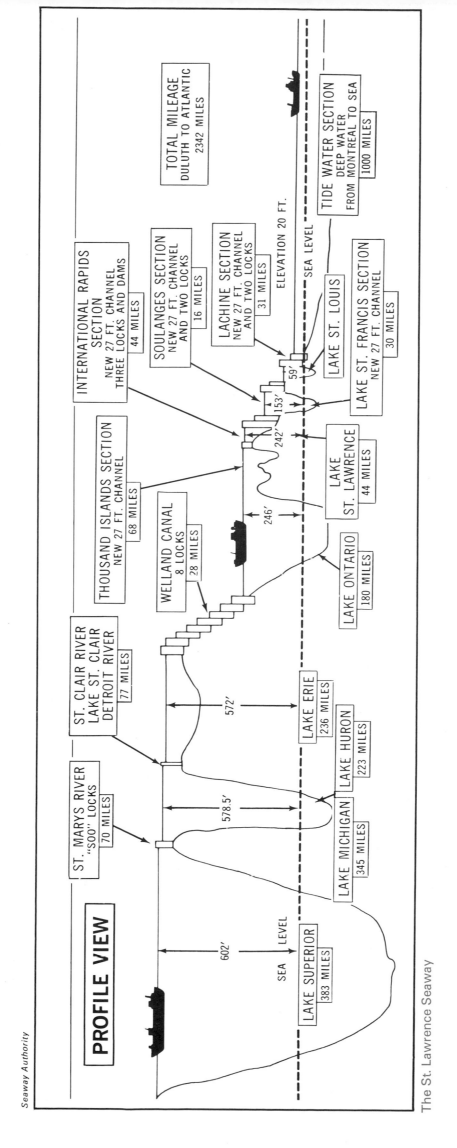

Seaway Authority

The St. Lawrence Seaway

PROFILE VIEW

TOTAL MILEAGE
DULUTH TO ATLANTIC
2342 MILES

TIDE WATER SECTION
DEEP WATER
FROM MONTREAL TO SEA
1000 MILES

INTERNATIONAL RAPIDS
SECTION
NEW 27 FT. CHANNEL
THREE LOCKS AND DAMS
44 MILES

SOULANGES SECTION
NEW 27 FT. CHANNEL
AND TWO LOCKS
16 MILES

LACHINE SECTION
NEW 27 FT. CHANNEL
AND TWO LOCKS
31 MILES

ELEVATION 20 FT.

SEA LEVEL

LAKE ST. LOUIS

LAKE ST. FRANCIS SECTION
NEW 27 FT. CHANNEL
30 MILES

THOUSAND ISLANDS SECTION
NEW 27 FT. CHANNEL
68 MILES

59'

153'

242'

LAKE
ST. LAWRENCE
44 MILES

WELLAND CANAL
8 LOCKS
28 MILES

246'

LAKE ONTARIO
180 MILES

ST. CLAIR RIVER
LAKE ST. CLAIR
DETROIT RIVER
77 MILES

572'

LAKE ERIE
236 MILES

LAKE HURON
223 MILES

ST. MARYS RIVER
"SOO" LOCKS
70 MILES

578.5'

LAKE MICHIGAN
345 MILES

602'

SEA LEVEL

LAKE SUPERIOR
383 MILES

cally, the seaway is considered to extend all the way from Montreal to Lake Superior, and all Canadian canals along the way are under the jurisdiction of the St. Lawrence Seaway Authority. The cost of the seaway was $460,000,000 (not including the hydro-electric installations), of which Canada paid $330,-000,000 and the United States $130,000,000.

Throughout its length the seaway can accommodate ships with a maximum length of 730 feet. As past experience would lead one to expect, shipowners have promptly added vessels of this size to their fleets. One of the newest of them, the *Canadian Progress,* owned by the Upper Lakes Shipping Company, can carry 25,000 tons of cargo, and has modern self-loading equipment that enables her to unload a cargo of coal at the remarkable rate of 4,500 tons per hour. Some of these big new ships are designed for deep-sea service; others expect to confine their voyages to the Great Lakes, the St. Lawrence and the Gulf of St. Lawrence.

Inevitably the completion of the seaway soon ended the careers of most of the "canallers" that had used the old 270-foot locks. But if one of the best-known types of ship on the Lakes began to disappear, a wide variety of new types took their place, as deep-sea vessels from all over the world began to come up through the new canals to the great inland sea. For with the completion of the seaway Toronto, Hamilton, Cleveland, Detroit, Chicago, Thunder Bay and many other cities suddenly became seaports in a new sense, with direct links with the oceans of the world.

The canals play a major part in Canadian transportation. Over 50,000,000 tons of cargo pass through the Welland Canal in a typical year; slightly less tonnage is carried in vessels using the seaway between Montreal and Lake Ontario. The Canadian and American canals at Sault Ste. Marie between them constitute the busiest waterway in the world. As much as 128,000,000 tons of cargo has passed through them in a single season.

The Advent of Radio

"Firsts" are often a matter of dispute. There is some difference of opinion regarding the date and place of the world's first regularly scheduled radio broadcast, but it was probably made in Montreal in December 1919 over station XWA (later CFCF), owned by the Canadian Marconi Company. Other stations were soon in operation, but for some time efforts were mostly local and sporadic. Those were the days when radio fans prided themselves on the number of different stations they had managed to pick up on their primitive battery-powered sets. What they heard and how well they heard it was a secondary consideration; to hear and record the station letters was the important thing.

The man who introduced a new era in broadcasting in Canada was Sir Henry Thornton, who became president of the Canadian National Railway late in 1922. Thornton had several ends in view. He hoped that radio would enable him to establish a personal contact with the railway's hundred thousand employees. He was confident that it would provide valuable publicity, and, last but not least, he was convinced that radio had much to offer Canada as a community and a nation. It could be a potent enemy of isolation and loneliness in remote areas, and it could promote a feeling of unity in the country as a whole.

A C.N.R. Radio Department was established in 1923, and radio-equipped cars were operating on the transcontinental trains early in 1924. That same year the C.N.R. opened the first of its own broadcasting stations, the ancestor of CBO, in Ottawa. If two stations linked together can be deemed to constitute a network, the C.N.R. had already made the first network broadcast when it arranged to have stations in Ottawa and Montreal linked for a special occasion in December 1923. And it played a large part in the much more spectacular broadcast that marked the 60th anniversary of Confederation on July 1, 1927. A network utilizing the wires of the C.N.R. and ten other telegraph and telephone companies enabled the ceremonies on Parliament Hill to be heard from one end of Canada to the other.

By the end of 1929 the C.N.R. had established a permanent nation-wide network of land lines and broadcasting stations that pioneered in many types of programming. The Toronto Symphony Orchestra, known on the air as the All-Canada Symphony, broadcast a series of concerts in 1930, and the next spring Tyrone Guthrie directed a succession of historical plays by Merrill Denison entitled *The Romance of Canada.* In 1930 the Canadian Pacific Railway completed a rival radio network, and used the orchestras in its hotels for many of its broadcasts.

These enterprising efforts were soon hard hit by the depression; parliamentary committees tended to take the narrow view that broadcasting was a frill that simply added to the C.N.R. deficit. Nor were privately owned stations faring well. Surprisingly, the possibilities of broadcasting as an advertising medium were not realized for years, and the stations were starved for revenue. Although the number of private stations in Canada jumped from 55 in 1926 to 84 in 1928, it declined thereafter.

Other countries had been struggling with the problem of national broadcasting policy, and it was clearly time that Canada did likewise. In the United States private ownership was the basic pattern; the National Broadcasting Company was formed in 1926 and the Columbia Broadcasting System followed in 1927. In Britain public ownership was chosen, and the British Broadcasting Corporation came into existence in 1927. Late in 1928 the Canadian Government appointed a Royal Commission that reported in the fall of 1929 and recommended that, in the public interest, nationalization should be the policy adopted.

The next three years were a troubled period of great uncertainty. The depression reached its

Sound effects in 1925 (above)

The special effects staff, complete with locomotive bell, ready for a broadcast at one of the C.N.R. broadcasting stations.

Station CNRO in Ottawa, 1925 (at right)

This station (now CBO of the CBC) was one of the ten stations comprising the pioneer trans-Canada network of the Canadian National Railways, which extended from Moncton to Vancouver.

depths; there was a change in government; Ottawa had many other things on its mind; those who had, or wished to have, an interest in privately owned radio were active. Yet it was obvious that some measure of public ownership was essential. From the national point of view, the first need was coverage that would be as nearly as possible nation-wide. Private stations would naturally concentrate on populous areas and take no interest in the backwoods, where costs would be high and revenues negligible. The case for public ownership at least found informed and persuasive support in the Radio League of Canada, founded in December 1930 by a small group headed by two able and disinterested young men, Graham Spry and Alan Plaunt. Their solution of the problem was a typically Canadian compromise: the proposal that public and private ownership should run in tandem. In no small measure it was due to the League's efforts that legislation was passed in 1932 creating the Canadian Broadcasting Commission. Networks were to be a monopoly of the Commission, but the local field was left open to private stations.

The Commission had a rather unhappy life of four years. For various reasons, some of them political, it failed to be an effective body. As a result, new legislation in 1936 replaced it with the Canadian Broadcasting Corporation—the familiar CBC —that was much more independent in structure. The change for the better was immediate. When the CBC took over, radio was reaching only 49 percent of the population; a year later this had been raised to 78 percent and it was soon increased further to 84 percent. It has since increased to nearly 99 percent.

CBC created three networks—two English and one French—and developed two special services. The Northern Service endeavoured to reach isolated settlements, and in recent years has included broadcasts in Indian languages and in Eskimo. The International Service, dating from 1945, seeks to spread knowledge of Canada, its people, and its point of view among nations abroad, particularly in eastern Europe. Notable both in CBC and the private stations has been the attention given to news and to current events. News and the weather reports are perhaps the things people now turn to first, yet both were strangely late in appearing, presumably because news agencies and newspapers feared their competition. News as a radio feature did not become common until 1933 or later.

The great new development in the postwar years was the advent of television. Broadcasts began in 1952, and colour television followed in 1966. Costs were high and CBC budgets increased enormously. In 1950 the Corporation's income was $9,447,000; by 1966 it had jumped to $165,338,000. In 1968 the CBC had 39 radio and 75 television stations, and in addition was operating 16 short-wave stations and 181 low-power relay transmitters —the latter being the means by which it reaches innumerable communities that lie beyond the reach of its standard networks.

The CBC as created in 1936 was a regulatory as well as a broadcasting body. All radio services are targets for criticism, but in addition to the usual charges CBC was inevitably accused of administering regulations in its own interest. For this and other reasons a Board of Broadcast Governors was set up in 1958 to take over the regulatory function. Its most memorable act was its decision to end the television network monopoly of the CBC and to permit the organization of the CTV privately owned network in 1961. The Board was superseded in 1968 by the Canadian Radio and Television Commission, which regulates and supervises all broadcasting, and licenses all private radio and television stations.

Broadcasting coverage in Canada is now thorough in all the populated areas. In 1968 there were 372 radio and 304 television stations in operation, making a total of 676 in all, of which 104 were owned by the CBC. Radio networks are still a CBC monopoly, but many of the private stations are affiliated with the networks and broadcast programmes from them.

Transportation in the Northland (Canada North of 55°)

Legend

∗	Far northern wireless stations
•	R.C.M.P. posts
•	Hudson's Bay Co. posts and stores
	Principal Highways
	Railways
	Scheduled Airlines
	Department of Transport supply routes

0   200   400
miles

ARCTIC OCEAN

ATLANTIC OCEAN

Davis Strait

Baffin Bay

Hudson Bay

James Bay

L. Superior

Yukon R.

St. Lawrence River

Fraser R.

Columbia R.

Athabasca R.

Churchill R.

Saskatchewan R.

Lake Winnipeg

CORNWALLIS I.

ELLESMERE ISLAND

DEVON I.

BAFFIN ISLAND

BANKS I.

MELVILLE I.

VICTORIA ISLAND

SOUTHAMPTON I.

Prince of Wales I.

Bathurst I.

Place names

Alert
Eureka
Isachsen
Mould Bay
Resolute
Grise Fjord
Alexandra Fjord
Cape Christian
Pond Inlet
Cape Dorset
Pangnirtung
Frobisher Bay
Lake Harbour
Sugluk
Port Harrison
Fort Chimo
Goose Bay
St. John's
Halifax
Montreal
Quebec
to Toronto
Timmins
Moosonee
Winnipeg
Regina
Saskatoon
Calgary
Edmonton
Great Whale River
Severn
The Pas
Flin Flon
Thompson
Lynn Lake
Churchill
Eskimo Point
Rankin Inlet
Chesterfield Inlet
Baker Lake
Coral Harbour
Repulse Bay
Igloolik
Spence Bay
Cambridge Bay
Holman Island
Coppermine
Port Radium
Sachs Harbour
Cape Parry
Tuktoyaktut
Aklavik
Inuvik
Herschel Island
Fort McPherson
Arctic Red River
Fort Good Hope
Norman Wells
Fort Norman
Fort Simpson
Fort Providence
Fort Liard
Hay River
Fort Reliance
Fort Resolution
Fort Smith
Pine Point
Yellowknife
Rae
Uranium City
Fort Chipewyan
McMurray
Peace River
Grande Prairie
Fort St. John
Fort Nelson
Watson Lake
Winter Road
Old Crow
Fairbanks
Dawson
Keno
Mayo
Carmacks
Whitehorse
Teslin
Carcross
Haines Junction
Juneau
Prince Rupert
Prince George
Vancouver
Victoria

40°
60°
80°
100°
120°
140°
160°
80°
70°
60°
50°
55°
55°

CHAPTER 18

Resources and Development

Wheat Faces Marketing Problems

WHEAT, long Canada's pride and joy and her premier export, is now proving to be a problem child. Its quality is as high as ever, but it is being produced in such large quantities that it cannot all be disposed of profitably.

Before the great immigrant influx to the prairies in 1897-1913 a wheat crop of 40,000,000 bushels was considered a bumper harvest. The first 100,000,000 bushel crop was grown in 1905. In 1911 production passed the 200,000,000-bushel mark. In 1915, owing to an exceptionally favourable growing season and a special effort to meet anticipated wartime demands, a crop of over 393,000,000 bushels was harvested.

Prices collapsed in 1920 and the wheat farmers experienced several very lean years. However, by 1924 the markets had recovered and the next five years were a boom period. They concluded with two record harvests in 1927 and 1928 (the latter totalling 566,700,000 bushels) that between them provided a foretaste of the problems that are facing wheat today.

Like most Canadian exports, wheat must be sold in a world market. The state of that market depends to a great extent upon the harvests in competing wheat-producing countries. It so happened that in 1927 and 1928 world production was unusually large, with the result that Canada was unable to market all her crops and acquired something that was to become painfully familiar in later years—a carryover, or unsold residue from previous harvests.

This is the situation that exists today, but on a far more formidable scale. In 1927 the carryover was only 51,000,000 bushels, and it had risen to no more than 112,000,000 bushels by 1930. By contrast, in the years from 1955 to 1963 the carryover averaged more than 575,000,000 bushels. It dropped to 420,000,000 in 1966, but a record harvest of over 800,000,000 bushels the same year made the problem of emptying Canada's grain storage bins and filling the pockets of the farmers more difficult than ever. When it is remembered that Canada's domestic consumption of wheat is only about 150,000,000 bushels, the extent to which the solution depends on world conditions and world markets will be apparent.

Some new customers for wheat have appeared. Since 1960 substantial sales have been made to Russia, China and Japan, but their continuity is uncertain as yet. Much of this wheat has been shipped through Vancouver, and this has emphasized the rise of grain exports through ports on the west coast. In 1966 Vancouver handled almost 25 percent more wheat than Montreal, long the country's traditional and greatest grain port.

In many respects grain growing is easier and more efficient than it used to be. Farms are larger; modern machinery is expensive, but it makes much better use of labour. Horses have been replaced by tractors; combines have taken the place of binders and threshing machines. Ironically, these various improvements have helped to push production to the point where the product cannot all be disposed of on the world market. Some scaling down of wheat acreage seems inevitable. Wheat growing will always be big business in Canada, but increasingly it will have to be confined to the finest crops on the best acres.

Already wheat is relatively less important in the over-all Canadian economy than it was for many years. In 1929 grain and grain products made up nearly 40 percent of the total value of Canadian exports. By 1966 they represented only about 10 percent. The value of newsprint alone exceeded that of wheat exports, and the value of forest products as a whole was far in excess of it. Changes of equal interest and importance are taking place in Canadian farming itself and in the economies of the

An old-time threshing scene

Public Archives of Canada

A typical threshing outfit in the days when the steam tractor was the chief source of power. The steam engine was somewhat of a nuisance because of its requirements for fuel and water, and as internal combustion engines developed, they took over. Combines — combination binder-threshers — have made the big threshers of an earlier day obsolete.

Dept. of Agriculture

Dept. of Agriculture

Grain storage

The huge wheat carryover that has accumulated in recent years presents staggering storage problems. In normal times elevators (to which storage sheds have often been added) could meet most storage needs. Now all manner of temporary storage buildings are used, and wheat must sometimes be left in huge piles in the fields until space for it can be found elsewhere.

prairie provinces, where wheat was long dominant. The value of livestock products now substantially exceeds that of all field crops; farm income from cattle and calves in 1966 was greater than that from wheat. Industry has come to the prairies. Oil has transformed Alberta, and in neighbouring Saskatchewan petroleum products were valued at over $200,000,000 in 1966. Such new discoveries as the immense potash deposits in Saskatchewan are giving the provinces a greater variety of resources. The day of the old one-crop economy is now long past.

Mines and Minerals

Gold, silver and precious stones were among the treasures that early explorers hoped to discover but failed to find in Canada. Instead, the fur trade developed and, in conjunction with funds sent from France to meet defence expenditures, was the mainstay of the colony for many years.

Mining developed very slowly; east of the Rockies, at the time of Confederation, the fur harvest problably still exceeded metal production in value. West of the mountains, gold had been discovered in quantity on the Fraser River and its tributaries in 1858-60, the most exciting event that had yet figured in the history of mining in Canada. The prosperity it brought was fleeting, and by 1867

the mines had passed their peak; but between 1858 and 1870 they produced gold worth at least $32,000,000—a very large sum in those days.

The mineral industry has grown to giant proportions relatively recently. In 1886, the first year for which statistics are available, production in all Canada was valued at only $10,221,000. By the end of the century it was still no more than $50,000,000. Growth was much more rapid thereafter, and the total had risen to over $310,000,000 by 1929. But even this substantial figure was dwarfed by developments after the Second World War. In 1945 production was valued at about $500,000,000. Only five years later the total exceeded $1,000,000,000, and it has since risen to over $4,000,000,000.

Some of the increase in dollar value has resulted from higher prices and inflation, but most of it reflects an enormous growth in the physical volume of mineral production. Only in the United States

Ship loading grain at Vancouver

British Columbia Government

Cominco

The Trail smelter about 1880

In 1898 the Canadian Pacific acquired the Columbia & Western Railway. The railway's charter was the thing of primary interest to the C.P.R., but the property included the original Trail smelter, which has since developed on a prodigious scale.

and the Soviet Union is production greater. The tonnage of such old standby products as nickel, copper and zinc has more than doubled in the last dozen years; asbestos production has risen by over 50 percent. The most important recent development in metals has been a great increase in iron ore shipments, particularly from the Quebec–Labrador border area. In 1945 iron ore production totalled only about 1,000,000 tons; it now exceeds 40,000,000 tons. In the fuels category, the western oil discoveries in Alberta and Saskatchewan have added a billion dollars a year to production totals. Uranium from Great Slave Lake and Elliot Lake, potash in Saskatchewan and a new molybdenum industry in British Columbia are other items that have swelled the total.

Many factors enter into the development of a successful mine. The mine itself must be discovered and its worth proven; any technical problems that its ores may present must be solved; capital must be found to finance development and, finally, transportation must be available to move the product to market.

Today prospecting is a highly technical undertaking; some types of exploration can even be done from the air. But several of the greatest discoveries in Canadian mining history were made virtually by accident. Excavations for new railways provided three famous examples. The asbestos deposits south of Quebec City, which now provide most of the western world's supply, were discovered by chance in 1877 by workmen excavating for the Central Quebec Railway. In 1883 a construction crew building the main line of the Canadian Pacific unearthed a nickel-copper deposit near Sudbury that resulted in the development of the world's largest nickel mines. And in 1903 workers building a railway for the Government of Ontario stumbled upon a fabulously rich silver-cobalt deposit that was first developed primarily as a silver mine and is still important as a source of cobalt. In 1896 chance of another kind had resulted in gold discoveries on creeks and rivers in the Yukon that touched off the great Klondike rush in 1897.

The role of chance in mining history must not be exaggerated; patience, systematic exploration and hard work have been much more productive. The Sullivan mine at Kimberley—one of the world's great mines—is a prime example of a major discovery whose wealth could not be tapped effectively until difficult technical problems had been solved. Its purchase by Cominco in 1910 was something of an act of faith; discovered in 1892, it had defeated

273

The Trail smelter today

Parts of the subsidiary chemical and fertilizer plants can be seen in the left background.

Sudbury today

The International Nickel Company's Copper Cliff reduction plant. As part of the Company's anti-pollution programme, the three stacks (two of which are 500 feet high) will be replaced by a single giant stack 1200 feet in height. It will be the highest in the world.

all efforts by four previous owners to devise a process that would separate the lead, zinc and other metals in its rich but complex ore. Success came finally in 1920 when R. W. Diamond perfected the differential flotation process. By 1923 a plant capable of treating 3,000 tons of ore a day was in operation at Kimberley, and the great expansion of the mine and the smelter at Trail was under way.

Gold is one of the few minerals whose value is so high that its transportation is rarely a serious problem; with the base metals it is quite otherwise. Rich ore deposits frequently must languish for years untouched if a reasonably cheap means of moving the ore to market is not available. Another Cominco property, the lead and zinc mines at Pine Point, near Great Slave Lake, is an instance of this. First noticed in 1899, the deposits were explored to some extent by Cominco in 1927-28, but nearly forty years were to pass before the construction of a railway north from the old end of steel on the Peace River provided a means of shipping out concentrates. A plant that could process 5,000 tons a day was built, and the first shipments were made in 1964.

Transportation was equally vital in the development of the vast iron ore deposits near the Quebec–Labrador boundary. They became of practical value only after the building of the 360-mile Quebec, North Shore and Labrador Railway from Sept-Iles, on the St. Lawrence River north to Schefferville. Construction and development costs were enormous, but so are the ore deposits from which the first shipments came in 1954.

As with many other Canadian products, the export market is vital to the mineral industry. Production far exceeds domestic needs. Nickel is perhaps the best example of a metal of which a very high proportion is exported; for minerals as a whole, which now comprise the largest category in Canadian exports, the proportion is about 60 percent. This seems likely to increase in the years to come, for production will probably increase more rapidly than Canada's own needs. The output of many minerals, notably nickel and iron ore, is scheduled to rise considerably; the demand for coking-coal in Japan is resulting in a great increase in coal production in British Columbia.

Mining is a depleting industry; once a mineral is extracted it can never be replaced. Some day Canada must come to the end of her mineral resources, which it was fashionable at one time to describe as inexhaustible. Certainly they are still vast and many rich discoveries will be made in due course; but it is to be hoped that industries will develop within the country that will absorb a substantially higher proportion of production than is possible at present.

The Forest Industries: Manufacturing Giant

The forest industries are the largest segment of manufacturing in Canada. They give employment totalling over 300,000 man years (and actually employ many more individuals, as some of the work is seasonal), and provide about a quarter of the total value of all Canadian exports.

The three major products are lumber, wood pulp and newsprint, and their story is largely the

The Copper Cliff Mine at Sudbury in 1888

This was the beginning of the vast industry that now produces a high percentage of the world's supply of nickel.

story of the industry. As the great pine forests of eastern Canada became depleted, lumber production there declined, and this became specially marked after the First World War. But the pulp and paper industry was developing, and eventually it far surpassed lumbering. Pulp mills added a whole new dimension to the forest industries, for they made use of kinds of trees and smaller trees that were not suitable for lumber production. This smaller growth, which existed over vast areas, had been regarded hitherto as being of little or no commercial value; the advent of the pulp mill made it saleable raw material. Later it was found that the mills could also make use of the slabs and edgings that had been burned as waste or at best sold for firewood by the lumber mills.

Pulp is made in two ways—by the mechanical or groundwood method, or by one of several chemical processes. The first groundwood mill in Canada seems to have begun operations in Valleyfield, Quebec, in 1866; the first chemical plant opened near Sherbrooke three years later. Early development was mostly in Quebec; 17 of the 24 mills

recorded in the 1891 census were in that province. In 1908 pulp production totalled 363,000 tons. Much of this was consumed by paper mills; the rest was exported. Export markets were vital, because pulp and paper production alike soon far exceeded the demand within Canada, and the growth of the industry on a large scale began in 1909 and the succeeding years, when American tariffs were first reduced and then removed altogether. Pulp production rose to 1,000,000 tons in 1915, it was over 2,150,000 tons in 1922, and reached 4,000,000 tons in 1929.

Papers of many kinds are made in Canada, but newsprint is the prime product of the paper mills; it accounted for 85 percent of paper production in 1929. This proportion has not varied greatly in later years, but the volume of both pulp and paper production has increased enormously. In 1949 Canadian mills produced 7,852,000 tons of pulp and 5,187,000 tons of newsprint. By 1966 pulp production had risen to nearly 16,000,000 tons and the newsprint output was 8,419,000 tons. About a quarter of the pulp is exported. The vital importance of the export market, and of the American market in particular, is made abundantly clear by three figures: in 1966, as just noted, newsprint production was 8,419,000 tons. The same year 7,764,000 tons were exported and of this total 6,340,000 tons went to the United States.

British Columbia Government

Cathedral Grove (upper left)

Cathedral Grove, a magnificent stand of virgin fir forest on Vancouver Island, which is being preserved permanently as a provincial park.

Modern lumber mill at New Westminster (bottom left)

For many years Quebec was by far the largest producer of pulp and paper, with Ontario ranking second. British Columbia, a latecomer in the field, now threatens to surpass Ontario, and British Columbia and Ontario between them produce substantially more than Quebec. The first paper made in British Columbia from wood pulp was not produced until 1912, and in 1929 paper production in the province was still only 229,000 tons, or about 7 percent of the Canadian total. It had more than doubled by 1949 and rose to 1,150,000 tons in 1960 and to 1,521,000 tons in 1965. Pulp production has risen even more steeply, and from a total of 3,275,-000 tons in 1965 is expected to reach 5,700,000 tons in 1970.

But lumbering continues to be the major forest industry in British Columbia, and more than three-quarters of Canadian lumber is cut there. In 1967 production totalled well over seven billion board feet. The same year the province produced 82 percent of the plywood made in Canada. (This is a relatively new development; the word "plywood" itself, now so familiar, dates only from 1917.) Until recent years lumbering in British Columbia was primarily a coastal industry, centred largely on magnificent stands of Douglas fir. The lumbermen have now moved inland, and about half the lumber produced comes from the interior.

About a quarter of North America's total stand of merchantable timber is in British Columbia; for Canada as a whole the proportion is substantially higher. But even these immense reserves (in many areas inaccessible at present) will require farsighted management if they are to support the forest industries in perpetuity. Better fire protection is one pressing need; the average annual fire loss now totals hundreds of millions of feet. Nor can anything ever replace the great primeval forests; but reforestation, selective cutting, and other conservation measures could in time ensure a high perpetual yield. With the current assault on the Canadian forests approaching four billion cubic feet a year (about 45 percent of which is cut in British Columbia), forest management is clearly a vital matter for Canada.

The Rise of the Petroleum Industry

The first commercial oil well in North America was developed in Canada in 1857, but it was not until 90 years later, in 1947, that oil fields were discovered that were to make a fundamental change in the Canadian economy.

Paper Mill at Powell River, B.C. (upper right)

The first newsprint produced in British Columbia was shipped from the small ancestor of this vast plant in May 1912. The Powell River mills are now one of the world's largest producers of newsprint.

Shipping lumber overseas (bottom right)

Loading lumber at a port in British Columbia for shipment to Great Britain.

MacMillan Bloedel

The pioneer well was at Black Creek (soon renamed Oil Springs), a small community about 18 miles southeast of Sarnia. It was brought into production by James Miller Williams, who later the same year built Canada's first oil refinery. Further oil discoveries were made in 1860 at Petrolia, a few miles north of Oil Springs, and the field proved to be of some consequence. Production reached a peak of 800,000 bbl in 1895, after which it declined and is now little more than a trickle.

Alberta was to be the first really large-scale source of oil in Canada. Both oil and natural gas were discovered in 1914 in the Turner Valley, south of Calgary, and for a generation this was the most important oil producing area in Canada. Production began to decline about 1942, but by 1949 total production in 35 years had totalled over 102,000,000 bbl.

For many years geologists prospecting for oil had had to depend very largely on evidence on or very near the earth's surface. By degrees knowledge increased and prospecting methods improved; areas that had been looked upon as being barren of oil were now given a second and more efficient searching examination. It became apparent that oil deposits were much more widespread than had been thought. Exploratory drilling began farther north in Alberta, and in 1947 a huge oil field was discovered near Leduc, 20 miles south of Edmonton. The next year another major field was found near Redwater, 36 miles northeast of Edmonton, and other discovereies followed.

Petroleum production now increased at a spectacular rate. In 1946 Canadian production had totalled 7,585,000 bbl. By 1948 it was 12,286,000 bbl and the next year it exceeded 20,000,000 bbl. Only seven years later production was over 113,-000,000 bbl and in 1961 it reached 157,811,000 bbl. Five years later, as the 20th anniversary of the Leduc discoveries approached, it had again more than doubled to 320,542,000 bbl.

Alberta contributed the lion's share to this total —203,339,000 bbl—but Saskatchewan produced 93,218,000 bbl. Extensive oil fields were first discovered there in 1952; the chief producing centres are around Weyburn, in the south east, and Fosterton and Coleville in the west. For a time it was hoped that large fields might be found in Manitoba as well, but nothing has yet developed beyond the wells around Virden, which produce about 5,000,000 bbl a year. British Columbia has been more fortunate. In addition to large natural gas resources, oil wells

British Columbia Government

Oil wells at Petrolia
This sketch was first published in 1871.

Imperial Oil

British Columbia Government

Imperial Oil

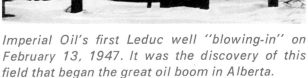

Imperial Oil's first Leduc well "blowing-in" on February 13, 1947. It was the discovery of this field that began the great oil boom in Alberta.

A vast network of pipelines now carries oil and gas from the wells in the West to many parts of Canada. Here, shown at top of page, a gas pipeline is being laid in the Peace River District. Two sections of the pipe are being welded together. When this has been completed and the pipe given a protective coating, it will be lowered into the trench prepared for it and buried.

Night view of part of the vast complex that comprises the Imperial Oil Company's Sarnia refineries.

in the northeastern part of the province, next to Alberta, produced 16,671,000 bbl in 1966 and over 19,656,000 bbl in 1967. Ontario still produces over a million barrels a year, and in 1966 the Northwest Territories produced 752,000 bbl.

An event of more than passing interest was the completion in 1967 of a plant to produce crude oil from the famous so-called tar sands of the Athabasca River valley. A pipeline carries this oil to the refineries in Edmonton.

The oil discoveries, especially those in Alberta and Saskatchewan, have not only been important for Canada as a whole, but have added substantial new sources of employment and revenue at a time when the old wheat-based economy of the prairies

is encountering grave difficulties. Nationally, the most significant result has been the substitution of home-produced petroleum and petroleum products for those imported from abroad, with a resulting major saving in foreign exchange. Before the Leduc discoveries every automobile and truck operating in Canada was placing a strain on the Canadian dollar and the country's financial reserves.

The turning point came in 1954, when for the first time Canada exported more oil than she imported. As this implies, the importation of oil has not ceased, for there are parts of Canada that can be supplied with oil from the United States and other foreign sources more cheaply and conveniently than from Canadian wells. But there are likewise areas in the United States that can best be supplied from Canada, and Canadian oil is exported to them.

What the future holds no one can tell, but it appears to be full of promise. Offshore drilling vessels are investigating the possibility that undersea areas off the coasts of Canada may have great lakes of oil beneath them. The discovery of extensive oil fields in Alaska, along the Arctic coast, has strengthened the belief of some geologists that Melville Island, in the Canadian Arctic, may be sitting on top of oil reserves of fabulous extent. Ellesmere Island is believed to be another excellent prospect. Certainly it would appear that Canadian oil production—now higher per day than it was per annum in 1928—may well become very much greater before many years pass.

The first electric street lights, Victoria 1883

British Columbia Archives

Ontario Hydro's Lakeview steam generating plant
Completed in 1968, it has a capacity of 2,400,000 kW.

Ontario Hydro

B.C. Hydro and Power Authority

Power to Turn the Wheels of Industry

Power is the basic essential for modern industrial development, and if the Canadian economy is to progress, it must be available in vast and ever increasing quantities.

Water-wheels were the first source of power; many of Canada's early sawmills and gristmills were driven by them. But their capacity was usually very limited, and they could be installed only if a suitable river was at hand. When the steam engine appeared, both these limitations were overcome to a considerable extent; an engine could be installed almost anywhere, and the power developed could be many times that produced by water-wheels. However, this power had to be distributed mechanically by shafts and belts and pulleys, which meant that it could be made available only over a relatively small area. In other words, every mill or factory had to have its own steam engine; nothing in the nature of a central source of power was yet possible.

This was the immense step forward provided by electricity—the power generated could be transmitted in any direction over a network of cables and wires. Electricity appeared on the Canadian scene about 1883, and was used progressively for street lighting, domestic lighting and street railways. In December 1883 arc lights mounted on 150-foot masts, which were intended to floodlight the centre of the city, were installed in Victoria. Pembroke is said to have had the first electric street lights in eastern Canada in October 1884; Ottawa turned on its first lights a few months later. Electric street cars began to run in Windsor in 1886, in St. Catharines in 1887, and in Victoria and Vancouver in 1890. Montreal and Toronto followed in 1892.

Electricity soon began to be used by industry, but large-scale application was delayed by the limitations of the old-style reciprocating type of steam engine, which could not generate power cheaply. The vital invention that made this possible was the turbine, which could rotate at high speed and could be coupled directly to an electric generator. Charles Parsons, the famous British turbine pioneer, built a small turbine in 1884 that drove a generator satisfactorily, and much larger installations followed quickly. Quite as important, turbines that could be driven by water were developed, and this new and sophisticated type of water-wheel made it possible to generate electricity from Canada's great rivers upon a scale hitherto undreamed of. Rapids and water-

W. A. C. Bennett Dam on the Peace River

No picture can convey adequately the size of the Bennett Dam, which is one of the largest earthfill structures in the world. It is a mile and a quarter wide, 600 feet high, and half a mile thick at the base.

falls that had been looked upon as being merely impediments to navigation, or at best as beauty spots, suddenly became potential sources of power for a thousand domestic and industrial uses. On the Ottawa River, for example, virtually all the rapids and falls between Montreal and Mattawa, around which the fur traders had to make laborious portages, have now given way to storage lakes behind hydroelectric power dams.

In 1900 electric generating plants in Canada developed a total of 173,000 hp. By 1910 the total had jumped to 997,000 hp, and this increased to over 2,500,000 hp in 1920. There was a five-fold increase during the next 30 years to 12,562,000 hp in 1950, and so rapid had expansion then become that the total had more than doubled to 26,330,000 hp by 1960.

It was abundant cheap power that made possible the development of the vast pulp and paper industry; it uses about a fifth of all the power developed in Canada by hydro stations. Mining and smelting use even greater quantities of electricity. To cite one important instance, the huge smelter at Trail, one of the largest in the Commonwealth, was made possible by the power that could be developed on the nearby Kootenay and Pend d'Oreille rivers. The asbestos industry in Quebec, which meets a major share of the world's needs, likewise depends upon an abundant supply of electricity.

The availability of power has even brought industries to Canada for which the country cannot provide raw materials. Most important of these is the manufacture of aluminum. There are no known deposits of bauxite in Canada, but cheap power makes it profitable to import it from abroad. Hydroelectric plants on the Saguenay River with an output of almost 800,000 kW supply the plants at Arvida, and since the Second World War a new aluminum manufacturing centre has been developed at Kitimat, on the coast of British Columbia. Power for the plants there was secured by creating a huge storage lake in the interior of the province and conveying water from it, through the mountains and miles of tunnels, to Kemano, which is at sea level. The generators there have a capacity of 812,800 kW.

Electricity has added much to the comfort, safety and convenience of Canadian homes. The change has been specially noteworthy in rural areas, where the 1966 census records that 88.7 percent of the farms had electric power available. In early years many small plants supplying homes shut down during the day because light was not required and domestic appliances were unknown. By contrast, in a recent year residences and farms between them used no less than 21 percent of all the electricity produced in Canada. Commercial use amounted to 15 percent and industry consumed 55 percent. The remaining 9 percent was classified as "losses and unaccounted for."

In many homes, business and industries, heat and power are also derived from three other major sources of energy—coal, oil and gas. All three provide fuel for thermal plants that generate electricity, for water power is not available everywhere. Prince Edward Island depends entirely upon thermal plants, and they are the major source of supply in Nova Scotia, New Brunswick, Saskatchewan and Alberta. In other provinces, notably Ontario, most of the rivers with large power potential that are reasonably near heavily populated and industrialized areas have now been harnessed, and as the demand for power continues to grow unrelentingly, thermal stations are being built to meet it.

Ontario has pioneered in the development of nuclear thermal generating plants. A demonstration station with an output of 20,000 kW was built at Rolphton, 20 miles from Chalk River, in 1962. This was followed by a 200,000 kW reactor that was completed at Douglas Point, on Lake Huron, in 1966. This was Canada's first full-scale nuclear power station. A much larger station, which will have a capacity of 1,080,000 kW is under construction at Pickering, near Toronto. A nuclear generating plant with a rated capacity of 250,000 kW is also being built in Quebec.

Experts believe that in the long run thermal plants will become the major source of power in Canada. The demand for power seems insatiable, and even in the water-rich provinces of Quebec and British Columbia there must be a limit to hydroelectric development. At one time it seemed that this day might come relatively soon, as many rivers, especially in the north, were so far away that power could not be brought from them economically. Transmission lines operating at fantastically high voltages have now made it practicable to transmit electricity cheaply for long distances. The result has been a series of spectacular projects that are changing the power map of Canada. In British Columbia the Peace River has been dammed at Portage Mountain and generators there, the first of which began to operate in 1968, will have a capacity of 2,270,000 kW. A 500,000-volt transmission line will carry the power 574 miles to Vancouver. In Manitoba a generating station at Kettle Rapids, on the Nelson River, will produce 1,224,000 kW—the equivalent of the total demand for electric power in the province in 1969. In Quebec a series of seven hydro plants on the Manicouagan and Outardes rivers will have a capacity of no less than 5,800,000 kW. Finally, at Churchill Falls, in Labrador, generators will produce 5,225,000 kW. Both in Quebec and Labrador the transmission line voltages will be 735,000.

On January 1, 1967, installed generating capacity in Canada totalled 32,993,000 kW. Of this 23,405,000 kW were produced in hydroelectric plants and 9,588,000 kW in thermal stations. New generating capacity then under construction or definitely planned for the next few years totalled 24,800,000 kW—15,200,000 kW in hydro plants and 9,600,000 kW in additional thermal stations. Total capacity will then rise to 57,793,000 kW—sufficient to turn many wheels in a myriad of industries, old and new.

CHAPTER 19

People and Politics

Fifty Years of Post-war Immigration: 1919-1969

IMMIGRATION is influenced by many factors; it reflects conditions and prospects both in Canada and abroad. It is checked by a depression, or even an appreciable recession, and a war can bring it virtually to a halt. Political events can affect it strongly. The flight of the Jews from Nazi-dominated countries is one example; the events in Hungary in 1956-57, which brought 35,000 Hungarians to Canada, is another.

The peak year in Canadian immigration history is still 1913, when 400,870 immigrants entered Canada, and its record is not likely to be surpassed. Indeed, only twice—in 1957 and 1967—has the number of immigrants been more than half that number.

The outbreak of war in 1914 halted the tremendous flow of people from Europe to America that had been in progress since the beginning of the century; only 36,665 persons came to Canada from all sources in 1915. The pace quickened again and the total rose to 107,698 in 1919, the first post-war year, and in the decade 1921-31 about 1,200,000 immigrants arrived. But even in the prosperous 'twenties a disconcerting number of the new arrivals later left Canada, and they were accompanied by many Canadian-born. In 1931, census figures revealed that roughly a million people had left Canada in the previous ten years. The population had risen by 1,558,000 since 1921, but no more than 229,000 of this could be attributed to immigration; natural increase accounted for the rest.

The years of depression and war that followed reduced the flow of immigrants even more drastically than the events of 1914. An order-in-council passed in August 1930 restricted immigrants to the wives and children of men already in Canada and to agriculturists possessed of some capital, and the

number of arrivals fell to 27,530 in 1931. Even that modest total was not to be equalled for fifteen years, and in 1942, midway through the Second World War, immigration reached its lowest point—7,576.

Many factors led to a sharp increase as soon as peace was restored. One of them was the problem presented by "displaced persons"; over the years Canadian sympathy was demonstrated by the admission of at least 300,000 refugees. In all, over 2,000,000 immigrants entered Canada in the years 1946-61.

Over 600,000 more arrived in the succeeding five years. This movement has differed markedly from the previous large migrations, especially in recent years. Few immigrants have come from eastern Europe; most of them have come from the west and the south. Much the largest numbers have come from the British Isles, the next largest from Italy. Other substantial groups have come from the United States, other Commonwealth countries, Germany, Portugal, France, Greece, the Netherlands and Switzerland, roughly in that order.

The character of the immigrants themselves has changed. They now include a large proportion of skilled workers and men with technical or professional qualifications. In 1966, when immigration rose to 194,743, the new arrivals were divided almost equally between wives, children and a few retired persons and "workers" of various sorts. Of the latter, just over a quarter had managerial, technical or professional qualifications, and the vast majority had occupational skills of some definite sort. The traditional "general labourers" numbered only 7,593, or no more than 9.6 percent of the "workers" seeking employment.

A much higher proportion of immigrants now remain in Canada; over the period 1946-61 not many more than one-fifth sought better prospects elsewhere. But 387,000 Canadian-born persons entered the United States during the same period, and this drain continues, usually at the rate of between 30,000 and 35,000 departures per year.

Changes in legislation and regulations have increased Canada's control of immigration; it is now possible to pick and choose much more care-

The Mennonites

The Mennonites have retained many of their customs. Here the congregation leaves the Mennonite Church at St. Jacobs, Ontario.

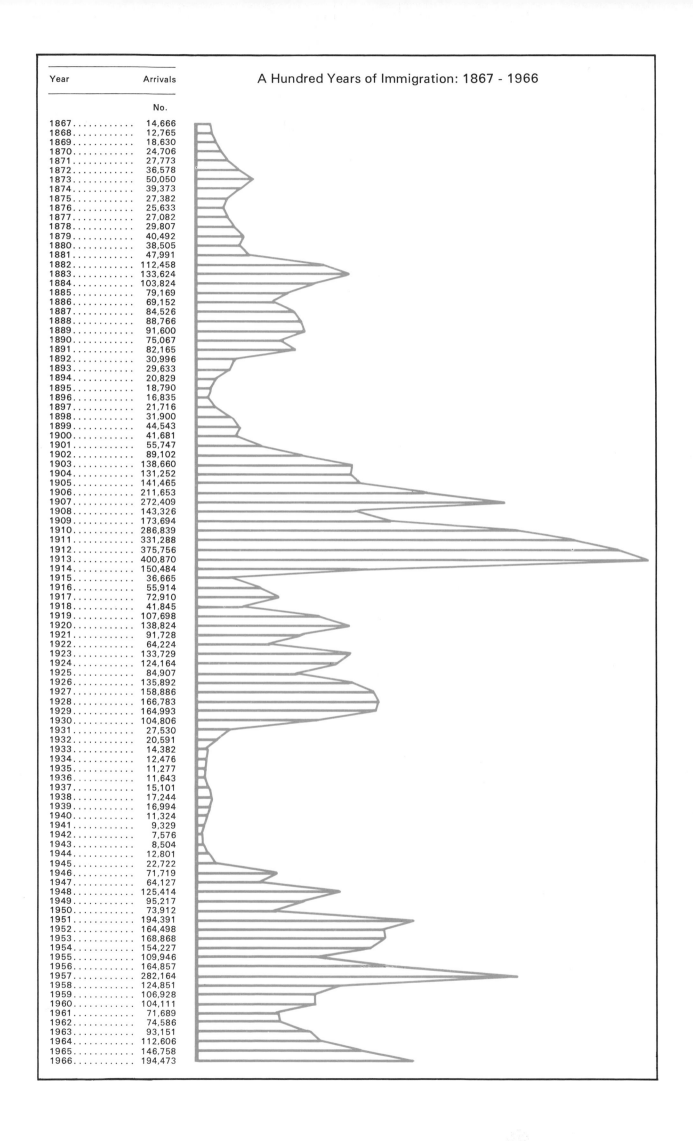

A Hundred Years of Immigration: 1867 - 1966

Year	Arrivals
	No.
1867	14,666
1868	12,765
1869	18,630
1870	24,706
1871	27,773
1872	36,578
1873	50,050
1874	39,373
1875	27,382
1876	25,633
1877	27,082
1878	29,807
1879	40,492
1880	38,505
1881	47,991
1882	112,458
1883	133,624
1884	103,824
1885	79,169
1886	69,152
1887	84,526
1888	88,766
1889	91,600
1890	75,067
1891	82,165
1892	30,996
1893	29,633
1894	20,829
1895	18,790
1896	16,835
1897	21,716
1898	31,900
1899	44,543
1900	41,681
1901	55,747
1902	89,102
1903	138,660
1904	131,252
1905	141,465
1906	211,653
1907	272,409
1908	143,326
1909	173,694
1910	286,839
1911	331,288
1912	375,756
1913	400,870
1914	150,484
1915	36,665
1916	55,914
1917	72,910
1918	41,845
1919	107,698
1920	138,824
1921	91,728
1922	64,224
1923	133,729
1924	124,164
1925	84,907
1926	135,892
1927	158,886
1928	166,783
1929	164,993
1930	104,806
1931	27,530
1932	20,591
1933	14,382
1934	12,476
1935	11,277
1936	11,643
1937	15,101
1938	17,244
1939	16,994
1940	11,324
1941	9,329
1942	7,576
1943	8,504
1944	12,801
1945	22,722
1946	71,719
1947	64,127
1948	125,414
1949	95,217
1950	73,912
1951	194,391
1952	164,498
1953	168,868
1954	154,227
1955	109,946
1956	164,857
1957	282,164
1958	124,851
1959	106,928
1960	104,111
1961	71,689
1962	74,586
1963	93,151
1964	112,606
1965	146,758
1966	194,473

The day of the crowded immigrant ship is long past. Here immigrants are shown arriving from the Orient at Vancouver International Airport.

Italian immigrants carrying a statue of the saint in a St. Anthony's Day parade in Toronto.

Chinatown in Vancouver (bottom left)
Vancouver's Chinese quarter is one of the oldest ethnic communities of this kind in Canada.

fully than in the past. Preference is given to younger people with skills and potential that will enable them to secure employment without great difficulty.

The average immigrant today is quite unlike his land-hungry predecessors who flocked to Canada at the beginning of the century. Most new arrivals now settle in urban centres, and a large number of them have swelled the populations of metropolitan Montreal, Toronto and Vancouver. Toronto and Vancouver have also grown as a result of important migrations of population that have taken place within Canada itself since the Second World War. In the quarter century from 1941 to 1966 migration to Ontario totalled 1,228,000, while 610,000 people moved to British Columbia. Quebec (256,000) and Alberta (117,000) were the only other provinces that gained population in this way. Inevitably there were losses in the other six, the most serious being in the Maritime provinces, which between them lost the very high total of almost 255,000 persons.

Ethnic Origins

The complex of ethnic groups comprising the population of Canada has been aptly termed the Canadian mosaic. Naturally the groups differ greatly both in size and characteristics. As a Centennial tribute to them, the Government's Citizenship Branch published an attractive monograph, *The Canadian Family Tree.* In addition to notes on the Indians and the Eskimos, 45 chapters were required to describe the groups who have come to Canada from Europe, Asia and other parts of North America, over a period of more than three and a half centuries.

The mosaic has become much more variegated since Confederation. In 1871 the pattern was still a simple one; 60 out of every 100 persons in Canada were of British origin, and on the average, 31 were French. The 202,000 persons of German origin (about 6 in every 100) were the only other ethnic group of any size, except the Indians and Eskimos.

Today the picture is very different. In 1961 slightly less than 44 out of every 100 Canadians traced their ancestry to Great Britain or Ireland, while just over 30 were of French origin. British and French together, who had made up 91 percent of the population in 1871, together comprised only 74.2 percent in 1961. Many expect that before long this figure might well drop to about 70. The other 25 or 30 percent of Canadians represent the great number of immigrants that have come to Canada, principally from Europe, but to some extent from all over the world.

As in 1871, people of German descent continue to be the largest group after the British and French. In spite of the two wars in which Canada and Germany fought against one another, German immigrants continue to flock to Canada. More than 300,000 came in the twenty years between 1946 and 1965, and by 1961 there were over a million people of German origin in the country.

This was by far the largest ethnic group that originated in continental Europe; the next in size— the Ukrainians—were less than half as numerous. The other large groups are the Italians, the Dutch, the Scandinavians (Norwegians, Swedes and Danes) and the Poles. Between them the five groups totalled just over 2,000,000. The Ukrainians (473,000) will probably soon be overtaken in numbers by the Italians (450,000), for their growth depends primarily on natural increase; very few people now come to Canada from the Ukraine, whereas Italian immigration continues at a high rate—about 375,-000 in the period 1946-65. The Dutch (429,000) have likewise added many immigrants to their number since the Second World War, and the same is true of the Scandinavians (356,000). Immigration has also added substantially to the Polish people in Canada, who numbered 323,000 in 1961. The Jews constitute a somewhat smaller but rapidly growing group which now numbers at least 250,000.

About a million Canadians spring from smaller ethnic groups, of which the Austrians, the Hungarians and the Russians are the largest. Asiatics (about three-quarters of whom were Chinese and Japanese in 1961) numbered nearly 122,000, and, as noted elsewhere, the native Indians and Eskimos now probably exceed 250,000.

People have come to Canada for all sorts of reasons, and those reasons have frequently determined the kind of people who have come. The first Germans who came to Canada were recruited in 1750 to help establish the new colony of Nova Scotia; it is interesting to recall that then and for many years thereafter the King of England was also King of Hanover. Difficult economic conditions in Iceland prompted emigration to Canada between 1875 and 1910. When times improved this source of excellent settlers dried up. Most of the Jews that came to Canada did so to escape pogroms and persecution of some sort. The Doukhobors, who first arrived in numbers in 1899 and succeeding years, came in the hope of finding a place where they could live in accordance with their own peculiar religious and social ideas, some of which were found to conflict with Canadian laws and customs. Chinese came to British Columbia at the time of the gold rush, and in greater numbers in railway construction days. Most of them hoped to amass their savings and return to China, but a good many remained. Some 4,600 veterans of the Second Polish

Army Corps came to Canada in 1946-47 because political changes at home made it impossible for them to return. But these and like circumstances did not motivate the vast majority of immigrants; the lure of a new and uncrowded country, where land, for a time at least, was cheap and opportunity was great, was the chief and enduring attraction.

Some groups scatter widely, others tend to hive together in communities where old languages and many customs can survive, at least for a time. Sometimes the basis of the community is religious, as in the case of the Mennonites, Hutterites and the Doukhobors. Sometimes it is racial, as with many of the Chinese and Japanese. An ethnic group will frequently show a geographical preference. By and large the Dutch, Norwegians, Swedes and Danes seem to prefer to settle in the West. Nearly all the East Indians in Canada are in British Columbia. The Jews and the Greeks are found mostly in the larger cities, and the Italians likewise prefer to live in urban centres. Here and there the detailed census returns reveal odd little pockets of population that are difficult to explain—like the Maltese community, 14,000 strong, that flourishes in the City of Toronto.

A discussion of immigration such as this is apt to give the impression that Canada's population is composed largely of people who have arrived in the country relatively recently, but this is not the case. In 1961, in spite of the heavy postwar immigration, almost 85 percent of the population had been born in Canada. And evidence that the many ethnic groups have taken root is shown by the prominence that individuals from almost all of them have attained in the life of the country. Art, music, literature, science, technology, banking, commerce, education and government—all these fields and many others have been enriched by leaders who trace their ancestries back to many and varied lands.

Northern Exploration Since 1867

In addition to myriads of smaller ones, there are three huge islands in the Canadian Arctic—Baffin Island, which is much the largest of the three, Victoria Island and Ellesmere Island. By mid-century a good deal was known about the first two. They were adjacent to the mainland, and were south of the sequence of broad waterways, extending from Lancaster Sound westward, in which much exploring had been carried out in search of the North West Passage, and, incidentally, in an effort to find the lost Franklin expedition. But very little was known about Ellesmere Island, which lay to the north and extended far into a region yet unexplored.

Ellesmere finally came to the fore when the interest of explorers began to shift from the North West Passage to the North Pole. The northern part of Baffin Bay separates the Island from Greenland,

The Queen in Ottawa, July 1, 1967

The climax of the Centenary celebrations; ceremonies on Parliament Hill.

The Queen and Prince Philip passing the centennial flame.

The Queen and Prince Philip pass between the sergeants-at-arm of both Houses, and the "Black Rod," at the Centenary ceremonies in Ottawa, July, 1967.

and it was hoped (with good reason, as it turned out) that a series of bays or channels would continue on northward between them, thus providing a waterway to the polar seas and an approach to the Pole itself.

One of the Franklin search parties put this theory to the test as early as 1853. It was led by Dr. Elisha Kane, an American, who thought that Franklin might have sailed far to the north into the Arctic Ocean. In an attempt to find him, Kane sailed from Baffin Bay through Smith Sound into what is now Kane Basin. Ice conditions prevented his ship from going further, but in 1834 a land party travelled to Kennedy Channel—farther north than anyone else had yet ventured.

The first attempt to reach the Pole by this route was made in 1860-61 by Dr. I. I. Hayes, who had been with Kane. He claimed to have reached latitude 81°35′ north, at the northern end of Kennedy Channel, but it is doubtful if he actually did so.

Ice conditions vary greatly from season to season, and they were exceptionally favourable in 1871 when the next expedition, led by another American, Capt. Charles F. Hall, crept up the coast of Ellesmere Island. Hall's ship, the *Polaris,* was able to get through to the northern end of Robeson Channel, which leads to the open Arctic; but there his expedition's good fortune ran out. Several short explorations were made by land, but Hall himself died of apoplexy, the *Polaris* began to leak alarmingly, and a party of 19 were marooned on an ice floe near Smith Sound. They survived an incredible drift southward that lasted 194 days and were rescued on the coast of Labrador.

The British Government now decided to sponsor an attempt to reach the Pole, and an expedition commanded by Capt. Sir George Nares arrived off Ellesmere Island in 1875. Like Hall, Nares was able to take one of his ships, H.M.S. *Alert,* through Robeson Channel, and she actually wintered on the northern coast of Ellesmere, near Cape Sheridan. An outbreak of scurvy defeated the expedition's effort to reach the Pole, but an exploring party traced most of the northern coast of Ellesmere, and discovered Cape Aldrich, the northernmost point in Canada.

Geological Survey

Geological Survey

R.C.A.F.

Showing the flag in the Arctic (upper right)

The Neptune *frozen in for the winter of 1903-04 at Cape Fullerton in the course of the first Arctic cruise in which Canada took definite steps to assert her sovereignty. The other vessel is the American whaler* Era.

Ellesmere Island, 1904 (centre)

Formal possession was taken and the Canadian flag raised.

Cape Aldrich (bottom right)

This photograph of the coast of Ellesmere Island shows Cape Columbia in the foreground and beyond it, to the east, Cape Aldrich, the northernmost point in Canada.

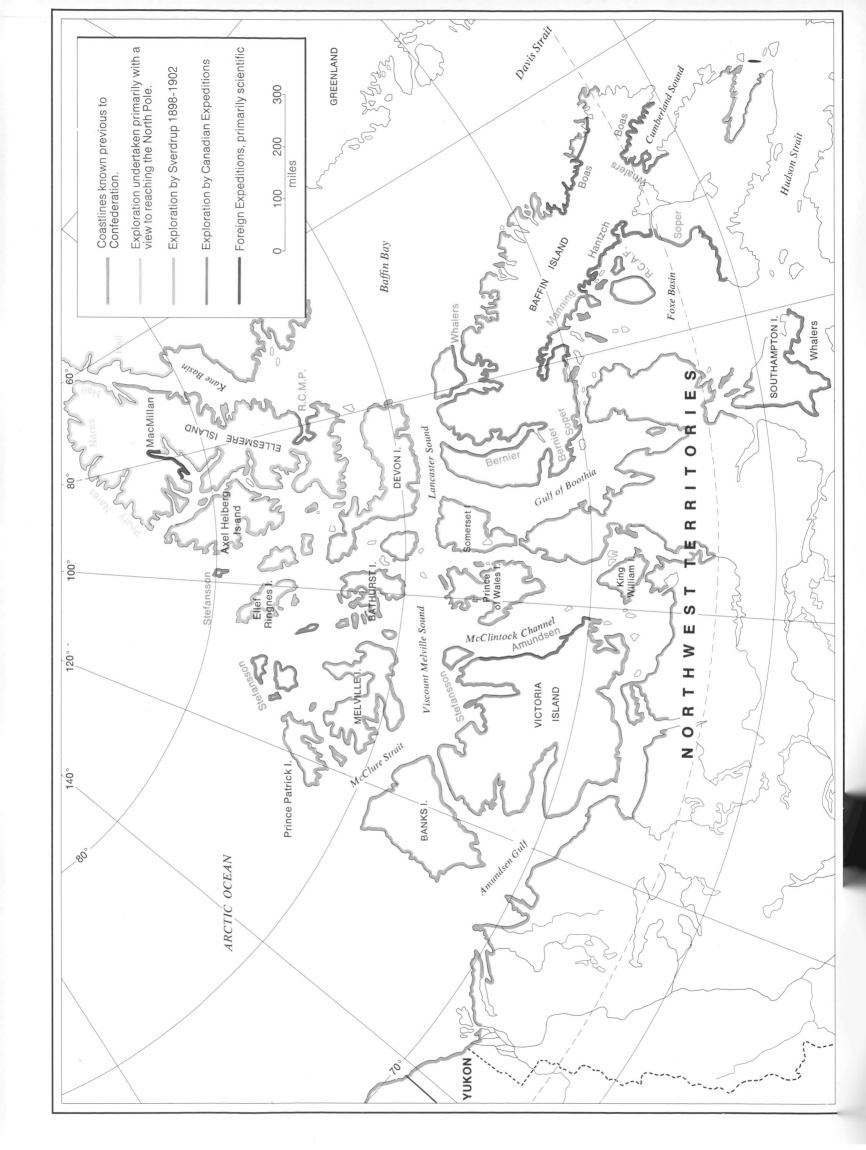

Legend

Coastlines known previous to Confederation.

Exploration undertaken primarily with a view to reaching the North Pole.

Exploration by Sverdrup 1898-1902

Exploration by Canadian Expeditions

Foreign Expeditions, primarily scientific

miles

0   100   200   300

GREENLAND

Davis Strait

Cumberland Sound

Boas

Boas

Whalers

Hudson Strait

Baffin Bay

BAFFIN ISLAND

Manning

Hantzch

R.C.M.P.

Foxe Basin

Soper

Whalers

Kane Basin

Hall

MacMillan

Nares

ELLESMERE ISLAND

R.C.M.P.

Whalers

Soper

Bernier

SOUTHAMPTON I.

Whalers

60°

Peary   Nares

Hall

80°

Axel Heiberg Island

Stefansson

Eller Ringnes I.

DEVON I.

Lancaster Sound

Bernier

Gulf of Boothia

Somerset I.

King William

100°

Stefansson

BATHURST I.

Prince of Wales I.

120°

Stefansson

MELVILLE I.

Viscount Melville Sound

Stefansson

McClintock Channel

Amundsen

VICTORIA ISLAND

N O R T H W E S T   T E R R I T O R I E S

Prince Patrick I.

McClure Strait

BANKS I.

140°

80°

ARCTIC OCEAN

Amundsen Gulf

70°

YUKON

A long pause now ensued in the search for the Pole by the Ellesmere Island route. It was resumed in 1898 by Robert E. Peary, who had already had experience in the Arctic, and who was to make three expeditions during the next eleven years. On the first of the three he made two attempts to reach the Pole—one from Cape Jesup, in Greenland, the most northerly land in the world, and the other from Cape Columbia. The first was frustrated by ice conditions and the second by an impassable expanse of open water. Peary's next expedition (1905-06) was notable on two counts. He explored the whole of the northern coast of Ellesmere Island, and in a second attempt to reach the North Pole from Cape Columbia he travelled as far as 87°06′ north, within 200 miles of his objective. Success came finally on his third expedition, when he reached the Pole on April 6, 1909.

Reaching the Pole was a great achievement, but it did not add materially to information about Canada's northland. An immense contribution on this score was made by Capt. Otto Sverdrup, whose ship was the famous *Fram*, which he had previously commanded for Nansen. Like Peary, Sverdrup set out in 1898 with the North Pole as his objective, and the two actually met during their first winter in the Arctic. Ice conditions frustrated Sverdrup's efforts, and he turned his attention to exploration by land. He soon became fascinated by the complex of islands he was discovering and abandoned his efforts to reach the Pole. The *Fram* was provisioned for five years and Sverdrup was able to spend four consecutive winters in the Arctic. By the time he returned to Norway in 1902 he had explored the southern and western coasts of Ellesmere Island, had followed almost the entire coast of Axel Heiberg Island, and had circumnavigated the Ringnes Islands, to the west. It was a great accomplishment, and very appropriately the whole group is known today as the Sverdrup Islands. Questions of sovereignty were raised by Sverdrup's discoveries, but these were settled finally in 1930, when Norway officially recognized Canadian ownership of the islands.

One area still remained unexplored—the region north of Melville Island and west of the Ringnes Islands. This and other areas in the western Arctic were visited in 1913-18 by the Canadian Arctic Expedition led by Vilhjalmur Stefansson. His discoveries filled in the last large blanks in Canada's Arctic map, but many of the outlines were still somewhat rough and ready, and an immense job of detailed charting still remained to be done. Aerial surveys were used in Hudson Strait as early as 1927, but air mapping did not develop on a large scale until after the Second World War. Planes and cameras had then reached a state of development that made a complete aerial survey of the Canadian Arctic practicable, and this has now been carried out.

Ownership can be made apparent and effective only by occupation, and by the turn of the century, with American and Norweigian expeditions active

Dept. of Transport

The Manhattan

The huge American tanker Manhattan *halted by ice in her first voyage through the North West Passage, in 1969. The Canadian icebreaker* John A. Macdonald *is working through the ice to free her.*

in the North, Canada prepared to exercise her sovereignty. In 1903 the steamer *Neptune* sailed to the Arctic under the command of A. P. Low, of the Geological Survey, accompanied by Major J. D. Moodie of the North West Mounted Police. The purpose of the voyage was to "show the flag," to investigate matters of law and order, and to make the Canadian presence felt in the North. Low took formal possession of the islands at several points, including Cape Herschell, on Ellesmere Island. This pioneer voyage was followed by several by the steamer *Arctic*, commanded by Capt. Joseph Bernier, one of the famous figures in Canadian Arctic history. By 1922 the Arctic voyages were becoming known as the Eastern Arctic Patrol, and they have continued on an increasing scale ever since. In 1950 a large new vessel, the *C.D. Howe*, was completed for the Arctic patrol service and in 1953 she was joined by the much larger and more powerful *D'Iberville*, which combines the functions of a supply ship and an icebreaker.

The North West Passage was not forgotten completely in the excitement about the North Pole. In June 1903 Roald Amundsen sailed from Norway in the little 47-ton herring boat *Gjoa* and by slow and cautious degrees worked his way through the Arctic islands to the Pacific. The voyage took three years, partly because its objectives included observations near the North Magnetic Pole.

This memorable first voyage was not duplicated until 1940-42, when the Royal Canadian Mounted Police patrol vessel *St. Roch*, commanded by Staff Sergeant H. A. Larsen, sailed from Vancouver to Halifax. Two years later, in 1944, favourable ice conditions enabled Larsen to sail the *St. Roch* from Halifax back to Vancouver in a single season —the first ship ever to accomplish this by the Arctic route.

Slowly, as knowledge of the Arctic and charts of its waters have improved, the possibility of using the North West Passage for commercial purposes has received consideration. In 1954 the Canadian ice-breaker *Labrador,* a substantial ship of 3,800 tons, repeated the feat of the *St. Roch* and sailed without difficulty from the Atlantic to the Pacific. Finally, in 1969, the capabilities of both ships and the Passage were tested on a huge scale when the American tanker *Manhattan,* of 115,000 tons deadweight, smashed her way through the Arctic ice, assisted by the ice-breaker *John A. Macdonald,* and succeeded in reaching the ports that will serve the new oil fields in Alaska.

What the future holds for the Passage only time can tell.

Politics
Between the Wars

Laurier and Borden between them dominated Canadian politics for over twenty years; both left the scene not long after the end of the First World War. Laurier died in 1919, at the age of 77. Borden, tired out by wartime strains, resigned in 1920.

Arthur Meighen, Borden's successor as prime minister and leader of the Union Government, an able lawyer and brilliant debater, soon encountered difficulties. The Union Government had been formed primarily to enforce conscription; with the coming of peace, compulsory military service ceased to be a rallying cry, and Liberals who had supported it began to drift back to the old party allegiance. The bitterness the issue had engendered lingered on in Quebec, where opposition to conscription had centred, and this worked to the advantage of Wil-

The founding conference of the C.C.F.
The delegates photographed in Regina in July 1935. J. S. Woodsworth, first leader of the Co-operative Commonwealth Federation (now the New Democratic Party) is seated in the front row, centre, in white.

liam Lyon Mackenzie King, who had succeeded Laurier in 1919 as leader of the Liberal Party. Meighen had drafted the Military Service Act of 1917; King had supported Laurier in his stand against it. This assured King a solid backing in Quebec, but when a general election was held in December 1921 the Liberals just failed to gain a majority.

This was due to the emergence of a new third party, the Progressives, who drew their main strength from various farmers' movements. Agriculture had been hard hit by the short but severe post-war depression, and the farmers turned to politics to combat the freight rates, interest charges and high tariffs that they felt were crippling them. The provincial United Farmers organizations won elections and formed governments in Ontario in 1919, in Alberta in 1921, and in Manitoba in 1922. The 65 Progressives returned to the House of Commons represented these same interests, and they outnumbered Meighen's Conservative followers, who were reduced to 50. With the general support of the Progressives, King became Prime Minister, and during the next few years he was able by degrees to lure many of them into the Liberal ranks. But the lot of a minority government is not a happy one, and in the election of 1925 the Liberals and Progressives between them lost over 50 seats and the Conservatives increased their representation to 116. Again with Progressive support, King was able to continue in office, but scandals soon erupted in the Customs Department that weakened his position still further.

This was the setting for the famous King–Byng crisis of 1926. King advised Lord Byng, the Governor-General, to dissolve parliament on the grounds that no party could gain a stable majority in the existing House. Byng declined, whereupon King resigned and Arthur Meighen formed a new government. Only three days later, under an odd combination of circumstances that is discussed and debated to this day, the Meighen government was defeated in the Commons by one vote. Meighen then asked Byng for a dissolution, and his request was granted.

Saskatchewan Archives

Public Archives of Canada

Public Archives of Canada

Saskatchewan Archives

In the ensuing election King astutely raised a constitutional issue, both because he believed in its soundness and because it conveniently diverted attention from the customs scandals. He contended that he should have been permitted to dissolve the House, and that when the Governor-General refused to agree to this he was declining to follow the advice of his Prime Minister, which constitutional custom required him to accept. There were other issues, but this one put the Conservatives on the defensive and played a considerable part in their defeat. Meighen lost his own seat and soon retired, and only 91 Conservatives were returned to the new parliament. True, the Liberals still numbered only 116— less than a majority—but they could count on the support of some 30 Progressives and others, some of whom had become Liberals in all but name.

King's second administration lasted four years. It is memorable chiefly because of the Imperial Conference of 1926, at which the independent status of the Dominions, later established formally in the Statute of Westminster, was agreed to in principle, and the onset of the great depression that was to mark the 1930s.

The Wall Street crash of October 1929 had serious repercussions in Canada, but it was the collapse of international trade and finance that was the really crippling blow. Exports were vital to the Canadian economy, and when both price levels and the volume of exports plummetted, a grave crisis ensued. A few figures will suffice to illustrate its disastrous character. In 1928 agricultural income had totalled $856,000,000; by 1932 it had fallen to only $233,000,000. In 1929 Canadian factories had

A depression scene in the dustbowl (above)
The depression coincided with a drought period in large areas of the prairies that greatly aggravated both human and economic distress. This typical dust storm was photographed in Saskatchewan near Lakenheath.

Arthur Meighen in 1912 (upper right)
At this time he was still a backbencher. He became Solicitor General in 1913, but this post did not carry Cabinet rank until 1915. So obvious and outstanding was his ability that he became leader of the Conservative Party and Prime Minister only five years later.

Richard Bedford Bennett
Prime Minister in the depression years from 1930 to 1935, and by temperament so much an individualist that he bore personally much of the brunt of the problems of the time. He eventually retired to Great Britain where he was created Viscount Bennett.

built 263,000 automobiles; in 1932 they produced only 61,000. In 1933 one-fifth of the labour force was unemployed. The United States, at least as hard hit as Canada, raised tariffs to protect home industries and ceased to be Canada's largest export market.

The government that bore the brunt of the depression was a Conservative administration headed by R. B. Bennett, who had succeeded Meighen as leader of the party in 1927. The popularity of the Liberals had declined sharply as eco-

293

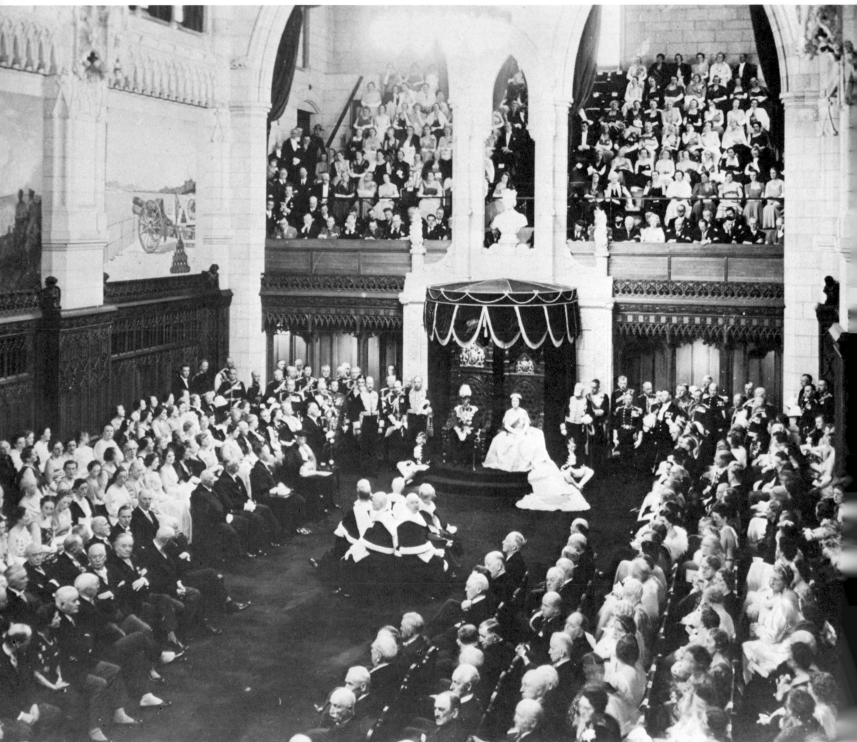

The Royal Visit of 1939
Their Majesties King George VI and Queen Elizabeth in the Senate Chamber on May 19, 1939. This was the first occasion upon which the reigning monarch presided over the opening of the Canadian Parliament and personally read the Speech from the Throne.

nomic conditions had worsened, and the Conservatives won a clear majority in the election of 1930. Bennett took steps to increase unemployment relief, and sought to stimulate production by tariff changes and by agreements on Commonwealth and world trade. An Imperial Economic Conference was held in Ottawa in 1932 and a World Economic Conference followed in London the next year. These were held at what proved to be the depths of the depression in Canada; the turning point in most industries came late in 1932 or early in 1933. By 1935 recovery had become substantial but it came too late to save the government. In January, Bennett announced a whole series of "New Deal" reform measures (many of which were later declared unconstitutional when enacted in legislation), but these frightened many Conservatives and attracted little popular support. Only 39 Conservatives were elected in the election held in October, and Mackenzie King and the Liberals, having at last won a clear majority, returned to office.

The opposition in the Commons included representatives of two new political parties. Just as the hard times that followed the First World War had seen the emergence of the Progressive Party, essentially as a party of protest, so the great depression caused various movements to crystallize in the Co-operative Commonwealth Federation and the Social Credit Party. Like the Progressive Party, both found their chief strength on the prairies. The C.C.F., based largely on labour and socialist groups, was organized in 1932, and adopted its famous Regina Manifesto at a conference there in 1933. The new party's leader was J. S. Woodsworth, an idealistic and highly respected reformer who had been in the Commons since 1921. The C.C.F. aroused much interest and some apprehension, but it elected only seven members to Parliament in 1935. The Social Credit movement, which centred in Alberta, grew up around William Aberhart, a high school teacher and radio evangelist who saw economic salvation and justice in the Douglas Social Credit monetary theories. As Aberhart interpreted them, these had a strong appeal to the middle class and to the fearful. In a general election held in August 1935, Social Credit won 56 of the 63 seats in the Alberta legislature, and the party has retained power in the province ever since. In the 1935 federal election it won 15 of the 17 Alberta seats, but only two Social Credit candidates were successful elsewhere.

The third Mackenzie King administration, destined to last 13 years, soon found that domestic issues were being slowly but inexorably overwhelmed by the rise of Hitler and the international crises that resulted. Ever mindful of 1917, and the latent opposition to overseas entanglements that existed in Quebec, King avoided commitments and insisted that Canada must be master of her own external policies and activities, both civil and military. It was not a policy that aroused enthusiasm, but it did prevent a split on foreign policy from developing within the country. When the Second World War broke out in September 1939, the Canadian declaration was delayed some days until Parliament could meet and approve the measure. This it did with remarkable unanimity, and Canada went to war a united nation.

Newfoundland: 1919-1949

The thirty years from 1919 to 1949 were a crucial period in the history of Newfoundland. They both began and ended in a time of postwar readjustment, but circumstances had changed greatly in the interval.

By 1919 the prosperity that the First World War had brought was collapsing. Economic difficulties were developing which, compounded by the great depression that began in 1929, were to make it necessary to suspend responsible government. In 1949, when self-government was being restored to a relatively prosperous Newfoundland, the people voted to throw in their lot with Canada, instead of resuming the more hazardous status of independence.

Newfoundland's entry into Confederation in 1949 might be termed a response to the third time of asking.

Two delegates from the island—F. B. T. Carter and Ambrose Shea—attended the famous conference at Quebec in 1864 at which the original terms of Confederation were drafted; but Newfoundland had taken no further action before the British North America Act was passed in 1867. However, the Act provided specifically for her admission to the new federation, and in 1869 a cabinet headed by Carter worked out terms of union with Canada. But by that time anti-Confederation feeling had become strong, and the Carter government was defeated at the polls.

The disastrous fire that swept St. John's in 1892 and bank failures and a financial crisis in 1894 prompted the second round of negotiations. These took place in Ottawa in April 1895 and came very close to success. Newfoundland's public debt proved to be the stumbling block. The Canadian Prime Minister, Mackenzie Bowell—not an imaginative statesman—allowed negotiations to lapse when a gap of less than $200,000 a year separated the minimum subsidies that Newfoundland felt she must receive and the maximum that Bowell was prepared to give.

More or less private discussions with Prime Minister Borden took place shortly before the First World War, but the confederation issue was not raised again in a serious way for a generation.

In some respects the 1920s were an encouraging time for Newfoundland. The Labrador boundary award of 1927 added greatly to her territory and to her economic potential. In 1931 the Statute of Westminster accorded her full Dominion status, on a par with that granted to Canada. Throughout most of

Government Travel Bureau

Fish "flakes" at a Newfoundland outport

These are still very like those shown in Herman Moll's engraving of 1719. The fish are split and exposed to the sun to dry, and the platform is so designed that air can circulate freely both above and below them.

her history Newfoundland had been almost entirely dependent on a single product—fish; in the 1920s pulp and paper mills and iron ore mines began to offer alternative employment and more diversified exports. But the impact of the depression of 1929 was devastating. Prices and the demand for exports fell drastically; by the winter of 1932-33 more than a quarter of the population were on relief, and the scale upon which relief could be given was no more than a few cents per person per day.

In desperate straits, Newfoundland asked the British Government to appoint a Royal Commission to consider her plight. It recommended that Britain should assume general responsibility for finances until Newfoundland could again become self-supporting, and that meanwhile self-government should be suspended and replaced by a special Commission of Government, presided over by the Governor, on which Britain and Newfoundland would have equal representation. This plan was adopted and a Commission assumed control early in 1934. Intended as a temporary measure, government by commission was destined to continue for 15 years.

Though funds were scanty, the Commission tackled Newfoundland's problems with some success. In the next few years expenditure on health and education doubled, welfare benefits increased, and roads were improved. But it was the Second World War, and the extraordinary needs to which it gave rise, that finally pulled the island out of the doldrums.

Exports were soon in brisk demand, and before long the economy was benefiting from large military expenditures. Newfoundland was virtually defenceless in 1939, and its geographical position made this a matter of grave concern alike to Canada and the United States. When Hitler's armies overran Europe, both took steps to remedy the situation. Canadian troops were sent to Newfoundland in June 1940; later Canada built large air bases at Goose Bay, in Labrador, and at Torbay, near St. John's. Canada also took over and enlarged the air stations at Gander and Botwood. A British-Canadian naval base developed at St. John's played an important part in the Battle of the Atlantic. The United States took comparable action. In 1941 sites for three large bases were leased to the Americans, the most notable being at Argentia, where a huge naval and air base was constructed. All these activities brought thousands of men and millions of dollars to Newfoundland, and the later war years were a time of great prosperity.

When the war ended, the question soon arose as to whether or not the commission form of government should be continued. Obviously the matter could be dealt with satisfactorily only by a representative assembly, and in June 1946 a special National Convention was elected to make recommendations to the British Government. Union with Canada was one of the possibilities considered. A delegation was sent to Ottawa to discuss terms of admission, and in October 1947 Prime Minister King outlined the terms he would be prepared to recommend to the Canadian Parliament. Throughout the negotiations Canada took pains not to try to persuade the Newfoundlanders one way or the other; the choice was to be their own decision. Perhaps this accounted for the fact that the National Convention proposed that a referendum should be held that ignored Canada and would offer only two proposals—the continuation of commission government or the restoration of responsible government. It was the British Government that felt that the people should have an opportunity to express an opinion on Confederation and added union with Canada to the ballot as a third choice.

A first referendum was held on June 3, 1948. Responsible government was favoured by 69,400 voters, Confederation by 64,066 and commission government by 22,311. In a second referendum, held on July 22 and limited to the first two questions, Confederation received 78,323 votes and responsible government 71,334.

Thereafter events moved rapidly. Terms of union were hammered out in negotiations in the autumn, and were signed in Ottawa on December 11. Both the Canadian Parliament and the Newfoundland Commission of Government approved them formally in February 1949. The British Parliament passed the necessary amendment to the British North America Act a month later, and at midnight on March 31 Newfoundland became Canada's tenth province.

In Newfoundland the two doughtiest fighters for Confederation had been Joseph Smallwood and Gordon Bradley. The former became the premier of Newfoundland's first provincial government, and Mr. Bradley became Secretary of State of Canada, and Newfoundland's first representative in the federal cabinet.

Newfoundland joins Confederation (upper right)

Viscount Alexander, Governor-General of Canada, signs the bill providing for the admission of Newfoundland. Mr. St. Laurent, the Prime Minister, is on his right and the Speakers of the Senate and House of Commons are on the left.

St. John's Newfoundland: A modern view (centre right)

Portuguese fishing vessels at St. John's (bottom right)
Portuguese fishermen still visit the Newfoundland banks each year, as they have done for centuries.

Public Archives of Canada

Government Travel Bureau

Government Travel Bureau

CHAPTER 20

The Second World War and After

The Second World War Overseas

THE outbreak of war in 1939 was not unexpected, but few in Canada can have foreseen how long and desperate the struggle was to be. It lasted nearly six years, and in the course of it over a million men and women served in the Canadian Army, Navy and Air Force—a prodigious effort by a nation with a population of only 12,000,000.

On land, Hitler seemed at first content with the conquest of Poland; the unnatural quiet of the "phoney war" settled over the western front. At sea it was otherwise. The torpedoing of the liner *Athenia* on the evening of the very day Britain declared war marked the beginning of the submarine warfare that was to reach its savage climax in the Battle of the Atlantic three years later. The *Athenia* had been sunk contrary to Hitler's orders, as he was still concerned about the opinion of neutral nations, particularly the United States; but the 40 ships that were torpedoed in September alone in the waters around Britain showed clearly what the German Navy—orders notwithstanding—had in mind.

The Canadian Navy had 6 destroyers and 5 minesweepers in commission when war was declared; its enlisted personnel was less than 2,000. Coastal defence was expected to be its chief duty, but before the war was a fortnight old Canadian destroyers were escorting convoys of merchant ships leaving Halifax. From this small beginning grew an anti-submarine force numbering hundreds of ships that was entrusted in 1943 with complete responsibility for operations in the Northwest Atlantic.

Ships were the prime necessity. A few yachts and other makeshift craft could be requisitioned, but only a large-scale building programme could meet the need adequately. With this same contin-gency in mind, the British had been experimenting with a new ship type that was soon to be given the old name *corvette*: a small patrol ship based on a whaler design that had proven to be lively and uncomfortable but remarkably seaworthy. Equally important, it could be built quickly. Sixty-four of them were ordered from Canadian shipyards early in 1940, and by September the first of them had been completed and commissioned. Some of the 64 were for the Royal Navy, as construction programmes were apportioned to take best advantage of the capabilities of different yards. Thus Britain built destroyers for Canada, while Canada built corvettes for Britain.

Later, as the Germans developed faster and more formidable submarines, the corvettes were first improved and then replaced by a larger and faster type of ship, the frigate. Meanwhile the destroyer force had been increased by new construction and by transfers from the Royal Navy. In addition, seven of the 50 over-age destroyers handed over to Great Britain by the United States in 1940, in return for the leasing of base sites, were assigned to the Canadian Navy. In the course of the war the Navy commissioned a total of 27 destroyers, 71 frigates and 122 corvettes. To these were added a few larger ships—three auxiliary cruisers, two escort aircraft carriers and two cruisers—and a host of smaller craft that brought the grand total to 471 ships. A few less than 100,000 men and 6,500 women (the famous WRENS) served afloat and ashore.

The Navy did many things in many places but the Battle of the Atlantic was always its prime concern; if men and supplies could not cross the ocean, defeat was certain. The worst days came in 1942, when war with Japan compelled the United States Navy to move many of its ships to the Pacific. Submarines were now crossing the Atlantic in force; shipping on the whole Atlantic coast was ravaged, and the war even reached the Gulf of St. Lawrence. A corvette, an armed yacht and fourteen merchantmen were sunk there in 1942. By the following spring the tide was turning; more and better patrol ships, and air cover provided by escort carriers and

Normandy 1944: clearing Falaise of German snipers

Canadian Armed Forces

Canadian Armed Forces

The R.C.A.F. in Normandy

A Spitfire attached to No. 416 Fighter Squadron photographed near Bazenville in June 1944. The plane is "at dispersal" — off by itself, to guard against the danger of mass destruction of aircraft in the event of an enemy attack.

long-range Liberator bombers, enabled the Allies at last to gain the upper hand. If the war with Japan had continued, the Royal Canadian Navy planned to form a 60-ship Pacific Fleet manned by 13,500 men. As it turned out, only the cruiser *Uganda*, which had been sent in advance to the Pacific, took part in operations there.

Like the Navy, the Royal Canadian Air Force was a very small force when the war broke out. But, again like the Navy, it grew very rapidly and accomplished remarkable feats.

Its first major task was in Canada. The Allies would require tens of thousands of pilots, navigators, and other aircrew, and in December 1939 the United Kingdom, Canada, Australia and New Zealand agreed to launch a large-scale British Commonwealth Air Training Plan. This was to centre in Canada, and the R.C.A.F. made a great contribution to it. Over 131,000 aircrew were trained, including almost 50,000 pilots; over half of them were Canadians. At its height the Plan had 97 flying schools. Their construction, let alone their operation, had been an immense undertaking. They required roads, runways, hangars, barracks, and innumerable items of equipment, to say nothing of some 12,000 aircraft.

In Canada, Eastern and Western Air Commands were organized, with a string of bases along the east and west coasts. Antisubmarine patrols, extending far out to sea as the war progressed and aircraft improved, were a major activity in the east. When the Japanese occupied Kiska and Attu, in the Aleutians, Western Air Command cooperated with the Americans in bombing and reconnaissance flights until the Japanese withdrew. A Northwest Staging Route was developed—an "aerial highway,"

Canadian Armed Forces

The R.C.A.F. over Germany

A Lancaster bomber of No. 617 Squadron scores a "grand slam" with a 22,000-pound bomb on a railway bridge at Arbergen, in March 1945.

as it has been termed—over which supplies and aircraft flowed to Alaska and to Russia. Traffic along it became so heavy that a special North-West Air Command was set up to control it.

R.C.A.F. units began to arrive in Britain in February 1940. Unlike the Army, the R.C.A.F. overseas was not under Canadian control. The Royal Air Force felt strongly that there should be one unified Commonwealth air force, and for most purposes it was able to make this view prevail. Sixty percent of Canadian aircrew overseas served in the R.A.F., and Canadian squadrons were under R.A.F. operational control. Even the largest R.C.A.F. formation—No. 6 Bomber Group, comprising eleven squadrons—was subject to R.A.F. Bomber Command.

This integration makes it difficult to gauge the full extent of the Canadian contribution, but it was immense. Canadian aircrew and aircraft took part in virtually every type of operation. Hurricane and Spitfire fighter planes, Typhoon dive bombers, light Mosquito bombers and heavy four-engined Halifax and Lancaster bombers were some of the aircraft flown. A Canadian fighter squadron arrived in time to take part in the Battle of Britain; later Canadian fighters intercepted nearly a hundred of the V-1 buzz-bombs directed against England. Canadian planes helped to bomb the battleship *Tirpitz;* they attacked bridges and locomotives and all manner of other targets on the continent. By the summer of 1942 R.C.A.F. Bomber Command could muster a thousand planes for a single operation, and it participated in the great saturation raids on Germany. In all, 48 squadrons were organized in Europe, of which 15 were bomber squadrons.

In the course of the war over 232,000 men and 17,000 women served in the R.C.A.F.—a total strength of just under 250,000.

The Army was the first of the three forces to arrive in Europe but, owing to the fall of France, was the last to engage in large-scale combat. The First Division went overseas in December 1939 and by February 1940 there were 23,000 Canadian troops in Britain. In mid-June one brigade landed at Brest, but it was so evident that France was collapsing that it re-embarked within 48 hours. After Dunkirk, when invasion seemed imminent, the Canadians were for a time the best equipped force in Britain, and they were held in readiness in the Midlands, where they could be moved quickly to any part of the coastline.

The invasion threat faded, and almost four years passed before the long awaited D-Day. In the interval, the Canadians suffered two tragedies. The first was at Hong Kong, to which nearly 2,000 troops were sent from Vancouver in the fall of 1941. The attack on Pearl Harbor came only a few weeks later and the Japanese attacked Hong Kong at dawn the next morning. The outcome was inevitable, but the defenders held out for more than a fortnight. Christmas Day was also Surrender day, and by that time a third of the Canadians had been killed or wounded. The survivors faced over three and a half years of imprisonment under dreadful conditions, and 557 of the men who had left Vancouver never returned.

The second tragedy was the raid on Dieppe, deemed necessary as the only means of testing the plans that were being prepared for the Allied invasion of Europe. British commandos were to take the batteries on either side of the town while the Canadians assaulted the headlands nearer it and landed on the beach in front of the town itself. Unhappily things went wrong. A chance encounter with a naval patrol alerted the Germans that something was afoot; neither the batteries nor the headlands could be seized as planned; a murderous fire therefore poured down on the infantry and tanks that came ashore on the beach. Withdrawal was the only course, but this was not easily accomplished. Of the 4,963 Canadians in the attacking forces, 907 were killed and 1,946 were taken prisoner. Much of value is said to have been learned at Dieppe, but the cost was high.

During the years of waiting the Army grew into a formidable force. In December 1940 a Canadian Corps was formed; in 1942 it was announced that a Canadian Army of two corps would be created, and this came into being early in 1943—the First Canadian Army, both in name and in fact.

Having formed an Army, the Canadians were naturally reluctant to break it up, but in order to gain battle experience and for other reasons it was decided that a Canadian infantry division and an army tank brigade should become part of the British Eighth Army and participate in the invasion of Sicily. The first landings took place on July 10, 1943, and the conquest of the island was completed late in August.

The Canadians had shown themselves to be a thoroughly trained and effective force, and they joined in the much larger struggle for the Italian mainland. Built up to corps strength, they were given several of the most difficult assignments of the campaign. The Adriatic port of Ortona was taken in December, after heavy fighting. In May 1944 the Canadian Corps—acting as a unit for the first time—broke the Hitler line and took Ceprano, south of Rome, but was withdrawn before the fall of Rome itself a few days later. Back once again on the Adriatic coast, the Canadians broke through the Gothic Line at the end of August and fought on northward until torrential rains checked their advance.

Meanwhile D-Day—June 6, 1944—had come in Normandy and 15,000 Canadians had been among the troops that went ashore the first day. Their point of landing was St. Aubin-sur-Mer and two other little seaside towns north and west of Caen. The First Canadian Army—in action as such for the first time—fought alongside the British Second Army and shared with it the task of pinning down as many Germans as possible, in order to ease pressure on the Americans farther west and enable them to capture Cherbourg and Brest.

The amazing artificial harbour that the invading forces brought with them served its purpose well, but adequately equipped ports through which men and vast quantities of equipment and supplies could pour into Europe were vital to the success of the whole campaign. Ports were made the special objective of the First Canadian Army, and in cooperation with the British Second Army, which advanced parallel to the Canadians but a little further inland, it spent the final eight months of the war fighting its way systematically from harbour to harbour along the French, Belgian, Dutch and German coasts. Dieppe, entered on September 1, was found to be undefended; Ostend, Boulogne and Calais were taken in the next month. Of far greater importance than these was Antwerp. The British had entered it on September 4 and had found its harbour installations virtually undamaged; but the Germans still held the mouth of the Scheldt, and so cut off Antwerp from the sea. The task of the Canadians was to dislodge them, and this they did after a long and bitter struggle. They had their reward on November 28, when the first Allied convoy arrived in Antwerp—an event that General Eisenhower declared brought "the end of Naziism . . . in clear view," for it opened a supply route of almost unlimited capacity.

In February 1945 the Canadian Corps that had fought in Italy began to move to the western front to join the First Canadian Army there, and the Canadians fought as a single united force until the war ended in Europe in May.

Although the Canadian Army in the Second World War was substantially larger than in the First—730,625 men and women served in it, compared with 620,000 in the Great War—casualties were much lower. The deadly stalemate of static fronts and trench warfare had been avoided; 22,917 were killed, compared with over 59,000 in

Public Archives of Canada

King, Roosevelt and Churchill at Quebec in 1943

1914-18. A grand total of 1,086,475 men and women served in the three services, and of these 42,007 lost their lives. It was once again a heavy and tragic price to pay for victory, but the contribution made to the Allied cause by the Army, Navy and Air Force was immense.

The Second World War and Canada

The Second World War affected daily life in Canada much more directly than the Great War. Some things had become scarce in 1914-18, but strict rationing was unknown until World War II. Gasoline, meat and sugar were perhaps the rationed items that people were most conscious of; many

other things, including new automobiles, clothing of various kinds, and a wide variety of foodstuffs, were not formally rationed but were either scarce or unobtainable.

The Second World War came much closer to Canada in a physical sense. Many ships were sunk off the East Coast, and in 1942 German submarines, as has been noted, added the Gulf of St. Lawrence to their theatre of activity. Sailing far inland, they sank ships within 60 miles of Rimouski. In October the passenger steamer *Caribou*, sailing between Newfoundland and Nova Scotia, was torpedoed in Cabot Strait and sank with the loss of 136 lives. Much of this U-boat activity was shrouded in wartime censorship, but enough became known to make it clear that the war had indeed come to Canada's front door.

After Japan entered the war, the West Coast also found itself on the fringe of enemy activity. Incendiary balloons, intended to set forests aflame, began to float in from the Pacific on the prevailing westerly winds. Fortunately they proved to be much more of a nuisance than a menace. In June 1942 the Japanese landed on Kiska and Attu. Both islands were far away in the Aleutians, and the Japanese presently abandoned them; but the fact remained that the enemy had landed on North America. The same month Japanese submarines appeared off Vancouver Island. The new freighter *Fort Camosun,* recently completed in a British Columbia shipyard, was shelled and torpedoed off Cape Flattery, and the next night the lighthouse and radio station at Estevan Point were bombarded briefly. But the attacks did not continue, and in spite of them five of the corvettes based on Esquimalt were sent to the Atlantic where the need for ships was desperate.

Prices were controlled with surprising success, thanks in great part to the Wartime Prices and Trade Board that was set up promptly in September 1939. Price increases were very much less than during the Great War. This was all the more remarkable because as the war progressed industrial activity increased enormously. By 1944 the value of production was three times what it had been in 1938. Owing to the false quiet that prevailed before the fall of France, the large-scale manufacturing of munitions and supplies was delayed for a time, but the volume of goods produced in later years was impressive. In round numbers, Canada produced 800,000 motor vehicles, 6,500 tanks and self-propelled guns and 16,000 aircraft. Shipbuilding, important even in the First World War, became even more vital in the second. About 400 merchant ships came from Canadian yards and more than that number of naval craft.

Industrial prosperity made high taxation possible, and no less than 56 percent of the cost of the war was paid for out of revenue—more than double the 25 percent that had been financed in this way in 1914-18. The remaining costs were met almost entirely by internal borrowing, with the result that Canada was not burdened with a heavy foreign debt.

Politically, the domestic issue that Prime Minister Mackenzie King and his government had to keep constantly in mind throughout the war years was the preservation of national unity. King had vivid recollections of the way in which the conscription crisis had rent the country in 1917, and his constant preoccupation was to prevent a repetition. It is easy to forget how complete the rift had been: the Union Government did not have a single French-speaking supporter in the House of Commons. King was convinced that if such a state of affairs recurred it would make it virtually impossible for Canada to contribute effectively to the war.

Both before the outbreak and in the debate in Parliament when war was about to be declared, King had given a "no conscription for overseas service" pledge. Recruitment for the armed forces would be voluntary, and he believed that volunteers would be sufficiently numerous to meet the nation's needs—a belief that was to be disappointed, but only by a very narrow margin.

By degrees the government's hand was forced by the course of events. In 1939 many Canadians, especially in French Canada, had not been convinced that Canada herself was in any great peril. After the fall of France the danger became much more obvious. In June 1940 the National Resources Mobilization Act authorized compulsory enlistment for military service within Canada. This would help to build up strength overseas, as conscripts could

"Wings Parade" at Uplands, Ottawa
Graduates of the British Commonwealth Air Training Plan receiving their wings in September 1941.

PBY "Canso flying boats" (bottom)
In production for the R.C.A.F. and the United States Navy at Canadian Vickers in Montreal.

303

Students of the Commonwealth Air Training Plan (top of page)

Australia, New Zealand, Britain, Newfoundland, the United States and Canada were represented in this group.

The corvette *Edmundston*

Sliding down the ways at the Yarrow shipyard, Esquimalt, early in 1941.

Public Archives of Canada

Public Archives of Canada

take over some defence duties and release volunteers who were ready to serve in Europe.

The situation became still more grave in December 1941 when Japan entered the war. No one could foresee what might happen, and King felt compelled to prepare for all contingencies. In April 1942 a national plebiscite was held, asking the people whether or not they were willing to release the government from its pledge not to conscript men for service overseas. The vote supported conscription overwhelmingly, and the clause in the National Resources Mobilization Act limiting compulsory service to Canada was struck out; but the plebiscite had raised the spectre of 1917. In English-speaking Canada 80 percent of the voters had approved the change; in Quebec, 72 percent had opposed it. King had expected as much, and would almost have welcomed greater opposition outside French Canada. On the eve of the poll he noted in his diary that he expected the Tories to vote "yes," but added: "Should any change to 'no' it will help to distribute the 'no's' more generally in the other provinces, and thereby not make Quebec quite so conspicuous."

Although released from its pledge, the government had no intention of instituting conscription if this could possibly be avoided. While the bill to amend the Mobilization Act was before Parliament, General A. G. L. McNaughton, commander of the First Canadian Army, was in Ottawa on leave, and he assured King that he preferred an army of volunteers and saw no necessity for compulsory service.

In spite of this, the full-scale conscription crisis that King feared arose in the fall of 1944. Considering the manpower that had been absorbed in the Navy and the R.C.A.F., the Army had perhaps grown larger than it should have been. When it went into action in Italy and Normandy, casualties were high, and both the army commanders and the Minister of National Defence, the Hon. J. L. Ralston, became convinced that adequate reinforcements could not be secured by voluntary enlistment. King refused to yield, and on November 1, Ralston resigned. King had privately consulted General McNaughton, who had retired as army commander, and had found that he still believed that sufficient volunteers could be found to meet the army's needs. When Ralston resigned, King asked McNaughton to become Minister of National Defence, and he accepted. But McNaughton's utmost efforts failed to produce the flow of volunteers he had expected, and the government was forced at last to adopt conscription.

The military results were relatively small; only about 13,000 conscripts were sent overseas, but the political stresses and strains had been acute. It was generally acknowledged that the King government had managed the war well, and that it had done its utmost to avoid conscription. No French minister resigned during the crisis, probably because they found such a convinced and courageous leader in Louis St. Laurent, who had joined the cabinet a few months after the death of King's earlier great French lieutenant, Ernest Lapointe.

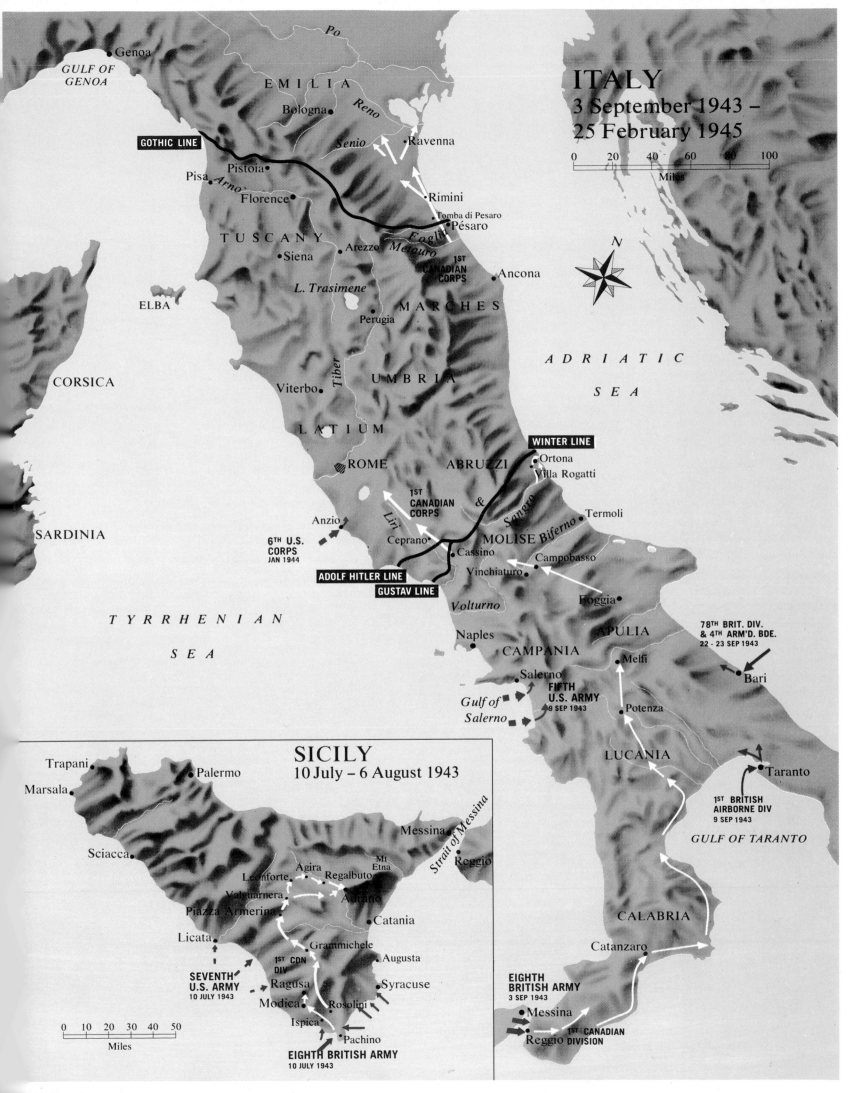

ITALY
3 September 1943 –
25 February 1945

GULF OF GENOA

Genoa

EMILIA

Po

Bologna

Reno

Ravenna

Senio

GOTHIC LINE

Pistoia

Arno

Pisa

Florence

Rimini

TUSCANY

Foglia

Tomba di Pesaro
Pésaro

Arezzo

Metauro

1ST CANADIAN CORPS

Siena

L. Trasimene

Ancona

ELBA

MARCHES

Perugia

ADRIATIC SEA

CORSICA

UMBRIA

Viterbo

Tiber

LATIUM

WINTER LINE

ROME

ABRUZZI

Ortona
Villa Rogatti

1ST CANADIAN CORPS

&

Sangro

Anzio

Liri

6TH U.S. CORPS JAN 1944

Ceprano

Cassino

MOLISE

Biferno

Termoli

Campobasso

Vinchiaturo

ADOLF HITLER LINE

GUSTAV LINE

Volturno

Foggia

78TH BRIT. DIV.
& 4TH ARM'D. BDE.
22 - 23 SEP 1943

TYRRHENIAN SEA

Naples

CAMPANIA

APULIA

Melfi

Bari

SARDINIA

Salerno

FIFTH U.S. ARMY
9 SEP 1943

Potenza

Gulf of Salerno

LUCANIA

1ST BRITISH AIRBORNE DIV
9 SEP 1943

Taranto

GULF OF TARANTO

SICILY
10 July – 6 August 1943

Trapani

Palermo

Messina

Strait of Messina

CALABRIA

Catanzaro

Marsala

Reggio

Sciacca

Agira

Mt Etna

Regalbuto

Leonforte

Adrano

Valguarnera

Piazza Armerina

Catania

EIGHTH BRITISH ARMY
3 SEP 1943

Licata

1ST CDN DIV

Grammichele

SEVENTH U.S. ARMY
10 JULY 1943

Ragusa

Augusta

Modica

Rosolini

Syracuse

Ispica

Messina

Pachino

EIGHTH BRITISH ARMY
10 JULY 1943

Reggio

1ST CANADIAN DIVISION

0 10 20 30 40 50
Miles

0 20 40 60 80 100
Miles

N

Italian Campaign

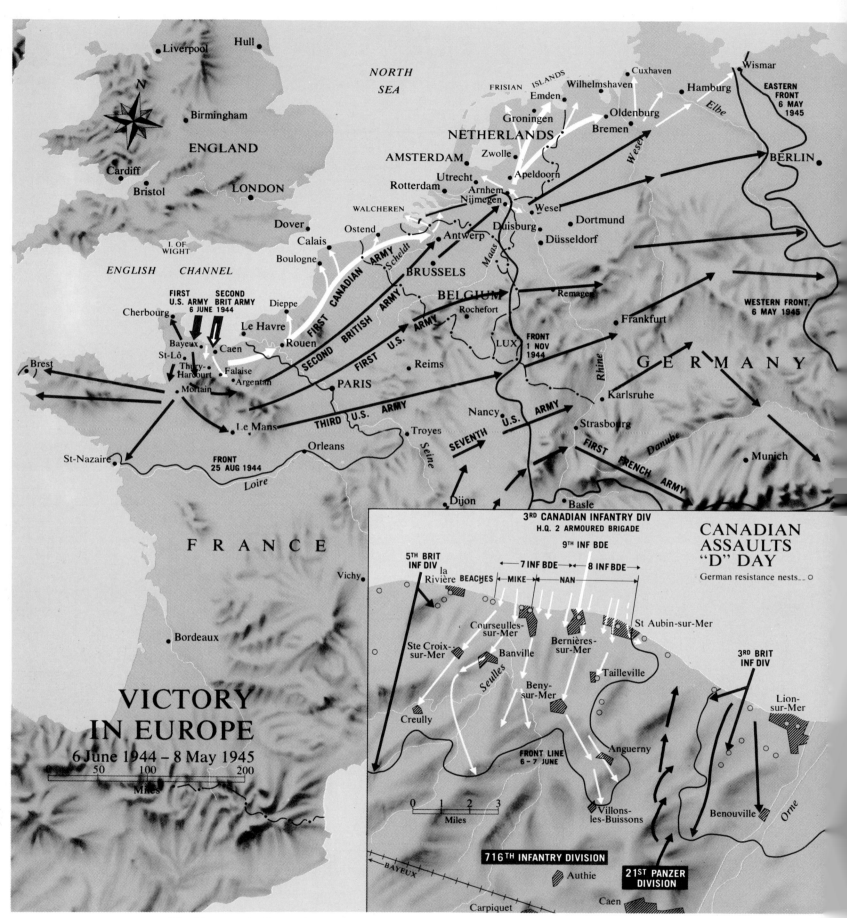

VICTORY IN EUROPE
6 June 1944 – 8 May 1945

0   50   100   200
Miles

The Normandy Campaign

CANADIAN ASSAULTS "D" DAY
German resistance nests...

3RD CANADIAN INFANTRY DIV
H.Q. 2 ARMOURED BRIGADE
9TH INF BDE
7 INF BDE   8 INF BDE
MIKE   NAN

5TH BRIT INF DIV

BEACHES

3RD BRIT INF DIV

FRONT LINE 6–7 JUNE

0   1   2   3
Miles

716TH INFANTRY DIVISION

21ST PANZER DIVISION

NORTH SEA
FRISIAN ISLANDS
EASTERN FRONT 6 MAY 1945
Liverpool
Hull
Birmingham
ENGLAND
Cardiff
Bristol
LONDON
Dover
I. OF WIGHT
ENGLISH CHANNEL
Ostend
Calais
Boulogne
Dieppe
Cherbourg
Le Havre
Bayeux
St-Lô
Caen
Thury-Harcourt
Falaise
Argentan
Mortain
Brest
Le Mans
St-Nazaire
FRONT 25 AUG 1944
PARIS
Orleans
Loire
Troyes
Seine
Reims
Rouen
FIRST CANADIAN ARMY
SECOND BRITISH ARMY
FIRST U.S. ARMY
THIRD U.S. ARMY
SEVENTH U.S. ARMY
FIRST FRENCH ARMY
FIRST U.S. ARMY 6 JUNE 1944
SECOND BRIT ARMY
Scheldt
Antwerp
BRUSSELS
BELGIUM
Rochefort
LUX
FRONT 1 NOV 1944
Remagen
Frankfurt
Karlsruhe
Strasbourg
WESTERN FRONT, 6 MAY 1945
GERMANY
Nancy
Dijon
Basle
Munich
Danube
Rhine
Cuxhaven
Wilhelmshaven
Hamburg
Emden
Groningen
Oldenburg
Bremen
NETHERLANDS
AMSTERDAM
Zwolle
Apeldoorn
Utrecht
Rotterdam
Arnhem
Nijmegen
WALCHEREN
Weser
Duisburg
Dortmund
Düsseldorf
Elbe
Wismar
BERLIN
Maas
FRANCE
Vichy
Bordeaux

la Rivière
Ste Croix-sur-Mer
Courseulles-sur-Mer
Banville
Creully
Seulles
Beny-sur-Mer
Bernières-sur-Mer
Taillerville
St Aubin-sur-Mer
Anguerny
Villons-les-Buissons
Lion-sur-Mer
Benouville
Orne
BAYEUX
Authie
Carpiquet
Caen

Urban Canada
in the Seventies

Recent views of Halifax, Montreal, Toronto, Ottawa, Winnipeg, Regina, Edmonton, Calgary *and* Vancouver.

Montreal

Regina

Winnipeg

Calgary

Ottawa

Edmonton

Halifax

Toronto

Vancouver

Party Representation in the House of Commons: 1945-1968

Date of Election	Liberal	Progressive Conservative	C.C.F. / N.D.P.	Social Credit	Other	Total Members
1945	125 MACKENZIE KING	67	28	13	12	245
1949	190 ST. LAURENT	41	13	10	8	262
1953	170 ST. LAURENT	51	23	15	6	265
1957	105	112 DIEFENBAKER	25	19	4	265
1958	47	208 DIEFENBAKER	8		2	265
1962	100	116 DIEFENBAKER	19	30		265
1963	128 PEARSON	96	17	24		265
1965	131 PEARSON	97	21	14	2	265
1968	155 TRUDEAU	72	22	14	1	264

Legend:

Colour	Party
■	Liberal
■	Progressive Conservative
■	C.C.F. 1945-1958; N.D.P. 1962-1968
■	Social Credit
■	Other

The Liberal majority in 1949 and the Progressive Conservative majority in 1958 were the largest since Confederation.

Politics and Leaders

Five prime ministers—Mackenzie King, Lous S. St. Laurent, John Diefenbaker, Lester Pearson and Pierre Elliott Trudeau—have held office in Canada since the Second World War. They offered interesting contrasts and their fortunes were as varied as their personalities.

Mackenzie King called an election in June 1945, and his Liberal government was returned, though with a much reduced majority. It was one of the very few wartime administrations to be re-elected in the democracies, and, more remarkable, under King and his successor as Liberal leader, Louis St. Laurent, was to retain office for another twelve years.

Most people expected the war to be followed by a depression, instead of the long period of expansion and prosperity that actually ensued. With this expectation in mind, the government had taken steps to prepare for the worst. A reconstruction programme had been drawn up which included fiscal arrangements, increased welfare services, and other measures intended to provide income and stimulate employment. Just as the war was ending family allowances were introduced. Though nominally a welfare service, the allowances were also a means of distributing purchasing power. Their effectiveness in this respect may be judged by the fact that nearly three million families now receive allowances totalling more than half a billion dollars a year.

In August 1945, King called a conference to present his reconstruction plans to the provinces. To them it seemed that the programme would strengthen further the increased authority that the federal government had acquired in the emergency period during the war, and they would have none of it. No agreement could be reached, and King found it necessary to make progress piecemeal, by discussing this proposal or that with individual provinces.

Federal–provincial relations have loomed very large in domestic politics in the postwar years. In general, two main issues have been involved. The first is financial, and centres upon the size of the subsidies and grants that are to be paid to the provinces, and the taxes that each level of government is to levy. Most of the other federal–provincial problems relate to health, welfare and education. These are fields reserved for the provinces under the terms of the British North America Act, but costs have become so great that federal aid has become essential. Moreover, some uniformity in health and welfare services in the various provinces is obviously desirable, and this can best be achieved by services that meet standards set by the federal government and are subsidized by it to whatever extent may be necessary to attain the standards. Only in this way can the poorer provinces provide benefits comparable to those available in the richer ones.

Wartime necessity gave rise to what became known as tax rental agreements. In return for vacating a tax field, notably that of income tax, a province received a guaranteed annual cash grant. In the case of health and welfare, a shared-cost plan was often agreed upon, under which the federal government paid a percentage of the cost of an approved programme. In this way the proper constitutional authority—the province—provided the service, while some or even the bulk of the money to pay for it could come from Ottawa.

Relations with Canada's enormous and, as it sometimes seems, all-pervading neighbour, the United States, have been another major preoccupation of Canadian politicians. Canadian dependence on the United States for continental defence soon became painfully clear; in addition, there was growing awareness of the extent to which Canadian industries were owned and controlled by American corporations. Uneasiness as to whether Canada was in danger of ceasing to be Canadian was one reason that prompted Louis St. Laurent to appoint a Royal Commission on National Development of the Arts, Letters and Sciences (the Massey Commission) in 1949, only a few months after he became prime minister. Its report, tabled in 1951, urged the government to subsidize the universities and encourage cultural activities in a comprehensive way. Many of the Commission's recommendations have since been implemented. Since 1952 the federal government has given direct assistance to the universities, and in 1957 it established and endowed the Canada Council, a semi-independent foundation concerned chiefly with the arts, letters and social sciences.

St. Laurent was prime minister from 1948 until 1957. Those were prosperous years, in which the gross national product more than doubled. St. Laurent himself, able, modest and charming, won an immense personal following that enabled him to win elections handily in 1949 and 1953. But thereafter the fortunes of the Liberals began to decline. The Prime Minister himself was getting old and tired. Prosperity was at a high level, but it did not extend equally to the whole country; the prairie farmers and dwellers in the Maritimes were not happy. The government had learned autocratic ways during the war, and tended to retain them in peace time; St. Laurent later admitted that the cabinet was apt to act like a board of directors. The famous pipeline debate of 1956, in which the government arrogantly resorted to closure to force approval of a pipeline construction loan, aroused an almost unprecedented storm of protest. By the time of the 1957 election the Liberals had been in office 22 years, and many felt that it was time for a change.

Meanwhile the Conservatives had acquired a dynamic and eloquent new leader in John Diefenbaker. A native of Saskatchewan, and a noted defence lawyer, he championed the cause of the prairie farmers and of the little man and the underprivileged everywhere. A magnificent campaigner, he stumped the country from coast to coast to such

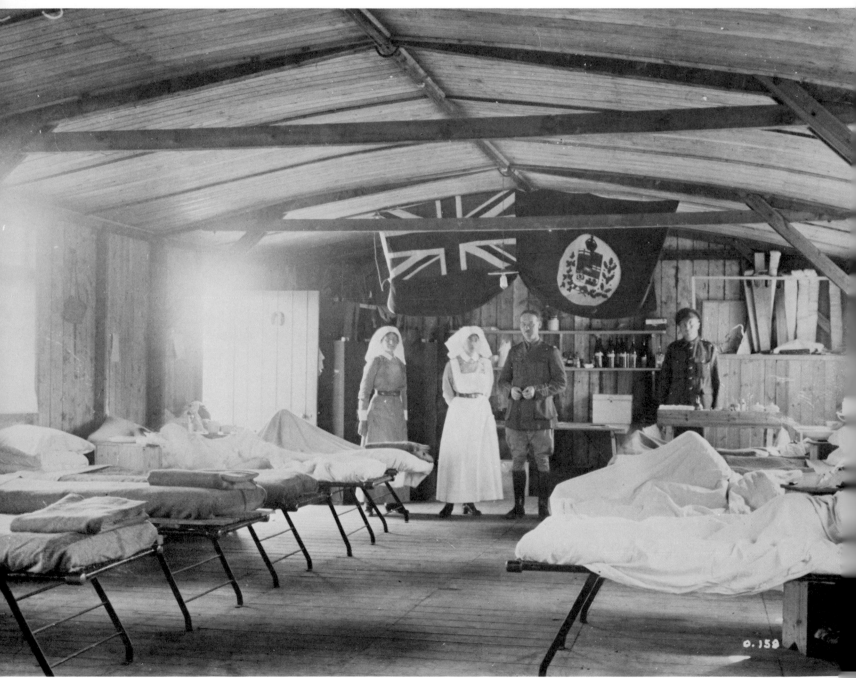

The Red Ensign

The red ensign, with a shield in the fly quartering the arms of the four original provinces, came into use unofficially as a Canadian flag soon after Confederation. As additional provinces came into being, their arms were added to the shield, which was surrounded by a wreath of green maple leaves. This photograph of a casualty clearing station in France in 1916 shows the flag under which Canadian troops fought in the First World War.

The arms of nine provinces made the shield crowded and complicated, and in 1924 they were replaced by the arms of Canada. About the same time, the wreath of maple leaves disappeared. The red ensign was for years thereafter almost universally recognized as the Canadian flag, and an order-in-council passed in September 1945 recognized it officially as such "until such time as action is taken by Parliament for the formal adoption of a national flag."

effect that the Conservatives in the Commons, only 51 in number in 1953, increased to 112 in 1957, while the Liberals fell from 170 to 105. Diefenbaker did not have a clear majority, but St. Laurent resigned within a few days, and Diefenbaker became prime minister. Nine months later, in a second election, the Conservatives won the unprecedented number of 208 seats, and the Liberal representation fell to an all time low of 47.

Diefenbaker was an individualist; his campaigns had been essentially personal. He never mastered the art of managing a team as large as that required to run the government of Canada. His many projects and promises did not add up to a coherent programme. He had difficulty in taking practical steps to advance toward the goals he had in view. Some of his measures—the "roads to resources" programme, for example, which reflected his interest in the North—appealed to the imagination; cash advances on their crops and large wheat sales to China and Russia won the loyalty of the prairie farmers. Perhaps the famous Bill of Rights of 1960, intended to protect the little man against the injustice of authority, is the measure for which he will be best remembered. But in spite of its huge and almost unwieldy majority—indeed perhaps in part because of it—the government slowly disintegrated. A recession added to Diefenbaker's difficulties; although the gross national product continued to rise, so did unemployment, budget deficits and the national debt. The climax came in 1962, when, in the midst of the election campaign, international pressures forced a devaluation of the Canadian dollar.

In the new House of Commons Diefenbaker's followers were reduced to 116 and the Liberals numbered 100. Ten months later, in a second election, the Liberals took the lead with 128 members—6 short of a majority—and the Conservatives held 96 seats. Diefenbaker thereupon resigned, and was succeeded as prime minister by Lester Pearson.

Pearson, certainly the most widely known Canadian of his day, came to politics after a most distinguished career in the diplomatic service. In most respects that career continued after he entered the King cabinet and subsequently served under St. Laurent as Secretary of State for External Affairs. His real baptism of political fire did not come until 1958, when he succeeded St. Laurent as leader of the Liberals shortly before the election that saw the party's representation in the Commons fall to 47.

The plight of a minority government is never a comfortable one, even when it is reasonably safe from defeat, as was the Liberal administration formed in 1963; but it proved impossible for Pearson to improve its position. In 1965 he was persuaded to try, but the net gain in the election for the Liberals was only three seats, leaving them still another three short of a bare majority. This third election in little more than three years showed that the country was still divided, with no strong political preference, one way or the other.

During Pearson's five years as prime minister many useful measures were passed, but the propensity of his government to live, or appear to live, in a state of almost perpetual crisis tended to obscure the fact. In addition, Pearson's methods were those of the diplomat rather than the politician. The diplomat advances a proposal in the full expectation that it will be met by a counterproposal, and that the final result will be some tenable compromise between the two. By contrast, when a government introduces a bill in the Commons, it normally expects to defend every jot and tittle of the text and to regard any material amendments as humiliations and victories for the opposition. Pearson, the diplomat, was prepared to have a measure torn asunder, always providing that the final bill represented a real advance toward the goal he had in view. The progress through Parliament of the Canada Pension Plan, approved in 1965, was a case in point; the debate on the flag issue was another. A pension plan was passed and a flag approved, but both differed materially from what the government had first proposed. The ends in view may have been gained, but the method was not effective politically.

Two matters that had long been simmering came to the boil during the Pearson regime. The first was the rise of a strong nationalist movement in Quebec, with an extreme left wing that became vocal, violent and separatist. The grievances that gave rise to it were many and varied. The province's outmoded educational system was one; the fact that Quebec provided labour rather than leaders for its own industries was another. These and other ills were mostly blamed on English Canada, and two demands quickly arose: Quebec must have a new constitutional status of some kind that would safeguard both her economy and the French culture she represents, and the French language must be given full legal equality with English throughout Canada. Pearson appointed a Royal Commission on Bilingualism and Biculturalism in 1963, and its first report was tabled in 1967. In accordance with its recommendations, English and French have been declared official languages by Parliament, but the constitutional issue is still in the early stages of discussion.

The second matter of moment was the extent to which Canadian industry had come to be owned and controlled by Americans. American capital poured into Canada after the war; everyone knew, for example, the large part it played in the development of the vast new oil industry in Alberta; the Canadian automobile industry, to cite another instance, is almost completely American owned. But it was not until the late 1950s that this state of affairs began to cause real uneasiness. Walter Gordon, Pearson's first Minister of Finance, brought the matter to the fore, and ever since some means has been sought whereby Canadian control of the country's industries can be assured without unduly discouraging the inflow of capital.

The Centenary of Confederation was 1967, and the occasion was marked by a singularly successful series of celebrations all across the country. Her Majesty the Queen participated in the ceremonies in Ottawa on July 1. Quebec's chief contribution took the nonpolitical form of a federally financed world exhibition in Montreal—Expo 67—which was attended by over fifty million people. These events tended to divert attention from politics, but developments of great interest nevertheless took place. In September, a national leadership convention of the Progressive Conservative party rejected John Diefenbaker's bid for a further mandate and chose as its leader Robert Stanfield, premier of Nova Scotia. And in the closing days of the year Lester Pearson announced that he would retire as soon as a new Liberal leader had been chosen to succeed him.

The retirement of Diefenbaker and Pearson marked the end of an era in Canadian politics, and the fact was emphasized by the completely different personality of Pierre Elliott Trudeau, who became prime minister in April 1968. Years from now scholars and politicians will doubtless still be discussing the cause and nature of the country-wide wave of "Trudeaumania" that swept him to the Liberal leadership and then elected the party in November with the long-sought clear majority that Pearson had never enjoyed. Quite apart from other qualities, Trudeau brought to politics an appearance of youth, an informality of manner and a gift for television that were new to the scene in Canada. And, as successor to Mackenzie, Laurier, King, St. Lau-

From San Francisco, May 8, 1945

This was "VE Day," and the conference that created The United Nations was in progress in San Francisco. From there the Prime Minister, Mr. Mackenzie King (left) and his successor-to-be, the Hon. Louis St. Laurent, then Minister of Justice, broadcast to the Canadian people.

rent and Pearson he happened to continue the Liberal propensity for choosing their leaders alternately from English Canada and French Canada.

Through the postwar years Canada has grown in status as well as stature. In 1931 the Statute of Westminster gave her virtually complete autonomy, but this has been underlined and amplified in a number of ways since 1945. On January 1, 1947, a Canadian Citizenship Act came into effect; Canadians continued to be British subjects, but the Act created the new distinct nationality of "Canadian citizen." Appropriately enough, the first citizenship certificate was presented to Prime Minister Mackenzie King at a ceremony on January 3, 1947.

In 1947 appeals to the British Privy Council were ended, and the Supreme Court of Canada became the final Canadian court of appeal. The same year the Parliament of Canada was given authority to amend the Canadian constitution—the British North America Act—with the exception of the clauses relating to the rights of the provinces. The demands of Quebec for the revision of these clauses have resulted in a search, not yet concluded, for an amending procedure that will be acceptable to all ten of the provinces.

In 1952 the Rt. Hon. Vincent Massey became the first Canadian to be Governor General of Canada. He was appointed before the death of King George VI, but did not assume office until after the accession of Queen Elizabeth II. The Great Seal of Canada designed for the Queen described her as Queen of Canada—the first time the sovereign had been so designated—and Canada was specifically mentioned in a new style and title adopted in 1953. Finally, in 1965, the long flag controversy was brought to a close when on February 15 a new Canadian flag, approved by the Parliament of Canada, was raised on the Peace Tower of the Parliament Buildings and on Canadian embassies and ships throughout the world.

Prime Minister John G. Diefenbaker admiring the portrait of Sir John A. Macdonald that hung over the fireplace in his office. The picture was taken shortly after he formed his ministry in 1958.

*School children crowded around Prime Minister
Lester Pearson when he visited Harts Corners,
Ontario, in 1965.*

*Pierre Trudeau delivering his acceptance speech
at the leadership convention, 1968.*

ABERCROMBIE, GENERAL JAMES, 65
Aberhart, William, 295
Acadia, 32, 47, 63
Acadian expulsion, 63, 78-9
Aerial Experiment Assn., 247
Aerial surveys, 253, 290
Air Canada (TCA), 251-2, 254, 257, 261
Aircraft manufacturing, 250, 253-4, 259, 303
Aircraft types, civil, 250-53, 257-9
Aircraft types, military, 257, 300
Air mail, 250, 253
Airports, 253, 257
Aix-la-Chapelle, Treaty of, 57
Aklavik, 253
Alaska, 19, 79, 83, 98, 100, 103, 162, 223, 248, 250, 279, 300
Alaska Highway, 248-9
Albanel, Father Charles, 36
Albany Fort, 39, 44
Alberta, 192, 247, 272, 277, 281, 292, 295
Alert (ship), 289
Alexander, Viscount, 297
Alexander VI, Pope, 16
Allan, Sir Hugh, 169
Angus, R. B., 169
Allen, Ethan, 68
America, first use of name, 29
American Revolutionary War, 68-70
Amherst, General Sir Jeffery, 65
Amundsen, Roald, 291
Angus, R. B., 169
Anian, Strait of, 28, 79
Annapolis Basin, 35
L'Anse aux Meadows, 16, 19
Anse Sablon, 228
Anson Northrup (ship), 152, 164
Anticosti Island, 24, 68, 228
Archangel, 232
Archibald, Sir Adams G., 162
Arnold, Benedict, 69
Arctic (ship), 291
Arctic exploration, 142-5, 286-92
Arctic islands, 162
Aroostock War, 120
Arvida, 281
Asbestos, 273, 281
Ashburton Treaty, 120
Astor, John Jacob, 100, 102
Astoria, 100, 102, 112
Athabasca tar sands, 279
Athabasca (ship), 188
Athenia (ship), 298
Atlantic, Battle of the, 296, 298
Atlantic and St. Lawrence Railway, 136
Aubert, James, 24
Automobiles, 244-8, 261
Aviation, 249-257, 261
Axel Heilberg Island, 291

BACK, LT. GEORGE, 143
Back River, 143
Baddeck, 250
Baffin, William, 26, 142
Baffin Bay, 142, 286, 289
Baffin Island, 15, 26, 142, 162, 286
Bagot, Sir Charles, 155
Baie des Sept-Iles, 16
Baldwin, F. W. (Casey), 249, 250
Baldwin, Robert, 113, 155
Baldwin, William, 113
Barkerville, 132
Baranof, Aleksandr, 100
Barrow Strait, 143
Bathurst Inlet, 143
Batoche, 182; battle at, 184-5
Battleford, 178, 184, 196
Beachey, Lincoln, 249
Beaumont Hamel, 226

Beechey Island, 143
Beechey Point, 143
Behaim, Martin, 13-15
Belcher, Capt. Sir Edward, 144
Bell, Alexander Graham, 249
Bennett, R. B. (later Viscount), 293, 295
Bering, Vitus, 79
Bering Strait, 19, 28, 79, 83, 143
Bernier, Capt. Joseph, 291
Big Bear (Indian chief), 184, 186
Bigot, François, 58
Bill of Rights, 315
Bishop, Major W. A., 230, 235
Bishop's Falls, 226
Black Hills, 53
Blossom (ship), 143
Bodega Bay, 100
Boothia, Gulf of, 143
Boothia Peninsula, 142-3
Borden, Sir Robert, 220, 223-5, 230, 238, 241, 247, 292, 295
Boscawen, Admiral Edward, 65
Botwood, 226, 296
Bougainville, Louis Antoine de, 57-8
Boundaries, in 1763, 66; in 1774, 68, 73; in 1783, 72, 74; with Maine, 72, 120; with Oregon, 126; with Alaska, 223; Quebec-Labrador, 228
Bowden, W. A., 264
Bowell, Sir Mackenzie, 226, 295
Braddock, General Edward, 63
Bradley, Gordon, 297
Bradstreet, Lt. Col. John, 65
Brant, Joseph (Mohawk chief), 69
Brébeuf, Father Jean de, 36, 42-3
Britain, Battle of, 300
British American Land Co., 88
British Columbia, 25, 79-83, 98-101, 103, 126, 129, 131, 160, 162, 165, 168-9, 192-3, 196, 249, 272, 276-7, 280, 281
British Commonwealth Air Training Plan, 257, 300, 303-4
British North America Act, 157, 159, 295, 297, 313, 316
Brobdingnag, Land of, 79, 83
Brock, General Sir Isaac, 108, 112
Brockville, 138
Brockville and Ottawa Railway, 138
Brown, George, 156-7
Brulé, Etienne, 34
Bryant, Mrs. Alys, 250
Bryant, Johnny, 250
Buffalo (animal), 19, 44, 174, 178
Buffalo and Lake Huron Railway, 138
Burgoyne, General John, 69, 70
Bus travel, 261
Bush pilots, 250
Butler, Col. John, 69
Butler's Rangers, 69, 86
Button, Sir Thomas, 26
Byng, Sir Julian (later Viscount), 230, 292-3
Bytown (Ottawa), 134, 138
Bytown and Prescott Railway, 138

CABLE, ATLANTIC, 160, 216
Cabot, John, 19, 22-3, 27-8, 34
Cabot Tower, St. John's, 217
Caen, 301
Calgary, 54, 196-7, 204, 250, 311
California, 100
Canada Company, New France, 39; Upper Canada, 88, 96
Canada Council, 313
Canada East, 155-6
Canada Highways Act, 247
Canada Jurisdiction Act, 174
Canada Pension Plan, 315

Canada West, 155-6
Canadian Arctic Expedition, 291
Canadian Army, 108, 218, 226, 230, 236-7, 239, 301-2, 304-6
Canadian Broadcasting Commission, 268
Canadian Broadcasting Corporation (CBC), 268
Canadian Citizenship Act, 316
Canadian Corps, World War I, 230; World War II, 301
Canadian Expeditionary Force, 226, 230, 236-7
Canadian Government Merchant Marine, 238
Canadian National Railways, 205, 260-62, 266; Radio Department, 266-7
Canadian Northern Railway, 189, 196, 202-5
Canadian Pacific Airlines (CP Air), 252, 254, 257
Canadian Pacific Railway, 154, 168-9, 173, 178, 184, 186, 189, 196, 200, 204, 223, 253-4, 260-62
Canadian Pacific Steamships, 217
Canadian Radio Television Commission, 268
Canadian Transport Commission, 261
Canallers (ships), 263-4, 266
Canals, 131-5, 160, 261-6
Canso Causeway, 249
Cape Aldrich, 289
Cape Bonavista, 22
Cape Breton Island, 22, 24, 27-8, 47, 88, 118, 249
Cape Canso, 27
Cape Columbia, 291
Cape Flattery, 81
Cape Herschell, 291
Cape Race, 22, 24, 27
Cape Ray, 27
Cape Sheridan, 289
Cariboo, 130-32
Cariboo Road, 131, 133
Caribou (ship), 302
Carignan-Salières Regiment, 45
Carleton, Sir Guy (later Lord Dorchester), 68-9, 75, 86, 88
Caroline (ship), 115-6
Carson, Dr. William, 124
Carter, Frederick Bowker, 225, 295
Cartier, Sir George Etienne, 156-7, 161
Cartier, Jacques, 19, 21, 23-4, 28
Cataraqui (Kingston), 87
Caughnawaga Indians, 220
C. D. Howe (ship), 291
Cedar Lake, 44, 53
Ceprano, 301
Chaleur, Bay of, 24
Chambly Canal, 135
Champlain, Samuel de, 32, 34-5, 39
Champlain and St. Lawrence Railway, 136
Chantrey Inlet, 143
Charles II, King, 39
Charlesbourg-Royal, 24
Charlottetown, 78, 120
Charlottetown Conference, 157
Chaste, Aymar de, 32
Chateauguay, battle at, 112
Chateau Laurier, 205
Chauvin, Pierre de, 44
Chesterfield Inlet, 72
Chignecto canal project, 131
Chirikof, Peter, 79
Cholera epidemic of 1832, 96
Churchill, Sir Winston, 302
Churchill Falls, 281
Churchill River, 26, 44, 75
Chrysler's Farm, 112
Civil War, 154-5, 157
Clarke, John, 174
Clergy Reserves, 88, 96, 113
Colbert, Jean Baptiste, 45

Collingwood, 136
Collishaw, Major Raymond, 230
Columbia River, 100-3, 126
Columbus, Christopher, 12, 14-5, 17, 22, 34
Commission of Government, Newfoundland, 296
Company of One Hundred Associates, 34
Confederation, 124, 152, 154-7, 225, 295, 297
Confederation, Centenary of, 287-8, 315-6
Conscription, 223, 225, 295, 303-4
Constitutional Act, 88
Constitutional issue, 315-6
Continental Congress, 68-9
Cook, Captain James, 77, 79, 81, 83, 98
Co-operative Commonwealth Federation
  (CCF), 292, 295
Coppermine River, 75, 81, 142-3
Cormack, William Epps, 123, 125
Corner Brook, 226
Cornwall, 91, 112
Cornwallis, General Charles, 70
Cornwallis Island, 143
Corte-Real, Gaspar, 22
Corte-Real, Joao Vaz, 16
Corte-Real, Miguel, 24
Countess of Dufferin (locomotive), 169
Coureurs de bois, 39
CP Air (Canadian Pacific Air Lines), 254, 261
Craigellachie, 186
Cree Indians, 21, 184, 186
Crimean War, 126, 142
Croft, Thomas, 22
Crown Point, 68
Crown Reserves, 88, 96
Crozier, Capt. Francis, 143
Crozier, Supt., 182
Cumberland House, 75, 102
Currie, General Sir Arthur, 232
Cypress Hills, 177-8, 180

Dakota (ship), 153
Davis, John, 26
Davis Strait, 26
Dawson City, 220
Dawson Creek, 262
Dawson Route, 180, 186
Day, John, 22
Dease, Peter Warren, 143
Deerfield, 45
Desceliers, Pierre, 28, 30
Denison, Merrill, 266
Dennis, Col. J. S., 161
Depression of 1929, 293, 295-6
Detroit, 36-7, 68, 108, 138
D'Iberville (ship), 291
D'Iberville, Pierre Le Moyne, 44-5
Dickins, Lieut. C. H. (Punch), 250
Diefenbaker, John G., 313-4, 316-7
Dieppe, 24, 28, 44; raid, 301
Diesel locomotives, 261
Discovery (ship), 81
Displaced persons, 282
Distributor (ship), 206
Dixon Entrance, 100
Dochets Island, 32
Dominion status, 293, 295
Dorchester, 140
Douglas, Sir James, 126, 131
Douglas Point, 281
Drake, Sir Francis, 14, 25, 79
Drummond, Lt. Gen. Sir Gordon, 112
Duck Lake, 182, 185
Duckworth, Sir John, 121
Du Creux, Father François, 38, 42-3
Dumont, Gabriel, 182-4
Dundas Street, 88
Dunkirk, 301
Durban army camp, 219

Durham, Earl of, 116-7, 124-5

Eaglet (ship), 39
Eastern Townships, 86, 96
East India Company, 98, 100
Eddy, Jonathan, 69
Edinburgh, H.R.H. the Duke of, 287-8
Edmonton, 178, 184, 189, 196, 201, 204, 310
Edward VII, King, 106, 144, 151, 178
Egyptian discoverers, 15
Electric power, 280-81
Elgin, Earl of, 155
Elizabeth I, Queen, 25
Elizabeth II, H.M. Queen, 243, 287-8, 315-6
Elizabeth, H.M. the Queen Mother, 294
Ellesmere Island, 279, 286, 289, 291
Elliot Lake, 273
Ellis, Frank H., 250
Empress of Britain (ship), 216
Erebus (ship), 143
Eric the Red, 15
Erie Canal, 113, 134, 136, 262
Ericsson, Leif (Leifr Eiriksson), 15-6
Ericsson, Thorsteinn, 16
Ericsson, Thorvaldr, 16
Eskimo, 19, 21, 26, 143
Esquimalt, 218, 220, 304
Essex County, Ontario, 90
Estevan Point, 303
Ethnic origins, 160, 285-6
European and North American Railway,
  138, 166
Expo 67, 316

FALAISE, 299
Family Compact, 113
Fathers of Confederation, 163, 225
Federal-provincial relations, 313
Fenians, 154
Finlay, James, 72
Fisher, Charles, 120-21
First Canadian Army, 301
Fisheries, 22, 24, 77, 121, 210-15, 225
Fishing rights in Newfoundland, 77-8, 121, 225
Flag, Canadian, 314-6, 321
Fleming, Sir Sandford, 166, 168-9
Fonte, Bartholomew de, 79
Forbes, Sir Francis, 121
Forbes, Brig. Gen. John, 65
Ford Model T car, 244, 247
Forest industries, 274-7
Fort Beauséjour, 63
Fort Bourbon, 53
Fort Calgary, 178, 196
Fort Carillon (Ticonderoga), 57, 65
Fort Carlton, 182
Fort Chambly, 57, 69
Fort Chipewyan, 179
Fort Cumberland (formerly Fort Beauséjour), 69
Fort de Chartres, 50, 65, 68
Fort Dauphin, 53
Fort Duquesne, 63, 65
Fort Edmonton, 196, 204
Fort Frontenac, 57, 65, 87
Fort Garry, 103, 155, 162, 164, 196
Fort George, Niagara River, 112
Fort Gibraltar, 196
Fort Howe, 78
Fort la Jonquière, 54
Fort La Reine, 53
Fort Lawrence, 63
Fort McLeod, 178
Fort Maurepas, 53
Fort Necessity, 63
Fort Nelson, 39
Fort Niagara, 57, 112
Fort Oswego, 50

Fort Pasquia, 53
Fort Ross, 100
Fort Rouille, 50
Fort St. Charles, 53
Fort St. John, 248, 262
Fort St. Louis, 53, 72
Fort St. Pierre, 53
Fort Saskatchewan, 178
Fort Selkirk, 220
Fort Simpson, 249
Fort Smith, 187, 253
Fort Ticonderoga, 57
Fort Vancouver, 103, 126
Fort Victoria, 126, 196
Fort Walsh, 177-8
Fort Whoop-up, 177-8
Fort William, 102
Fort William Henry, 65
Foxe, Luke, 27
Foxe Basin, 142
Fram (ship), 291
Francis I, King, 24
Franklin, Sir John, 128, 142-4, 289
Franklin, Lady, 144
Franklin Strait, 143
Fraser River, 101, 126, 205, 210; gold rush,
  106, 126, 129, 196, 272
Fraser, Simon, 101
French-Canadians, 47, 63, 68, 75, 88, 113, 160,
  186, 218, 223, 225, 285-6, 303-4, 315-6
French explorers, 37
French River, 34, 264
French Shore, Newfoundland, 77, 121, 225
Freydis, 16
Frobisher, Joseph, 75
Frobisher, Sir Martin, 25, 27
Frobisher, Thomas, 75
Frobisher Bay, 26
Frog Lake, 184
Frontenac, Louis de Buade, Comte de, 45
Fuca, Juan de, 79
Fundy, Bay of, 28, 131
Fur trade, 36, 39, 44-5, 50, 52, 58, 72, 75,
  98-107
Fury and Hecla Strait, 143

Gabriel (ship), 25
Galt, Sir Alexander T., 156-7
Galt, John, 96
Gama, Vasco de, 12
Gander, 296
Gaspé, 21, 24
George V, King, 151
Geoge VI, King, 243, 294, 316
Georgian Bay, 34, 36, 135-6
Georgian Bay Canal, 264
Geography, early conceptions, 14-15
Ghent, Treaty of, 113
Gibson, Paddy, 144
Gibson, W. W., 250
Gilbert, Sir Humphrey, 25-6
Gjoa (ship), 291
Glace Bay, 217
Goderich, 96, 138
Golden Hind (ship), 14
Goose Bay, 296
Gordon, Walter, 315
Gothic Line, Italy, 301
Grain elevators, 188, 272
Grain trade, 232, 270-72, 315
Grand Falls, 226
Grand River Valley, 86
Grand Trunk Railway, 136, 138, 166, 204-5
Grand Trunk Pacific Railway, 205, 210
Great Eastern (ship), 216
Great Slave Lake, 262, 273-4
Great Slave Railway, 262

Great Western Railway, 136-8
Greenland, 15, 26
Green Mountain Boys, 68
Grimshaw, 249
Groseilliers, Médard Chouart des, 36, 39
Guelph, 96
Guthrie, Tyrone, 266

HAIDA INDIANS, 21
Haig, Field Marshal Sir Douglas, 232
Haldimand, General Sir Frederick, 75, 88
Halifax, 57, 69, 79, 136, 138, 166, 218, 220, 254, 307
Hall, Capt. Charles F., 289
Hamel, Theophile, 24
Hamilton, 136-7, 244, 247, 266
Hamilton and Toronto Railway, 136
Hampton, Maj. Gen. Wade, 112
Hanna, Capt. James, 98
Haviland, Brig. Gen. William, 65
Hawaiian Islands, 83, 98, 100
Hay River, 249
Hayes, Dr. I. I., 289
Hayes River, 44, 127
Hays, Charles M., 204-5
Head, Sir Francis Bond, 113
Hearne, Samuel, 75-6, 81, 142-3
Heart's Content, 216
Helluland, 15, 20
Helmcken, Dr. J. S., 165
Henday, Anthony, 54
Henry VII, King, 22
Herjulfsson, Bjarni, 15
Hezeta, Bruno de, 81
Hill, James J., 154, 169
Hind, Henry Youle, 152, 154
Hitler Line, Italy, 301
Hochelaga, 24
Homen, Lopo and Diego, 28, 30
Homesteads, 187-8
Hong Kong, 301
Hope, 131
Howe, C. D., 254
Howe, Joseph, 118, 120, 136
Howe, General Sir William, 69
Hoy, Capt. Ernest, 250, 257
Hudson, Henry, 26
Hudson Bay, 26, 36, 39, 47, 102-3, 128, 152
Hudson's Bay Company, 39, 40-41, 44, 47, 53-4, 72, 75, 101-6, 126, 143, 152, 160-61, 174, 187, 196
Hudson River, 26
Hudson Strait, 26, 228, 253, 290
Hughes, Sir Sam, 230, 232
Hull, Maj. Gen. William, 108
Huron Indians, 17, 19, 21, 34, 36, 39, 45
Huron Tract, 96
Huronia, 21, 36, 38-9
Hydro-electric power, 280-81

ICELAND, 15
Ile-à-la-Crosse, Lac, 75
Ile St. Jean, see Prince Edward Island
Ile Sainte-Croix, 32
Immigration, 89, 96, 160, 187-8, 189-93, 223, 282-6
Imperial Conference of 1926, 293
Imperial defence plans, 220, 223
Imperial Economic Conference of 1932, 295
Imperial Munitions Board, 232
Indians, as wartime allies, 65, 108; population, 19, 21, 180; reserves, 178, 180; treaties, 179-81; tribal distribution, 19; see also names of individual tribes
Ingstad, Helge, 16, 20
International Joint Commission, 264
International Pacific Halibut Commission, 210

International Pacific Salmon Commission, 210
Intercolonial Railway, 166-7, 205
Irish discoverers, 15
Iroquois Indians, 19, 19, 32, 34, 36, 39, 45, 69, 86
Island of St. John, see Prince Edward Island
Italian campaign, 301, 305

JAMES, THOMAS, 27
James Bay, 26-7
Japan, 298, 300, 302-4
Jay, John, 22
Jesuit missions, 36, 42-3
Jesuit Relations, 36
John A. Macdonald (ship), 292
Johnson, Sir John, 69, 91
Jolliet, Louis, 36-7

KAMINISTIQUIA, 50
Kamloops (ship), 263
Kane, Dr. Elisha, 289
Kane Basin, 289
Kelsey, Henry, 44
Kemano, 281
Kennedy Channel, 289
Kent Peninsula, 142
Kimberley, 273-4
King, W. L. Mackenzie, 292-3, 295, 297, 302-4, 313, 315-6
King-Byng crisis of 1926, 292-3
King's Posts, 106
King's Royal Regiment of New York, 86
King William Island, 142-4
Kingston, 87, 112, 134, 144, 147, 218
Kirke, David and brothers, 34, 39
Kiska and Attu islands, 300, 303
Kitimat, 281
Klondike gold rush, 178, 220
Kootenay River, 281
Krenitzin, Captain, 79

LABRADOR, 15, 16, 68, 106, 228, 281, 296
Labrador (ship), 292
Lachine, 45, 103
Lachine Canal, 134-5
Lacolle, 116
La Corne, St. Luc de, 54
La Cosa, Juan de, 27-8
Lafontaine, Sir Louis H., 155
La Jemeraye, Sieur de, 50, 53
Lake, Brig. Gen. Sir Percy, 218
Lake Athabasca, 75
Lake Champlain, 32, 57, 108, 112
Lake Erie, 34
Lake George, 32, 57
Lake Huron, 34
Lake Michigan, 36
Lake Nipissing, 34, 36
Lake Ontario, 34
Lake St. John, 36
Lake Simcoe, 34, 36
Lake Superior, 34
Lake Winnipeg, 44
Lalement, Father Gabriel, 42
Lancaster Sound, 142-3, 286
Langlade, Charles, 59
Lapointe, Ernest, 304
Laprairie, 136
Larsen, Staff Sgt. H. A., 291
La Salle, René-Robert Cavelier de, 36-7
Laurentian Shield, 89
Laurier, Sir Wilfrid, 189, 204, 217, 241, 292, 316
Laval, Bishop, 59
La Vérendrye, François Chevalier de, 53
La Vérendrye, Gaultier de Varenne, Sieur de, 50, 51, 53

La Vérendrye, Louis Joseph, 53
Law and order in the West, 174
League of Nations, 238
Le Caron, Father Joseph, 34
Leduc oil field, 277, 279
Lemoyne (ship), 263
Lévis, Chevalier de, 65
Lincoln Highway, 248-9
Little, Philip Francis, 125
Lord Mayor Bay, 143
Lord Strathcona Horse, 218
Louis XIV, King of France, 45
Louis XV, King of France, 56
Louisburg, 47, 54, 57, 65
Low, A. P., 291
Lower Canada, 88, 108, 113, 117, 142, 174
Loyalists, 86-8, 91
Lumbering, 207-9, 275-7
Lundy's Lane, 112

MCCURDY, JOHN A. D., 249-50, 255
Macdonald, Sir John A., 156-61, 168-70, 180, 184, 186, 204, 223, 225, 316
Macdonald-Cartier Freeway, 249
McDougall, William, 161-2
McGillivray, William, 101
Mackenzie, Sir Alexander, explorer, 34, 101-3, 134, 142-3
Mackenzie, Alexander, prime minister, 169, 218, 223-4, 316
Mackenzie, Sir William, 204-5
Mackenzie, William Lyon, 113-4, 116
Mackenzie Highway, 249
Mackenzie River, 19, 101, 142-3, 206
McLeod, A. N., 174
McNaughton, General A. G. L., 304
McTavish, Simon, 101, 103
Magdalen Islands, 24, 78, 228
Magellan, Ferdinand, 25
Magnetic Pole, 142, 291
Maine, 113; boundary, 118, 120
Maldonado, Lorenzo, 79
Mandan Indians, 53
Manhattan (ship), 292
Manicouagan River, 281
Manifest Destiny, 116, 152-5, 157, 168
Manitoba, 162, 179, 223, 277, 281, 292
Manitoba Act, 162
Mann, Sir Donald, 204-5
Marco Polo (ship), 140, 142
Marconi, Guglielmo, 217
Markland, 15, 20
Marquette, Jacques, 36-7
Martinez, Estéban, José, 98
Massey, Vincent, 316
Matthew (ship), 22
May, Capt. W. W. (Wop), 250
Meares, Capt. John, 98
Meighen, Arthur, 292-3
Melville Island, 142, 269, 291
Mennonites, 94, 283
Mercator, Gerard, 27, 29
Metcalfe, Sir Charles, 155
Métis, 161-2, 182
Michilimackinac, 36, 50, 68, 108
Middleton Sound, 182, 184
Military Service Act, 223
Militia, Canadian, 108, 218
Mines and minerals, 272-4, 281; aluminum, 281; asbestos, 273, 281; coal, 126, 274; cobalt, 273; copper, 273; gold, 26, 106, 126, 129, 131, 196, 272, 274; iron, 273-4; lead, 274; nickel, 273-4; silver, 273; uranium, 273
Minnesota, 152, 180
Miquelon, 47, 65, 77, 121
Mitchell, John, 72

Moll, Herman, 78, 296
Monckton, Brig. Gen. Robert, 63, 65
Moncton, 138, 166, 205, 254
Montcalm, Louis Joseph Marquis de, 63, 65
Montgomery, Brig. Gen. Richard, 67, 69
Montreal, 21, 24, 32, 39, 45, 58, 61, 65, 92, 103, 108, 112, 134, 136, 138, 144, 147, 157, 249-50, 254, 262, 266, 270, 280, 285, 303, 308
Monts, Pierre Du Gua de, 32
Moodie, Major J. D., 291
Moors, 12
Moose Factory, 39
Munitions of war, 232, 303
Munk, Jens, 27
Murmansk, 232
Murray, Brig. Gen. James, 65-6, 68
Murray Bay (ship), 264
Musgrave, Sir Anthony, 165

NANAIMO, 126
Nares, Sir George, 289
Nass River, 210
National Policy, 223
National Resources Mobilization Act, 304
National Transcontinental Railway, 205
National Transportation Act, 261
Navy Island, 116
Nelson River, 26, 281
Neptune (ship), 291
Neutral Indians, 36
New Brunswick, 78, 86, 118, 120-21, 136, 138, 142, 157, 281
New Caledonia, 103
Newfoundland, early history, 15-17, 22, 24, 26, 45, 47, 77-8, 121-5, 160; fisheries and fishing rights, 77, 121, 125, 210, 225 since 1867, 157, 225-9, 295-7;
Newfoundland Railway, 225, 227
New France, 32-65
Newsprint, 275, 277
New Westminster, 125, 276
New York, 24, 26, 86
Niagara, 86, 108, 112
Niagara Falls, 115, 134, 136, 264
Nicholson, Francis, 45
Nicollet, Jean, 36-7
Nile Voyageurs, 220
Niobe (ship), 220
Nonsuch (ship), 39, 44
Nootka Convention, 100
Nootka Sound, 81, 98, 100
Normandy campaign, 299, 301, 206
Norsemen, 15
North Pole, 286, 289-91
Northern Pacific Railway, 166, 169
Northern Railway, 136
Northumberland Strait, 165
Norway House, 103
North West Company, 100-4, 112, 126, 131, 174, 196
North West Mounted Police, 175-6, 178, 182, 184, 186, 241, 291; *see also* Royal Canadian Mounted Police
North West Passage, 25, 72, 142-3, 286, 291-2
Northwest Rebellion, 178, 180, 182-6
Northwest Staging Route, 300
Northwest Territories, 162, 178
Nova Scotia, 27-8, 77-9, 86-8, 118, 120-21, 131, 136, 138, 142, 157, 166, 210, 281
Nova Scotia Railway, 166
Nuclear power, 281

OHIO VALLEY, 57, 59, 63, 65-6, 68, 72
Oil Springs (Black Creek), 277
One Big Union, 240

Ontario, 136-8, 244, 247, 249, 276-7, 279, 281, 292
Oregon, 103, 126; boundary, 103, 126, 152
Ortelius, Abraham, 28, 30
Ortona, 301
Ottawa, 134, 141, 144, 149, 155, 249, 287-8, 309
Ottawa River and Valley, 32, 36, 138, 264, 281
Otter, Colonel, 184
Outardes River, 281

PACIFIC FUR CO., 100, 102
Pacific Great Eastern Railway, 262
Pacific railway surveys, 166
Pacific Scandal, 169, 223
Pacific Western Airlines, 257
Palliser, Capt. John, 152, 154
Palliser's Triangle, 154
Papineau, Louis Joseph, 113, 117
Paris Peace Conference, 238
Paris, Treaty of 1763, 65
Paris, Treaty of 1783, 70, 73, 121
Parliament Buildings, Ottawa, 144, 155-6, 222, 241, 287, 294, 321
Parry, Lieut. W. E., 142
Parry Channel, 142
Parsons, Charles, 280
Passchendale, Battle of, 232-3
Patriotes, 113
Peace River, 101, 280-81
Pearl Harbor, 301
Pearson, Lester B., 313, 315-6, 318, 320
Peary, Robert E., 291
Peck, Capt. Brian, 250
Peel Sound, 143
Pembina Branch, C.P.R., 169-70
Pembroke, 280
Pepperell, William, 57
Perez, Juan, 79
Permanent Force, Canadian Army, 218, 239
Perry, Commodore Oliver H., 112
Perth, 96
Petawawa, 250, 256
Peterborough, 96
Petrolia, 277-8
Petroleum industry, 272-3, 276-9
Phips, Sir William, 45
Phoenician discoverers, 15
Pickawillany, 59
Pickering, 281
Pictou, 136
Piggyback transport, 261
Pine Point, 274
Pinta (ship), 15
Pipeline debate of 1956, 313
Pipelines, 261
Pitt, William, 64-5
Placentia, 45
Placentia Bay, 27
Plattsburg, Battle of, 112
Plaunt, Alan, 268
Plywood, 276
Point Barrow, 143
Polaris (ship), 289
Pond, Peter, 75
Pontgravé, François, 138
Pontiac (Indian chief), 68
Pontiac insurrection, 68, 72
Port Arthur, 188, 204
Port aux Basques, 225
Port Colborne, 134
Port Royal, 32, 45, 47, 138
Portland, Maine, 136
Potash, 138, 272-3
Portuguese discoverers, 12, 16, 22, 28, 79
Portuguese fishermen, 22
Poundmaker (Indian chief), 184
Powell River, 277

Prairie du Chien, 112
Prescott, 110, 138
Prevost, General Sir George, 108
Prince Albert, 184
Prince Edward Island, 24, 78, 118, 120-21, 157, 165, 244, 281
Prince George, 262
Prince of Wales (later Edward VII), 241
Prince Rupert, 205, 210
Princess Louise, 204
Princess Patricia's Light Infantry, 230
Prince William Sound, 98
Progressive Party, 292-3, 295
Ptolemy (Claudius Ptolemaeus), 13-15
Pulp and paper industry, 226, 275-6

QUADRA, JUAN FRANCISCO DE LA BODEGA Y, 81
Quebec (city), 21, 24, 32-4, 39, 45, 47, 54, 58, 60, 62, 65, 67, 108, 136, 140, 144, 146, 166, 218
Quebec (province), 66, 86, 88, 247, 249, 275-6, 281, 315, 316
Quebec Act, 68, 75, 228
Quebec Conference of 1864, 157
Quebec-Labrador boundary, 228
Quebec, North Shore and Labrador Railway, 262, 274
Quebecair, 257
Queen Charlotte Islands, 21, 81
Queen Elizabeth Way, 247-8

RADIO BROADCASTING, 266, 268
Radio League of Canada, 268
Radisson, Pierre, 36-7
Rae, Dr. John, 143
Railways, 120, 136-8, 154, 160, 165-6, 182, 188-9, 204-5, 244, 257, 261-2
Rainbow (ship), 220
Ralston, J. L., 304
Rationing in wartime, 302
Rebellions of 1837, 110, 113-7
Rebellion Losses Bill, 144, 155
Reciprocity issue in 1911, 223-4
Reciprocity Treaty of 1854, 120, 152
Recollet missions, 34, 36
Red Deer, 54
Red River carts, 154, 186-7
Red River Expedition of 1870, 162, 218
Red River Resistance or Rebellion, 161-2, 179
Red River Settlement, 102-3, 106, 152, 161-2, 174, 196
Redwater, 277
Reformers of 1837, 113, 116-7
Regina, 176, 178, 186, 199, 204, 292, 310
Regina Manifesto, 295
Reid, Robert, 225
Renaissance, 12
Repulse Bay, 143
Resolute (ship), 144
Responsible government, attitude of the British Government toward, 113, 116-7, 155; British Columbia, 131, 165; Canada, 113, 155; New Brunswick, 120; Newfoundland, 124-5, 296-7; Nova Scotia, 118, 120; Prince Edward Island, 120
Resolution (ship), 81
Richardson, Dr. John, explorer, 143
Richardson, John, fur trader, 174
Richelieu, Cardinal, 34
Richelieu River, 32, 57, 68-9, 108, 112, 135, 137
Richmond, 136
Rideau Canal, 134-5
Riel, Louis, 161-2, 165, 182-6, 223
Ringnes Islands, 291
Riss, François, 24
Rivière du Loup, 138, 166

Roads and highways, 88-9, 160, 244, 247-9, 261, 315
Roads to Progress project, 249, 315
Roberts, Capt. Charles, 108
Roberval, Sieur de, 24
Robeson Channel, 289
Robinson, John Beverley, 113
Robinson, Peter, 96
Rocky Mountains, 53-4

Roosevelt, Franklin D., 302
Ross, Capt. John, 142
Ross, James Clark, 142
Rouyn, 253
Royal Air Force, 230, 235, 250, 300
Royal Canadian Air Force, 239, 300, 301
Royal Canadian Mounted Police, 178;
    see also North West Mounted Police
Royal Canadian Navy, 220-1, 223, 230, 239, 296, 298, 300
Royal Commission on Bilingualism and Biculturalism, 315
Royal Commission on National Development of the Arts, Letter and Sciences (the Massey Commission), 313
Royal Military College, 218
Royal Navy, 218, 220
Royal Newfoundland Regiment, 226
Rupert River, 36
Rupert's House, 39
Rupert's Land, 39, 102, 106, 160-61, 178, 180, 186
Russia, 36, 70, 80, 103, 240, 300
Russian American Company, 100, 126
Ryerson, Egerton, 113
Ryswick, Treaty of, 45

SAGUENAY RIVER, 32, 36, 281
St. Alban's raid, 154
St. Andrews and Quebec Railway, 136
St. Brendan, 15
St. Catharines, 280
St. Charles, 113
St. Croix River, 32
St. Denis, 113
St. Eustache, 113, 115
St. Germain-en-Laye, Treaty of, 34
St. Jean River, 228
Saint John, N.B., 119, 138, 142, 166
St. John River, 86, 88
St. John's, Newfoundland, 24, 26, 45, 65, 77, 122, 125, 217, 226, 229, 295, 297
St. Johns, Quebec, 69, 136
St. Joseph Island, 108
St. Lawrence (ship), 112
St. Lawrence, Gulf of, 24
St. Lawrence River, 24, 32, 131-5
St. Lawrence Seaway, 261, 263-6
St. Lawrence Seaway Authority, 266
St. Lawrence and Atlantic Railway, 136, 138
St. Laurent, Louis S., 297, 304, 313, 315-6
St. Malo, 24
St. Paul, 152, 154-5, 169, 186, 188, 196
St. Paul and Pacific Railway, 169
St. Pierre, 47, 65, 77, 121
St. Roch (ship), 291-2
Sainte-Marie, 36, 39
Salaberry, Col. Charles Michel de, 112
Samson (locomotive), 137
Sandwich Islands, 83, 98
Santiago (ship), 79-80
Saratoga, British surrender at, 69-70
Sarnia, 138, 277, 279
Saskatchewan, 192, 249, 272, 277, 281, 293
Saskatchewan River, 53-4
Saskatoon, 201, 204

Sault Ste. Marie, 36, 50, 112, 131, 134, 154, 262, 266
Saunders, Admiral Sir Charles, 65
Saunders, Dr. Charles, 186
Scarpe, First Battle of, 226
Schultz, Dr. J. C., 161
Scott, Thomas, 162
Sea of the West, 79, 82
Sea Otter (ship), 98
Sea otter, 98, 100
Sealing, 58, 121
Seigneurial tenure, 88, 96
Selkirk, Earl of, 102-3, 106, 152
Settlement, 57-8, 77, 88-9, 91, 93, 120-21, 178, 187-8
Seven Years War, 55, 59, 63-5
Severn Fort, 44
Shaughnessy, Sir Thomas, 204
Shea, Ambrose, 225, 295
Shediac, 138, 166
Shelburne, 88-9
Sherbrooke, Sir John, 113
Sherbrooke, 136, 275
Shipbuilding, 58, 138, 232, 238-9, 298, 303
Ships, early, 14
Sicily, 301
Sifton, Sir Clifford, 189
Silver Dart (aeroplane), 250, 255-6
Simcoe, Lt. Col. John Graves, 88
Simpson, Sir George, 103, 106, 126, 143
Simpson, Thomas, 143
Sioux Indians, 36, 180
Skeena River, 210
Skidegate, 21
Smallwood, Joseph, 297
Smith, William, 88
Smith Sound, 142, 289
Social Credit Party, 295
Society for the Propagation of the Gospel, 124
Somme, Battle of the, 226, 230-31
Sonora (ship), 81
Sorel, 86
Soulanges Canals, 131, 135
South African War, 218-9, 223, 238
Southampton Island, 26
Spain, 16, 79-81, 98, 100
Spry, Graham, 268
Stadacona, 24
Stanfield, Robert, 316
Stanhius, Sigurdus, 20
Starvation Cove, 143
Steam power, 280
Steele, Maj. Gen. Sir Samuel, 178
Stefansson, Vilhyalmur, 291
Stephanius, Sigurdus, 20
Stephen, Sir George (later Lord Mountstephen), 166, 169
Sternwheel steamers, 206
Stikine River, 220
Stoney Creek, 112
Strachan, Rev. John, 113
Strange, Maj. Gen. T. B., 184
Stratford, 96
Strathcona, Lord, 218
Submarine warfare, 298, 300, 302-3
Submarines, built in Canada, 238
Subways, 249
Sudbury, 273-5
Sullivan Mine, 273
Supreme Court of Canada, 316
Sverdrup, Capt. Otto, 291
Sverdrup Islands, 291
Sydenham, Lord, 155

TALBOT, COL. THOMAS, 96-7
Talbot Settlement, 96
Tadoussac, 32, 39, 44, 106
Talon, Jean, 45-7

Television broadcasting, 268
Terror (ship), 143
Telegraph lines, 160, 182
Temperance Colonization Society, 204
Thom, Adam, 174
Thompson, David, 101-2, 126
Thompson River, 205
Thordarson, Thorfinnr, 16
Thornton, Sir Henry, 266
Thorvaldsson, Eirikr (Eric the Red), 15
Thunder Bay, 266
Ticonderoga (Fort Carillon), 68
Tilley, Sir Leonard S., 156-7
Timber trade, 118, 120, 138
Tirpitz (ship), 300
Tobacco Indians, 36
Torbay, 296
Tordesillas, Treaty of, 16, 22
Toronto, 108, 113, 116, 138, 144, 148, 244, 247-9, 257, 266, 280, 285, 308
Tracy, Alexandre de Prouville, Marquis de, 45-6
Trail, 273-4, 281
Trans-Canada Air Lines (TCA, now Air Canada), 251-2, 254, 257, 261
Trans-Canada Highway, 227, 249, 261
Transportation, 186, 269, 273-4; policy, 257;
    see also the various forms of transport
Trent (ship), 154
Trent Canal, 135
Trenton, N.J., British defeat at, 69
Trois-Rivières, 59
Trudeau, Pierre Elliott, 313, 316, 319-20
Truro, 166
Trutch, Sir Joseph W., 165
Tupper, Sir Charles, 157
Turnagain Point, 142
Turner Valley, 277
Typhus epidemic of 1847, 96-7

Uganda (ship), 300
Uniacke, James B., 120
Union Government, 225, 292, 303
United Farmers' movement, 292
United Province of Canada, 93, 117, 138, 144-9, 155-7
United Nations, 316
United States, 108-13, 136, 223, 225, 238, 279, 293, 296, 313, 315
United States ownership of Canadian industries, 313, 315
Upper Canada, 88, 108, 113, 117, 138, 141, 180
Utrecht, Treaty of, 46-7

VALLEYFIELD, 275
Vancouver, Capt. George, 98
    Survey of the West Coast, 101
Vancouver, 169, 173, 198, 204, 244-6, 250, 254, 270, 280, 285, 311
Vancouver Island, 79, 126-31, 196
Van Horne, Sir William C., 166, 169, 184, 186
Vaudreuil, Pierre de Rigaud, Marquis de, 57-8, 64
Venezuelan crisis of 1895, 218
Verrazzano, Giovanni da, 24, 26
Versailles, Treaty of, 238
Vespucci, Amerigo, 27
Victoria, Queen, 85, 144
Victoria, 132, 196, 250, 280
Victoria (ship), 142-3
Victoria Bridge, 138
Victoria Cross, 218
Victoria Island, 143, 286
Victoria Strait, 143
Victory Point, 144
Vikings, 15, 24
Viking ships, 16
Vimy Ridge, Battle of, 230, 232-3

Vinland, 15, 16, 20
Virden, 277
Vladivostok, 232

W. A. C. BENNETT DAM, 280
Walker, Sir Hovenden, 45
Waldseemuller, Martin, 27, 29
War of 1812, 108-13, 118, 131
Warner, Seth, 68
Wartime Prices and Trade Board, 303
Wascana Creek, 204
Washington, George, 63, 69
Washington (city), 112
Washington, Treaty of, 218
Water-wheels, 280
Watling Island (San Salvador), 15
Webster-Ashburton Treaty, 120
Welland Canal, 134-5, 262-4, 266
Wellington Channel, 143
Western Front, World War I, 234

Westminster, Statute of, 293, 295, 316
Weyburn, 277
Wheat, 186, 189, 270-72
Whisky traders in the West, 174
White Horse (ship), 206
White House, 112
White Star (ship), 142
Williams, James M., 277
Wilson, John A., 253
Windsor, N.S., 136
Windsor, Ont., 136, 249, 280
Winnipeg, 164, 169, 172, 184-6, 189, 196, 199, 205, 239-41, 309
Winnipeg General Strike, 239-40
Wireless, first trans-Atlantic message, 217
Wisconsin, 152
Wolfe, Maj. Gen. James, 64-5
Wolfe's Cove, 138, 262
Wolseley, Col. Garnet, 162, 218, 220
Woodstock, 136

Woodsworth, J. S., 292, 295
World War I, 223-6, 230-38, 250
World War II, 248-9, 295-6, 298, 306
WRENS, 298

X Y COMPANY, 174

YALE, 131
Yarmouth, N.S., 142
Yellowhead Pass, 196, 205
Yellowknife, 249
Yonge Street, 88
York (Toronto), 108
York Factory, 44, 103, 107
Yorktown, 70
Ypres, Battle of, 230, 235
Yukon, 178, 220
Yukon Field Force, 220-21
Yukon River, 206

The text material in this book
is set in 10 point Baskerville
and the headings in Helvetica Light

The book was designed by Brant Cowie
and produced in Toronto:
composition by Wareham & Hutton Limited
lithography by Ashton Potter Limited
and binding by T. H. Best Printing Co. Limited.